Utah
the Light Fantastic

FRONT COVER:
Some of Utah's most fantastic light illuminates the limestone pinnacles of Fairyland Canyon in Bryce Canyon National Park.

BACK COVER:
Bridal Veil Falls splashes into a small forest of bigtooth maples in Provo Canyon.

INTERNATIONAL STANDARD BOOK NUMBER:
978-0-9712555-4-8

LIBRARY OF CONGRESS NUMBER:
2006910383

PRINTED IN CHINA BY:
Everbest Printing Co. through Four Colour Imports, Ltd., Louisville, Kentucky.

PUBLISHED BY:
Fable Valley Publishers, Inc.
P.O. Box 337
Moab, Utah 84532
435-259-5327

BOOK PRODUCTION:

DIGITAL IMAGING, DESIGN, LAYOUT, PRODUCTION, & PREPRESS BY
Duncan and Caroline Mackie, Mackie Visions, Inc.

PRODUCTION ASSISTANCE BY
Lata Shambo and Marcy Till

TEXT EDITING AND PROOFING BY
Marjorie Miller

EXCEPT FOR PRINTING AND BINDING, THIS BOOK WAS PRODUCED SOLELY IN MOAB, UTAH, USA

OTHER BOOKS BY TOM TILL

Colorado: Images from Above
Outcroppings
Utah: Magnificent Wilderness
Utah Compass Guides
New Jersey: Images of the Landscape
Visions of the Colorado Plateau
American Southwest
Utah: Celebration of the Landscape
The Woven Spirit
Visions of the North
Utah Reflections
Utah Wildflowers
Slickrock Country
Iowa: Smithsonian Guides to Natural America
Sacred Images
Always in Season
Colorado Plateau: The Land, The Indians
New Mexico Wilderness
Seasons in the Rockies
Utah: Then and Now
Great Ghost Towns of the West
Along New Mexico's Continental Divide Trail
Continental Divide Trail, New Mexico
In the Land of Moab
Fodor's Utah Guide
Plateau Province

Utah
the Light Fantastic

Photography by Tom Till
Essays by Mikenna Clokey

FABLE VALLEY
publishers, inc.
Publishing the Photography of TOM TILL
PO BOX 337, Moab, UT 84532
Tel: 888.811.2436 ~ Fax: 435.259.7409
WWW.TOMTILL.COM

Foreword

"My soul can find no staircase to heaven
unless it be through earth's loveliness"
— Michelangelo

by Tom Till

A few more trips down the river, and a few more hikes around the bend of the canyon find me with a plethora of new Beehive State images which I hope will inspire, educate, and delight those who happen to spend a few minutes looking at what I've found in my recent photographic explorations.

Why keep doing this? Well, first of all, it's fun. I love my job, I love Utah, and my fervent hope is that my images will lead to a deeper appreciation for the natural world and Utah's singular portion of it. But more important, the places depicted here are almost all endangered in some way, and it's my hope that my Utah imagery can continue to foster the majority view in Utah, which is that most of us would like to see our natural and historical heritage saved for future generations through national parks, wilderness designation, wild and scenic rivers, and through preservation of roadless areas and open space. Only both the government and private citizens working together can do this.

Though there are many images of classic Utah locations in this book, my original idea was to include as many photographs as possible of subjects and locations that could not have appeared in a book done, say, 30 or even 10 years ago. The best example of this is the photo essay on the reemergence of Glen Canyon, whose short-lived return revealed marvels long inundated and new ones rising phoenix-like from their previously submerged depths.

Because of the help of many state agencies, especially the Division of Wildlife Resources, I was able to visit Range Creek Canyon, a scenic and archaeological treasure hidden from the prying eyes of the public until 2004, when its existence was revealed to the world. Though only one image from that wonderful trip has been included, subsequent volumes will show more.

Our national parklands, sadly, have not grown significantly in recent years, I've added a photograph of a magnificent arch in the Lost Spring Canyon section of Arches National Park. This addition to the park encompasses a spectacular canyon and a number of arches. Though some Moabites thought that the attention given the area by adding it to the park might cause a destructive rise in visitation, this has not happened, and Congressman Chris Cannon should be congratulated for his help with this needed expansion of the park.

Other new subjects include the gardens at Thanksgiving Point, surely the best in the Intermountain West, as well as crop circles in Spanish Fork and wonderful places that have been given protection by groups like Utah Open Lands. The Swaner Preserve, a stunning high-altitude wetland near metastasizing Park City, is a perfect example of these successful private/public sector initiatives to save these magical and highly photogenic places.

Also new this time are some magazine-style photo essays. I found that I had small portfolios on some fascinating subjects and that to tell their story, a grouping of images with text was the best way to utilize them. I hope you'll like it.

This attempt to do something that hasn't been done before also spills over into the technical realm. Though I'm still a strong advocate for large format cameras and analog

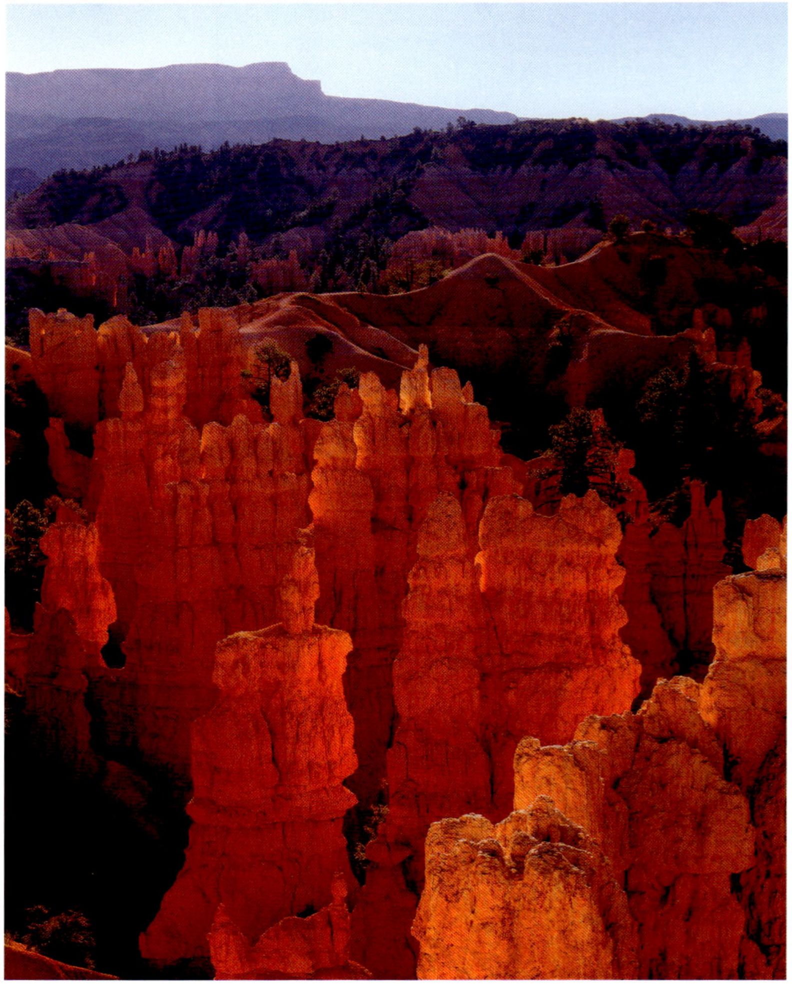

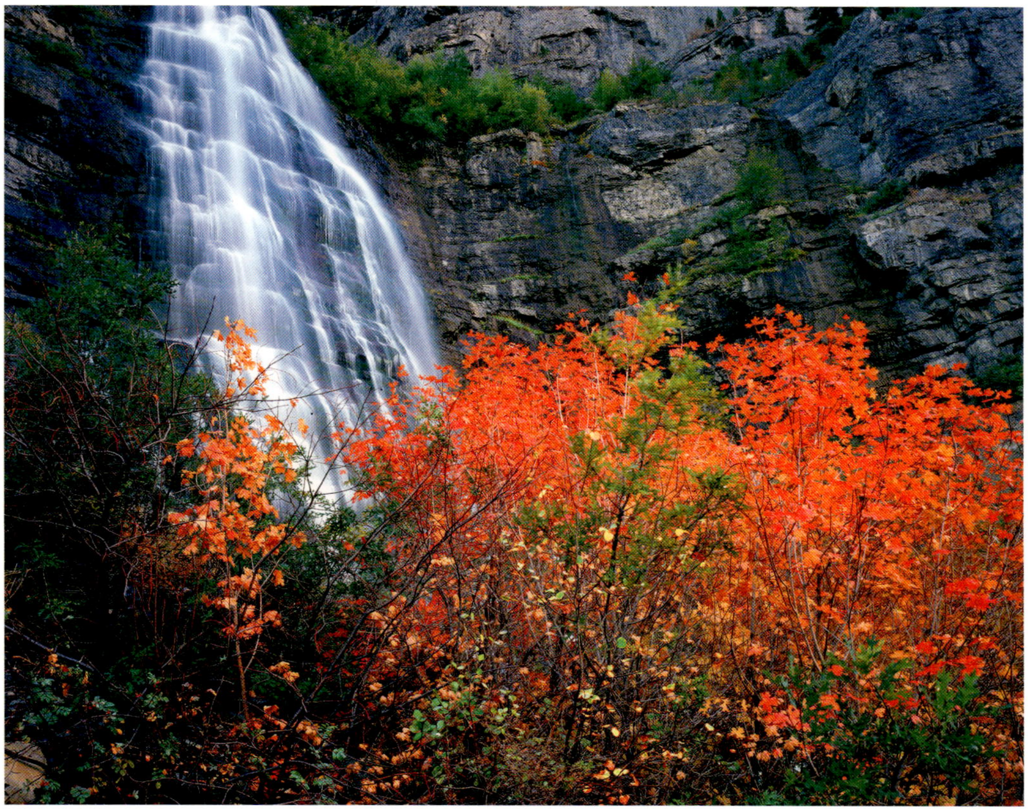

rather than digital photography, I'm excited about the advances in book printing that are apparent in the fidelity of the photographs included here. The richness and sharpness of my original 4x5 transparencies are finally given their due, so much so that the difference between this book and some of my first efforts is like the difference between viewing a regular old broadcast television and a new plasma HD screen. When years of work in the field can pay off so well with printed reproductions that capture the light and color I spend my life stalking, it is fulfilling and satisfying.

Those who have looked at my work over the years may find that I have favorite places, and as in past efforts, those areas have been given emphasis in this collection. Since all my work is self-assigned, and since I am drawn to subjects out of love for them, you'll see my prejudices again. Mount Timpanogos is well represented here, as is the area near my home in Moab. You'll also find lots of shots of Zion National Park, as well as lesser-known gems of the West Desert. I have also included a large number of images from Box Elder County, and, for the first time, a picture from beautiful Morgan County.

I try to make each book a collection of images that have been unpublished, at least in books of my own. I've been bitterly disappointed in purchasing books by photographers I admire, only to find that a small percent of the work is new to me. Due to popular demand, a couple of images that appeared as very small insets in my last Utah book, *Utah: Then and Now*, are displayed here in a larger format, otherwise everything is new. Also, I intend to make this book the flagship for a large series of books on the state, which if all goes as planned, will follow on a regular basis. For information about these books, check my website, www.tomtill.com.

As I finished work on this book, I took a photographic flight over the badlands near Factory Butte and Capitol Reef National Park. Several days of some of the most intense rain on record had turned these normally dull earth-toned areas into a kaleidoscope of saturated color. The flight took me over a small swath of Southern Utah, passing over places like the Red Desert, the Muddy River, Factory Butte, Goblin Valley, and the San Rafael Swell. Just this short flight drove home again the amazing size and diversity of the Utah landscape. Even after a lifetime of exploration, there's so much I haven't seen and so much I haven't explored. I also know that many of these areas are endangered, as is most of the state's public land.

It has been wonderful to collaborate on this project with my daughter, Mikenna, who has followed in my footsteps as an educated river guide. I don't know what made me more proud, her degree from one of the finest journalism schools in the country or her guide permit for the Colorado River in Grand Canyon. Our affinity for this amazing land is a strong bond between us, and I'm very proud of her.

I want to thank my wife Marcy and son Bryce, and my mother Effie for their help, inspiration, and encouragement. Thanks also to Duncan and Caroline Mackie, Lata Shambo, Kristi Paul, Chinle Miller, Sandy Barr, Glen Lathrop, Lisa Patterson, Steve Mullligan, David and Theresa Wilson, Monica and Bill Solawetz, Debby Berdan, John Botkin, Photocraft, Inc., Richard Jackson, Hance Partners, Singh-Ray Filters, Aramark Lake Powell, Utah Division of Wildlife Resources, Thanksgiving Point, Utah Open Lands, Canyonlands Natural History Association, Back of Beyond bookstore, Arches Book Company, Colorado River and Trail Expeditions, Dave and Vicki Mackay, Ann Carter, Carolyn Turkanis, Kimo Nelson, SUWA, and Lisa Hendy.

DEDICATED TO THE GREATEST PHOTOGRAPHER OF THE GREATEST GENERATION, PHILIP HYDE.

LEFT:
Some of Utah's most fantastic light illuminates the limestone pinnacles of Fairyland Canyon in Bryce Canyon National Park.

ABOVE:
Bridal Veil Falls splashes into a small forest of bigtooth maples in Provo Canyon.

NEXT PAGE:
Maples and oaks glow with an almost mystical light in the Mt. Naomi Wilderness in extreme northern Utah. When conditions are right, the maple trees of Utah (which extend from Zion in the south to the Idaho border) provide one of the most spectacular shows of fall color on the planet.

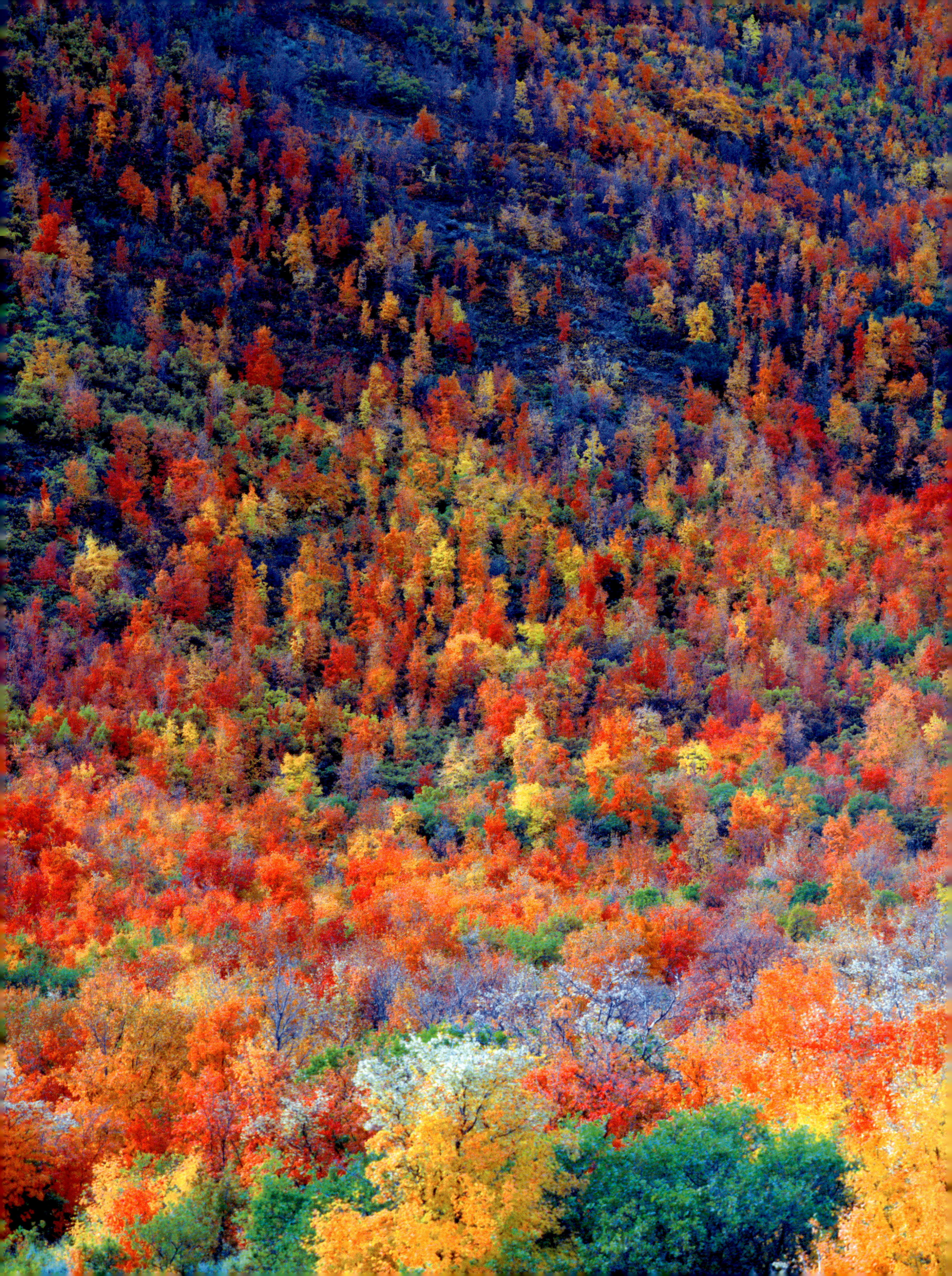

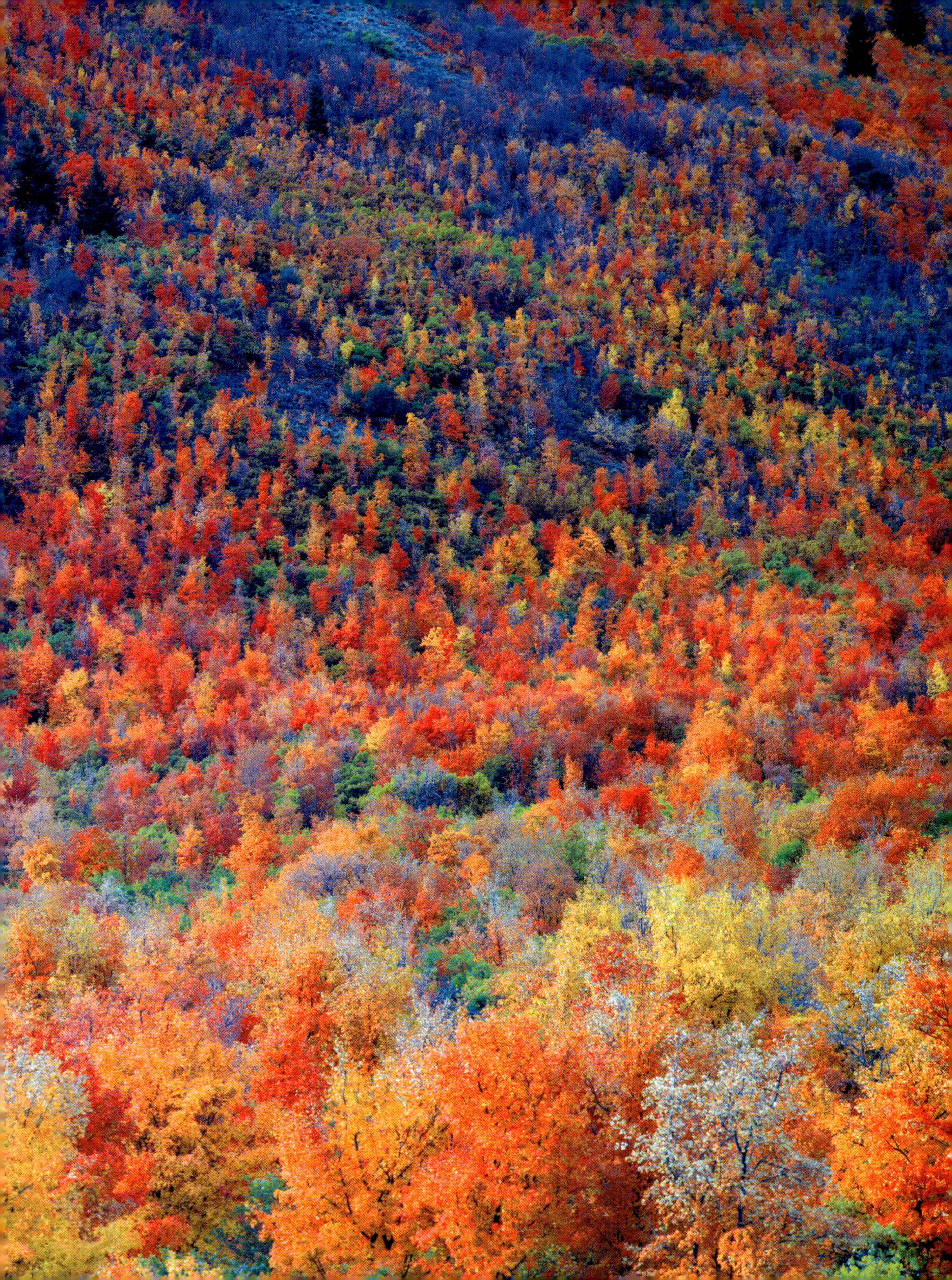

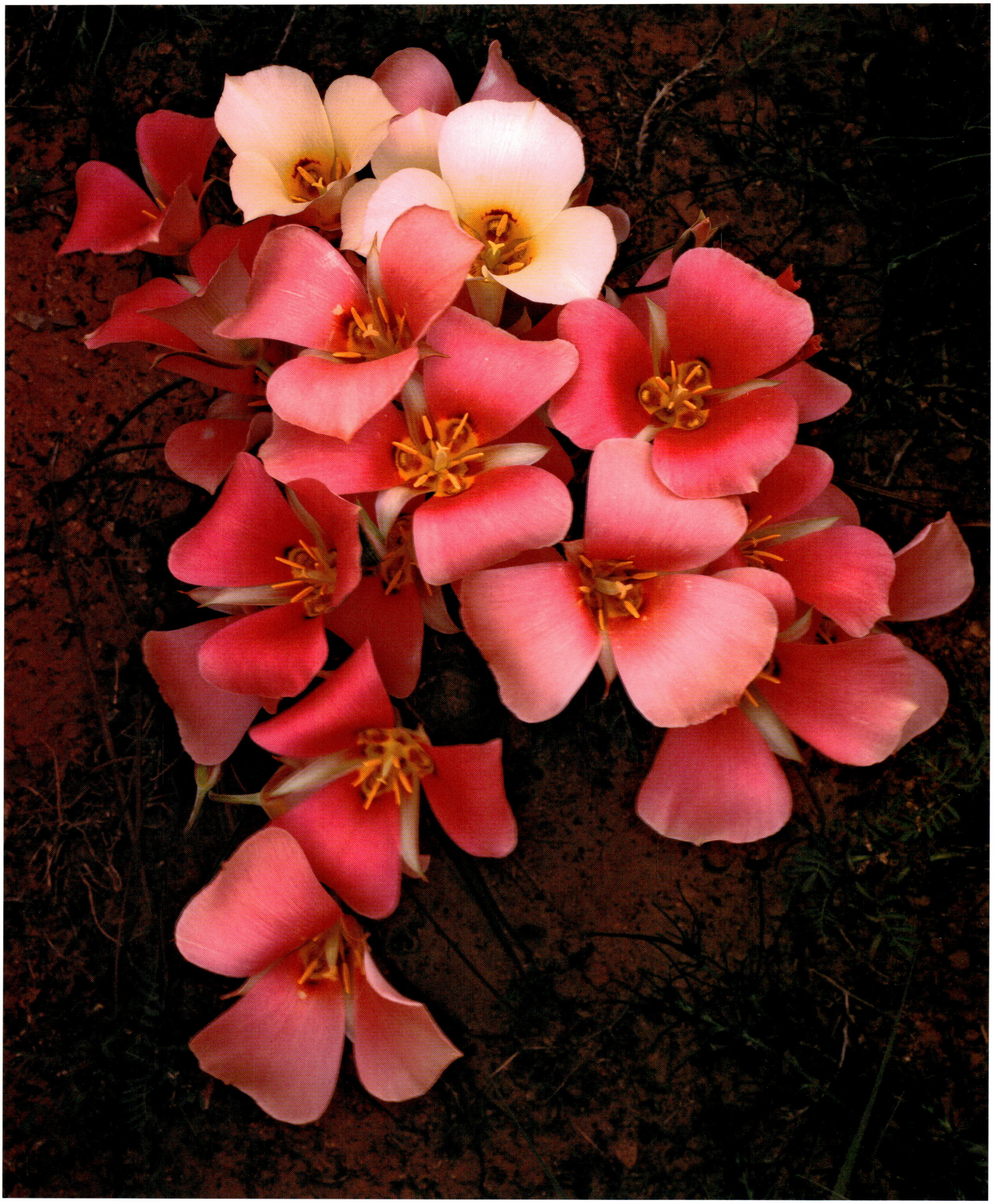

ABOVE:
This bloom of Sego lilies, the state flower, are some of the most colorful I've ever found. Normally a dull white, on rare occasions the flowers hybridize and become brown, orange, and maroon. I made this image in an intense windstorm, using a large sheet of linoleum stretched around the plant to control the gusts. When I returned the next day, the plants were gone, victims of grazing mule deer.

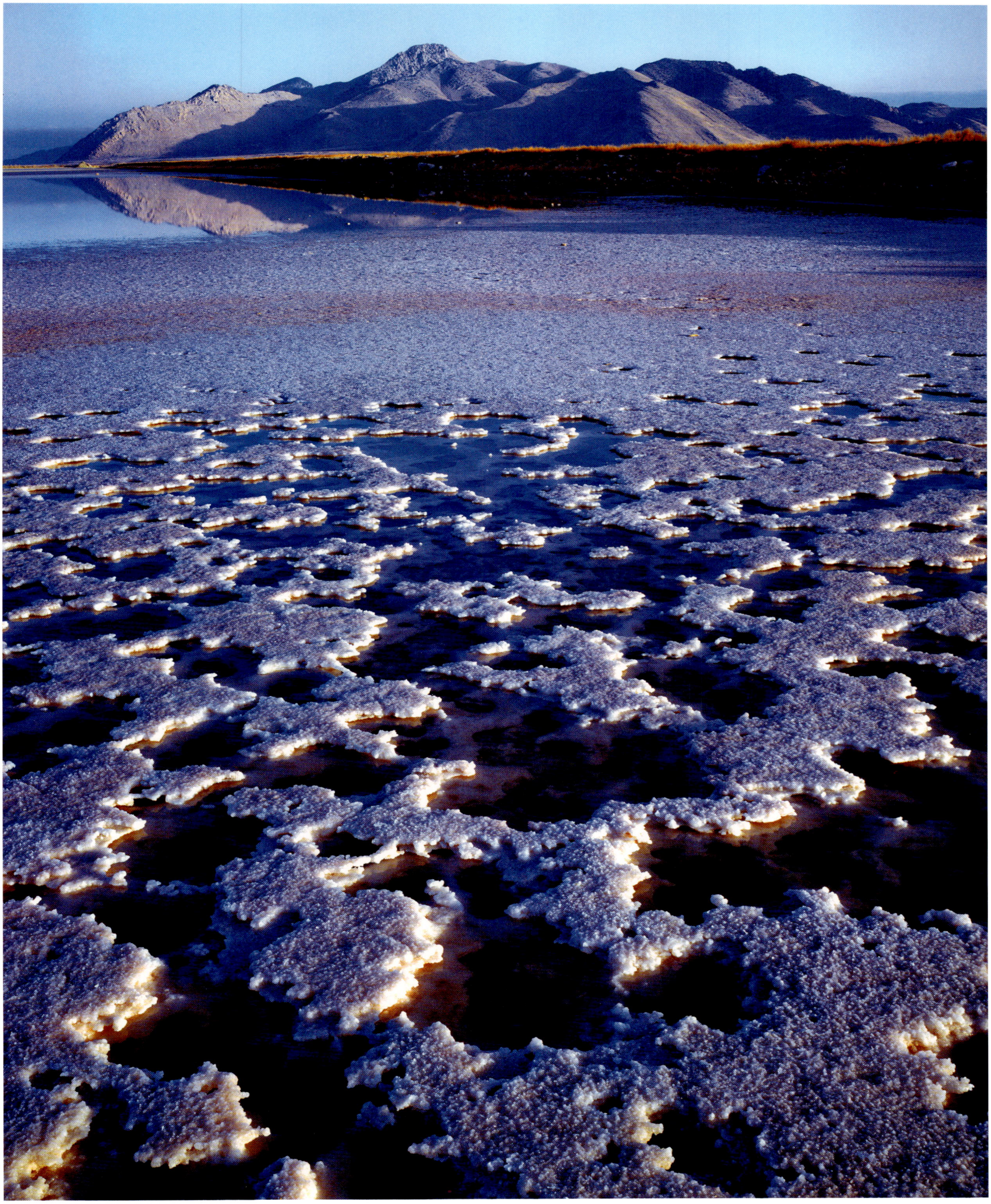

ABOVE:
I found these bizarre salt formations along the Great Salt Lake near Stansbury Island. They reminded me of almost identical features I had seen along the Dead Sea.

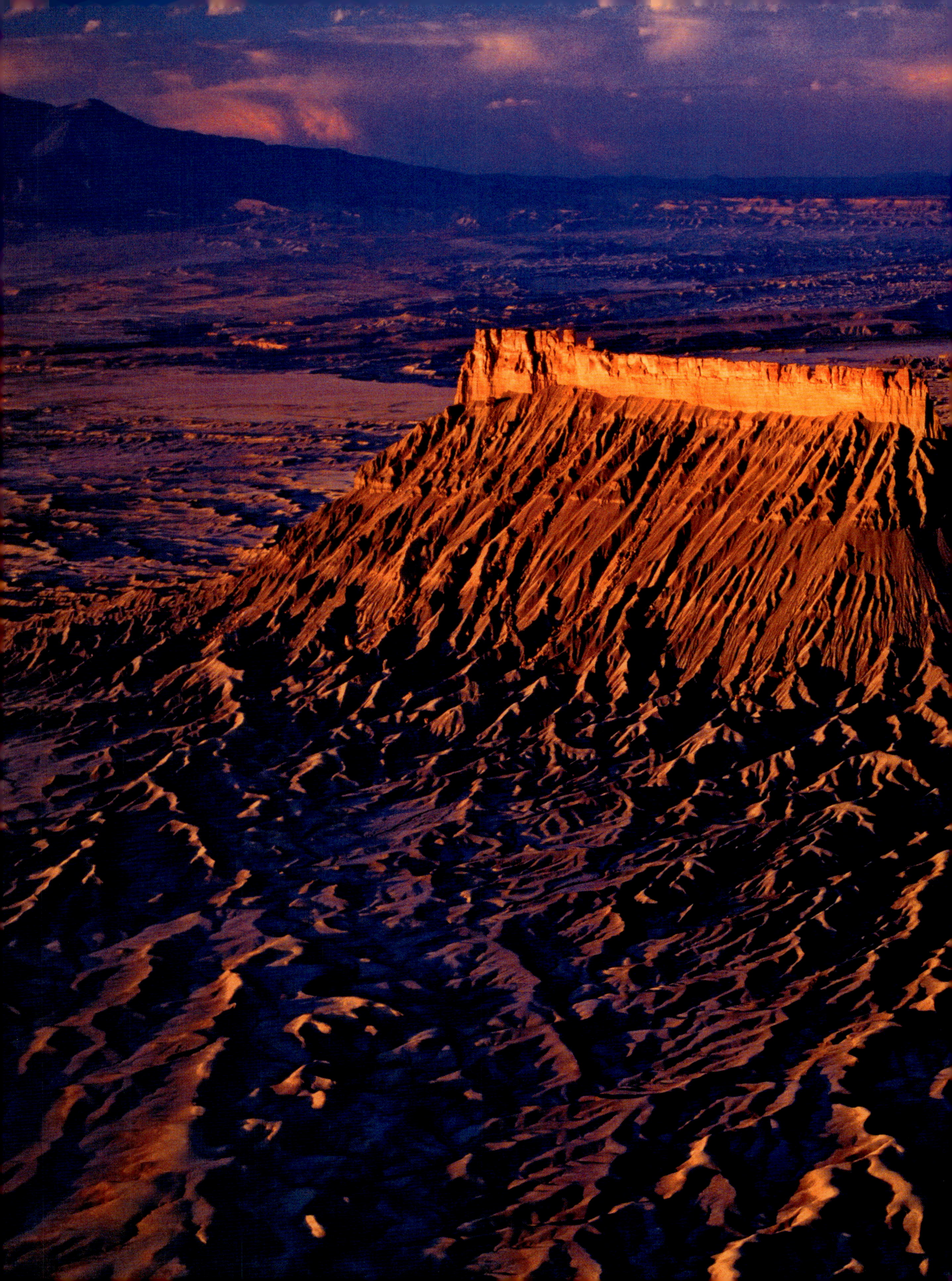

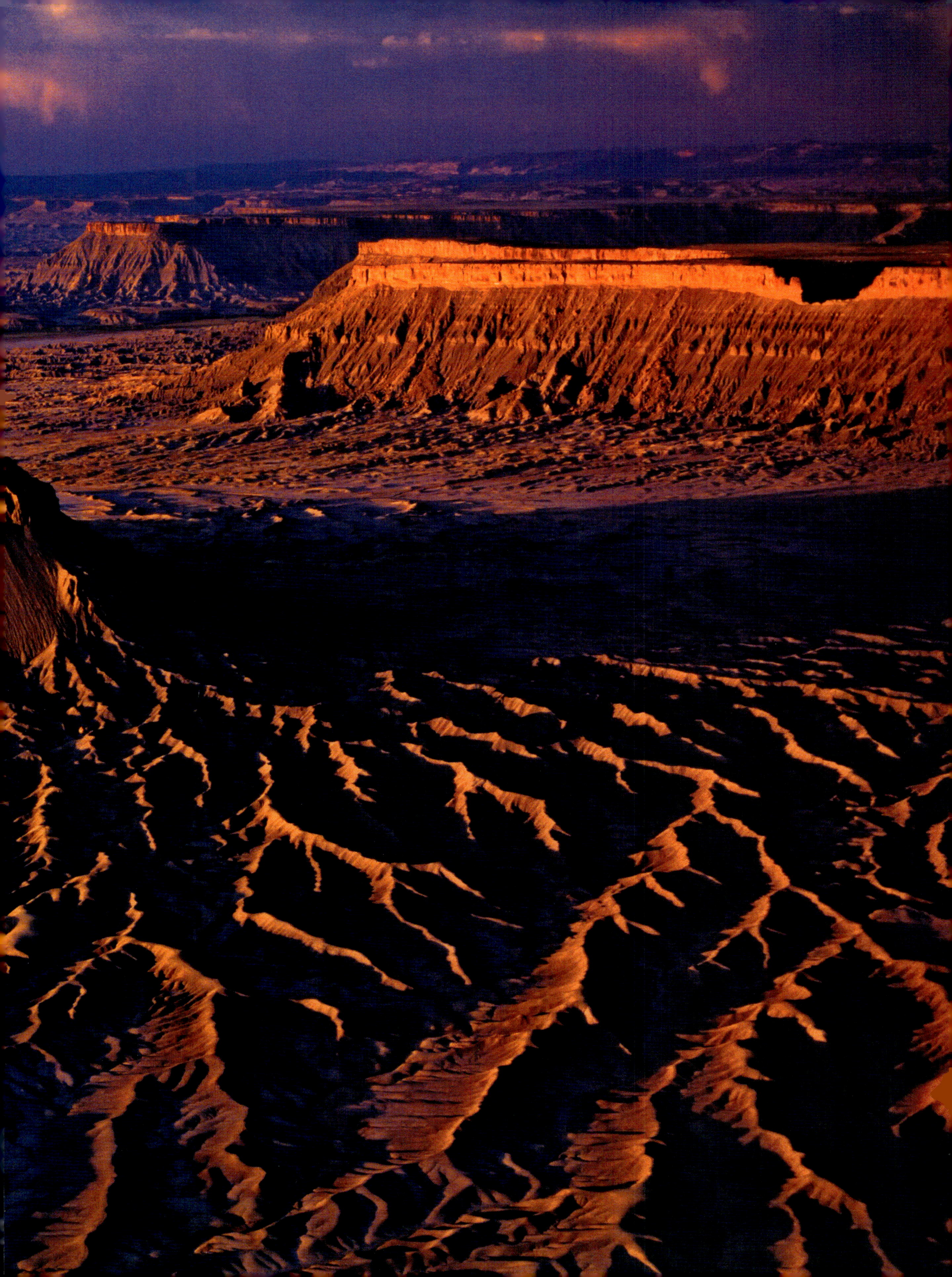

PREVIOUS PAGE:
Factory Butte has been the epicenter of a bitter conflict between environmentalists and off-road vehicle enthusiasts. Due in part to the impact of this aerial photograph, thus far courts have sided with those trying to preserve this beautiful and sensitive area from damage.

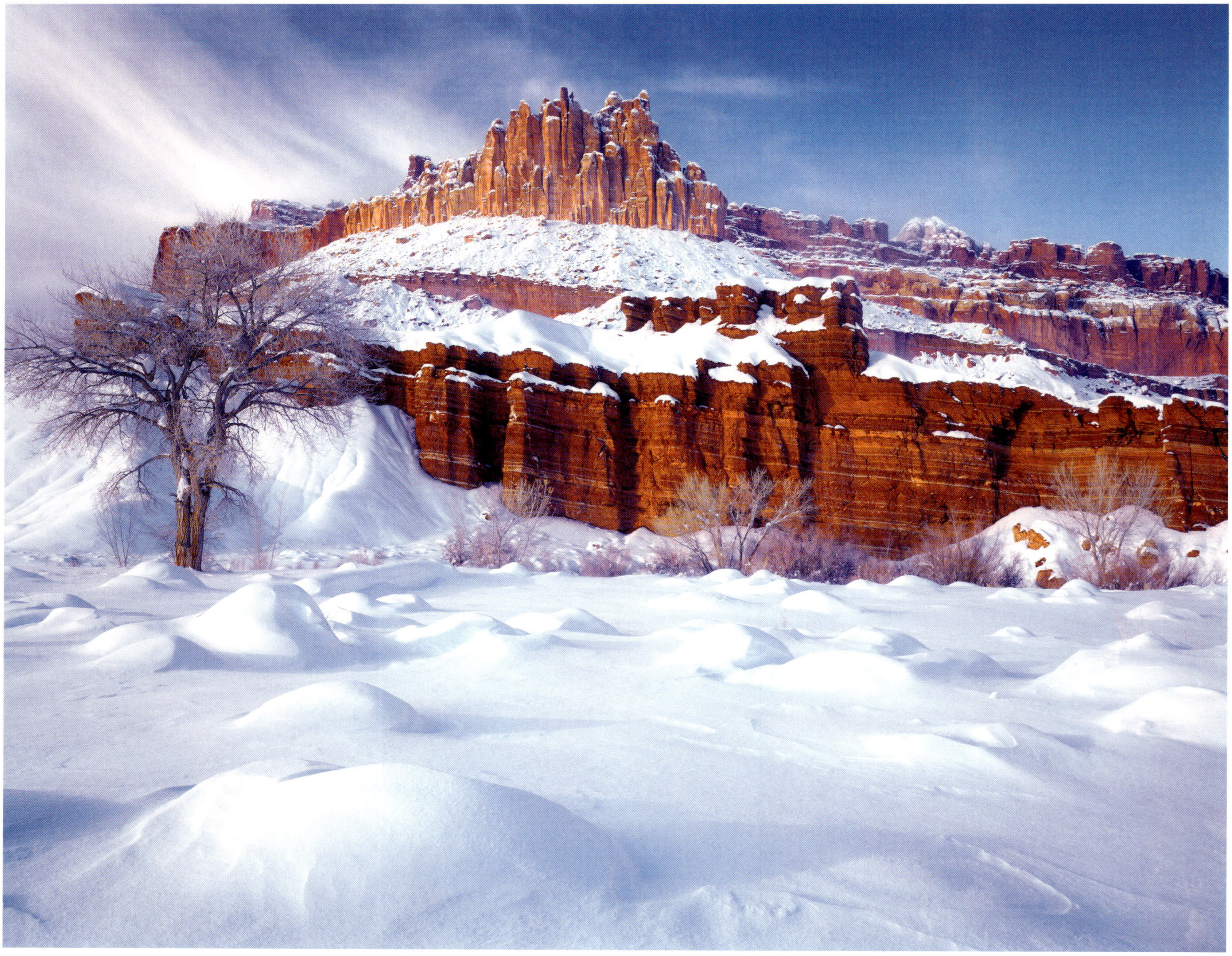

ABOVE:
After nearly 30 inches of snow, a rare event, Capitol Reef emerges from the onslaught. The difficulty with photographing this beautiful moment at the Castle was not the cold or an impassable highway. Though the road was plowed, there were no shoulders and no place to park a vehicle. I was forced to stop my car on the tarmac (traffic was nonexistent) and shoot from there, since leaving the road in the waist deep snow was also an impossibility.

RIGHT:
Indian paintbrush is my favorite wildflower, and this patch in Swaner Preserve near Park City is the most prolific bloom I have ever happened upon. Getting the final shot took several attempts as I waited several days for calm winds and good light on the Wasatch Mountains at sunrise.

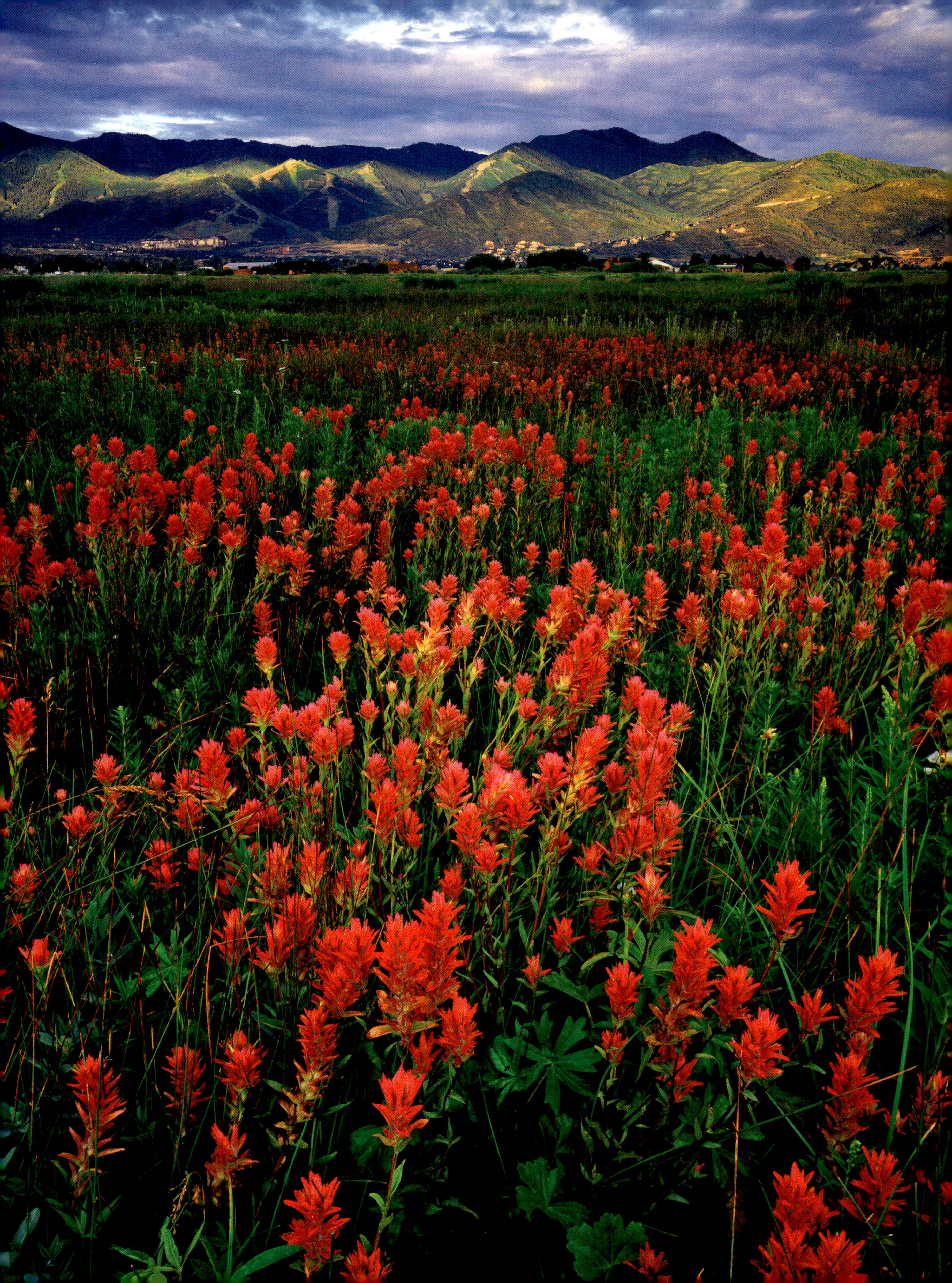

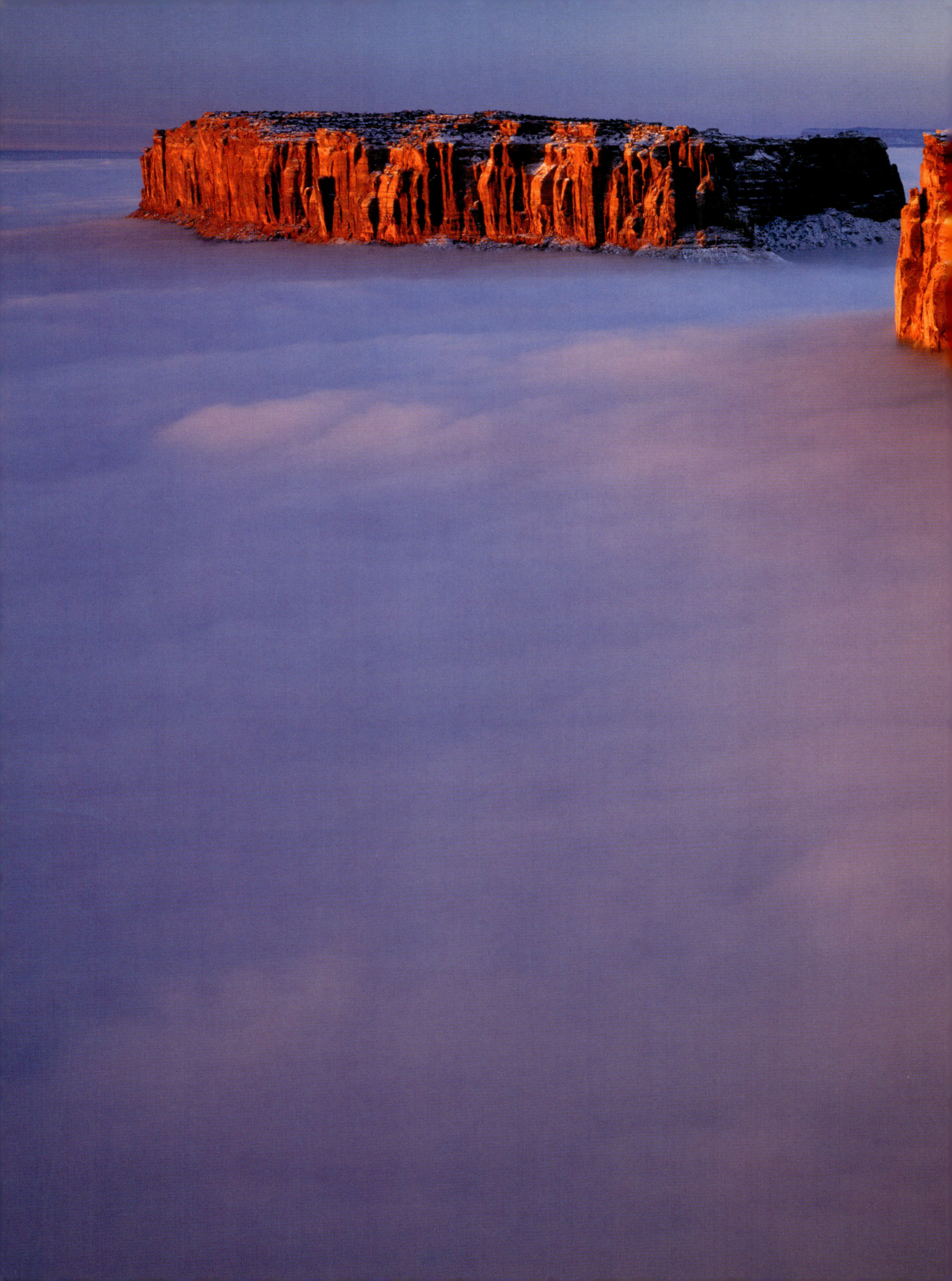

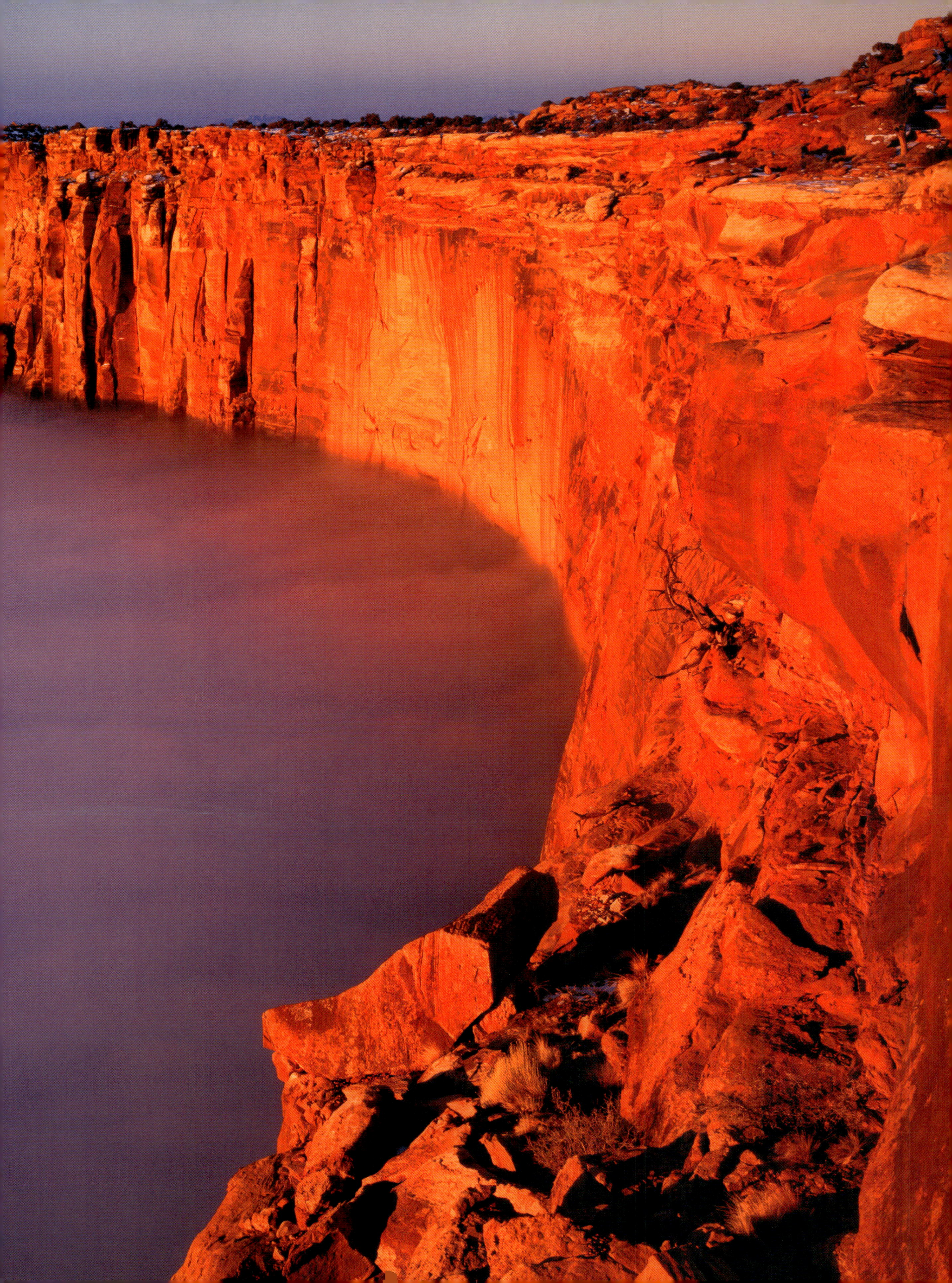

PREVIOUS PAGE:
Fog fills Canyonlands National Park at Grandview Point. Over the years I've spent a lot of time photographing fog ands its interaction with the landforms of Utah. In the Canyonlands, this has mostly been a frustrating series of failures because the fog level always seemed to sit right at the level of the canyon rims, obscuring any view below. One short-lived fog regime in 2004 was different. During this event, the fog formed several hundred feet below the rim, allowing the mesas and buttes to rise above what looked like an ocean. As the sun rose, the intense red from the Wingate cliffs reflected on the blue fog, lending it a fiery glow.

BELOW:
Balanced Rock in Arches National Park is a favorite subject. I've shot it in almost every conceivable way: at night, with lightning, with incredible clouds, in fog, during rainbows, and, in this case with a slight telephoto to enhance its size.

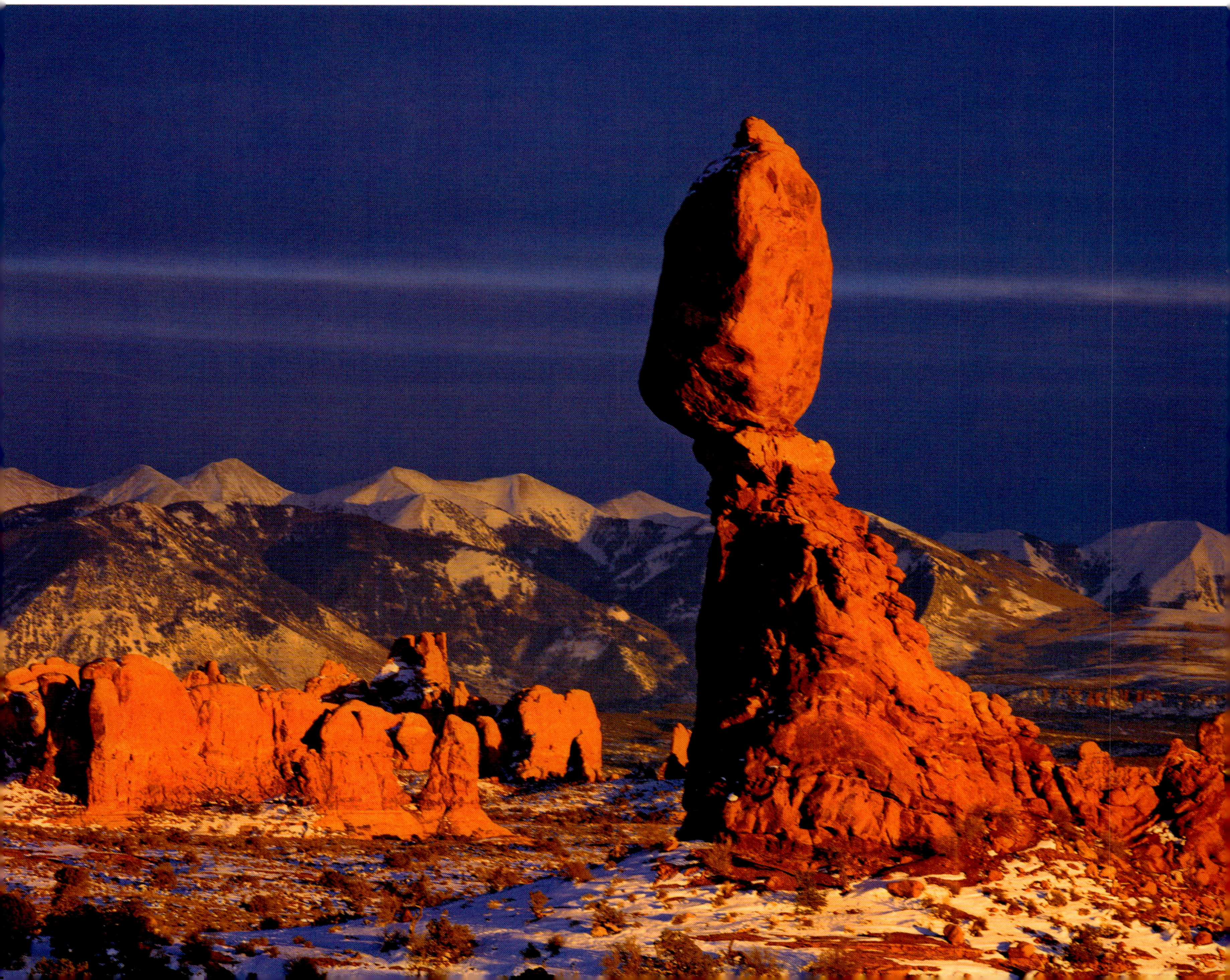

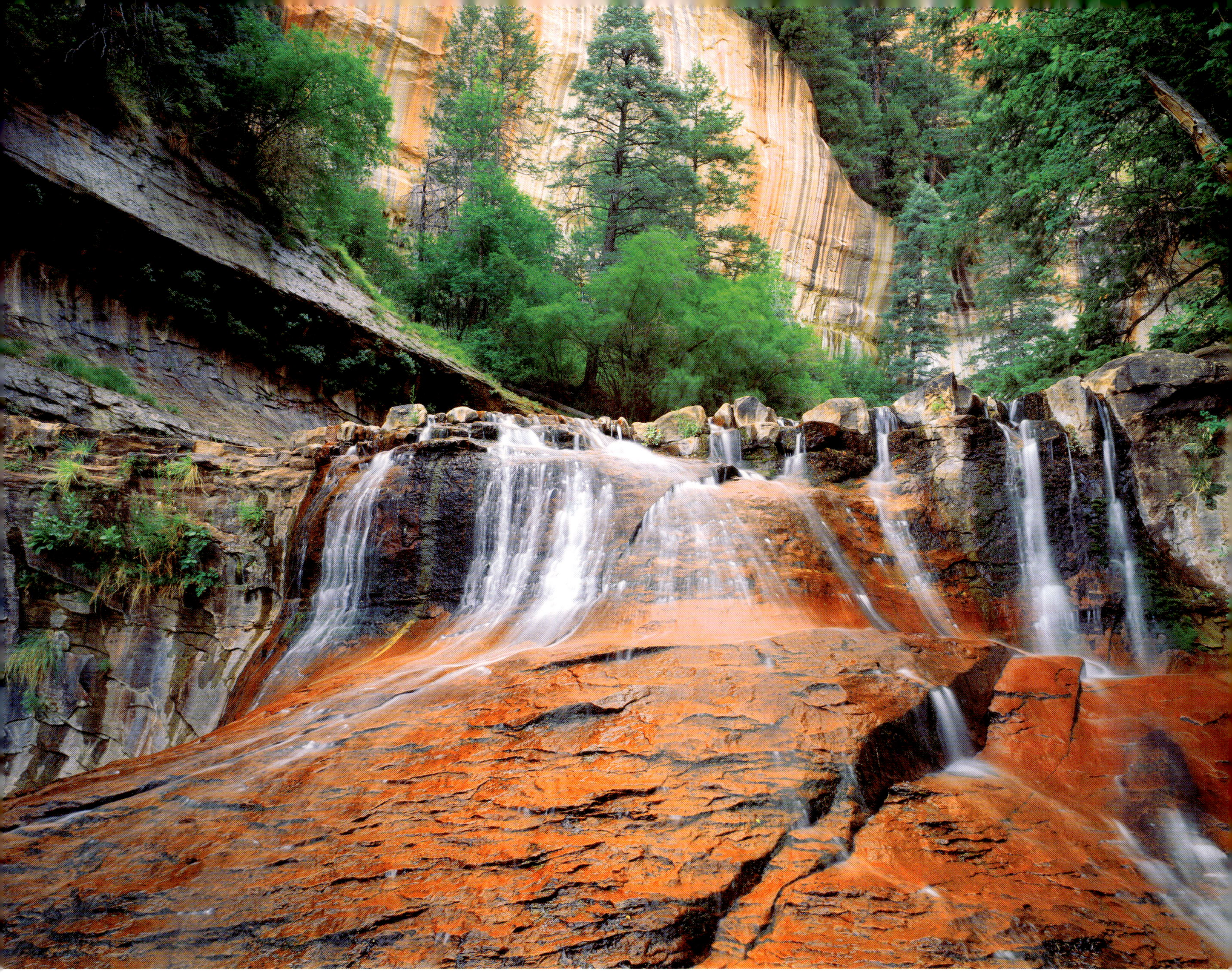

ABOVE:
These falls tumble out of the Subway in Zion National Park. I made the shot after climbing down all the way from the top. I believe I was the first photographer to take a large format camera into the Subway, in 1985.

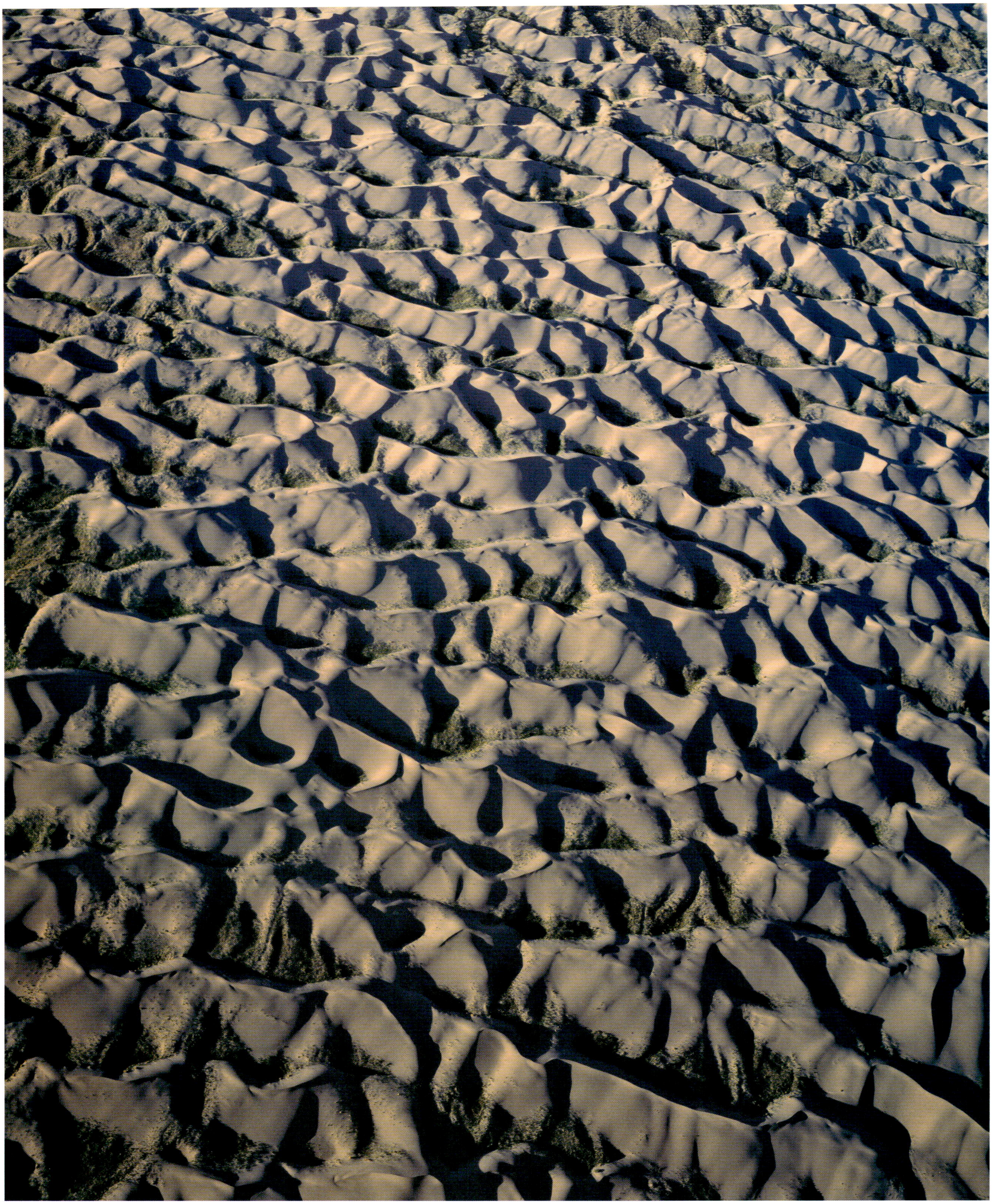

ABOVE:
Though much of the Little Sahara Sand Dunes north of Delta are a recreation area for OHV's, part of the area is a proposed wilderness. The beauty of this austere place explains why.

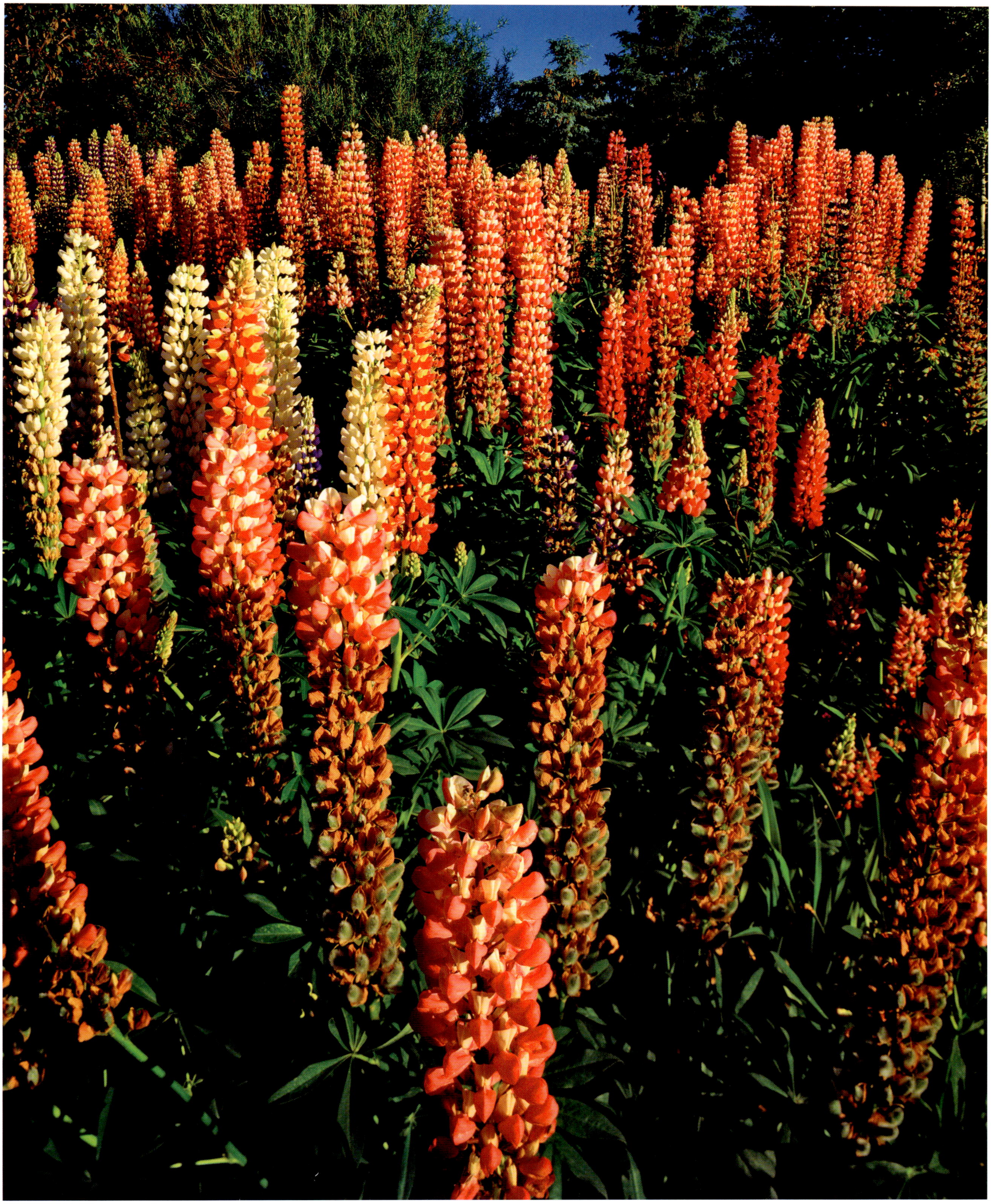

ABOVE:
Giant lupine create a colorful tableau in Park City.

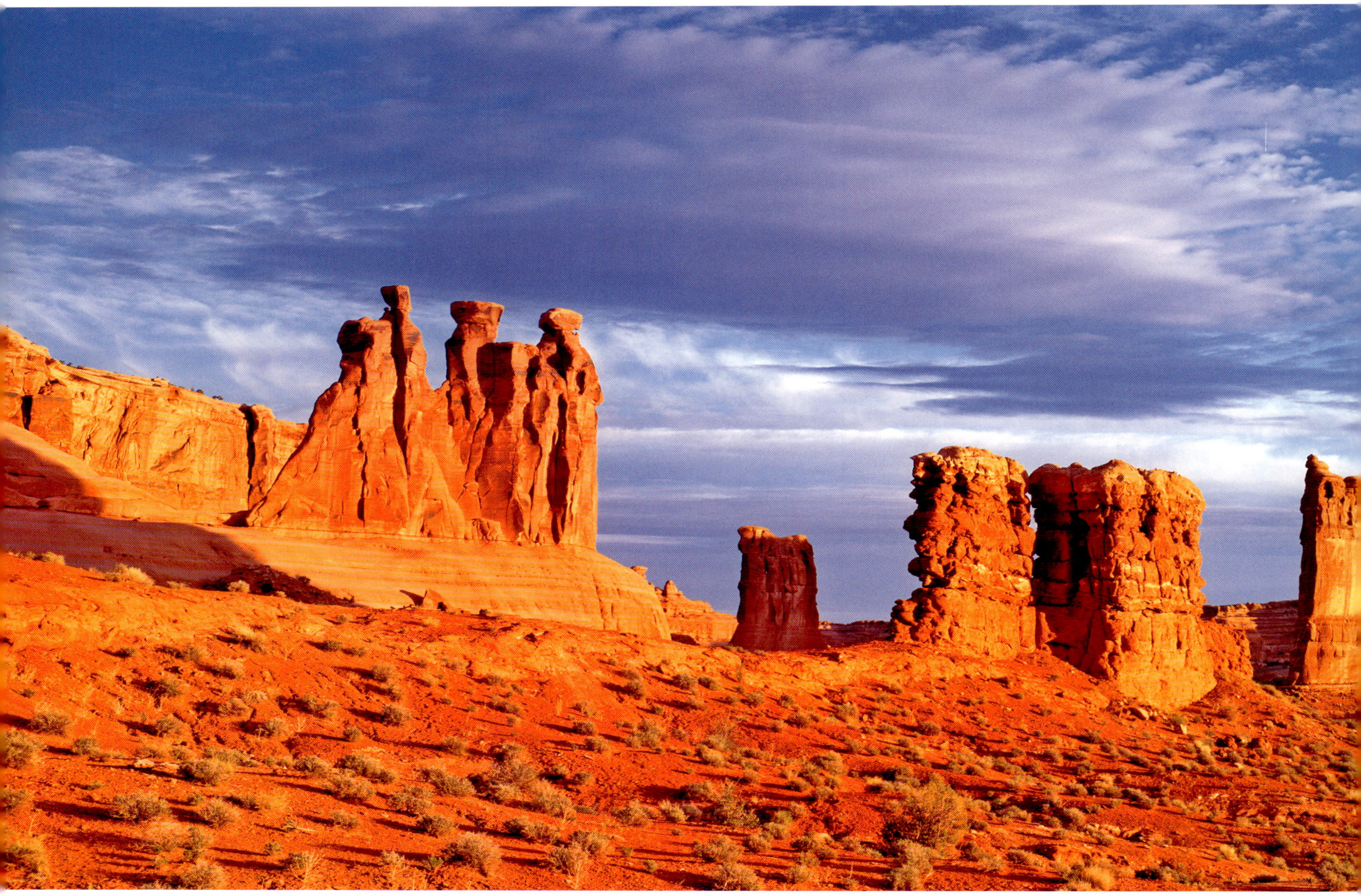

ABOVE:
The towers of Arches National Park create a wide vista during a summer sunrise. I photograph panoramic images with a Fuji 6x17 camera, which creates an image 6x17cm in size. As a frequent visitor to Australia, I'm amazed sometimes that landscape photography there is almost completely done in this format. This is the first of several true panoramic images in the book.

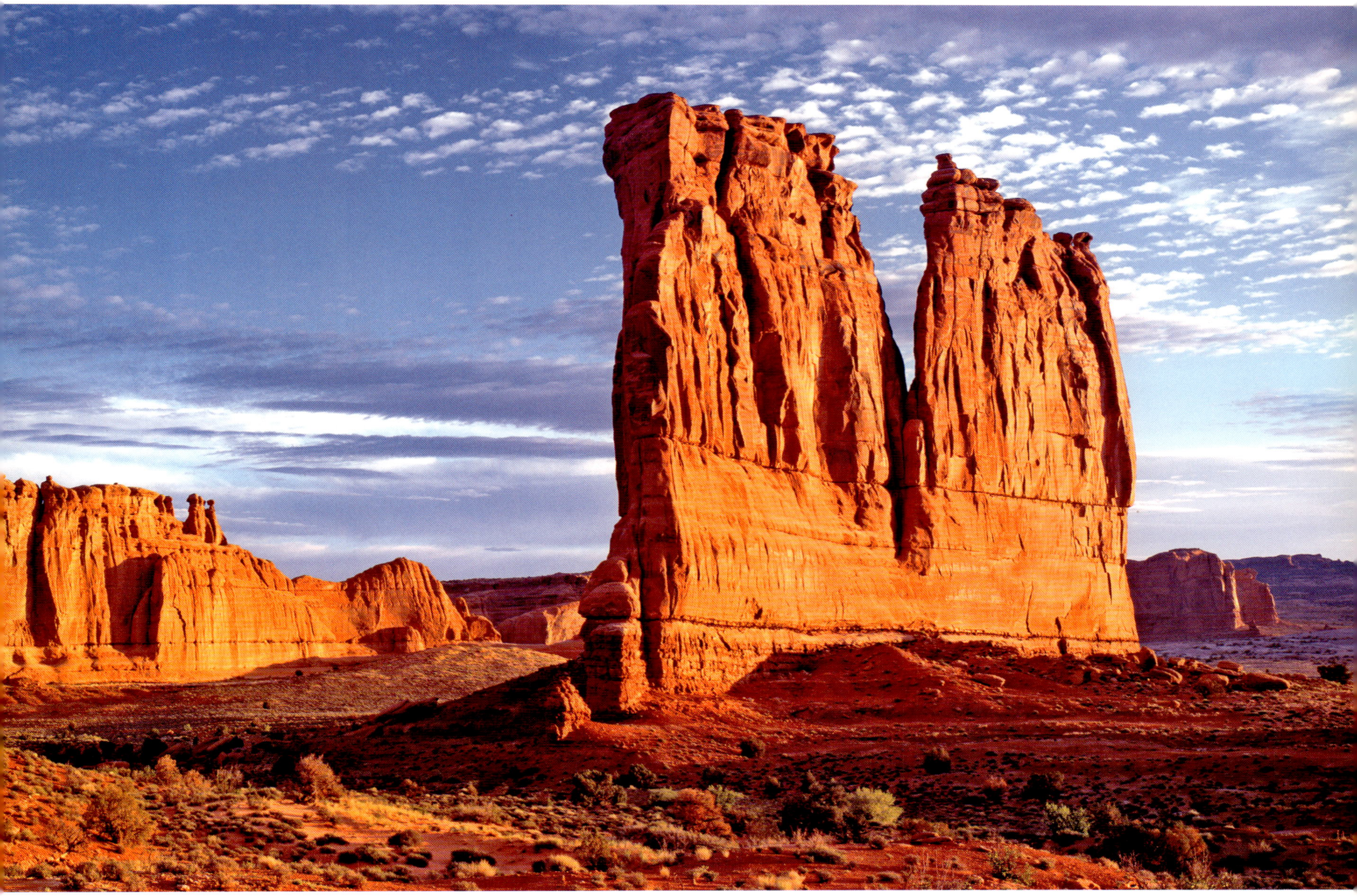

The Return of Glen Canyon

For what appears now as a short blip in the climatic calendar, several years of drought in the Rockies and the Southwest drew down the waters of Lake Powell in Glen Canyon National Recreation Area to historic lows. As the reservoir became more like a river, I was able to explore the reemergence of Glen Canyon for the short periods when the lake was at its nadir.

The wonders I saw include Cathedral in the Desert, drowned for fifty years, natural arches that had formed underwater in fifty years rather than five million, trees submerged for half a century that still stood tall, and beautiful new streaking on the "bathtub ring."

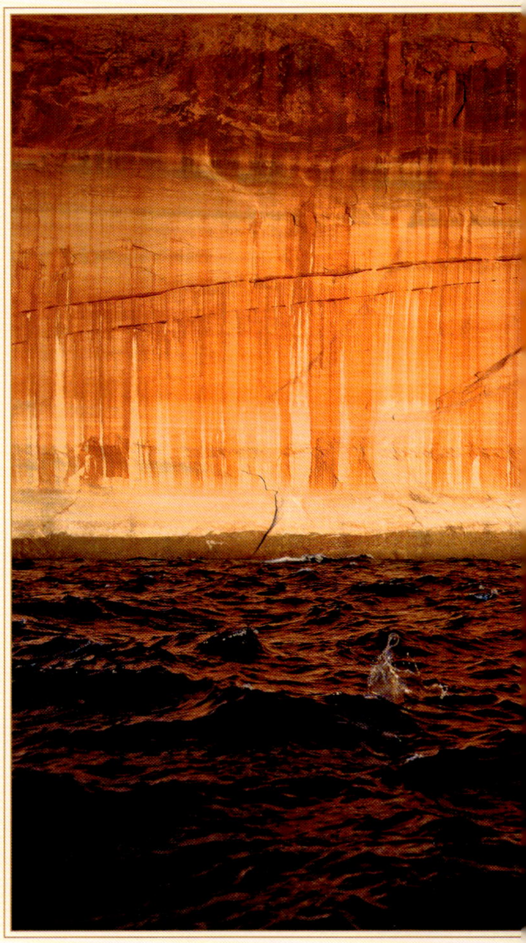

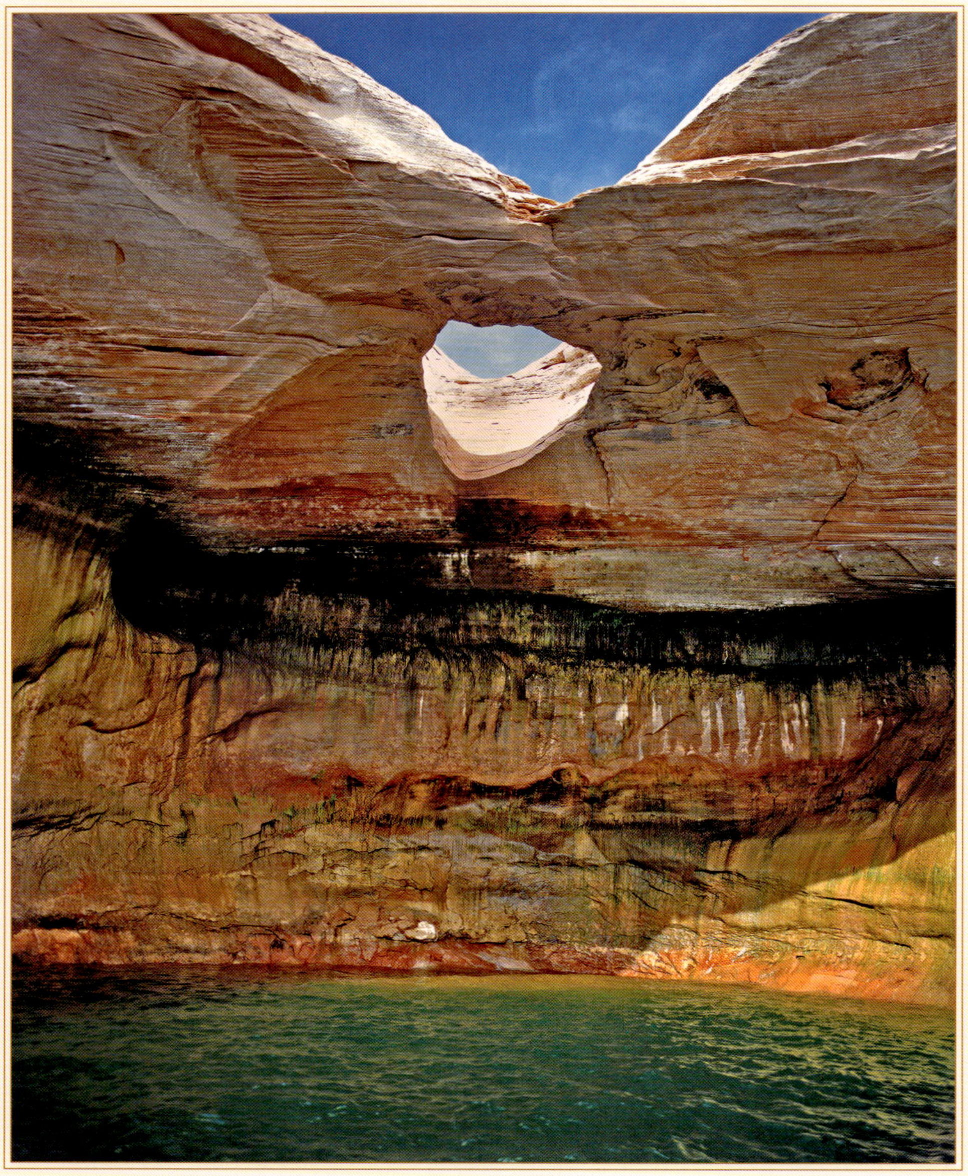

Normally, natural arches take millions of years to form, but when the waters of Lake Powell receded in the springs of 2004 and 2005, explorers were amazed to find dozens of new arches formed "overnight" in geologic terms. This arch near Wahweap is one of many examples.

The walls of Lake Powell, bleached white by the rising waters, create the "bathtub ring" when the water drops. In many areas rainstorms have redecorated the ring with colors that stand out like candy stripes.

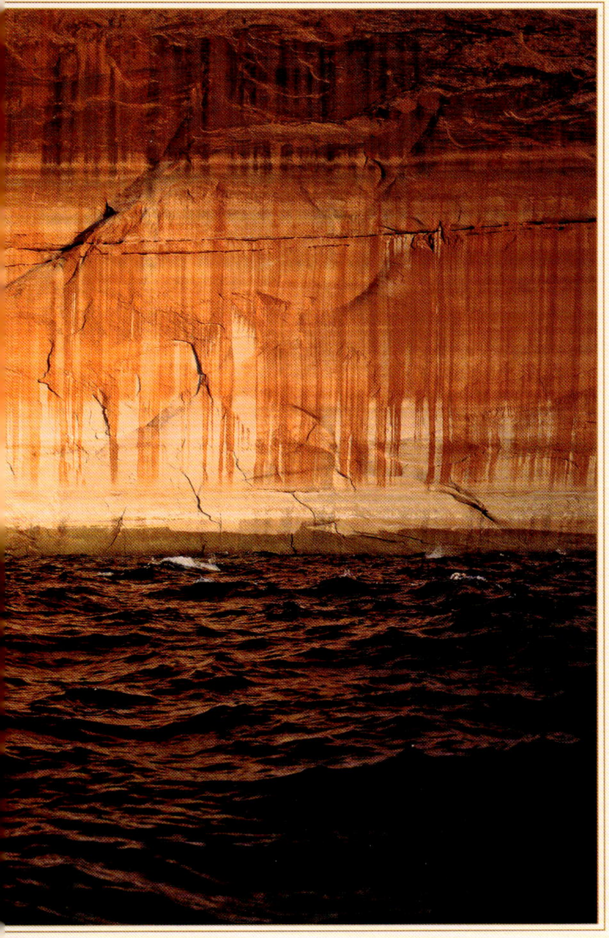

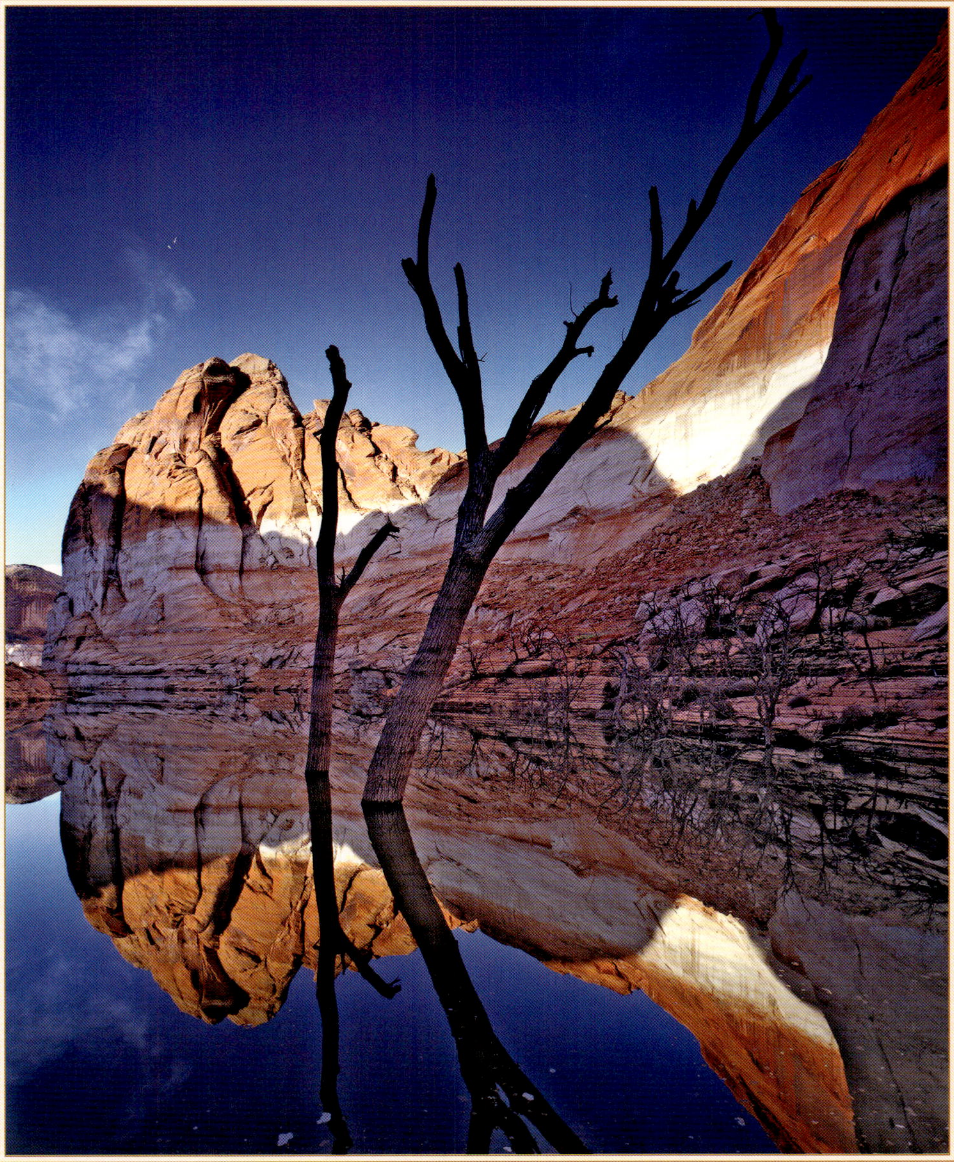

Left dry after being submerged for half a century, cottonwood trees still stand where they grew before Lake Powell was filled.

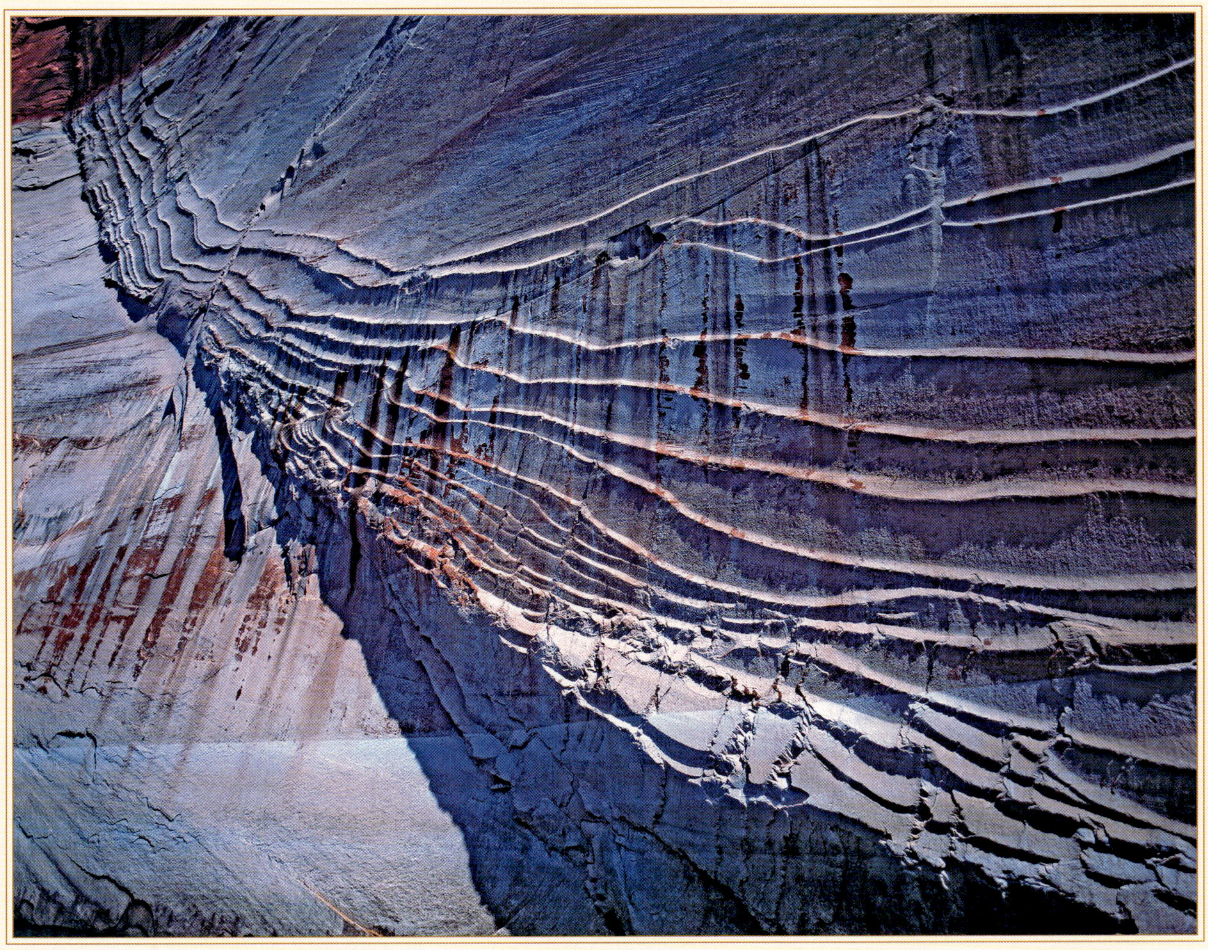

Besides natural arches, falling waters also revealed wonderful patterns and textures on the canyon walls like this example near Halls Crossing.

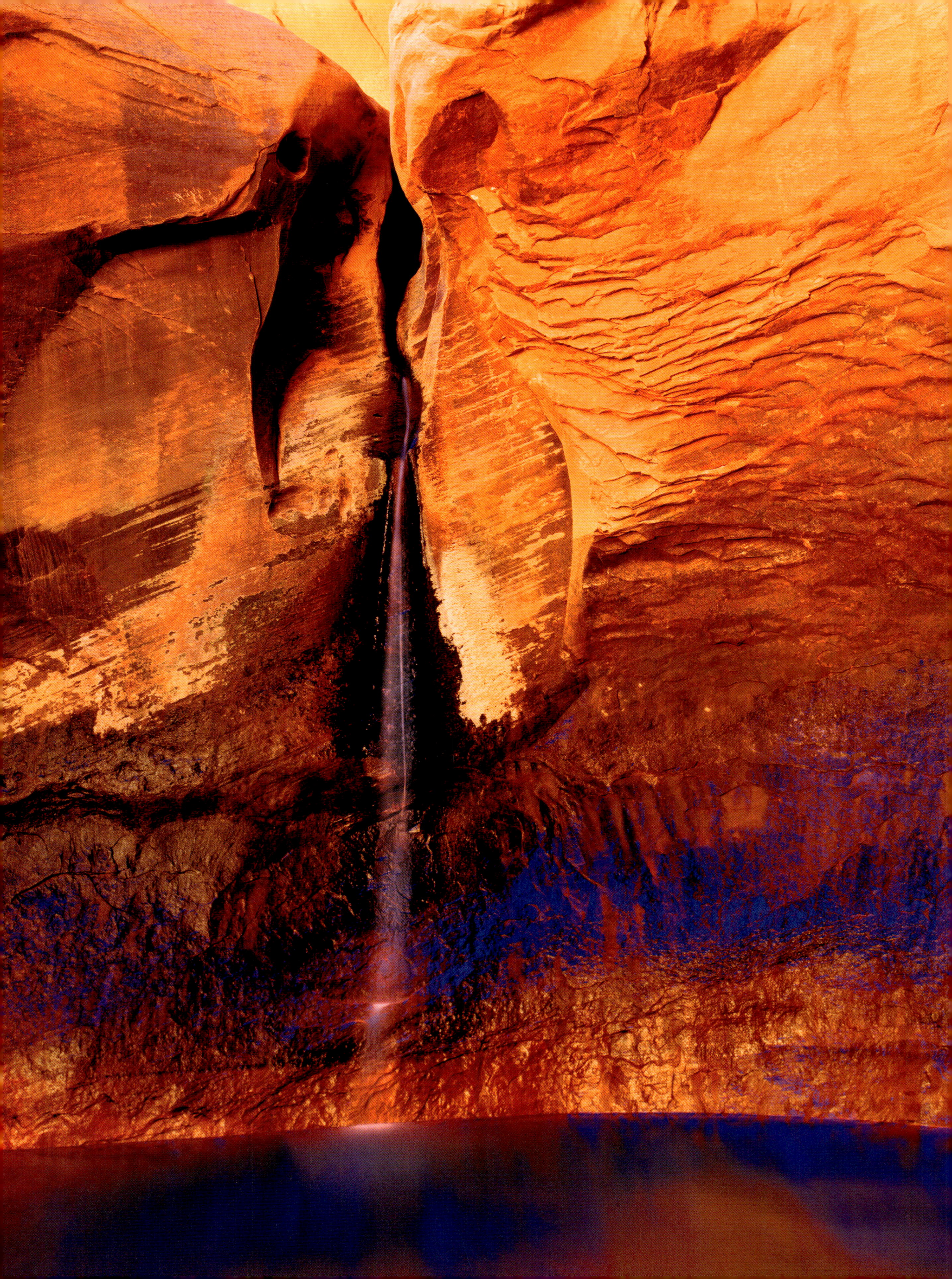

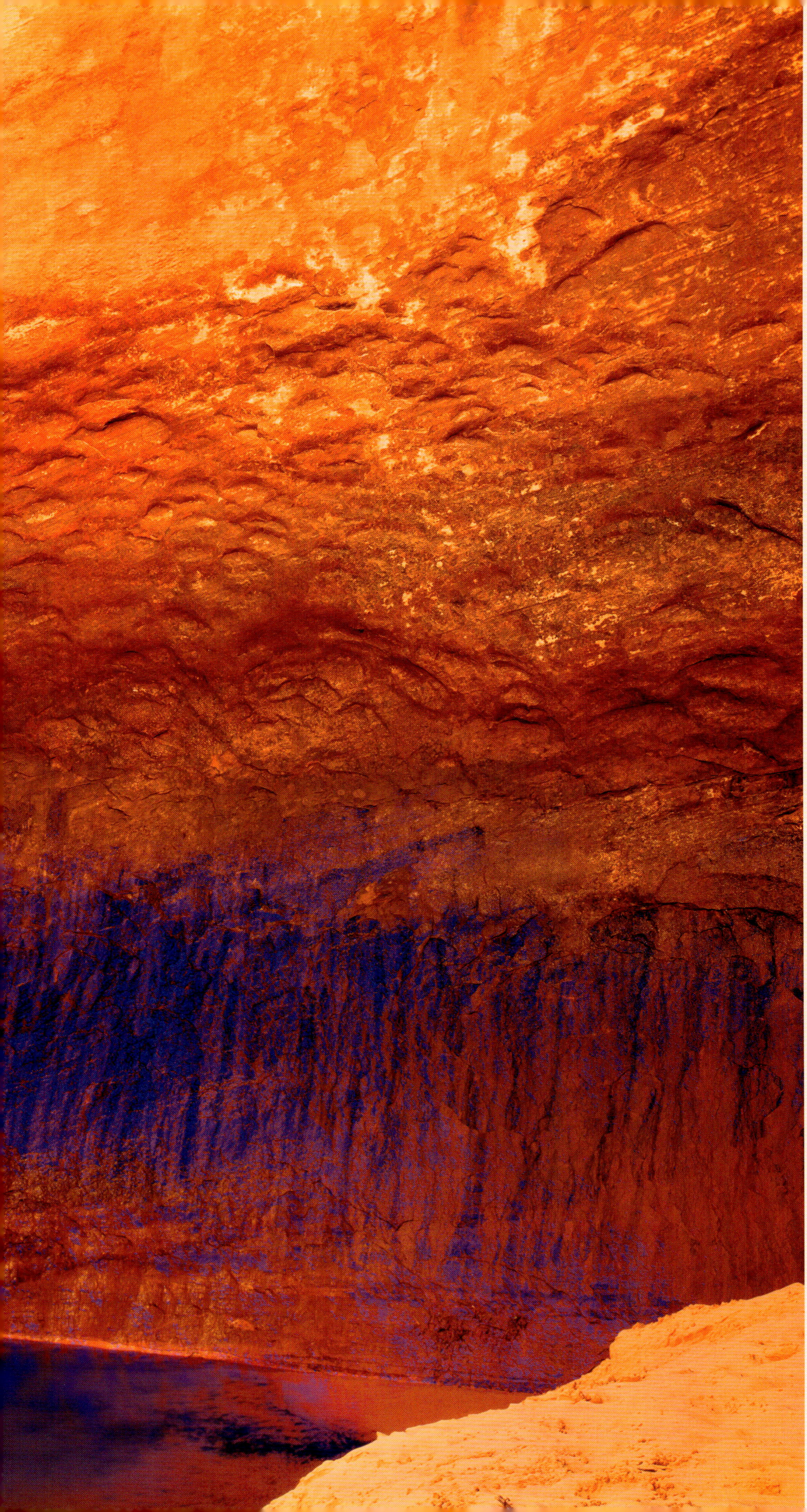

Cathedral in the Desert was the jewel of old Glen Canyon. I visited it twice, in 2004 and 2005.

In 2005, when the lake reached its lowest point, a sandbar appeared which allowed me to set up my 4x5 view camera.

This photograph was actually pointed out to me by my friend Bill Solawetz. In my excitement at photographing the slot canyon and waterfall in the Cathedral, I had set up my camera without looking around much. He quickly insisted I come across the creek to where he was.

Deep in the slot canyon, the weeping wall along the waterfall was reflecting blue sky, and the warmth of the slot canyon light was turning it purple.

Although what we saw was just a little of the magic of the old Cathedral in the Desert, it was amazing.

BELOW:
High above Naturalists Basin in the High Uintas Wilderness, a snow fed waterfall rushes from the top of a peak. I visited the beautiful basin with llamas carrying the seventy pounds of camera gear I needed for a week's shooting session.

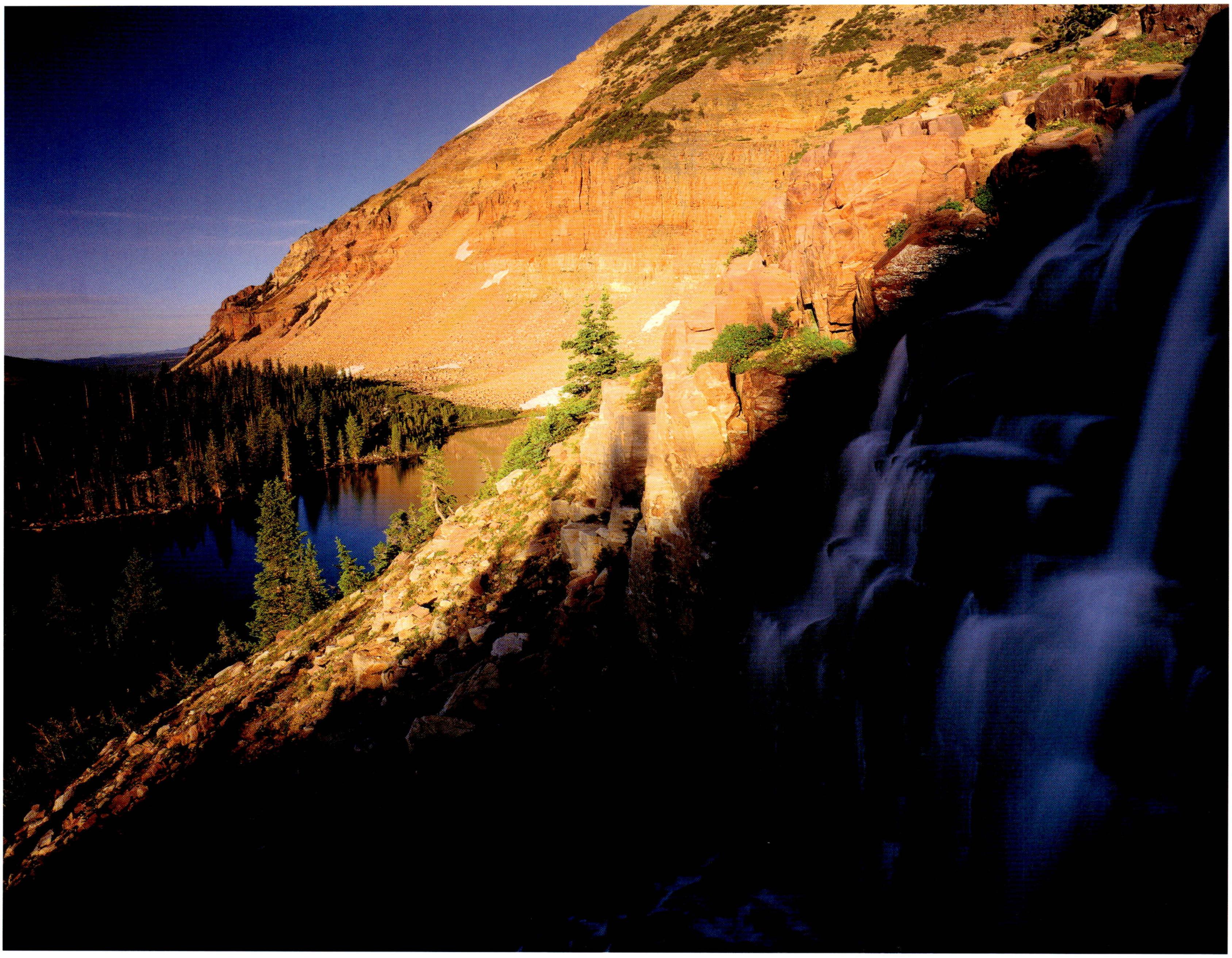

RIGHT:
A light ray enters a slot canyon in a proposed wilderness in Southern Utah. These rays penetrate the depths of these defiles only on the longest days of the year.

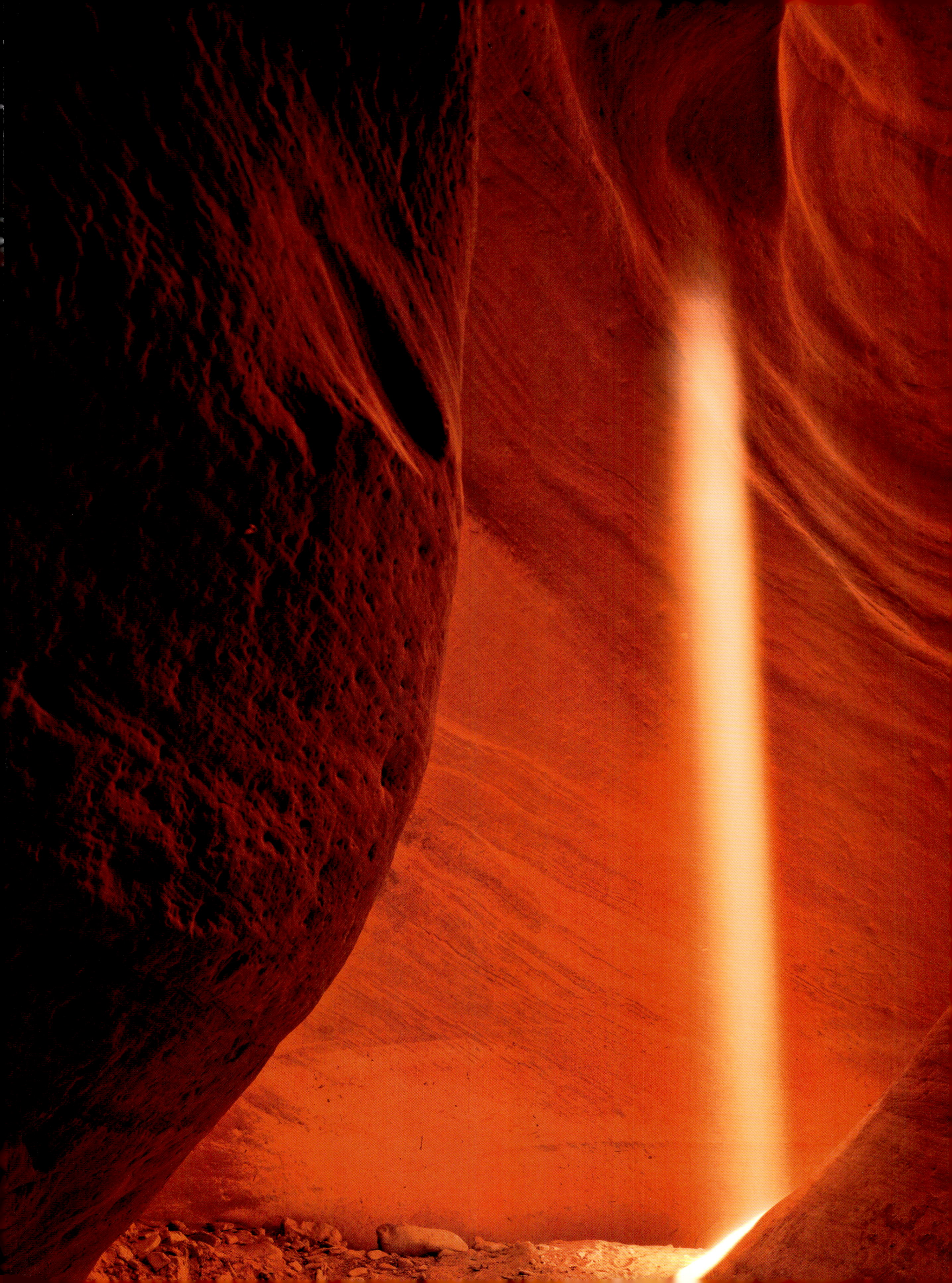

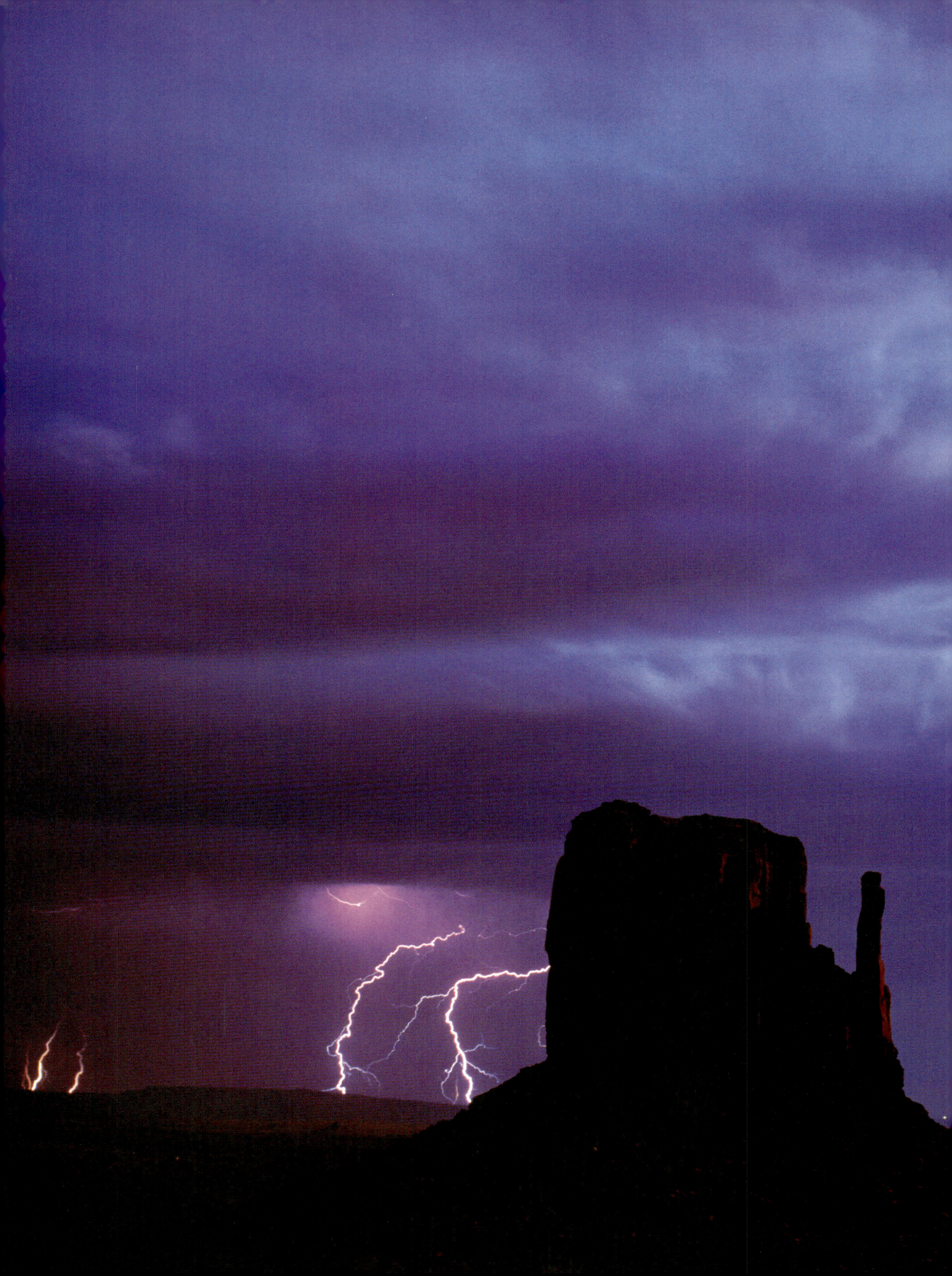

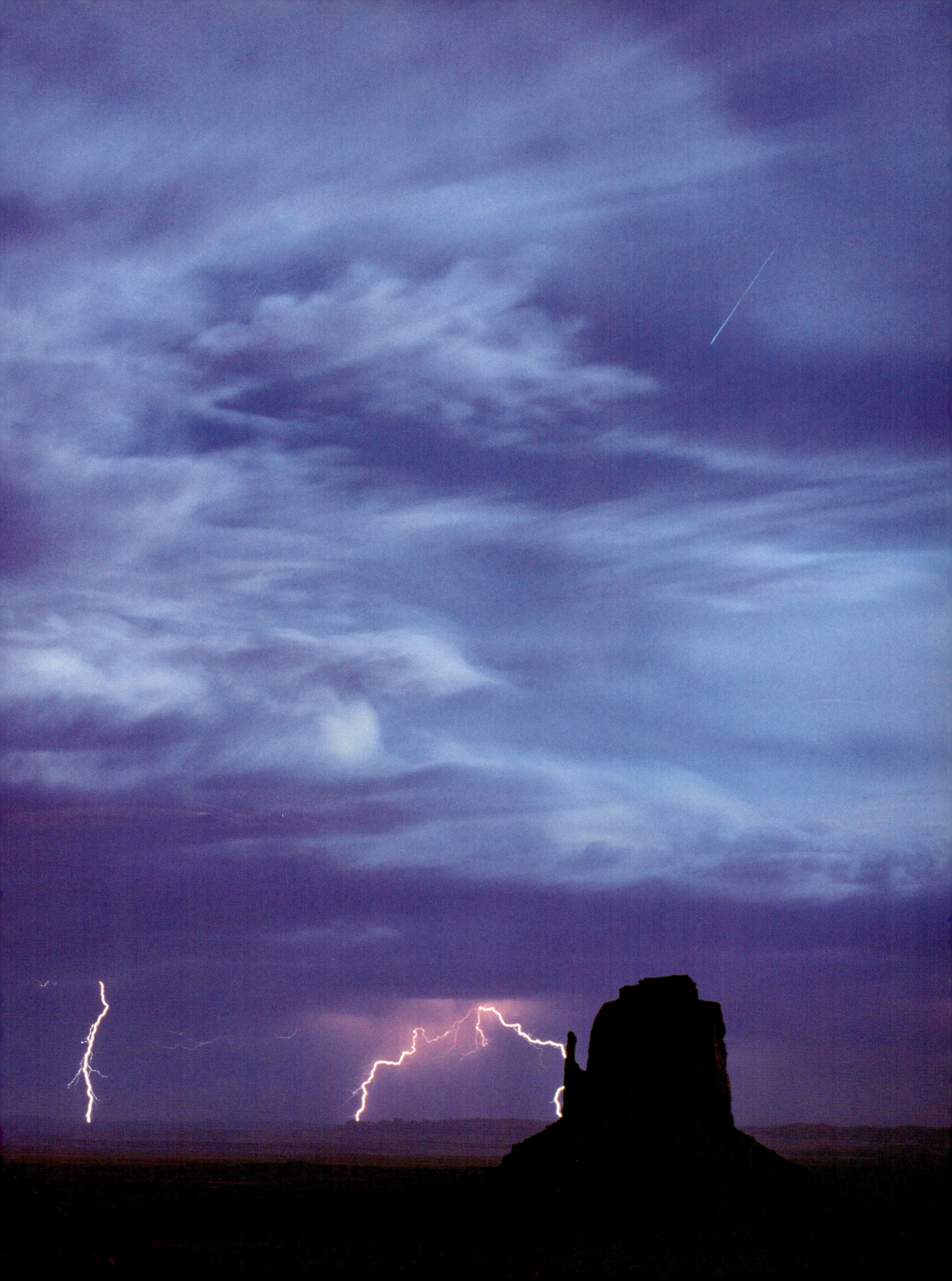

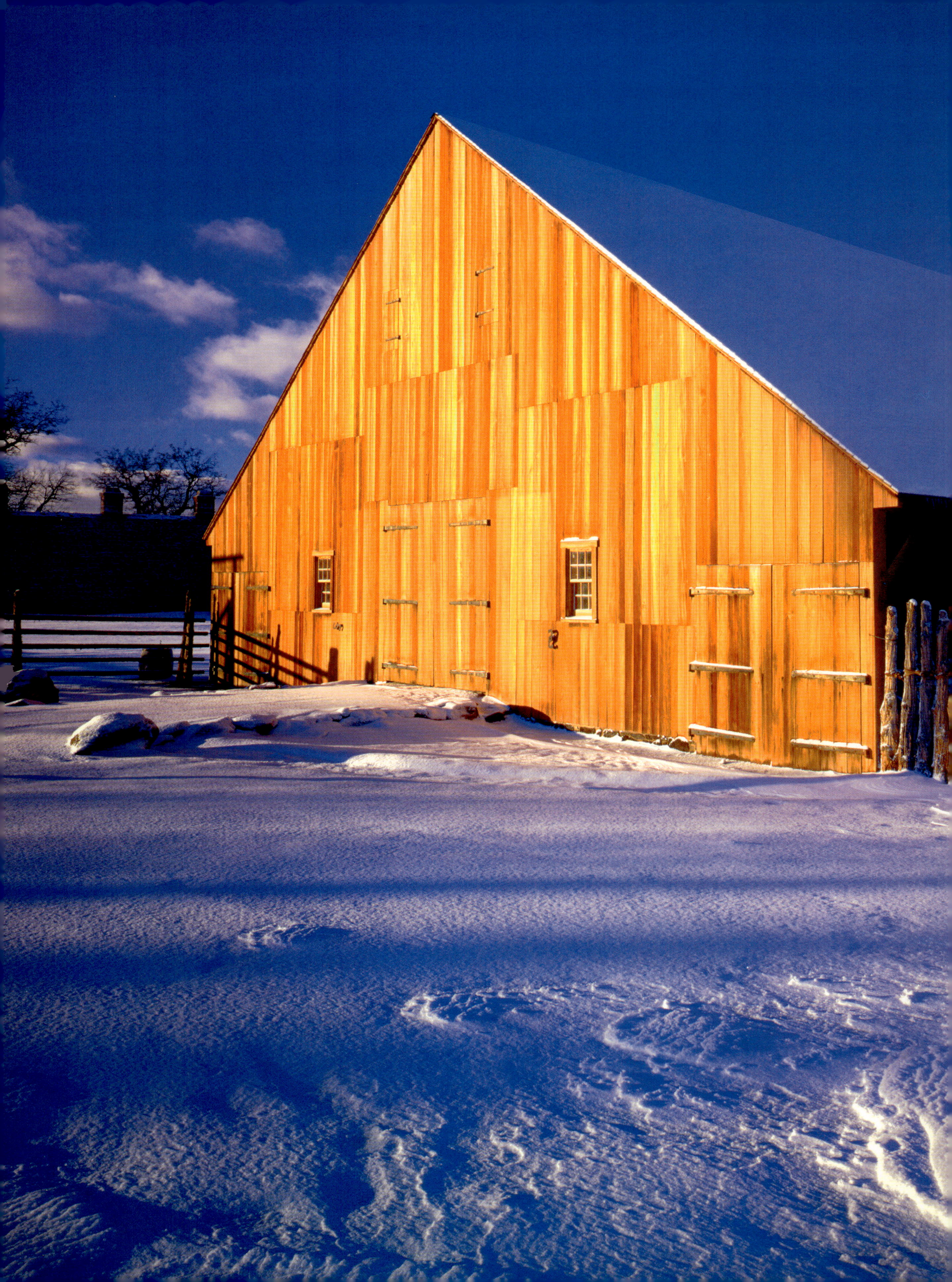

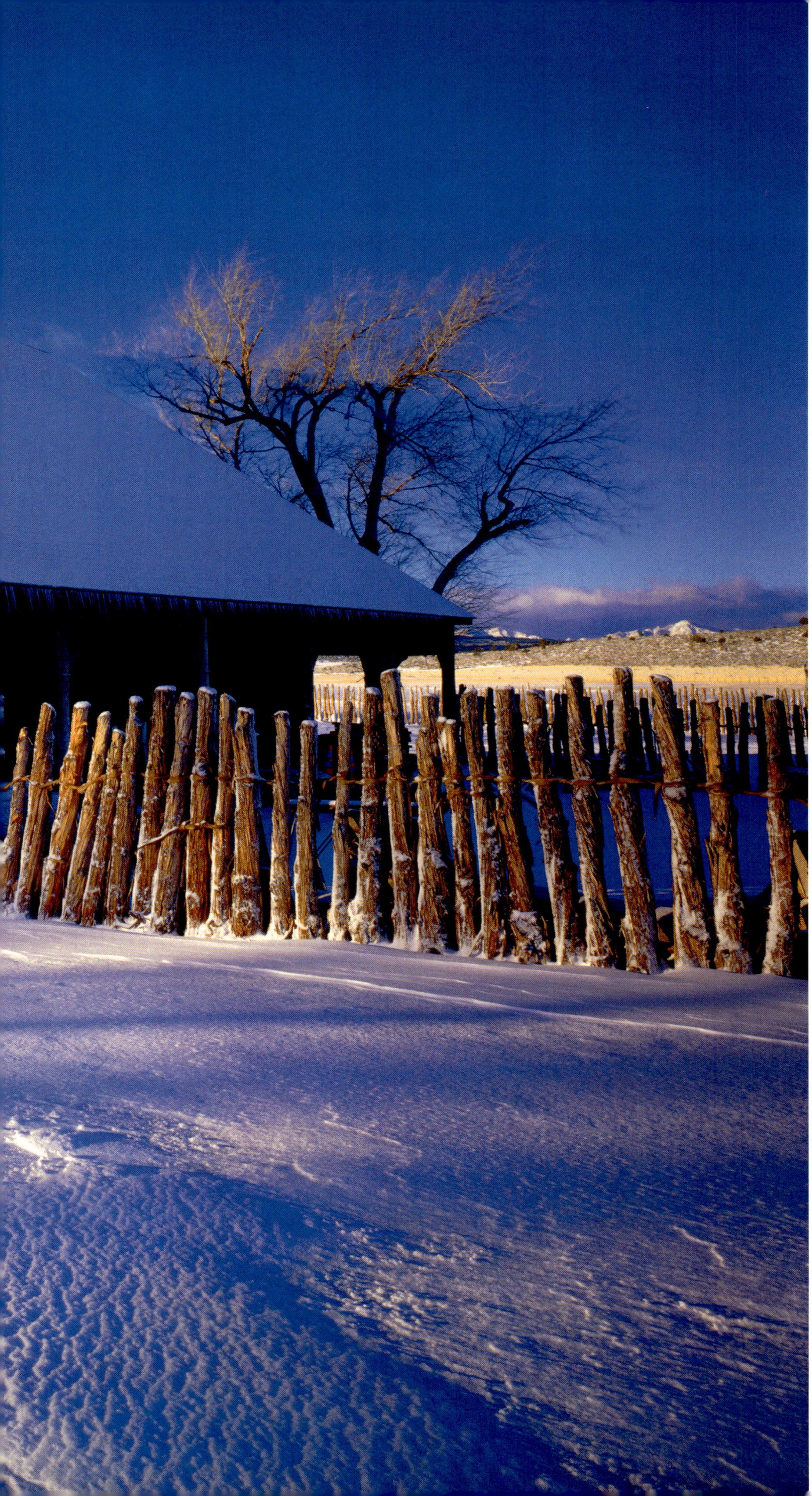

PREVIOUS PAGE:
Lightning plays among the Mittens in Monument Valley. I made the image with a Pentax 6x7 camera and a two-minute exposure.

A rising moon, not covered by the storm, provided enough illumination to light the buttes of the valley. The streaks are star trails.

LEFT:
One of America's most beautiful barns, the Cove Fort barn is placed perfectly to pick up the early rays of the rising winter sun.

I braved subzero temperatures to get the image and pre-visualized the beautiful mesh of blue snow and the warm-colored barn wood.

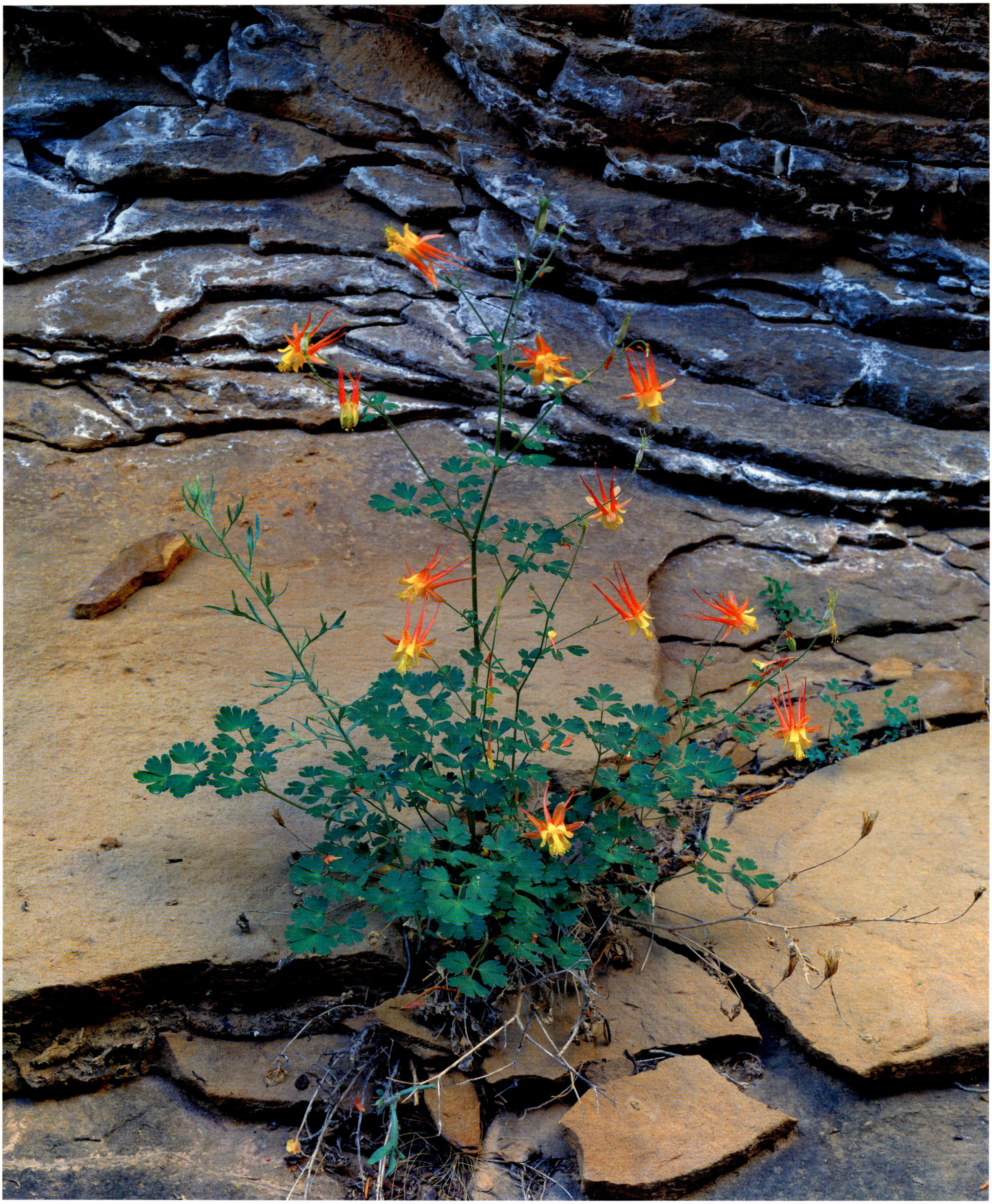

ABOVE:

A columbine clings to a rock wall in a small side canyon of Desolation Canyon, a proposed wilderness along the Green River.

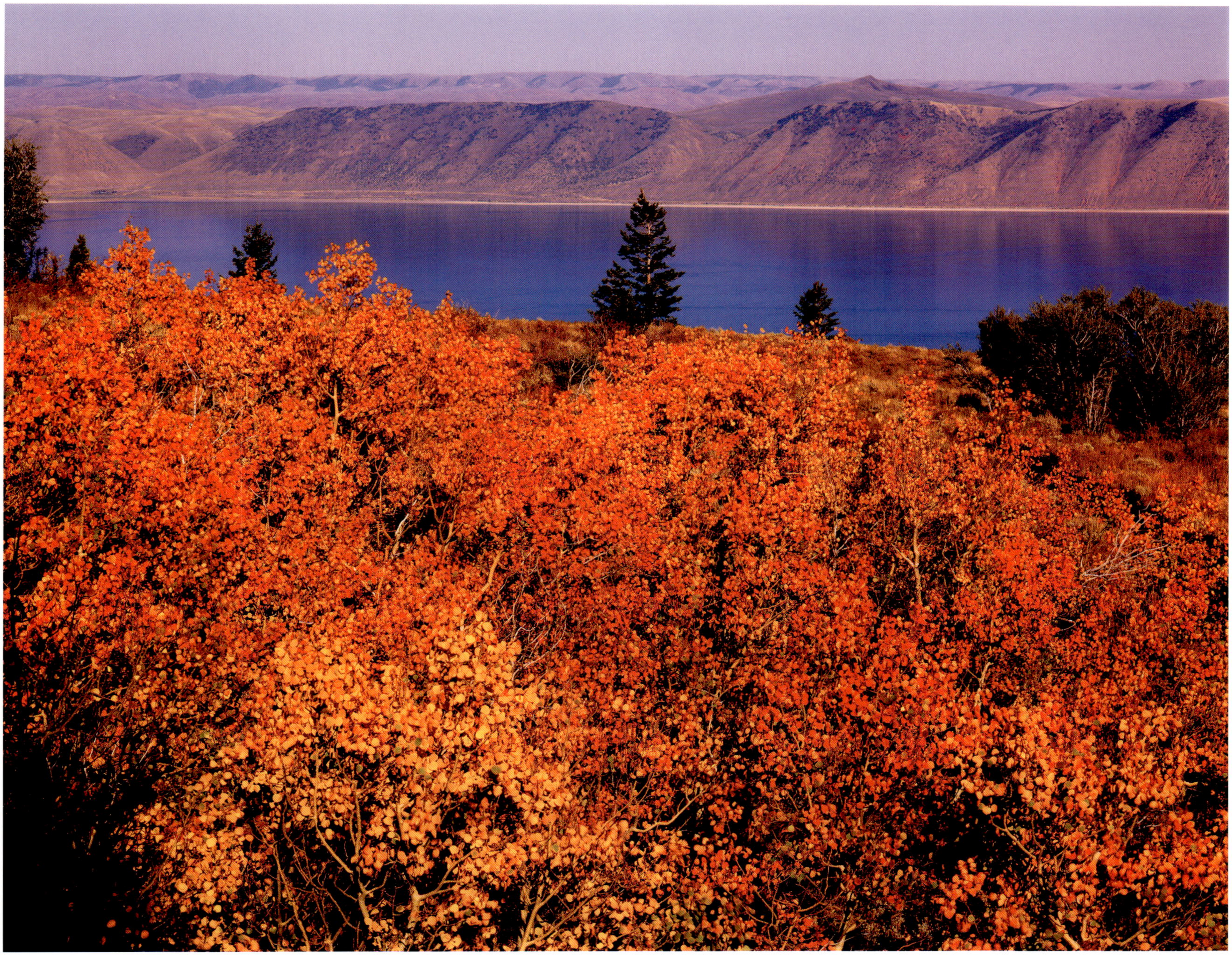

ABOVE:
Bear Lake's deep blues contrast with the intense fall colors of the Wasatch/Cache National Forest.

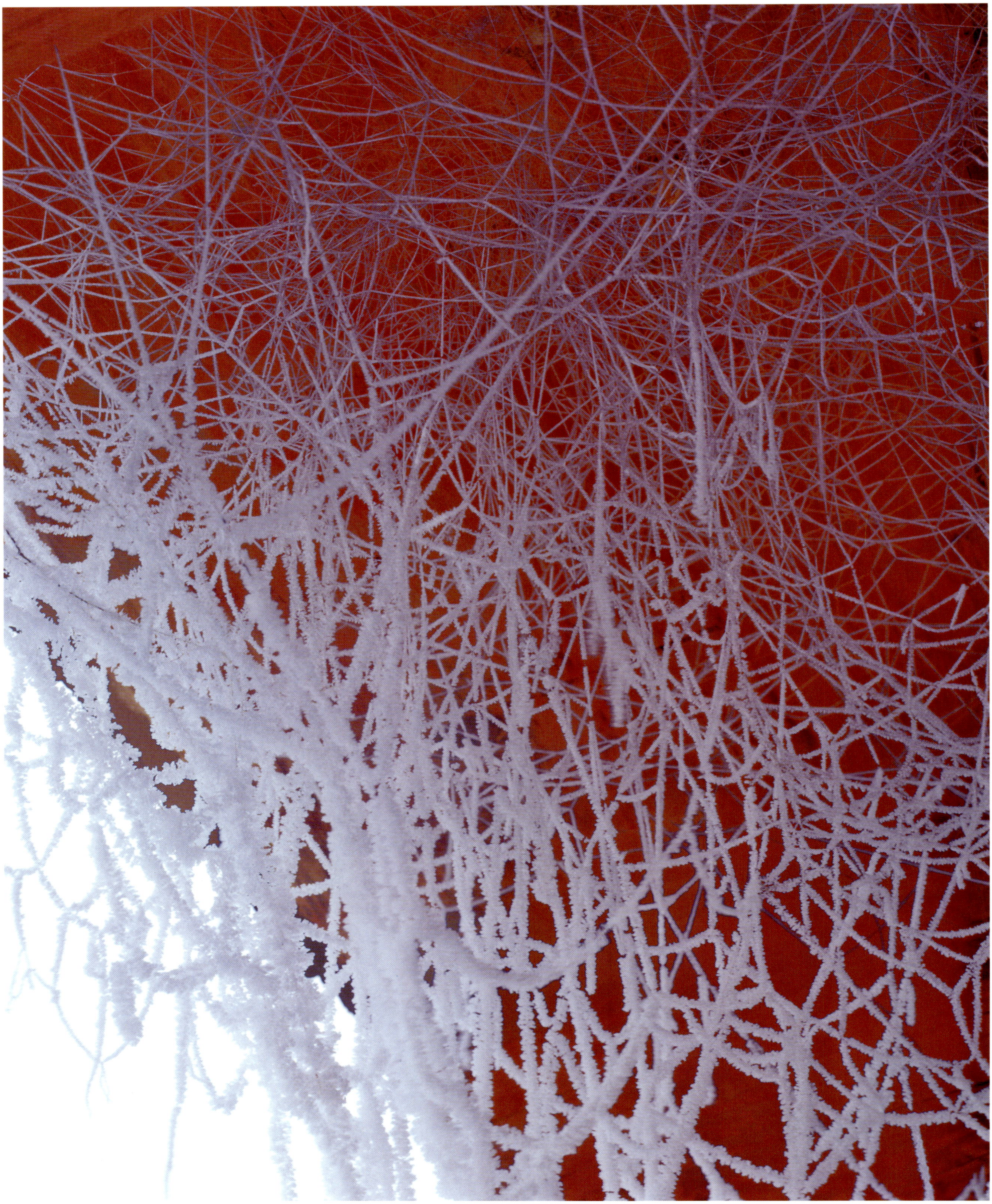

ABOVE:
An example of a favorite image that has never sold, this spider web was coated with a week's worth of rime ice from fog.

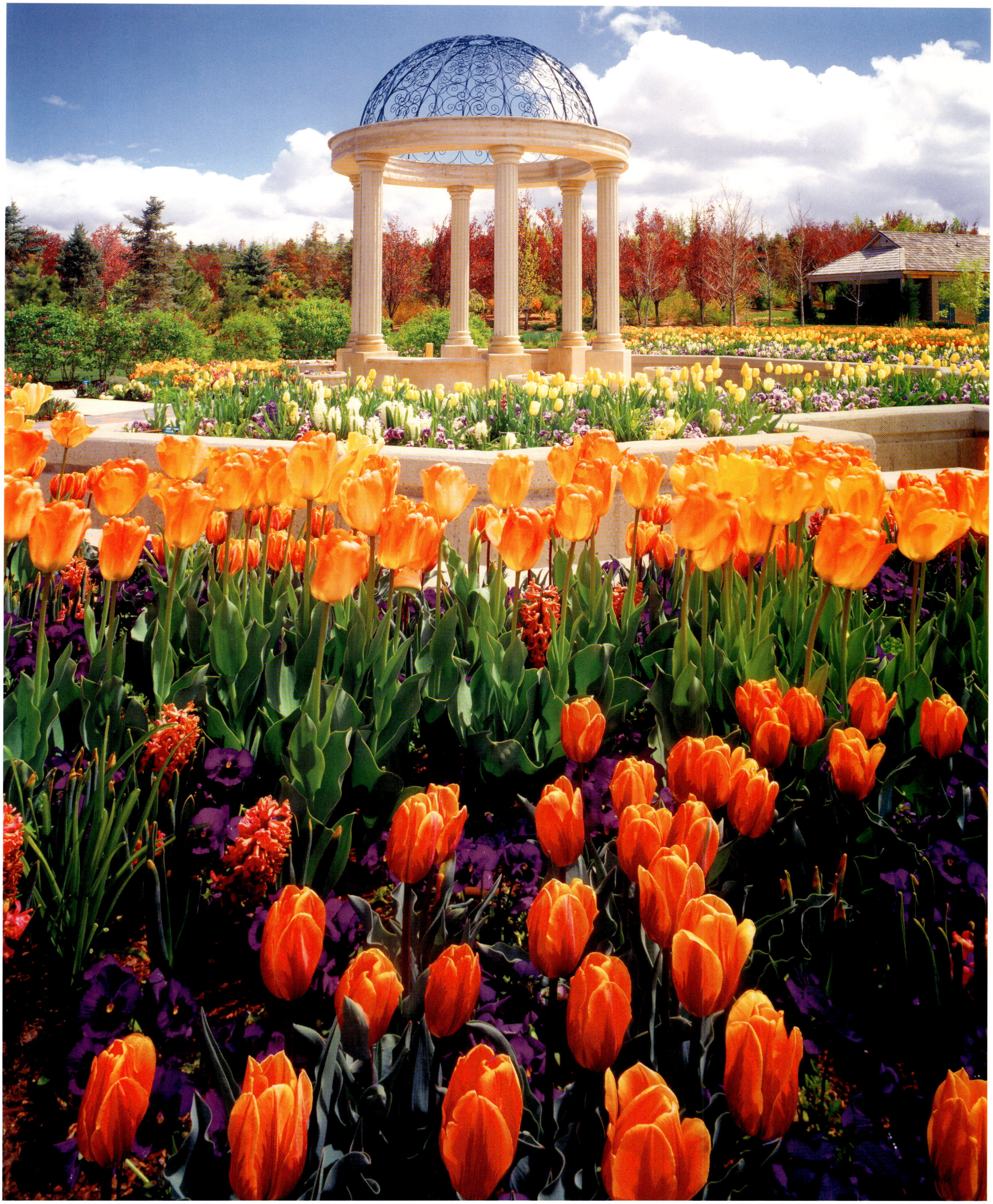

ABOVE:
The Thanksgiving Point tulips are a wonder to behold. My 4x5 camera allows me to hold focus from only a few inches from the camera out to infinity, but wind must be calm as my exposures can be quite long with this technique.

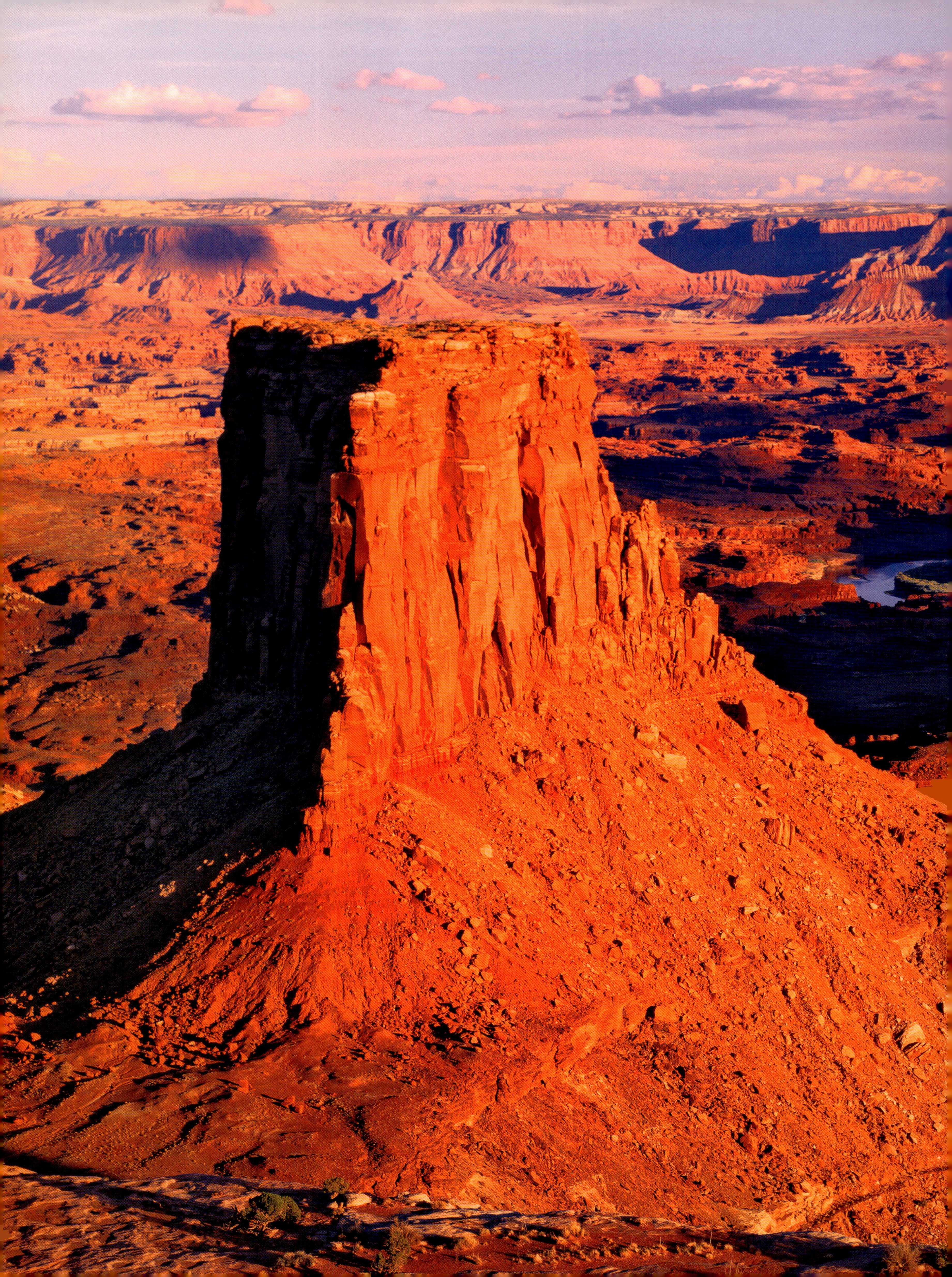

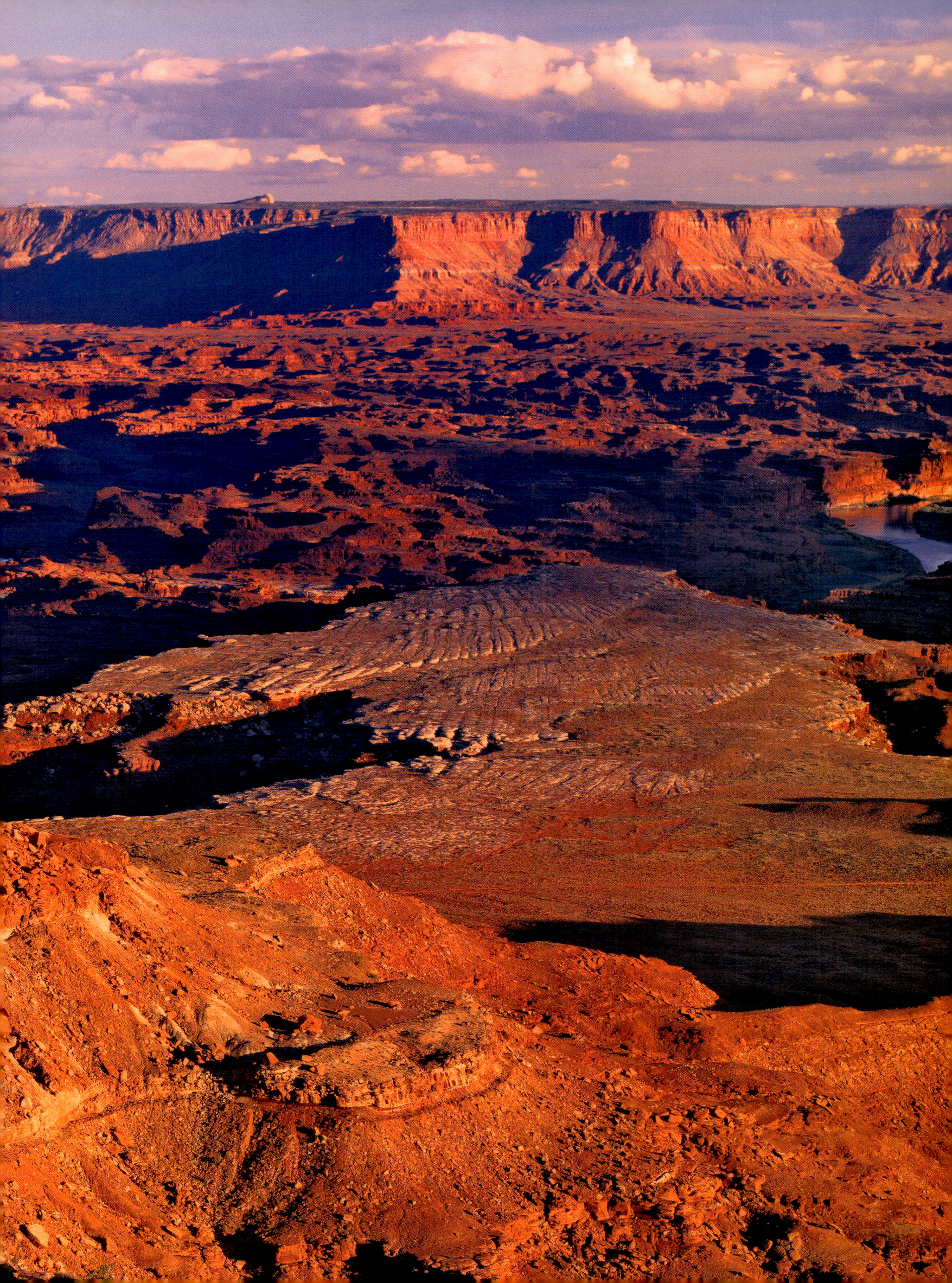

PREVIOUS PAGE:
Monster Tower looms above the Colorado River below the White Rim in Canyonlands National Park.

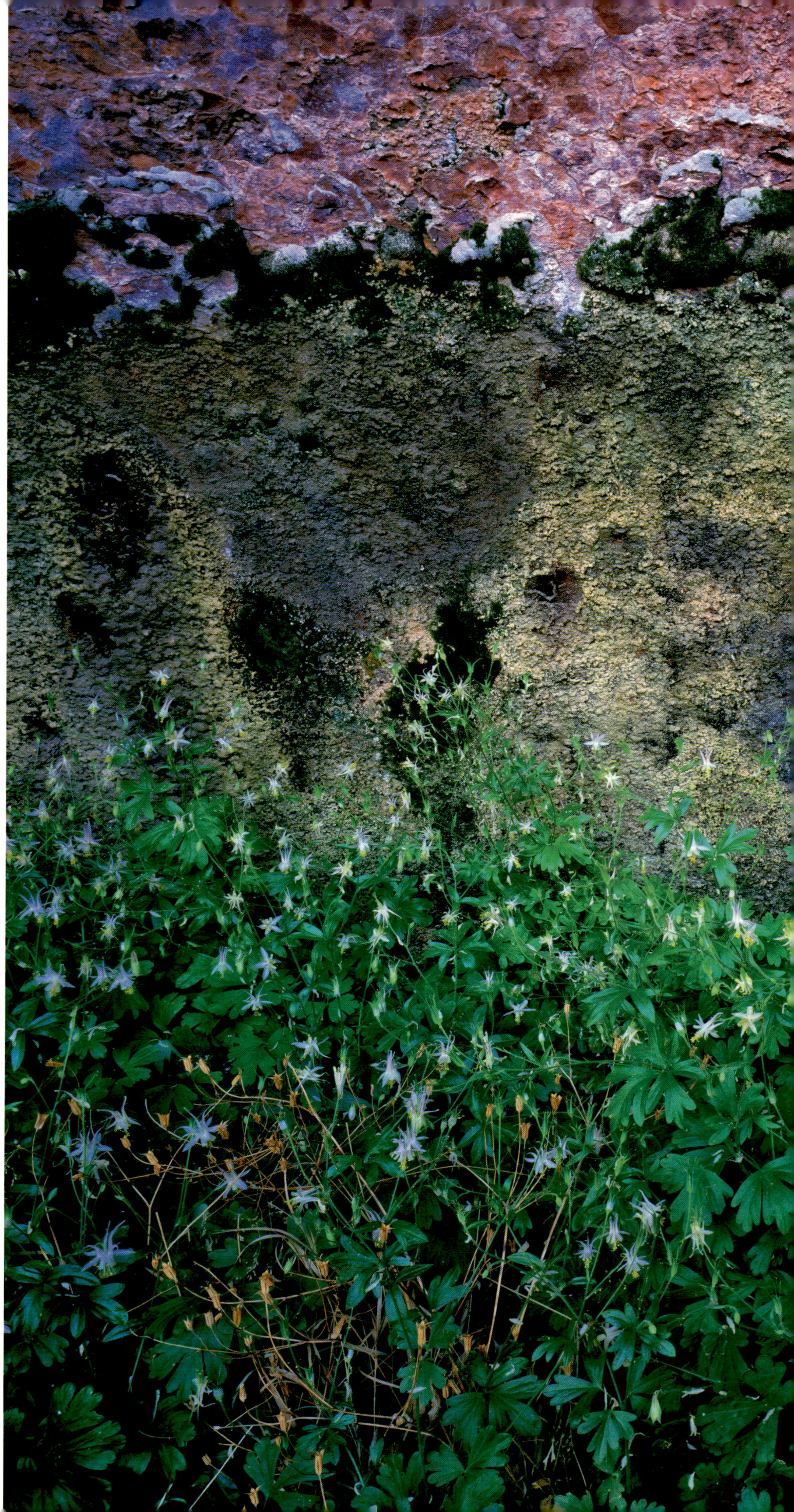

RIGHT:
A dense bloom of columbine adorns a wall in Moquith Mountain Wilderness Study Area.

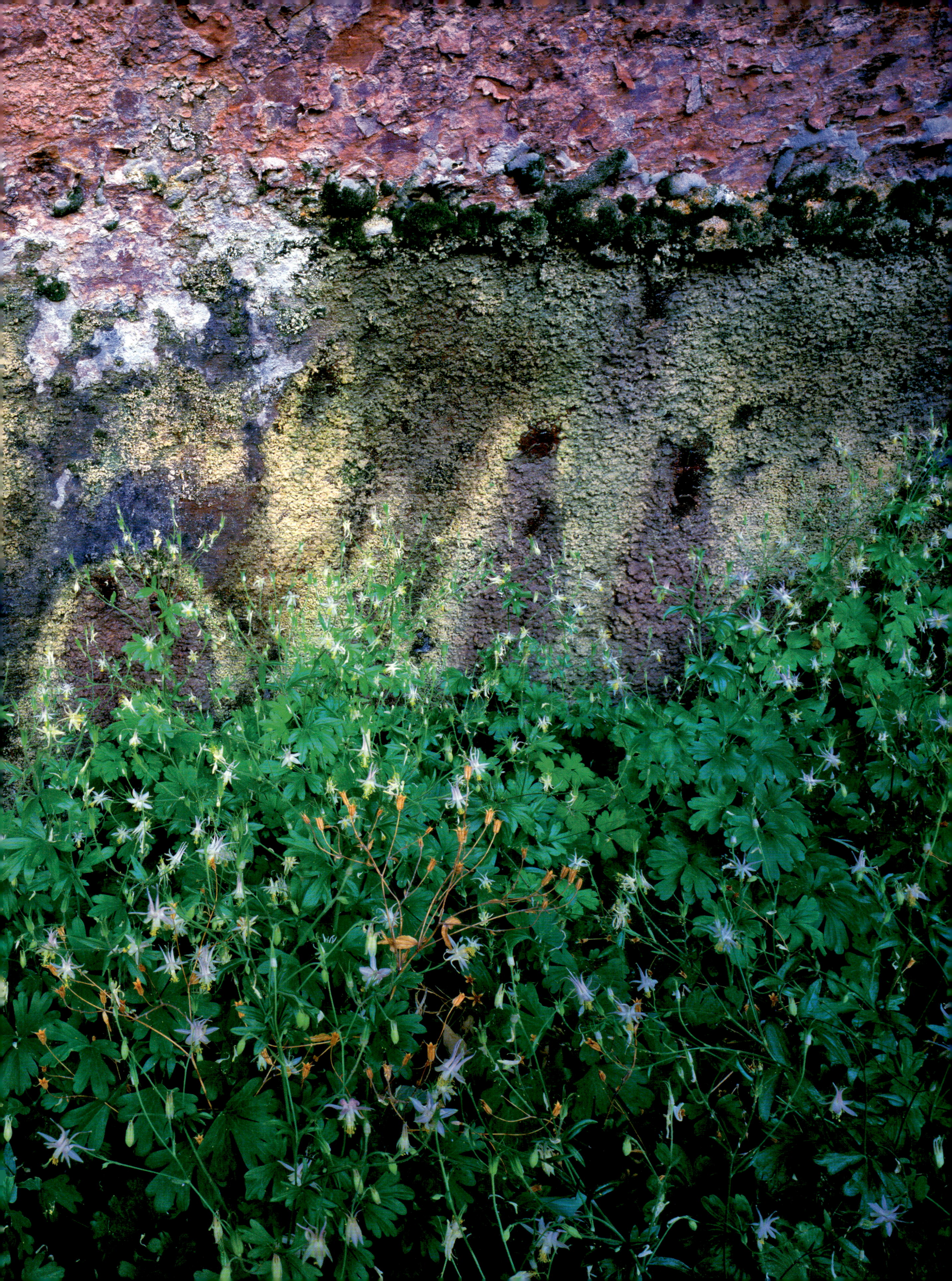

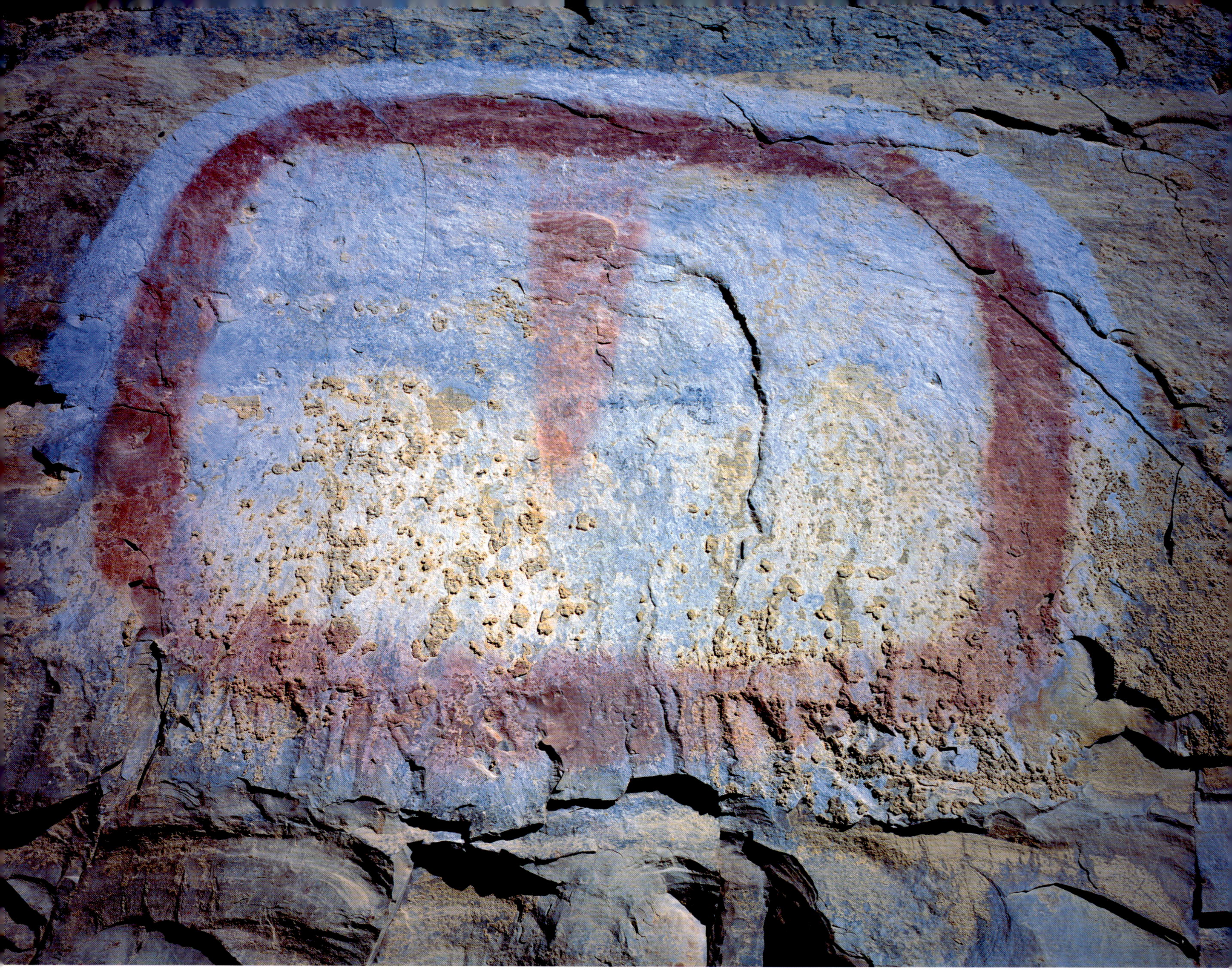

ABOVE:
The so-called "TV Screen" is an interesting pictograph panel in the newly designated Range Creek Canyon Wildlife Management Area. The ghostly Fremont culture image appearing on the "screen" makes for a compelling and mysterious experience. There is some precedence, for better or worse, for naming a rock-art panel after a modern entity — witness the All-American Man (a red, white, and blue pictograph) and "The Beach Boy Panel," my name for a group of pictograph images that seem to have striped shirts.

BELOW:
This mysterious crop circle appeared overnight in a Spanish Fork field. Though crop circles are common in Europe, a number have appeared in the Intermountain West, and a few have been recorded in Utah before this one. Though many crop circles have been determined to be man-made, some defy easy explanation, and this circle is of unknown origin.

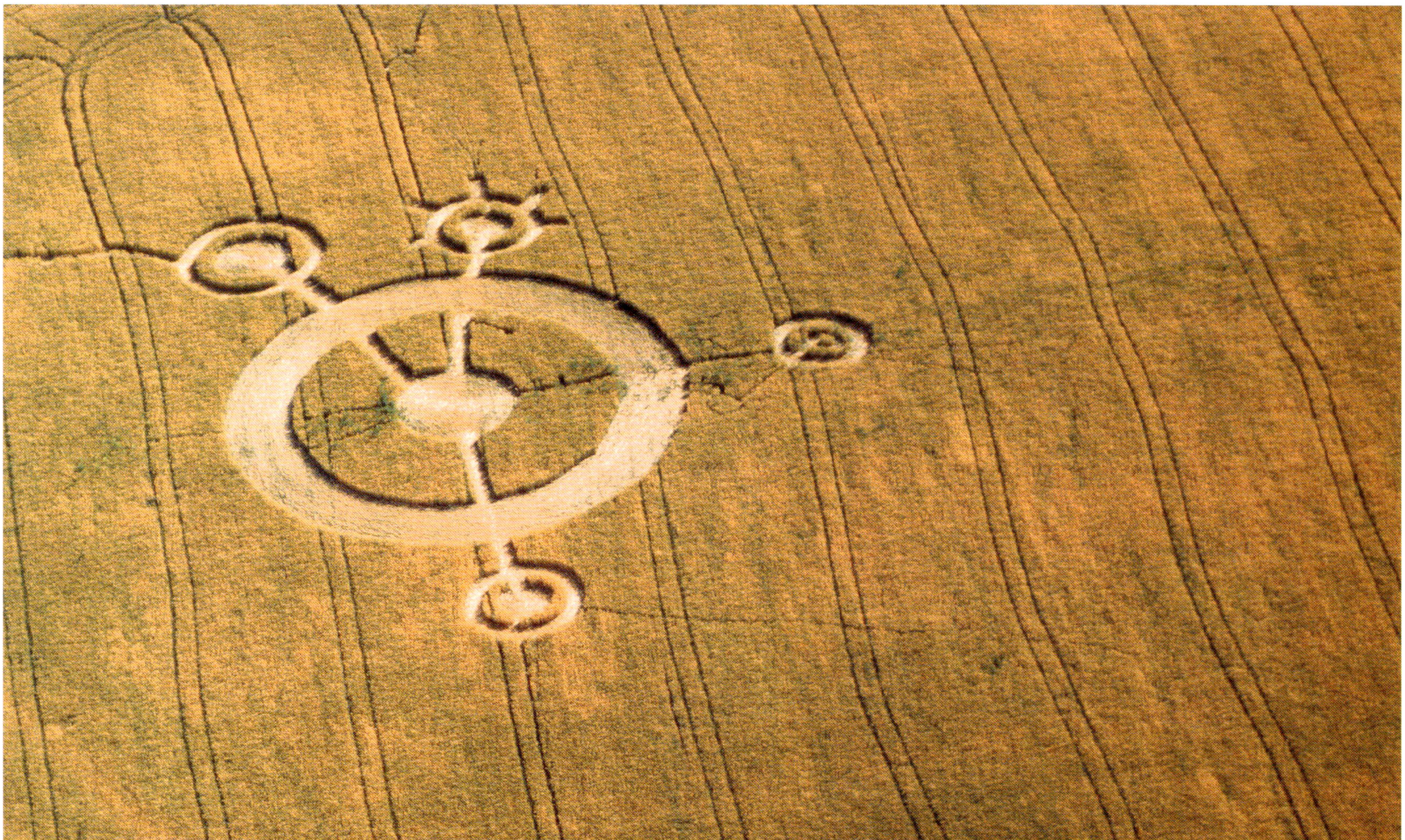

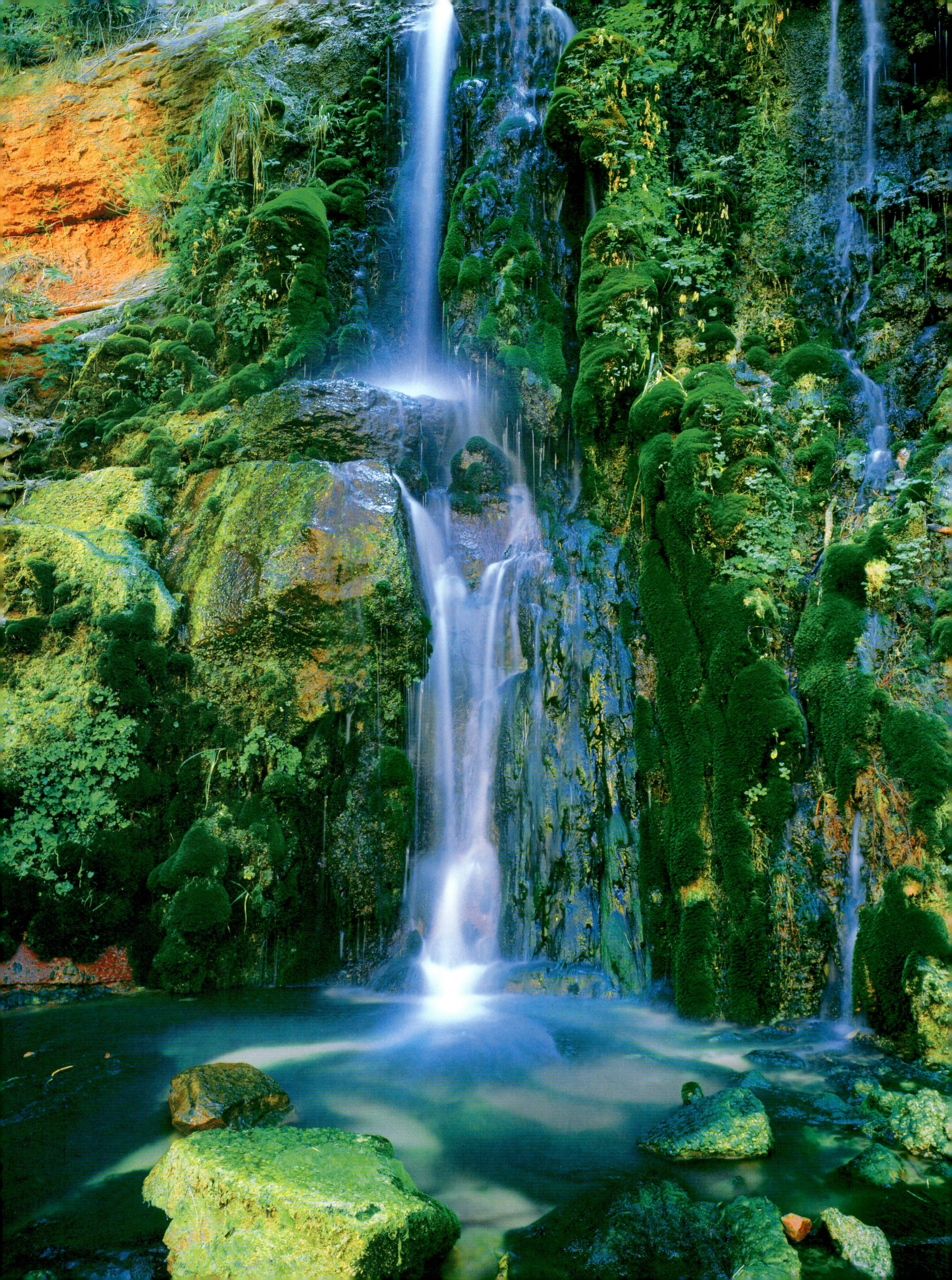

LEFT:
A splash of green draws the eye in Zion National Park, home of some of the West's most beautiful springs. Gushing from cracks in the canyon walls, the water surges freely for only a few seconds before being captured by the Virgin River.

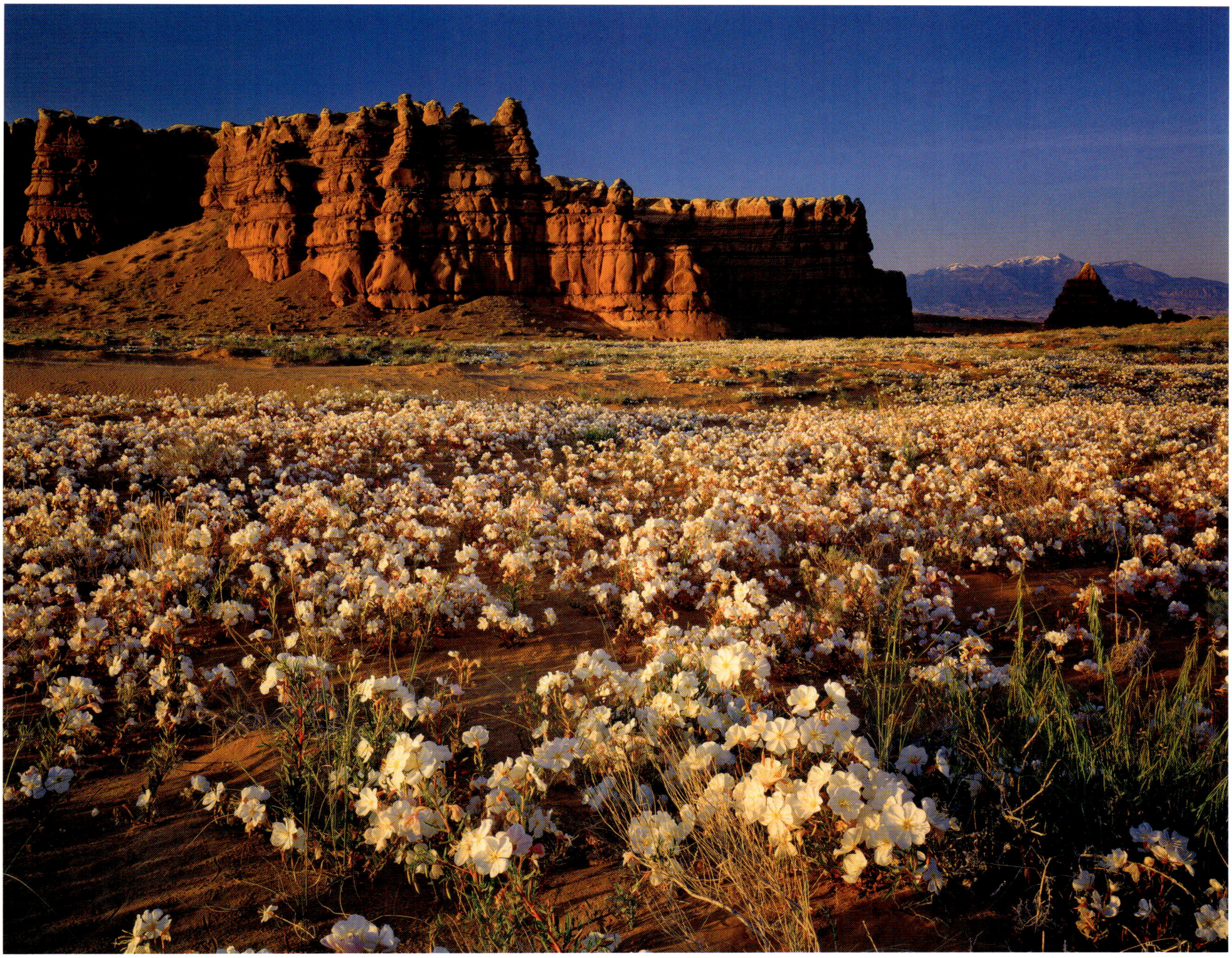

ABOVE:
A prolific bloom of evening primrose covers the desert near the San Rafael Swell. A rare occurrence, this amazing display came after a winter with a three-foot snowfall in the area. I planned out the shot, preferring dawn for the lack of wind and for the best chance of having the primrose petals open wide.

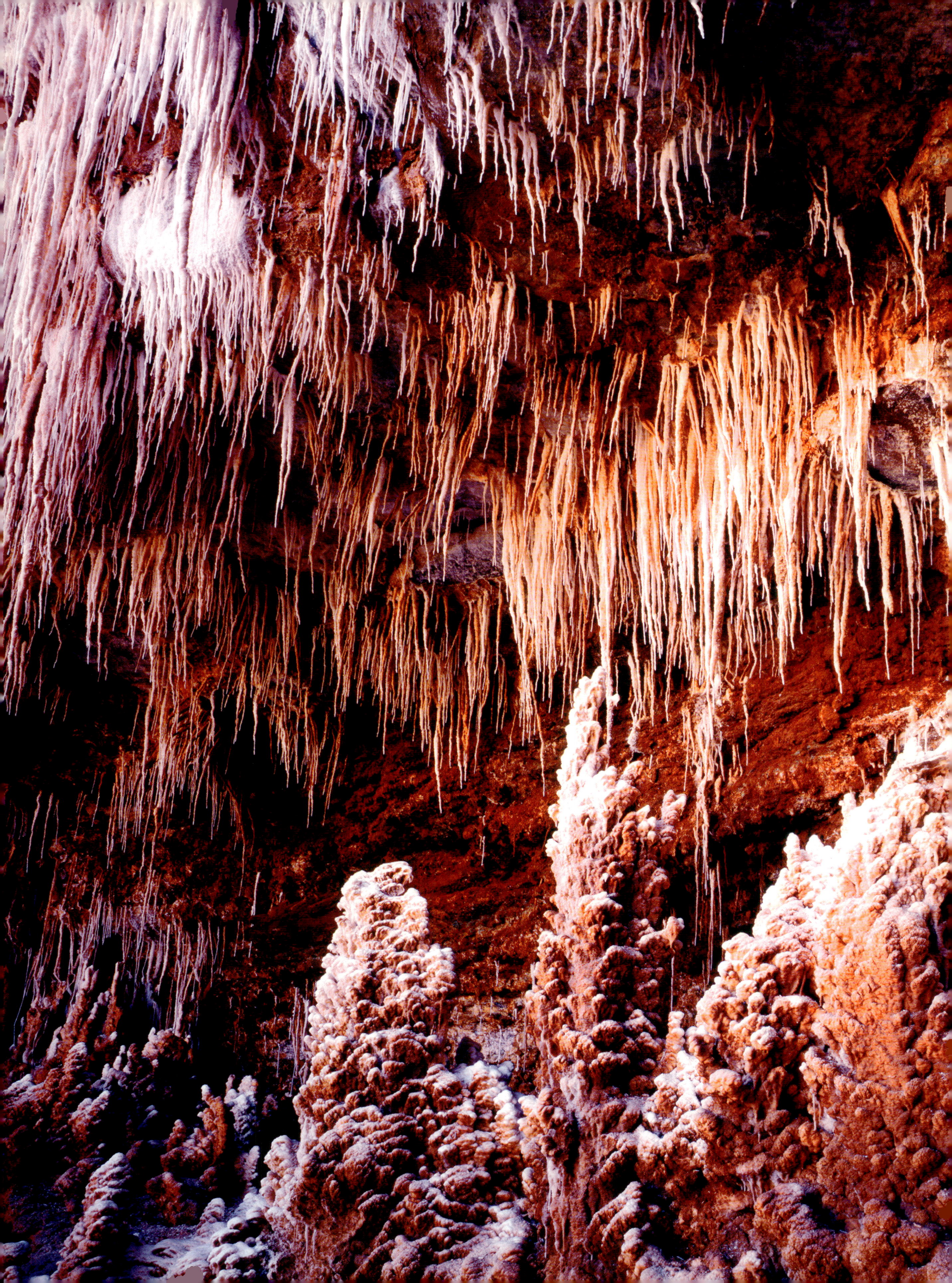

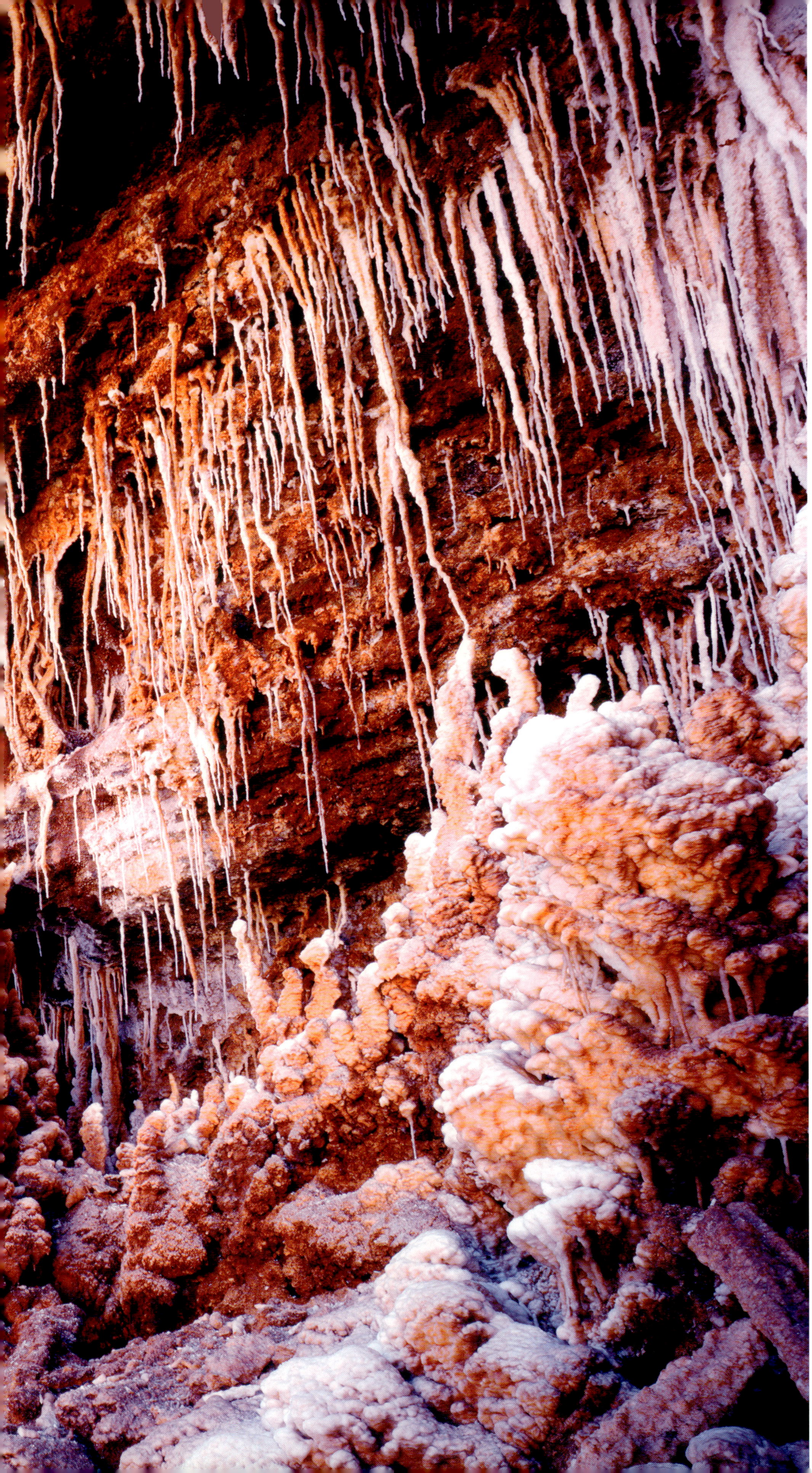

LEFT:
An amazing display of above ground stalactites and stalagmites decorates an open-air cave in Steve's Canyon. I know of no other such display in the world.

RIGHT:
At the beginning of the White Rim Trail in Canyonlands National Park, a short path leads to the edge of the inner river canyon. A giant hoodoo rock that I've photographed many times stands on the canyon's edge.

NEXT PAGE:
The islands of the Great Salt Lake contain some of the most prolific fields of cactus in America. Some islands are so covered with the spiny plants that just walking around is dangerous. When the plants bloom, the normally drab islands become carpets of color.

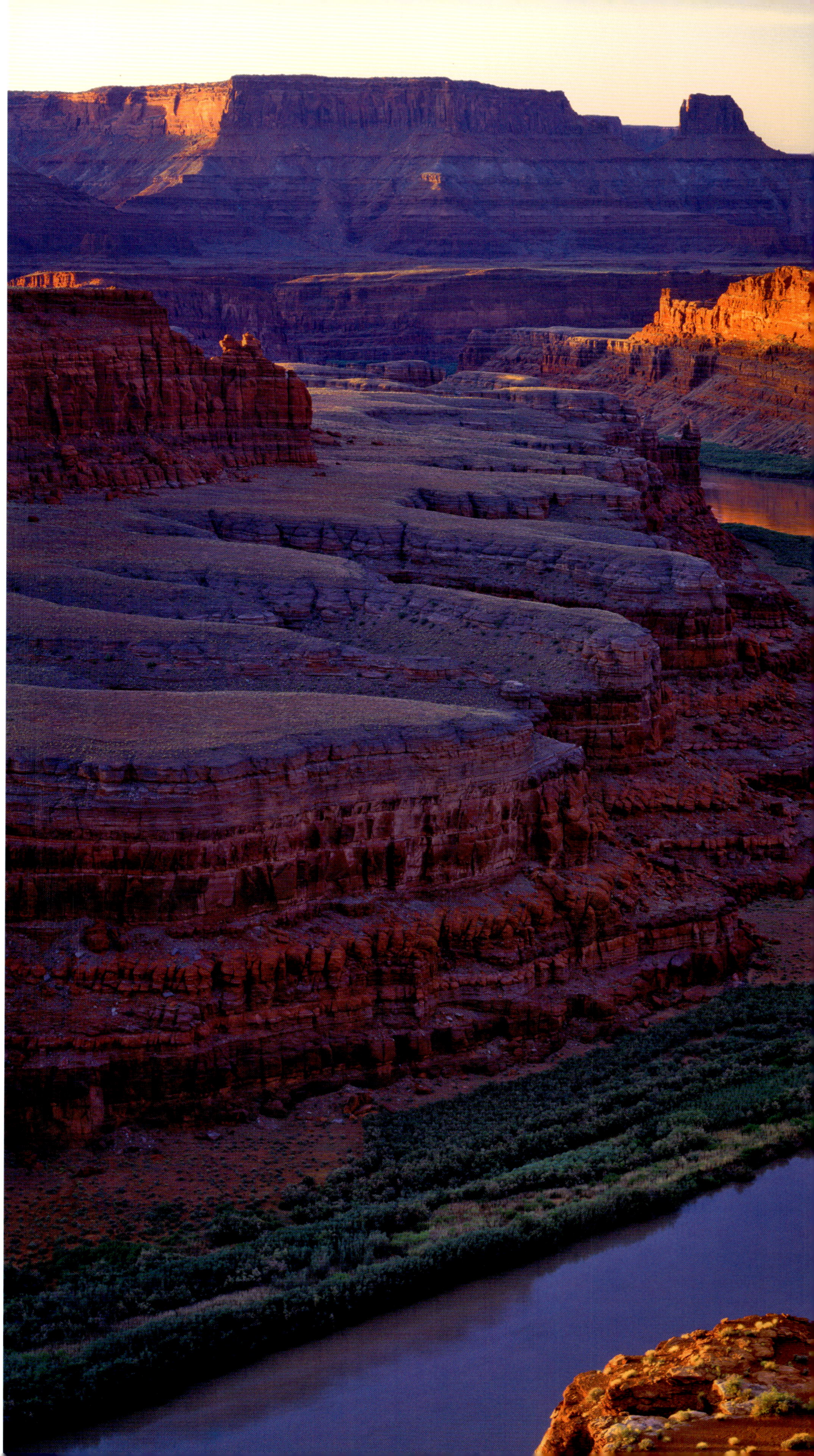

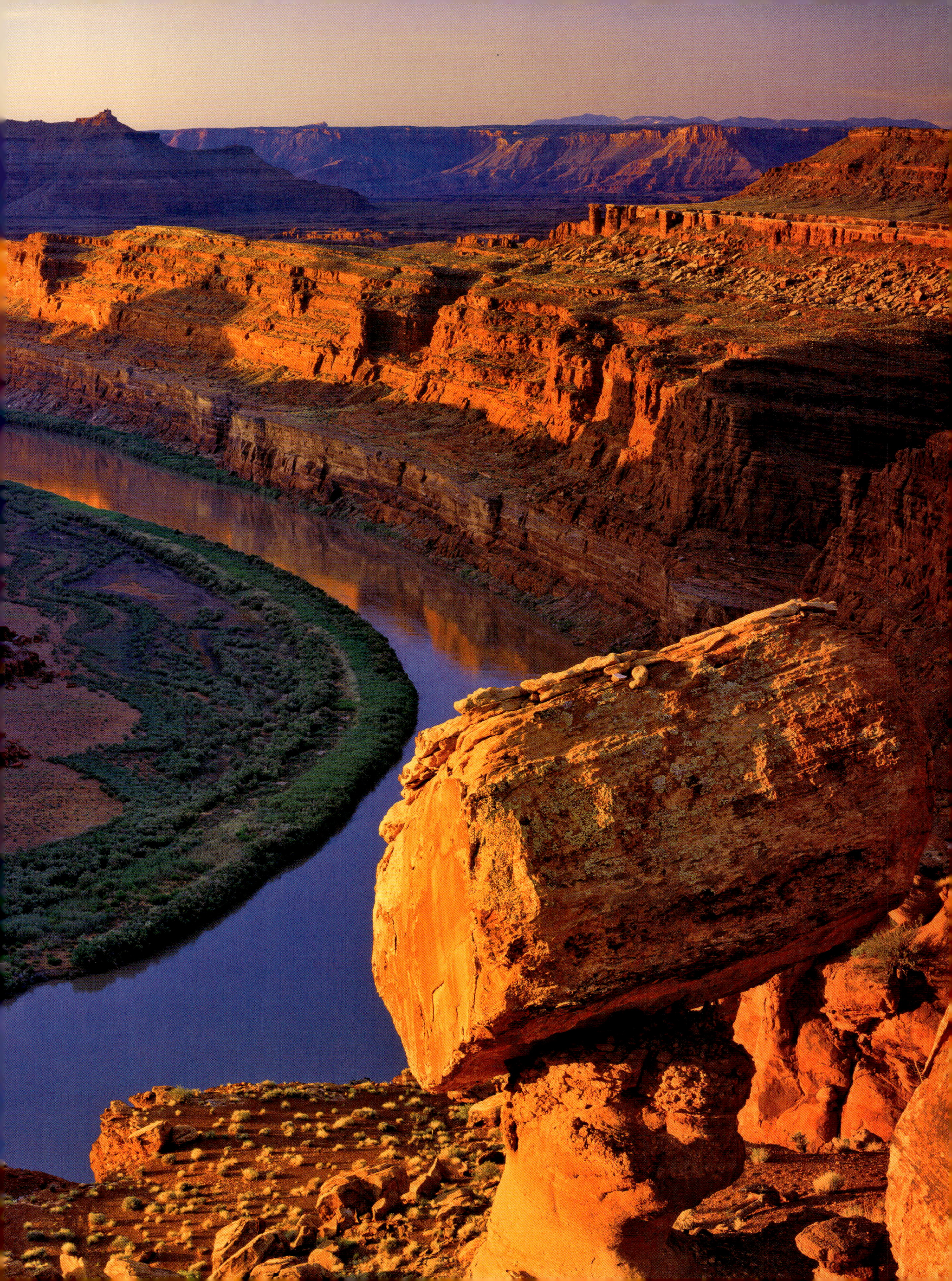

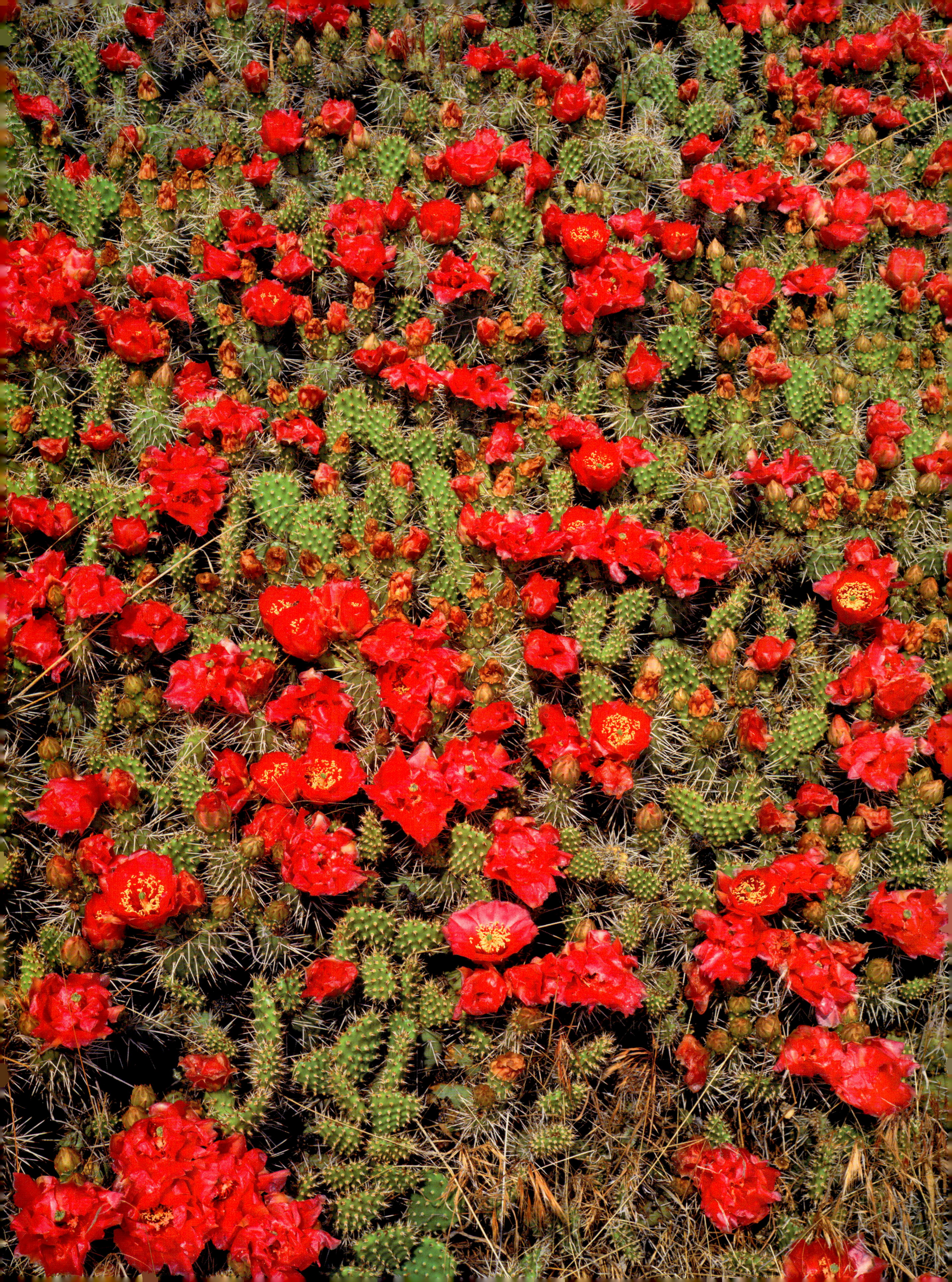

Characters & Canyons

by Mikenna Clokey

Our summer home was a pop-up camper. Nestled in the back of our truck, it was fifty square feet of thin wood and fiberglass, with a three-burner stove and a little sink to serve our little family — Mom, Dad, Bryce and me — on summer camping excursions around the country.

If I think hard about that camper, I can remember how it smelled — a slightly stale combination of the modest wooden cabinets and last night's dinner of rice and beans. I can remember sitting around the small table inside it, watching Toronto win the '93 World Series. We had a tiny portable television that, even with both antennae stretched like giant feelers in two directions, picked up bad reception at best. And I will always clearly remember the cue we gave Dad upon each night's stop when it was time to turn the crank that erected our little home: "Pop 'er up Dad!" — and he would.

Most mornings the truck shook to a start before dawn, my brother Bryce and I still asleep on the bed/dining area in the camper. For the next twenty minutes I would be half awake, rolling around with the rumble of whatever dirt road we were on at the time, trying not to push my snoozing little brother onto the linoleum floor. When the truck finally stopped and all was quiet, a peek out the window would reveal a desert just waking up like we were. Countless times I stumbled out the door of the pop-up onto a scene of pink and orange sandstone, a sheer canyon still dark in early shadow, or high desert flowers open to the cool morning air.

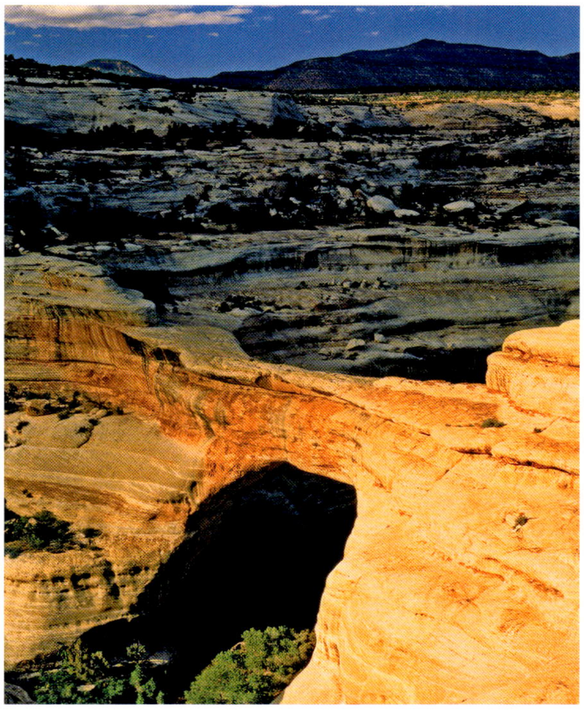

In our home state of Utah my family and I saw the sunrise over Bryce Canyon, Goblin Valley, and what is now Grand Staircase-Escalante National Monument. We watched the cliffs light up at Zion and Hovenweep, Flaming Gorge and Lake Powell. And always in the foreground was my father, looking like a phantom in a cape and hiking boots under his camera's dark cloth, as he tried to capture the scene on a few 4x5 sheets of film.

I am convinced that there is not much that can beat a Utah redrock sunrise. And I am continually amazed by the natural neon entertainment of Utah's canyon country at dawn. Perhaps this explains why my favorite colors are the burnt reds, coppery oranges, and deep lavenders of the desert.

While we always seemed to wake up looking at a Utah sunrise from the camper, we woke up to glowing redrock at our home in Moab as well. Moab, a thirty-mile detour off Interstate 70 in Southeastern Utah, is set in a small valley flanked by sandstone cliffs on two sides and the Colorado River and the La Sal Mountains on the others. Moab is spectacular. In the evenings the sun retreats across a pattern of redrock fins before lighting up the silvery peaks and green hills of the La Sals and finally setting, a nightly performance that is easily visible from almost anywhere in town. I have always counted the fact that I grew up in Moab, Utah, as auspicious dumb luck, for which I am very thankful.

Moab was, before my time and while I was growing up, mostly home to the descendants of early pioneers and the remaining residents brought to the area by a uranium rush that blew through town in the early 1950's. After the Three Mile Island disaster the demand for the metal died, leaving Moab with a hodgepodge mix of good-old-boy ranch types, a few outdoor recreationists, desert lovers and Mormons.

If you have ever read Edward Abbey's Desert Solitaire, a classic in this part of the country, you have an idea of how Moab has changed in the last few decades. Abbey described working in Arches National Monument before the skinny strip of arches and fins outside Moab became a national park. He detailed the beauty and wonder of a place nearly vacant of human visitors and the eccentric city of Moab a few miles outside of it. But Abbey also saw the explosion and exploitation of his desert coming and lamented the area's growing popularity.

The popularity that was just picking up in the early eighties is in full swing now. Grand County, where Moab lies, is home to more than 8,800 residents, a number that can double or triple during certain weekends in the spring and fall. An abundance of recreational opportunities — river rafting, rock climbing, mountain biking, hiking and four wheeling just to name the more popular activities — plus the draw of two world-class national parks nearby — Arches and Canyonlands — bring a flood of people toward the town.

Rows of cloned condos for new residents are going up in the fields and open desert where my friends and I used to ride our horses as kids. Moab is now home to every major fast food chain. New motels and hotels seem to be sprouting from the ground on both ends of the growing town, and now bike and raft companies litter Main Street. Tourists pour in during spring, summer, and fall to visit a small town and big landscape that have attained a kind of celebrity reputation for outdoor recreation and beauty. Moab is beyond being discovered, now it's exploding.

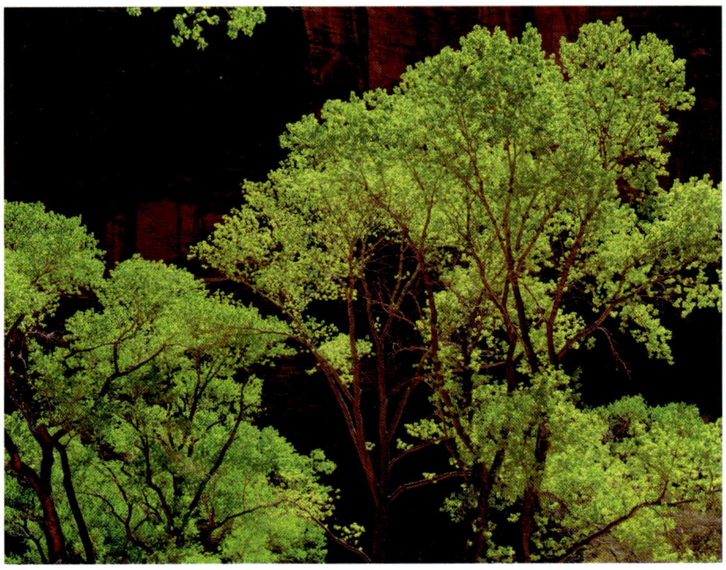

I have been heartbroken by much of the new development, including a subdivision on the hill where my best friend and I built "forts" and went sledding, and the recent addition of Starbucks to the local coffee scene, but I still love this town almost as much as I ever have. And I am somewhat comforted by the idea of an insider's scoop I like to think I have on the place.

I have found I get one of two reactions upon telling a new acquaintance where I am from: "Moab?" some ask, voice cracking in high crescendo. "The Moab? No one actually lives there, do they?" At which point I explain that I have grown up in the mountain-biking Mecca since I was four and yes, quite a few people actually do live, year round, in Moab. Then the conversation generally turns to a series of obvious questions like, "Have you ever been to Arches National Park? Doesn't it get really hot there?" or "I biked this trail once called the Sli…Slickrock Trail. Have you ever heard of it?"

The other reaction and one I like just fine is, "Huh? Never heard of it," followed by a shrug and a look that questions, "Utah, eh? You mean that parched, backward, Mormon piece of land in the middle of the West? Glad I don't live there." And that is that.

In true Ed Abbey vein, I have tried to make my own reaction to both responses as he said, "like a rattlesnake's, to warn you off," but I know that I am never very convincing. I want to tell potential visitors that Moab is a terrible place to visit, that if it's not hot enough to melt the dashboard in your car, it's cold enough for ice to freeze and drift along the surface of the Colorado River near town. Then there are the crowds — armies of spandex-clad bikers, thick-soled hikers, daredevil climbers and jeepers — nearly everywhere you go.

I always feel like these are facts I should emphasize when describing what my hometown is like, in the hopes that whoever is asking will opt to take their family to Disneyland or on a cruise instead. Unfortunately, I love the canyon country so well that it is hard to genuinely warn someone off.

Spring weekends, in my mind, are some of the worst times to live in Moab. A trip to town yields a show in testosterone on par with a WWF wrestling match. Men wear mirrored sunglasses and drive souped up, jacked up, beat up, four-wheel-drive-vehicles over every inch of stone, sand and concrete possible. They crawl in long trains across country that should only be seen via hiking boots. And after conquering a few miles of nearly impossible driving terrain in the desert, they come into town to conquer Main Street. This mighty feat requires enough gas money to roast laps from one end of town to the other for hours on end, as well as enough gall to stare down those with bigger tires while stopped at a stoplight. All of this is aside from the painful fact that many of the jeep enthusiasts who visit Moab are lacking the environmental ethic to resist the temptation to cut cross-country through the fragile desert or crush a patch of Sego lilies near the road.

Motorized vehicles are certainly not alone in their destruction of the desert. A hike through many canyons inevitably leads to patches of cryptobiotic soil, the delicate desert crust that holds much of this ecosystem together, striped with the criss-cross pattern of bike tire tread. The portion of land that is home to one of Moab's most popular bike races is sometimes stripped to dust when the race is finished. It seems to be reality around here that sports come first, environment comes second.

Weekends with jeep events and bike races make me want to warn those even loosely considering a visit to this little town to stay away. "We're full," I want to say — or, like every motel in town during Memorial Day weekend, "No Vacancy." But it is also weekends like those that help keep Moab afloat. The crowds are our economy and the commotion is enjoyed by some of the people who have spent their lives here. I know that, and am forced to begrudgingly tolerate such events. I know how much I am attracted to this land and beyond my own selfish wishes to keep it a secret, can hardly blame others who fall for its lure.

What I do hope is that people who visit Moab, or any natural area in Utah, gain a basic appreciation for a landscape that is infinitely unique and fragile, and in most areas is under attack. If natural gas exploration does not continue to taint its beauty then those seeking thrills on its slickrock, sand dunes, or sheer canyon walls will. But I remain optimistic that the tourists who come to experience this place will also think twice about their environmental philosophies and how they treat this or any land in the future.

As for me, I cannot even call it affection I have for this harsh desert; it is a fervent respect that is just a part of me. This respect reveals itself through the feeling of home I get winding through the Wingate sandstone while floating on the Colorado River. It is the happy calm that the desert of Utah evokes in me, even when I am just driving through it or looking out the window of the house I grew up in. It is the excitement and energy I feel before a summer storm, which I imagine is comparable to other girls my age getting excited about a clothing sale or new cell phone. This respect is why I never hike without carrying water because I realize what this climate can do to the unprepared, but also why I am not scared of this desert, never unwilling to sleep on the ground with the critters.

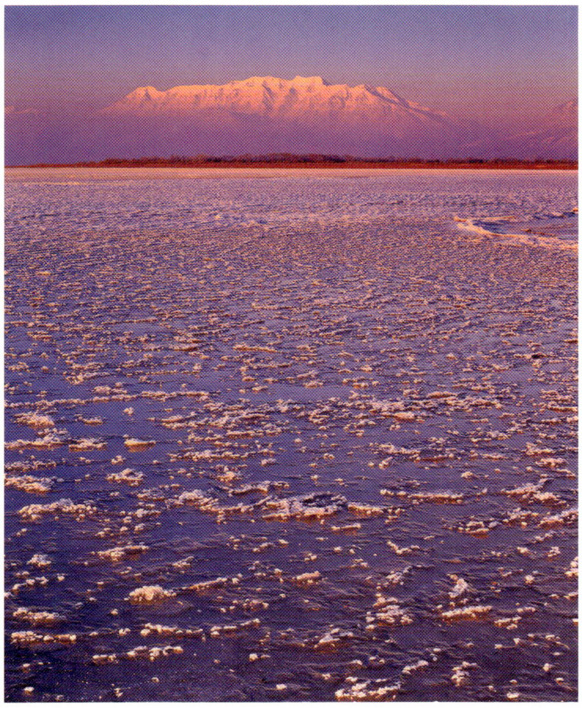

Though I love this land, I am a bit embarrassed to say that I have met outsiders who may know its geography better than I do. I've driven scores of random dirt roads with my dad, driving toward and through endless layers of Jurassic strata, but I cannot remember the names of each of the places I have been. Occasionally I hear a name mentioned that seems so familiar that I am almost certain I've been there, but have I? And where exactly is that? Utah is so vast and littered with crags, canyons, gulches, peaks, valleys and vistas that to see them all in a lifetime would be nearly impossible.

And I say nearly impossible, not altogether impossible, because my father has almost done it. I have been fortunate enough to be with him on several of his excursions.

Often, if there were a heavy autumn rain at our house, Dad would rush out to the car, yelling an invite to Bryce and me on his way out the door before speeding off to catch fleeting flash floods and waterfalls around town. Though there were many of these every-day-brand Tom Till excursions, I have a vivid memory of one specific such adventure, when I managed to get myself into his jeep before he sped out of the driveway on his way to chase and photograph the aftermath of a desert downpour.

If you've never experienced a Utah monsoon, it feels like a giant valve in the sky has suddenly been opened and water is pouring down onto the dry earth below it. Dark clouds roll over the edge of whatever canyon you may be in, and suddenly everything is soaked, often before there is time to prepare. I have tried, too many times, to scramble for my raincoat in such an event and always end up drenched before I can pull its thin protection over my head and shoulders.

But ending up sopping wet does not matter much anyway, because rain in the desert feels pleasantly cool and tickles running down your back and dripping off your eyebrows. It is almost always a welcome washing from sweat and dirt and an instant air conditioner, not to mention a much-needed rejuvenation for the parched soil onto which it falls.

During a hard rain, desert washes swell as ground that has been dry for months becomes quickly saturated and shunts gallons of water downhill. It is a comforting sight. I have often felt like I can see the frail vegetation and over-dried dirt gulping up the moisture and being revived with each drop.

Small storms give the desert a healthy dowsing. Large storms breed flashfloods that carry truck-sized boulders and carve away at the soft sand. In some places, the flood eats the dirt into steep-cut banks on both sides of the flow. In other areas it deposits truckloads of silt where there had been none before. In either case one is lucky to witness what keeps this tenuous canyon country alive, because just as they come, monsoons are quickly gone and the relentless sun is back.

On this particular afternoon, as my dad and I drove through Moab, every crack and crevasse in the stone walls that tower over our town was a red falls, and every gutter, wash and creek was running with thick brown mud and rocks. Sizeable pieces of cliff had been washed out into the road and were strewn through the lanes of traffic like scattered marbles. In a few places small cars could not drive due to deep silty water inundating the street. Desert downpours are fleeting and never seem to last long enough, so the sun was beginning to peak out from the edges of the black clouds as they passed overhead and everyone was coming out of their stores and houses to survey the damage.

Dad and I drove through town and out to Highway 189, The River Road, where, as expected, every drainage was raging with a brief flood on its way to the river. The wet stone had been temporarily tinted with shiny shades of light lavender and deep purple because of the rain, and the dense smell of wet dirt sprayed into the air as floods washed over the canyon rims above us. Dad and I pointed out each ribbon of falling water to one another and stopped beside the larger waterfalls, necks straining to see their origins through closed car windows. I cannot even remember if Dad took any pictures that afternoon, but I remember his hoots of excitement about the event and the exhilaration that the afternoon provoked in me.

I went on another type of Tom Till excursion last winter that is also particularly poignant in my mind. It's a prime example of how he does some of this work.

We drove three hours down to the Utah/Arizona border in the early morning dark and arrived at the valley of stone towers around 8:30 am. Monument Valley looks like a classic western movie set, and several classic western movies have been set in Monument Valley, characterized by its series of solitary stone formations. There are The Mittens, two buttes each naturally sculpted into the shapes of short, fat mittens set apart, thumbs facing each other. Behind the Mittens is the skinny finger of the Totem Pole, and behind that more freestanding pinnacles and buttes. Around each formation lies a featureless expanse of flat sandy desert. Everything is a variation of the color of rust, except after winter storms when a blanket of snow caps the crimson rocks in a display of striking contrast. The valley has been designated a tribal park and lies on the Navajo Indian reservation, half in Arizona and half in Utah.

Dad, my boyfriend Kimo, and I pulled into Bluff, had breakfast and waited to meet our guide. My dad was delighted. Today he was hoping to visit an Ancestral Puebloan ruin on a dwindling list of places in Utah he had never seen. Because the ruin lies on private land, he had called the landowner for special permission to visit and photograph the site and had arranged a guide who the landowner trusted. But reservation life seems to be on a different clock than the stringent Anglo time system surrounding it, so such excursions always involve several variables. What time will the guide arrive, or will he or she show up at all? Will they allow all of us to see the ruin? And how much is this all going to cost? The price always seems to be negotiable on the reservation, but mostly only negotiated higher and higher for anyone who's not a local.

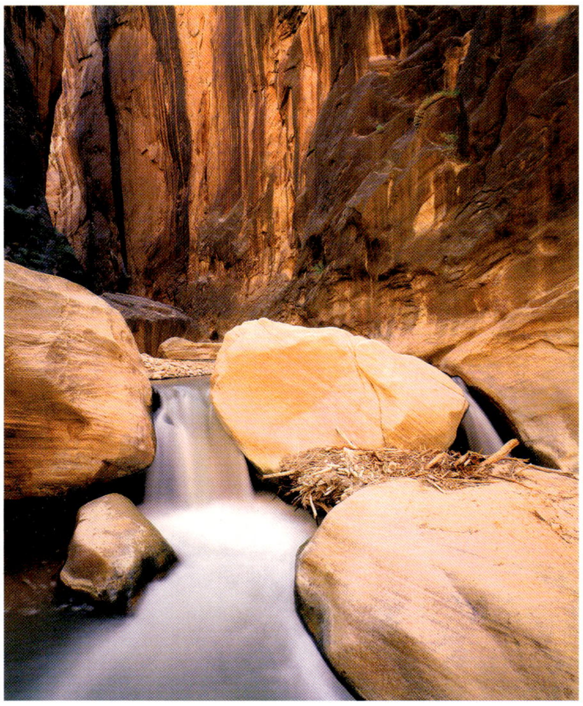

We got lucky that day, and a beat-up Suburban with only one working door pulled up next to us, driven by Bill, our guide. Bill was a weathered local, a Caucasian, but a 40-year resident of the area. He could not have been more than forty-five years old, but his skin, his mouth, his eyes all looked sandblasted and sunfaded from years spent in a harsh climate. He was skinny, and a cigarette hung loosely from his wrinkled lips.

However, after a quick, firm handshake, I realized that Bill's most striking features were his hands. Mounds of dry visible calluses jutted from the base of each finger; his hands seemed to have twice as much skin as they needed. The excess was twisted into knots and deep wrinkles that covered the tanned backs and fleshy palms of each. Then an unconformity: tacked onto the ends of his worn digits were the long, slender points of neatly groomed fingernails.

Bill wore a faded NAPA Autos Parts ball cap and clutched a coffee mug filled with coffee or a cocktail, I couldn't tell which. He would later set it on our long sought-after ruin like the structure was his living room coffee table.

Bill filled the ten-minute drive to the landowner's trailer with stories of camping and hiking in the nearby cliffs. It became obvious that he had developed a strong relationship with the land in this place where little else seemed to be outstanding. He and his friends used to hike to and camp in the ruins of the ancestors, he told us. And since he had been able to drive he had been guiding tourists into the desert to those same ruins. He rattled off names of mesas and canyons I had never been to. He had moved to the area as a boy and as he put it, "Everyday had been an Indiana Jones adventure since."

We passed through several gates, stopping at each one to drag it open and close it behind us, finally coming to the residence of the man whom we hoped was going to allow us on his land. Bill said he was a medicine man, and though the land belonged to the Navajo tribe, he owned the grazing rights to this portion.

The deal took a bit of negotiation. Dad had brought Kimo and me, two bodies the medicine man had not planned on. He had only one arm, and we watched as he spoke to Bill, motioning with his arm toward the desert and then toward the car where we were waiting. Luckily, $200 later we were allowed to cross through yet another gate and were on our way. We waved goodbye and said thank you. The medicine man stood on the porch of his trailer and waved back. His wife would escort us from there.

In the world I grew up in, it seems that there is a road leading to most destinations. Where there is not one, it is time to hike. But with Bill in the driver's seat, we rumbled into the open desert following a white SUV with low tires and children's heads bobbing in the back seat. Our two-car caravan drove cross-country, not toward anything in particular that I could see, picking our way through washes and over small hills. We wound on for about 15 minutes, past the skeletons of several rusty cars left to decay. The land had been used to graze cattle and had been chewed to the point of a neatly mowed lawn, making driving easy. Soon we climbed the last small hill to where we would park.

That hill, Bill told us, was a midden, an ancient trash pile, now covered with red dirt and scraggly patches of Mormon tea. I glanced at the ground and noticed that our Suburban was parked on thousands of ancient pieces of Native American pottery. This would never fly in the heavily regulated world outside the reservation. Bill reached down among the shards of handcrafted clay and picked up a tiny bead, which he rolled around in his wrinkled hand and promptly shoved into his jean pocket. That bead was probably 900 years old, but Bill said he had been collecting them for years now and had nearly enough to make a necklace. I doubt if he would have been offended if I had done the same, scavenged the earth for an ancient souvenir, but I have been too long conditioned in the "leave only footprints, take only pictures," school of thought to ever consider it seriously. But I did wonder what Bill's necklace was going to look like.

From the midden-turned-parking-lot we hiked up a short canyon of light-colored sandstone striped with dark weepy streaks of desert varnish. The canyon narrowed quickly and in less than an hour the ruin we had come to see appeared. In an alcove about thirty feet from the wash, stood the almost perfect two-story tower and several tiny rooms of a seldom-visited Anasazi or Ancestral Puebloan ruin. In front of the tower a small round kiva had been dug into the earth. The structures were almost flawlessly intact. Wooden beams framed doors much smaller than any window we would build today, and only a few walls of the ancient residence had fallen. The back wall of the alcove doubled as the back wall of the dwelling and was strewn with small pictographs.

I thumbed some shards of pottery that lay on the ground — black and white, red and black, raised patterns of unpainted clay — and began to explore. Dad set up his tripod, and Bill wandered around, perhaps looking for more beads. Kimo explored the continuation of the canyon. This ruin had a second level, housed in another alcove above the one we were in, and I began a few cautious steps up the vertical face to the second story. I quickly decided I did not really want Bill carrying me with a broken leg out of the canyon, so I down-climbed to safety. Ancient peoples are known to have been skilled climbers, but safe human passage here seemed impossible, and I stood there puzzled by how they would have accessed that second tier.

After looking past the initial awe and grandeur of this well-kept ruin, I noticed more modern signs of life: a shiny discarded can of Busch beer, some tinfoil and the name "Tammy" along with a smiley face, written in bold charcoal lettering on the back wall. Each piece of what I might call graffiti or garbage made a loud statement in a place I expected to be pristine. A packrat had also made this alcove her home since its ancient tenants had gone and had begun to solidify pieces of pottery along with pieces of trash into her cement of mud, sticks and urine. This place was by no means deserted.

I had to raise a few questions to myself. How far should we go in the name of conservation and protection? Was Tammy wrong for declaring her modern presence in this ancient place in big loopy letters? Or was Tammy just part of a progression, a continuation of use for this structure? Should the local teenagers respect ruins like these by picking up their beer cans or is this their land and their heritage to do with what they please? Should Bill return his clay beads to the ground where they fell 1,000 years ago?

I decided that I certainly was not in a position to make these decisions for the people of Monument Valley. I settled on being satisfied making decisions like these for myself and pondering the preservation ethics of others. Bill saw me staring at Tammy and seemed to have a simple solution to my questions.

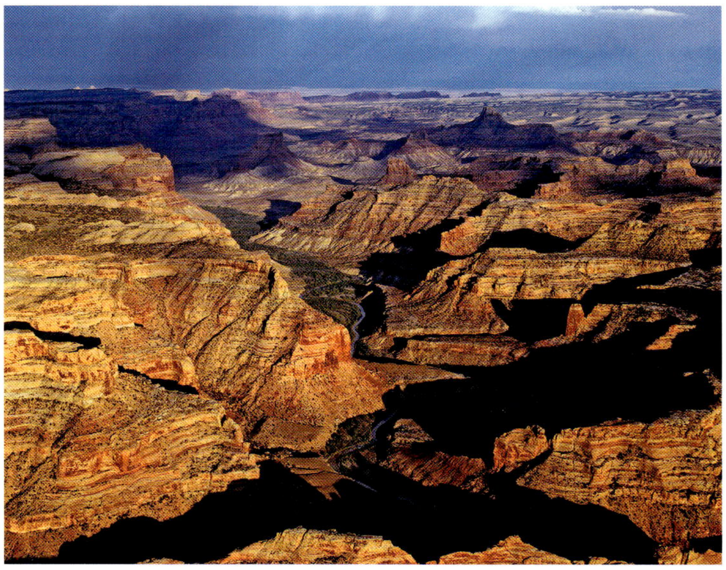

"Must be their (the medicine man's) kids," he said casually. Then he shrugged his shoulders somewhere underneath his baggy hooded sweatshirt and turned his attention back to bead hunting.

By that time Dad had managed to set up a shot that conveniently placed Tammy behind a stone wall and out of mind. He was patiently waiting for the science fiction-like glow of sunset. And as predicted, an hour later the light he'd been expecting lit the alcove in bright burnt orange and he began snapping one photo after another before its brilliance faded. Kimo and I assisted, one holding film, the other digging through his bottomless backpack to find this filter or that lens. We watched quietly as each hand-placed stone in the tower in front of us became flush with neon glow.

In a few short minutes the sun was down. It continued to climb the wall above the alcove and left the small canyon in a quiet grey evening. We retraced our steps, hiked back across the potshards, opened and closed each gate in reverse order, passed the one-armed medicine man's home, and arrived back into town. And after tipping Bill, who took the cigarette out of his mouth long enough to promise to take us to more hidden canyons whenever we returned, we headed back to Moab in the dark.

Tom Till excursions like these in my youth have set me up for a lifetime of outdoor exploration and recreation. I am happiest in the seclusion of the wilderness, among the sounds of its residents: the noisy ravens, the lizards rattling dry sticks, and the occasional chipmunk or roving coyote. As far as civilization goes, I will take a small town's quirks, faults, and genuine character over big city stretches of Bed Bath and Beyond and The Home Depot.

During my high school years I thought I would leave Moab for the big city life, seeking the excitement and stimulation that I thought I had not found in rural Utah. I attended a large university, but soon found myself overwhelmed and generally annoyed with the commotion and crowding. I have since pinpointed my frustrations to a kind of "cluster phobia" that I feel among endless expanses of buildings and parking lots, without an open space or tree in sight. I have realized that I am a small town girl at my core.

I have satisfied this desire by spending my summers in Green River, Utah, a dying desert town on Interstate 70 near the San Rafael Swell, in the central part of the state. Though reason to do more than simply keep driving through Green River may be hard to find upon first glance, I have grown to love the place. Of just under 1,000 people who live there, most are farmers or melon growers, a fact that has allowed the town to proclaim itself the Watermelon Capital of the World. Who wouldn't love a town that holds a melon festival complete with square dancing and the crowning of a Melon Queen each September?

Looking up from one's square-dancing feet while in Green River reveals that the town is surrounded by a pastel palette desert rockscape, disrupted only by the strip of brightly colored trees that line the Green River flowing through town. Isolated by the long-standing rows of the Book Cliffs to the east and west, the high altitude ridges of the Tavaputs Plateau to the north and the expanse of the Green River Desert to the south, Green River is precariously placed among the harshness that surrounds it. The nearby cliffs of brittle Mancos Shale and Morrison Formation are painted in thick perfectly parallel stripes of yellow, red, and blue that resemble how I imagine the world's largest layered cake might look before getting frosted. But the colorful silt and mudstone formations are relatively temporary and unstable, and they have crumbled into tall flattop towers along the outskirts of town.

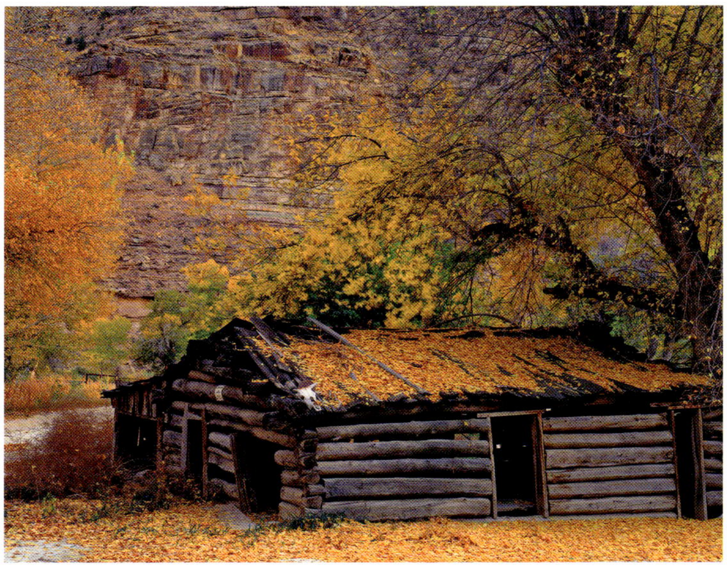

Setting off this beautiful and strange landscape are some of the most consistently brilliant sunsets in the state. Nearly every summer night, as my friends and I finish our work and settle down with a cheap can of beer, the sun illuminates the foregrounds of melon fields and distant tiers of rock and clouds in fluorescent hues that are otherworldly. I have found myself in Green River from May through August since 2002, working as a river guide on the nearby Green and Colorado Rivers.

Initially, the town of Green River appears to be more of a truck stop than a community, with abandoned buildings outnumbering the businesses along Main Street and weeds that have grown thick through old asphalt parking lots. Most of the successful establishments are the chain motels near the freeway that cater to the majority of Green River's visitors, those just passing through. But a closer look reveals a small population saturated with local charm.

In middle of town, next to an empty old-timey building with block lettering that says BANK, is Hal's Service Shop. I have taken a flat tire to Hal's numerous times, and Gary, the shop's sole owner and operator, has done everything he can to fix it right then, in a matter of minutes. Hal's is across the street from the Green River Coffee Company, a far cry from Starbucks, a fact most Green River residents are thankful for. The shop has filled an unlikely niche in Green River, and I've often enjoyed an icy frapaccino and an update on local gossip among the hand-painted murals on the walls inside. Then there is Ray's Tavern, perhaps Green River's most famous establishment. Giant hamburgers, famous fries and busy atmosphere define Ray's along with a staff that never seems to get a day off, and always recognizes and welcomes the river guide crowd.

But my favorite example of Green River charm is an off-beat little pizza bar that sits at the end of what once was Green River's busiest street, in a building that I have heard out-of-towners mistake as abandoned.

The cracked sidewalk in front of the joint is cluttered with old appliances and twisted pieces of metal that Frank, the character who owns the establishment, is saving for a future project he has yet to determine. A rusty children's wagon and a washing machine are among the recognizable fixtures in the pile of what most would call junk. Last summer the miscellany served as a platform for rows of tiny tomato plants that Frank told us he had rescued from inside a dumpster somewhere. By the end of the summer, he had cared for them enough to plant them.

For a long time there was a white piece of paper hanging in the middle of the establishment's front door that said something like, "SMOKING IS ALLOWED HERE IN ITS ENTIRETY," followed by an abundance of exclamation marks, a statement made in blatant defiance of recent legislation that bans smoking in Utah bars. The sign was only a prelude of what's inside.

Inside, it's smoky — smoky and dark. But eventually one's pupils dilate enough to really take in the place and notice its eclectic decor. I am certain it's like no other pizza place in existence. Among various neon Budweiser signs, bumper stickers make up the main design scheme, supplemented by quotes and cartoons that have been printed from the Internet. Through the stickers and sayings, an outspoken Frank tells patrons his take on some current issues, a combination of right-wing politics mixed with heavy contempt for any authority. It is not hard to form a clear idea of just who runs the place.

A white bumper sticker with bold red writing hangs from a thumbtack among several others in crooked formation behind the bar: "Save a child, shoot a drug dealer." The back of the door sports a picture of former President Clinton in front of a large marijuana leaf. On the ceiling, a few short strands of Christmas lights that I have never seen turned on dangle above a row of orange booths. There are a pool and a foosball table, along with some arcade games from the 1980s, to accompany your pizza if you can find the light switch that illuminates the back of the restaurant where they sit. The place's wood floor is made of the salvaged boards of an old school basketball court, three-point line included. You get the idea.

But Frank, who also acts as the hideaway's lone pizza chef, bartender, server, maintenance man and entertainment, is always a gracious host — as gracious as he can be anyway — and he works doggedly to get you what you need. He turns from watching Fox News when you walk in to greet you with a half-smile and a nod before he rushes to start filling a pitcher of Budweiser. He always figures that we, my friends and I, want a pitcher, which we do. Then he asks us briefly about out rafting season before disappearing into the kitchen.

In half an hour he emerges, sweating, carrying a stack of huge molten pies. Frank's pizza is always exceptional — mounds of melted cheese, onions, olives, peppers, homemade crust, and warm slices of sweet garden-ripe, locally grown tomato to crown each piece. In addition to making great pizza, Frank makes for pretty good dinner company. He stands behind the bar smoking a cigarette while we eat, telling us what he has found to rant about that week, between spurts of hoarse chuckling. And before too long, you have enjoyed a genuine Green River cheese plug, as my friends and I call it. We love the whole experience.

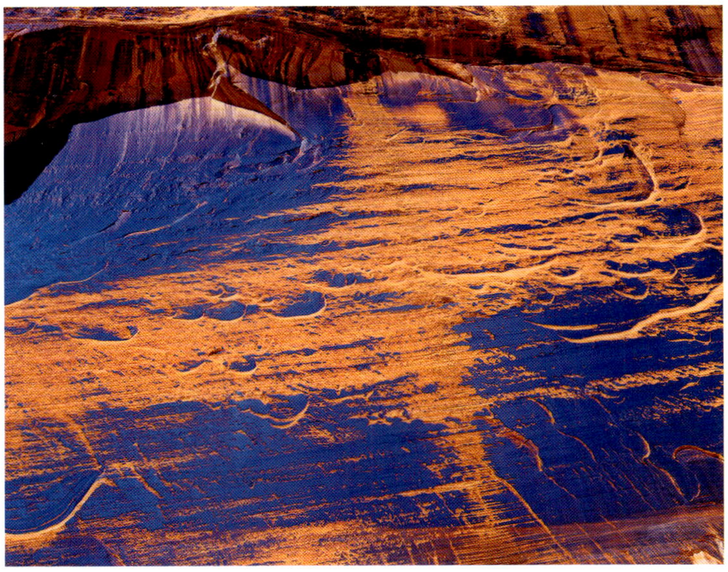

Though I have developed an affection for the community and people of Green River, I would much rather be running the Green River itself than spending much time in town. I love the hues, sounds, especially the scents of the desert Colorado Plateau and the bodies of water that sustain it. The sound of the river, gurgling in thick muddy harmony with the canyon wren, always makes me grin. The smell of the water after a storm, when it seems like the oars of your boat are pushing through chocolate pudding, gives me cause to inhale deeply. I feel like stretching my lungs and inflating them to capacity with the silty smell. And I never tire of the sight of the painted, crumbling canyon meanders that have housed the river for millions of years and continue to erode, allowing it to pass. Their shelter always makes me thankful to be in a part of the canyon country where there are no roads, where travel is made possible only by the water.

As a river guide, I encounter each of these wonders nearly every day. But equally satisfying for me is watching others fall for the same splendor and wilderness that I have. I am pleased to help others appreciate the spectacle of a place they might never have seen otherwise.

This is not to say that some river trip passengers do not make me want to zip on my lifejacket, plop into the murky water, and leave the entire trip on a beach somewhere. Some days I am desperate enough that I might not bother to put my life jacket on at all. But there are also those passengers who, when they leave our river trips, I can honestly say I have enjoyed and have made a new kind of friendship with, however short lived. A couple of examples:

Alan, a sensible looking man in his early forties, arrived at the Sand Wash boat ramp, the beginning of Desolation Canyon on the Green River, wearing an outfit straight off the rack at REI. He glanced quickly at the hands on his large watch and curtly inquired, "How many hours will we be on the river today?"

I stood with two other guides near the boats. Both had heard the question along with me. Patrick didn't even attempt an answer. He did not have a watch and quickly turned to me, but I sure didn't have one either. I have never worn a watch, so after a few awkward seconds I looked to Sybrena, the trip leader. She looked toward her wrists with a sly smile like a watch might magically appear, but it didn't. And none of us really minded because for the next five days we knew we would not be following a strict schedule.

"Well, don't you have an estimate?" our new passenger asked, eyebrows raised into sharp arcs. We all smiled, trying not to make him feel uncomfortable.

"A few hours," and "Until about dinner time," were the only honest answers we could give him.

Beside the fact that there is no way to know how long a day on the river might be, one of the best aspects of being on a river trip is the absence of a stringent timetable. No appointments, alarm clocks, or any other mandatory engagements can be kept and are therefore unimportant and hard to justify worrying about. As guides, we can estimate what time lunch might be or what time camp might get set up, but the numbers are never concrete and those looking for a strict schedule of events can be sorely disappointed. Wind, rain, swimming breaks, hiking, and other river parties are just a few of the variables that change with each trip, making any kind of time estimate a wild guess at best.

We stop for lunch when there is a good beach with some

shade and the kids on the trip are beginning to get rumbles in their bellies. We get to camp when we find a spot where everyone can sleep semi-comfortably and when there will be time to prepare dinner before the group goes to bed. For some, this can be a hard concept to grasp.

Alan asked again at lunch that day, "How many hours before we get into camp?" Again we estimated. He asked the next morning. "How many miles today?" We told him our ideas, hikes we would like to take, and the area we were aiming for that night, but explained that the plan always seems to change.

It was not until the morning of day three on our five-day excursion that I watched Alan take a deep breath and let go of his appointment-driven routine. He unwound 180-degrees and surrendered to the circumstances of his vacation. Alan quit awaiting the next stop and timing our meals like he was checking them off on a master list of to-dos for the trip. He stopped breaking Desolation down into increments of hours and miles and began to realize its scale. When he finally loosened up, even his physical appearance went through a transformation: his hat tipped to the side a little, his shoulders fell in relaxed slopes, and the white strip where his watch had been soon showed off a pink sunburn.

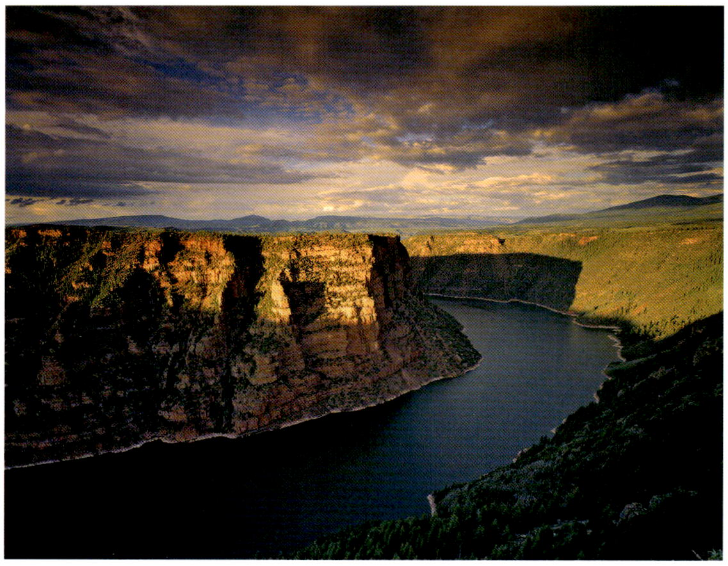

Alan's trip down the Green River was a few hundred miles and a few worlds apart from his high-rise life in Seattle, but when he let go of the rules that govern what most passengers on our trips call their "real lives," he seemed to take on a more complete appreciation of the experience. I chatted with him about the details of the canyon, wildlife, geology and vegetation. He told me about his wife and youngest son who were waiting for him at home. He and his older son matched shapes and shadows in the cliffs to familiar animals or objects. He took short naps on the boat and seemed completely content watching Desolation Canyon slowly roll by. Alan didn't ask about our schedule again. Instead he spent the remaining days of his river trip using the dry bags on the boat as his personal lounge chair.

There are also those river trip passengers who find the excursion to be not only a necessary getaway, but also an accomplishment they had never expected. Some of the people we meet surprise themselves.

Wendy was one of those people. She had wiry blond hair that was pulled neatly into two small hairclips behind her ears. Her bangs hung in the perfect curves of curling iron training and she spoke with a thick Texas accent that was quickly infecting the rest of the passengers on the trip. By dinnertime on day one, nearly everyone in the group, including me, had added a subtle twang to their tone and spoke with a subconsciously imitated drawl. I wondered if Wendy had noticed, but decided she had other things on her mind because she had chosen to undertake the three-day river trip having never camped in her life. Wendy was one giant leap outside her comfort zone.

On the second day of the adventure, she revealed that she had originally scheduled the trip as a Fathers Day and birthday present for her husband. Together they had saved up the cost of the trip and airfare and arranged the details for the trek to Green River. Then something came up. Her husband was called to serve in Iraq, training the country's fledgling police forces, and chose to go. But in the end, after agonizing apprehension, she chose to go on the originally scheduled river trip without him.

Wendy got herself on a plane to Phoenix and with a rented car wound up at the Motel 6 in Green River. She did not really know anyone on the trip. She had never even been to Utah. She was nervous. Wendy told me on the boat over the next few days that she was worried that she would slow the group down, that she was a little overweight, and that she might need help and become a nuisance. But to me, her determination was obvious, and she turned out to be an asset to the trip like she could never have imagined.

Every morning her bags were packed and sitting in front of the boats before we, the crew, were through cleaning up breakfast. She was dunking herself in the muddy water all day long and giggling about it the entire time. In the evenings, her stories left the rest of the group in constant rolling laughter in the hours after dinner.

And she had a sharp eye. For the entirety of the three-day float she sat on the stern of the raft, with a ceaseless grin on her face. Periodically she would pipe up, and in her strong accent point out wildlife that I surely would have floated past without note.

"Um...there's a pretty big bird sitting on that rock over there," she said. It was a redtail hawk. She later spotted two river otters, a species we do not often see, and what we decided must have been the tail end of a muskrat disappearing into the tamarisk trees along the bank. She was so attentive to the canyon and her surroundings that she made me feel I was taking them for granted.

Wendy stood on the dock at our boathouse and cried when the trip ended — big tears rolling down her rounded cheeks. She said she never would have thought she could pull off something like rafting down the Colorado River by herself, coming all this way, eating outside, sleeping outside, using the bathroom outside, and having a wonderful time at it. She is an example of my favorite type of passenger, those who discover some new talents in themselves and rediscover a little confidence that has been overshadowed or forgotten.

A river trip, for people like Wendy, though certainly not for all of our customers, can become an experience that alters their approach to everyday life and becomes much more than the thrill of the rapids or a rugged outdoor adventure. Even if their transformation only lasts for the few short days they are on the trip, some people recognize character they have forgotten or priorities they have disregarded.

I have found that this holds true for me as well. The river has a distinct way of placing my own priorities back where they belong each summer. It is easy to fall into a mindset where silly things seem to hold great importance. I admit that I have strained my own nerves in order to earn more money or look a certain way, for example. During the off-season, I have found myself wishing for things, possessions, that I would never take a second look at during the summer months, when acquiring more stuff means hauling it around, packing and unpacking it and having to find a place to put it. I have placed a project or a job above my family and myself, and what makes me genuinely happy. These are all issues that I've found easily remedied when I take the oars for a float.

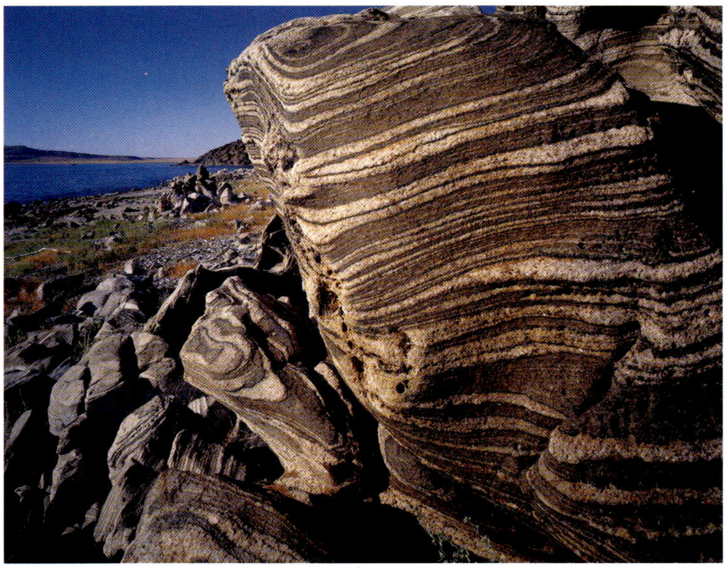

Everyday, the river reminds us that what really matters is staying safe, maintaining a full belly, getting much needed rest, absorbing the rugged surroundings, and occupying oneself with good, loving company.

Utah is not all rocky red desert dotted with a series of small towns, however. As our license plates boast, we have "the greatest snow on earth" and plenty of mountains to catch it.

One fall I climbed to the 12,721-foot summit of Mt. Peale, in the La Sal Mountains near Moab, with a good friend. Peale's apex offers a helicopter view of Castleton Tower, a famous pinnacle that rises six stories from its solitary talus pedestal near the town of Castle Valley, Utah. We sat on the mountain, enjoying the vista, drinking the best raspberry tea I have ever had, and I do not like tea.

The Abajo and the Henry Ranges are neighbors to the La Sals. The Henrys appear suddenly on the horizon, framed by narrow canyon walls at the head of Lake Powell after the rapids of Cataract Canyon. Their alpine contrast to the bottom of the canyon signals that the takeout is near and gently reminds river parties that they will soon be leaving Cataract. The Henry range is also home to the only herd of wild, huntable bison in the continental United States. Some of the chubby bison that line the roadways in Yellowstone National Park have been transplanted there from Utah's Henry Mountains.

Just as desertscapes demand a second look in southern Utah, mountains command the open space in the northern part of the state, where the peaks of the Uinta and Wasatch mountain ranges sit side by side.

The Uintas, which run for about 100 miles near Utah's northern border with Wyoming, hold some of my favorite mountain terrain, admittedly because it echoes what I love about the southern reaches of Utah. Though the range features the highest peak in the state, King's Peak, towering at more than 13,500 feet, the Uintas do not look like a classic alpine environment.

The higher peaks of the Uintas stand as ancient testaments of the unstoppable forces of erosion. Rebels of the Rocky Mountains, they run a peculiar east to west, between the towns of Vernal and Heber City. Remnants of what once were a band of sharp crests and deep fissures, they have been eaten away by insistent wind and countless seasons of freeze and thaw. Though they are high, the peaks of the Uintas have been weathered into the shapes of giant sand dunes with large vertical cliff faces, where it appears colossal chunks of the mountain have fallen away all at once. Below them lay foothills that roll on like the snow-covered backs of a herd of sleeping dinosaurs.

The lower elevations of the range stretch in rounded hills toward Flaming Gorge Reservoir, 91 miles of standing water created by Flaming Gorge Dam on the Green River. The area near the lake is a clash of desert rock and mountain forest, with a sizeable man-made body of water that has filled the canyons somewhere in the middle.

Major John Wesley Powell, the man credited with the exploration of the Green and Colorado rivers in 1869, named the canyon that is now under the reservoir, Red Canyon, for the brilliant colors of the strata. The geology near Flaming Gorge includes the same Wingate and Entrada formations that define the Moab area, and the Morrison and Green River formations of Desolation Canyon, but they sit at a higher elevation. Brittle clumps of sagebrush and blackbrush share the hillsides nearby with stands of pinion, juniper and lodgepole pine trees. Together, the rock layers, the lake, and the coexisting plant life make the area an earth-toned collage.

The lake itself drowns what would have been a beautiful section of the Green River. A glance over the edge of the dam down to the bottom of its plunging concrete panels shows the beautiful meanders of a narrow gorge of dark stone. I have stood there, trying to imagine what the river might have looked like where the lake is now, but seeing through the deep blue water, even in my imagination, is difficult. I like to think of it as Powell and his party saw it: a deep canyon of rainbow rock flowing fast with muddy water, mountain hillsides visible on the canyon rim, and no idea what to expect beyond the next eddy.

Today the area serves recreational and power generation purposes. During the summer months, the lake's waters are crowded with fishermen and water skiers, with the power lines that run in long rows up the hillsides from the dam humming in the background.

I have spent a good deal of my childhood hiking and playing near the lake and in the tiny town of Dutch John, three miles from Flaming Gorge Dam. Some of my family's best friends lived in that community of barely 200 residents, in government housing built for those who maintain the dam and work in the recreation area. With not much else to do, we were outside a lot.

My family and our long-time friends used to set up on the shore of the reservoir just like it was a white sand beach on the Pacific, with towels, umbrella, toy buckets, shovels and all. We would spend all day with the parents talking and watching the boaters, while the kids ran endlessly in and out of the water. When you grow up in Utah, the word beach means the gravely shore of a lake, or the sandy banks of the river, not the crash and salt of the ocean, but it is equally as satisfying on a scorching summer afternoon.

During the cooler months in Dutch John we had to bundle up to enjoy our time outside. Halloween was always spent in the snow, costumes hidden beneath layers of heavy clothing. We found that every costume seemed to go with snow boots as we went trick or treating a few houses at a time before retreating back home to warm up. I have a memory from that time stamped like a vivid photograph on my mind of elk, who seemed to tower at unearthly heights compared to my child-size stature, eating the Halloween pumpkins we had carved the night before right out of the front yard. I stood inside, watching in fascination as they made a quick snack of our careful craftsmanship.

Neighbors to the Uintas and big brothers to Utah's smaller southern ranges are the peaks of the Wasatch Mountains. Considered the western edge of the Rockies, the Wasatch resemble the Tetons of Wyoming with steep summits, mountainsides streaked with treeless gullies and patches of snow, which offer a stunning contrast to the deserts down south. The giant peaks of the Wasatch are sheer, bare faces of rock that, in some places, rise at near vertical angles from the range's foothill foundation. They jut abruptly from the bowl-shaped valleys where Salt Lake City, Provo, Park City and the suburbs of each lie. The Wasatch Range allows Utah to brag deservingly about some of the most steep and rugged ski and wilderness terrain in the country.

Mount Olympus is the most recognizable, at an altitude of 9,000 feet. It overlooks the Salt Lake City suburbs of Holladay and Olympus Cove in bold command of the valley. Timpanogos and Lone Peak follow suit. The cities below each have pushed as far up the foothills as they can, lapping at their bases. Mt. Nebo is the highest peak in the Wasatch, standing at 11,800 feet at the southern end of the range. And from the high peaks of the Wasatch another notable natural wonder of northern Utah can be seen, the Great Salt Lake.

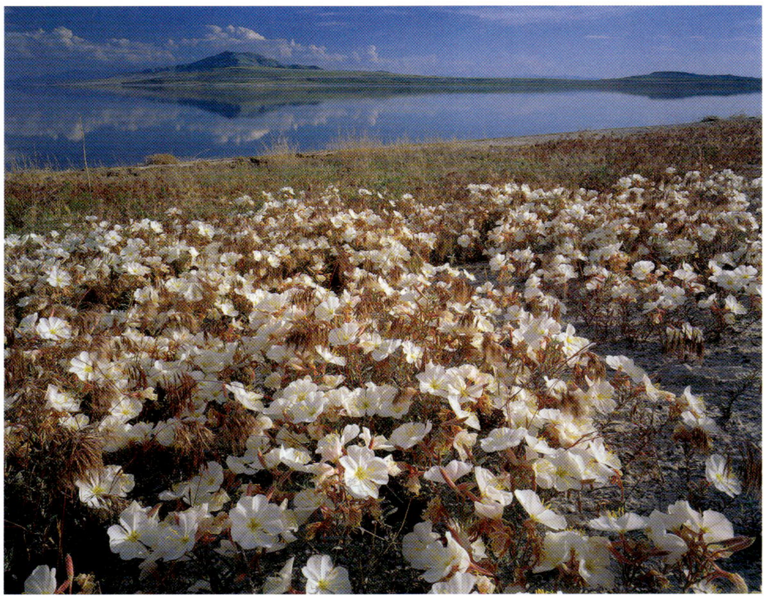

It is the lake that helps coat Utah winters in an abundance of soft light snow. The Great Salt Lake is the largest saltwater lake in the Western hemisphere and because its only outlet is evaporation, it is far saltier than any ocean. As cold winter winds cross the shallow, much warmer waters of the lake they pick up water vapor. That water vapor then freezes and is deposited as the winds are forced upward over the nearby mountains. The end results are frequent storms during the winter months that deliver welcome buckets of ideal skiable snow to the Wasatch.

Upon personal comparison of shooting down a ski run in Brekenridge, Colorado and cruising the terrain at Solitude Ski Resort up Big Cottonwood canyon in the Wasatch, I found the Utah license plate boasting to be true. We do get exceptional amounts of nearly perfect snow. The lake effect snow and overall low humidity in the region make the snow in the Wasatch almost weightless as it piles on the range's slopes and benches. It looks like movie snow gathering in downy mounds of porcelain white and blowing into feathery drifts. Unlike the wet snow of Summit County, Colorado, or the sharp icy particles of snow in the East, Utah snow floats a snowboard smoothly and quickly down an untracked gully, flying out from under it on both sides as it is disturbed from where it fell the night before.

Sharp and striking, the Wasatch Mountains cannot be ignored or overlooked as a vital asset to the diversity, draw and effortless beauty of this state.

I heard an unusual Utah story recently that made me think a bit.

On a particularly warm May afternoon, a volunteer ranger patrolling at the Westwater boat launch, the put-in to a popular whitewater rafting stretch on the Colorado River near Cisco, Utah, was confused by what appeared to be a giant piece of Styrofoam floating toward him upstream of the ramp. As the unidentifiable craft drifted closer, bobbing in the swift current of the spring runoff, the ranger realized that the white blob was some kind of a boat. He could see that it was manned by someone standing up using only one oar, in the style of an Italian gondolier.

It should be said that Westwater Canyon, which begins just a few miles downstream of the boat ramp mentioned above, is a narrow gorge of slick black stone. During the spring, when the water is flowing high and carrying whatever it has plucked from the banks upstream, the current in Westwater speeds through the canyon, plunging over boulders to form rapids with names like Staircase Rapid, Funnel Falls, and Skull Rapid. As it races through the canyon the water gets caught in boiling eddies and piles against the chasm walls at every turn. Once a boat reaches the gorge there is no bank on which to pull over and little time to regroup between rapids. The drops of each rapid are short but steep, and a few harbor obstacles like the Rock of Shock, Skull Hole and the Room of Doom that are best avoided all together. It is an exciting and wonderful ride with a little knowledge of the canyon and the proper equipment.

The foam boat was far from appropriate whitewater equipment. As it neared the ramp, it became apparent that the rest of the outfit's gear was no better. The man piloting the craft held a long four-by-four post of wood, onto which was fastened the lid of a plastic garbage can. He dipped his one oar awkwardly into the water and used long strokes to steer the boat, but he had little control. It would come out later that they had begun the trip with an actual paddle but had lost it to the river in one of the small riffles upstream.

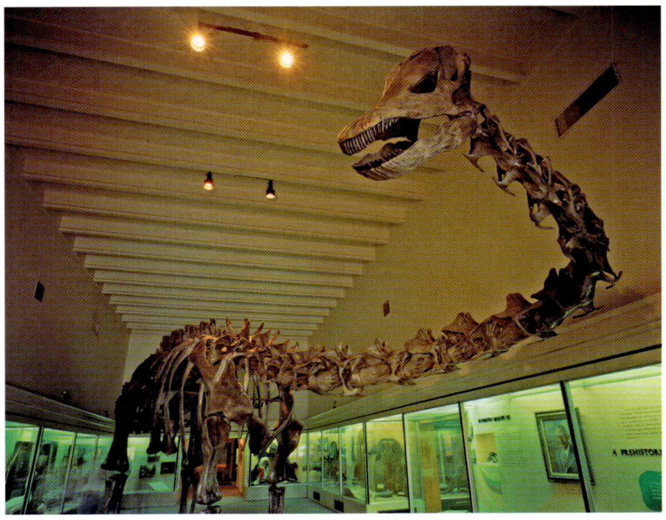

Upon coming into view, the ranger could see that the boat was constructed of a series of large rectangular pieces of foam, which made the boat a rectangle shape itself, the whole thing lashed together with thin white cord and duct tape. All together it looked like an oversized foam cooler with no lid. One piece of rope encircled the boat twice and was tied off in a haphazard knot at the front corner. Strips of Duct Tape in various sizes stretched over the sides and around the bottom. The boat's engineer had lined the inside with a large sheet of clear plastic and erected a sunshade made from a blue tarp suspended from poles at each corner of the raft. One pole was a piece of rebar. One was a ski pole. The last two were crooked sticks. In all its glory the boat was about ten feet long and almost that wide. The homemade raft had obviously taken a significant amount of labor and planning, and so far it had held together.

As the foam masterpiece approached the put-in, the ranger signaled its captain to pull over. The ranger, who relayed the story to me in person, said the man waved a hand at him as if to say, "Na, we're fine," and kept rowing. The ranger beckoned to him again, and again the man said he did not need any help. Finally the volunteer ranger resorted to yelling that the man and his companions, who appeared to be his wife and his dog, would most likely die if they continued down the corridor. After the ranger, who had run down the bank as the boat passed the ramp, threw the river party a rescue rope, the whole haphazard outfit reached the shore.

Upon hauling the boat onto land, the couple explained that they had been living in Grand Junction, Colorado, 35 miles upstream. They had run into some "hard times" as they put it, and planned to call on relatives who lived near Lake Powell for help. Their plan was simple. They looked at a map and saw that the Colorado River flowed through Grand Junction and continued directly to their destination. Without money or any other means of travel, they had decided to build a boat and float on down there, maybe even see some scenery along the way. They gathered jugs of water and cans of food, all of which were labelless and scored with a sloppy permanent marker question mark instead. It was a plan that, on the surface, made perfect sense. They had already made it four days from where they had launched their craft directly in the middle of downtown Grand Junction, to Westwater.

But the rangers at Westwater could not let them continue as they were. They would have surely been swimming within the first few miles, their boat reduced to floating chunks, their dog tossed into the churning water of rapids they did not know were coming. Without life jackets, it is unpleasant to think of what could have happened to the couple once they were in the water without a raft.

But it was the spirit and basic enthusiasm behind their improvised journey, along with the basic hilarity of the whole idea, that made me smile when I heard this story. When I recount the couple's tale in my mind I cannot fault them for the plan they put together. In the vein of western explorers before them, they targeted the river as a preferable means of travel and devised a way to use it. With an unusual boldness they did what they could to make their journey comfortable and safe. They knew it was imperative to protect themselves from the sun. They gathered inexpensive, non-perishable food, even improvised a working paddle when theirs was lost to the river. They had lined their boat with plastic and built a bench of Styrofoam inside it for sitting. They had obviously thought things through.

Their overall strategy was not without intelligence. It was just lacking the necessary research, or the simple purchase of a map perhaps, that would have alerted them of the steep rapids churning between them and their destination. I wonder if they were at all nervous about setting out on an unknown course, or if they were completely oblivious to the power of the Colorado. I wonder if they felt a little like modern-day explorers themselves, guessing at what was beyond each snaking meander.

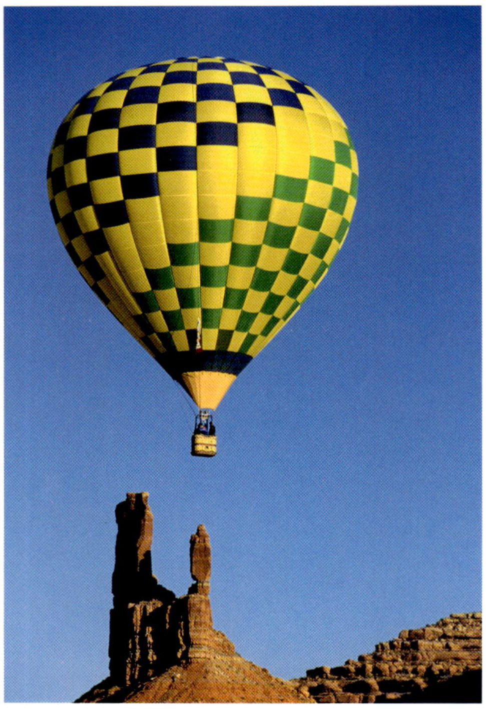

In this way, the story of the foam boat stirs up feelings of the adventurous western character that Utah and much of the west has been built upon. In a time period that can leave one feeling like there is nothing left to be discovered, like the wilderness has all been conquered and that our lives are doomed to be consumed by possessions and politics, this story is a reminder of the basics in this part of the country. It is a reminder of the reasons why we all live here.

I have occasionally felt like the attitude and wilderness spirit of the original frontier west are dead — as if the notions of discovery and a life lived in accord with the land are not real anymore. It seems these ideals have been sold to advertisers and Hollywood, or commandeered by them, as a means to sell us all cigarettes, four-by-four trucks, swanky cowboy clothing or imitated Native American style art. But then I hear a story like the foam boat or spend time in a captivating place like Desolation Canyon that revitalizes my hope in the American West and makes me optimistic that western adventure is still more than just an advertising slogan.

I remember what makes this desolate land matchless when I think about Bill and his friends having camp outs in 1,000 year-old Ancestral Puebloan ruins, or the medicine man who carries on centuries-old Navajo tradition. I think about myself staring out at the towers of Monument Valley and realizing that for most they are just the cliché landscape of movies, but in Utah they stand in our back yards, and we can visit them — really see, feel and appreciate their grandeur — whenever we like.

I recall Green River's one-man-show pizza bar and the front door attempt to defy a culture that is increasingly regulated. I laugh to myself and know that only in Green River could Frank get away with that sign. Though he is a gruff and stubborn character, and harbors a strong disdain for many of the rules most of us blindly obey, he would be the first to show up if any of his friends were in need. Amused, I am thankful that similar establishments punctuate small towns all over this state.

I am also comforted by the elk, standing in muscular command of the mountains, eating the Halloween pumpkins outside the front door of the little brick house in Dutch John. Even as I write this, those elk are grazing in deceptively docile herds in the Uintas and roaming the fields of the modest ranches that dot the foothills.

And I know that the West is not lost when I think of my father, who fell in love with this state as a child, peering out the window of his father's Chevrolet on family vacations from Iowa. My dad has said that this land touched him like nowhere he had ever been, and now he spends his time seeking out and capturing those scenes, light and colors that he fell for years ago. The places and grandeur in his lasting photographs are those that some say don't or can't exist, but they do, in his work and in Utah.

This state of western grit, curious charm, splendor and diversity, is like no other I know. And from the snowy cirques and impressive summits to the orange glow of the desert canyon lands, it is striking on every level.

I heard a first time visitor to Moab describe in stunning simplicity what struck him about this place recently. "You people live in a painting," he said.

Though I would have never so clearly articulated it myself, his interpretation of Utah rings soundly true. We are surrounded by a collage of colors that appear as if they could only have been mixed by hours of careful artist's strokes. We live among wonders like the Colorado River, the Wasatch Mountains, the towers of Monument Valley and Utah's patchwork of quirky communities, all of which are scarcely found together in one place except in the fantasy of art. But here, those unbelievable shades of color are the backdrop to the everyday, and those rugged people of western fables are our friends. We can enjoy and immerse ourselves in it all through a simple glance out the window, conversation at the grocery store, or summer excursion in a pop-up camper. So, for now, life in this Utah painting is pretty good.

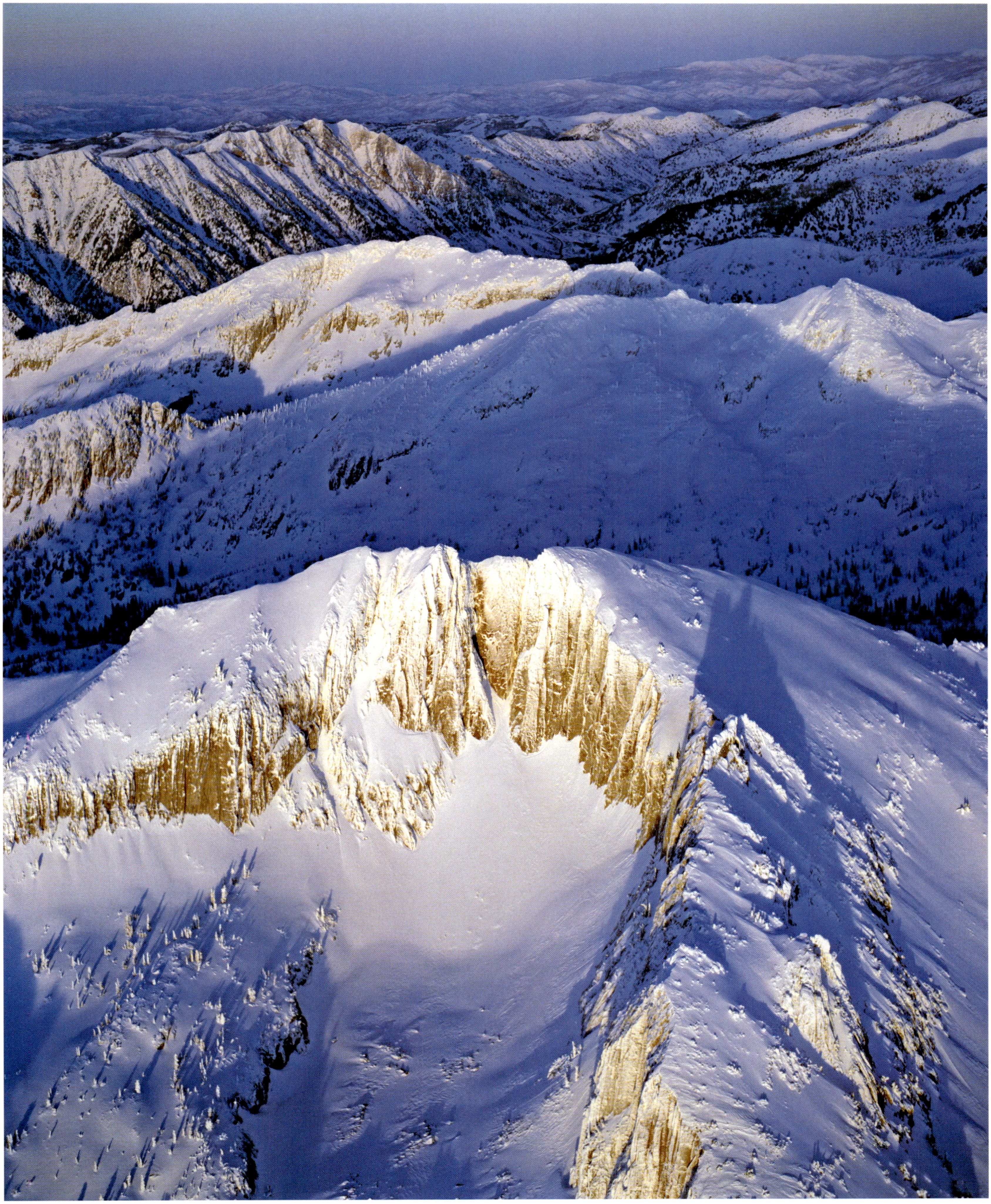

ABOVE:
After days of heavy snow, Lone Peak emerges from clouds in the Lone Peak Wilderness. I used a Pentax 6x7 to shoot through an open airplane window to obtain the image. The wind chill was about minus 50°F.

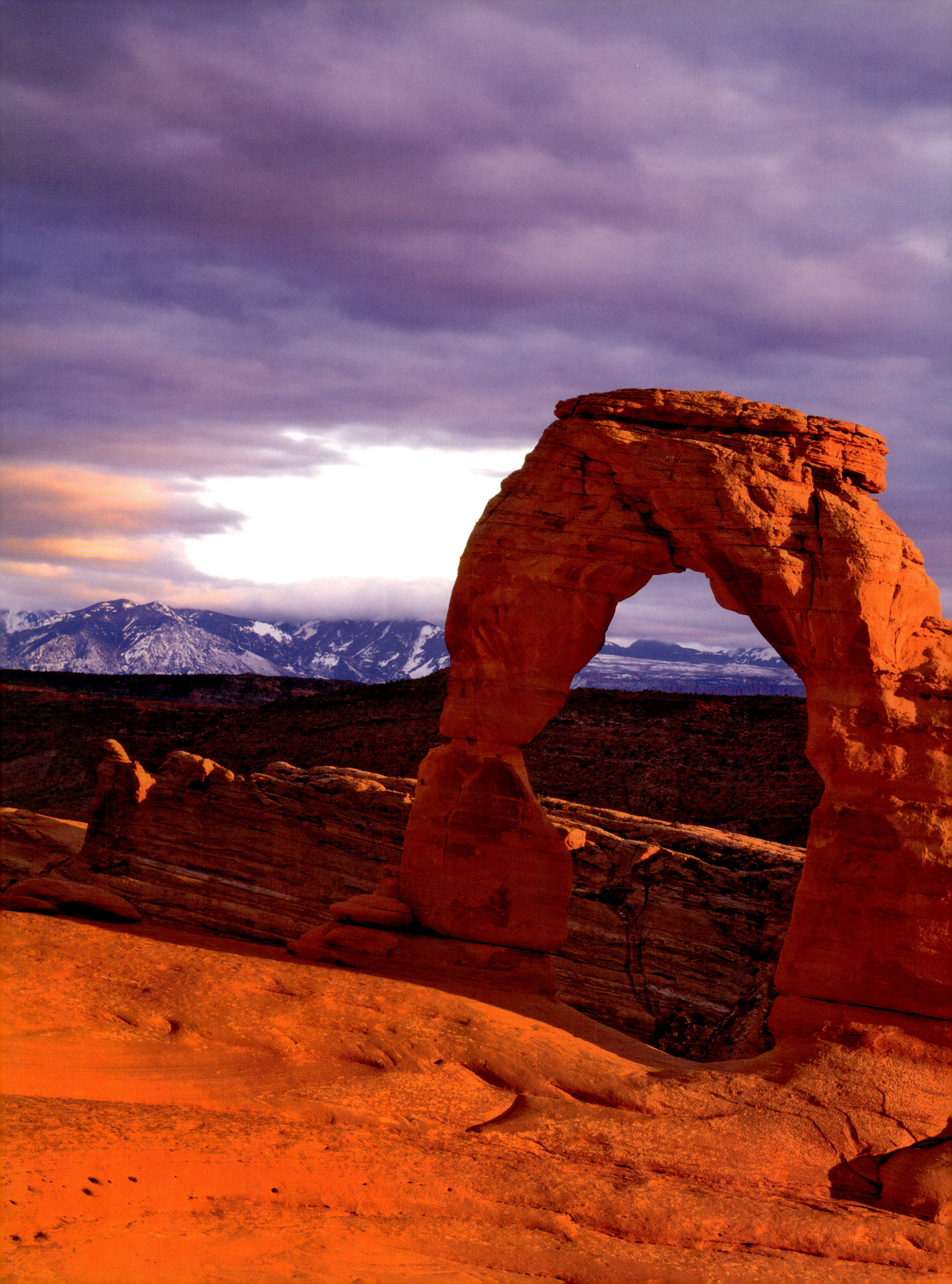

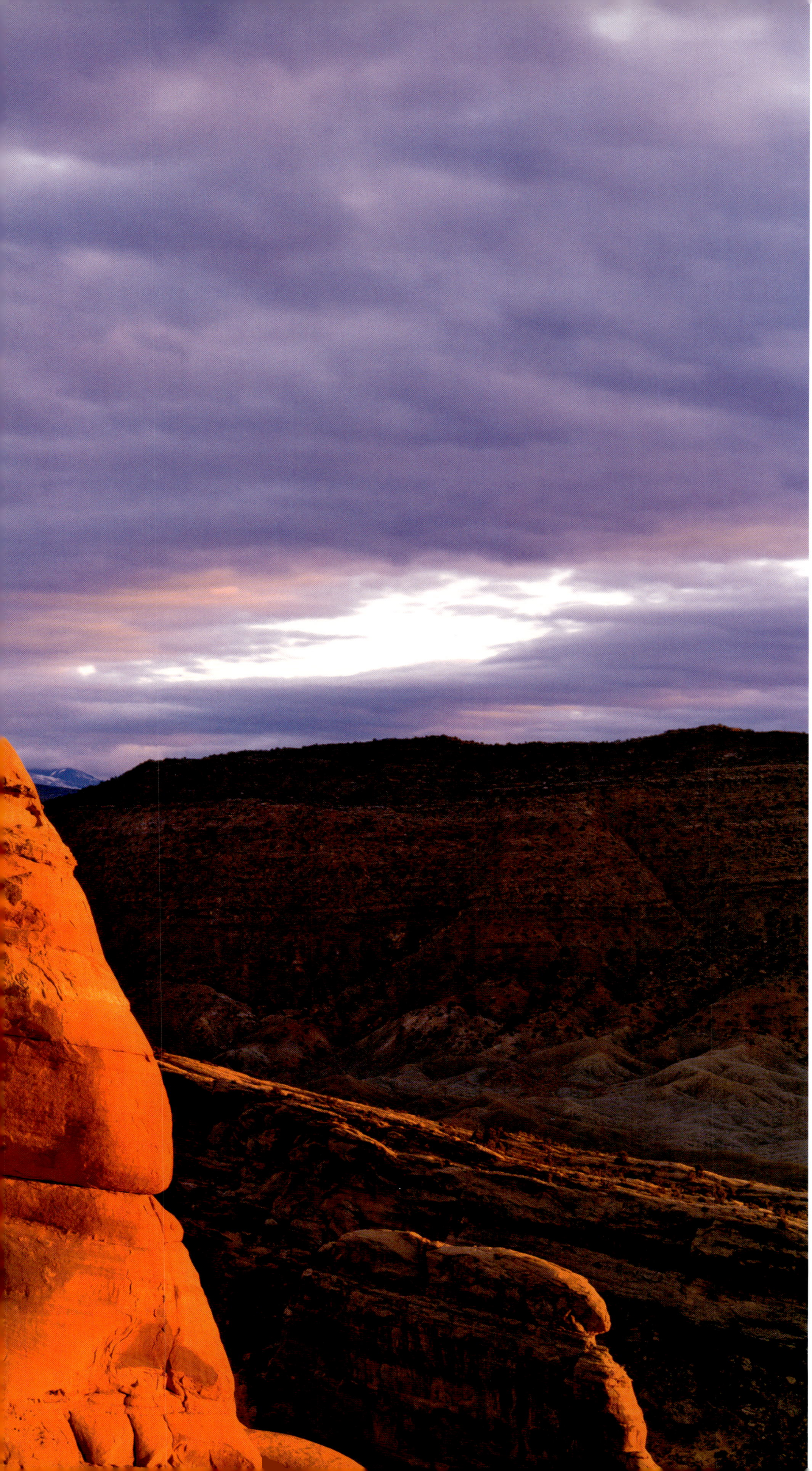

LEFT:
Storm clouds build behind Delicate Arch in Arches National Park.

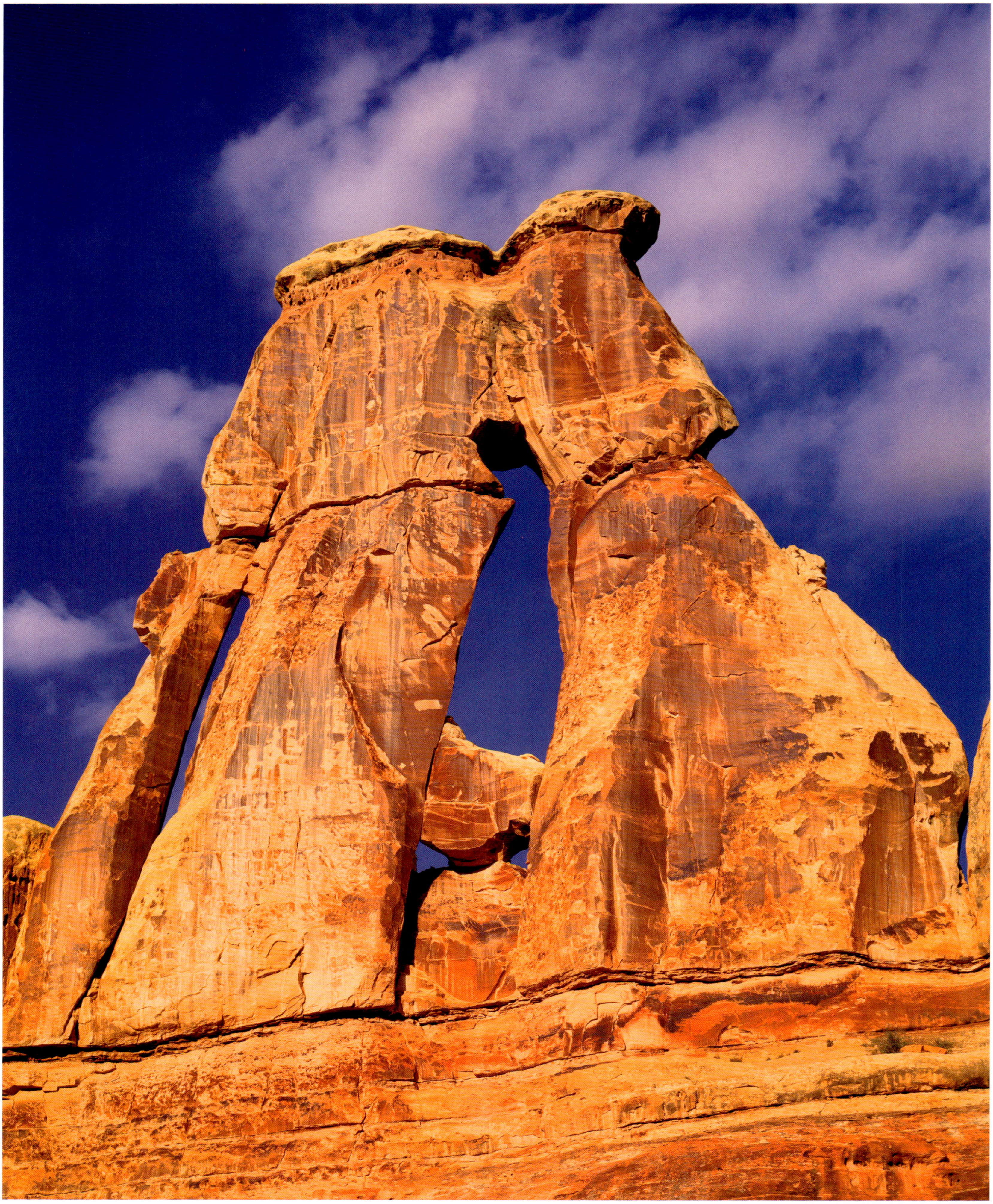

ABOVE:

Hiking the five miles to Druid Arch is one of my favorite activities. I first did it in the late 1960s, just a few years after Canyonlands National Park was designated. Everyday I thank heaven for this park, and I thank those that were instrumental in its creation—a few of whom, thankfully, are still with us. Canyonlands is a treasure of Utah, and I plan to spend a great deal of the rest of my life exploring the few corners I have not yet seen.

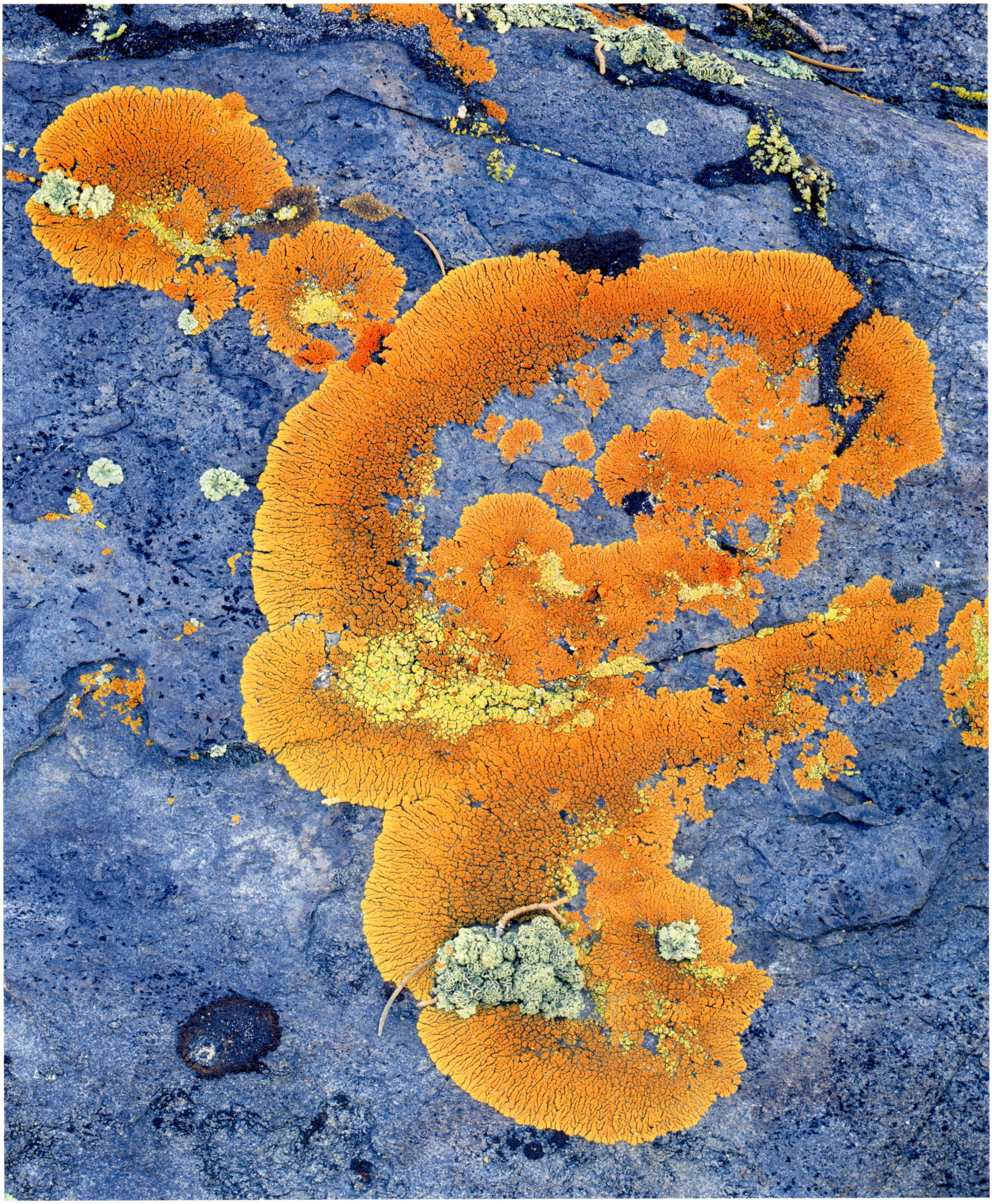

ABOVE:
Lichen in the Deep Creek Mountains is bursting with water and color after several days of spring rains.

NEXT PAGE:
Utah's wildflower nexus, Albion Basin, is always different and ever changing. I've never seen the same blooms twice in dozens of visits. I carry no expectations except to be surprised by what I find, and I always am.

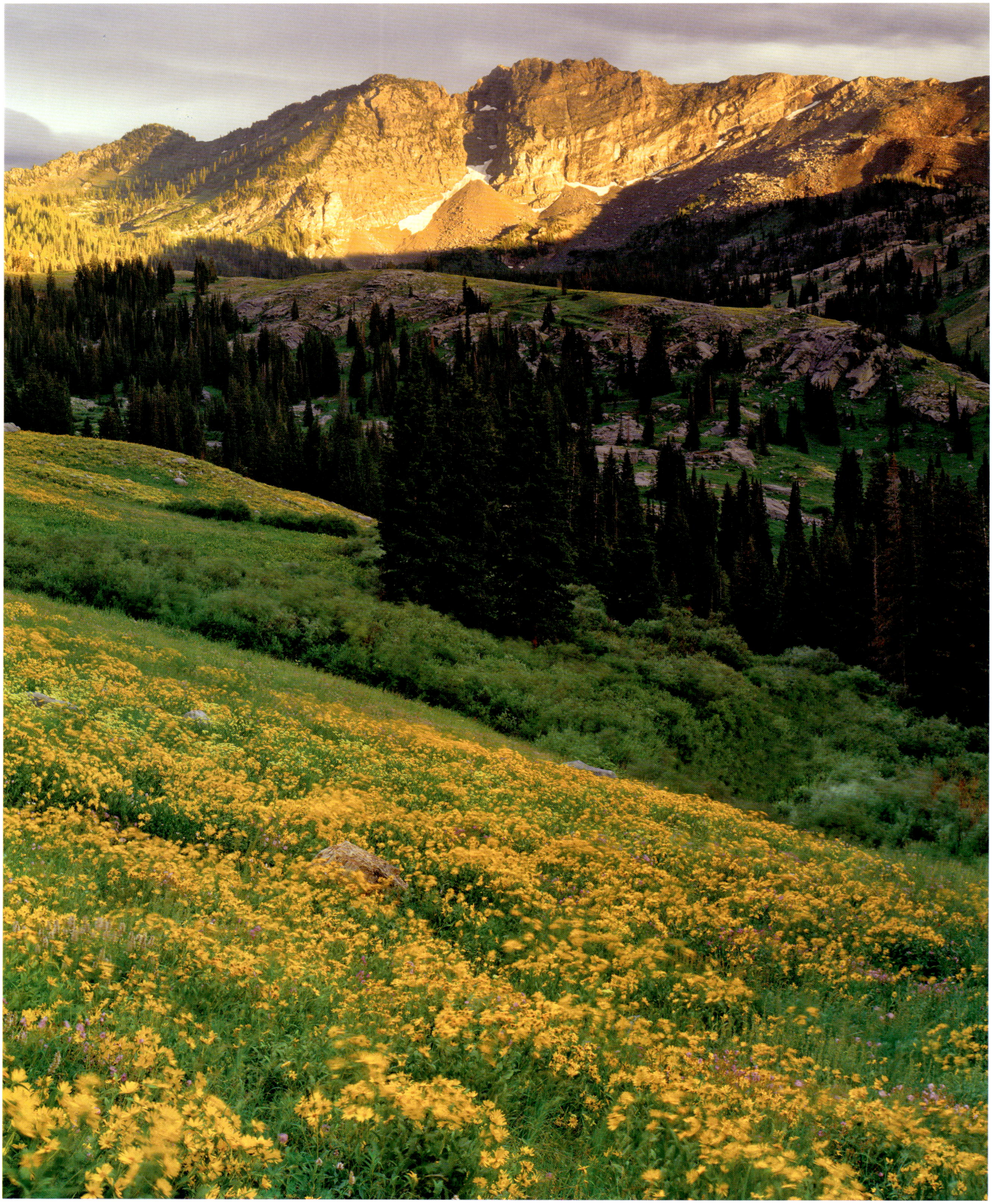

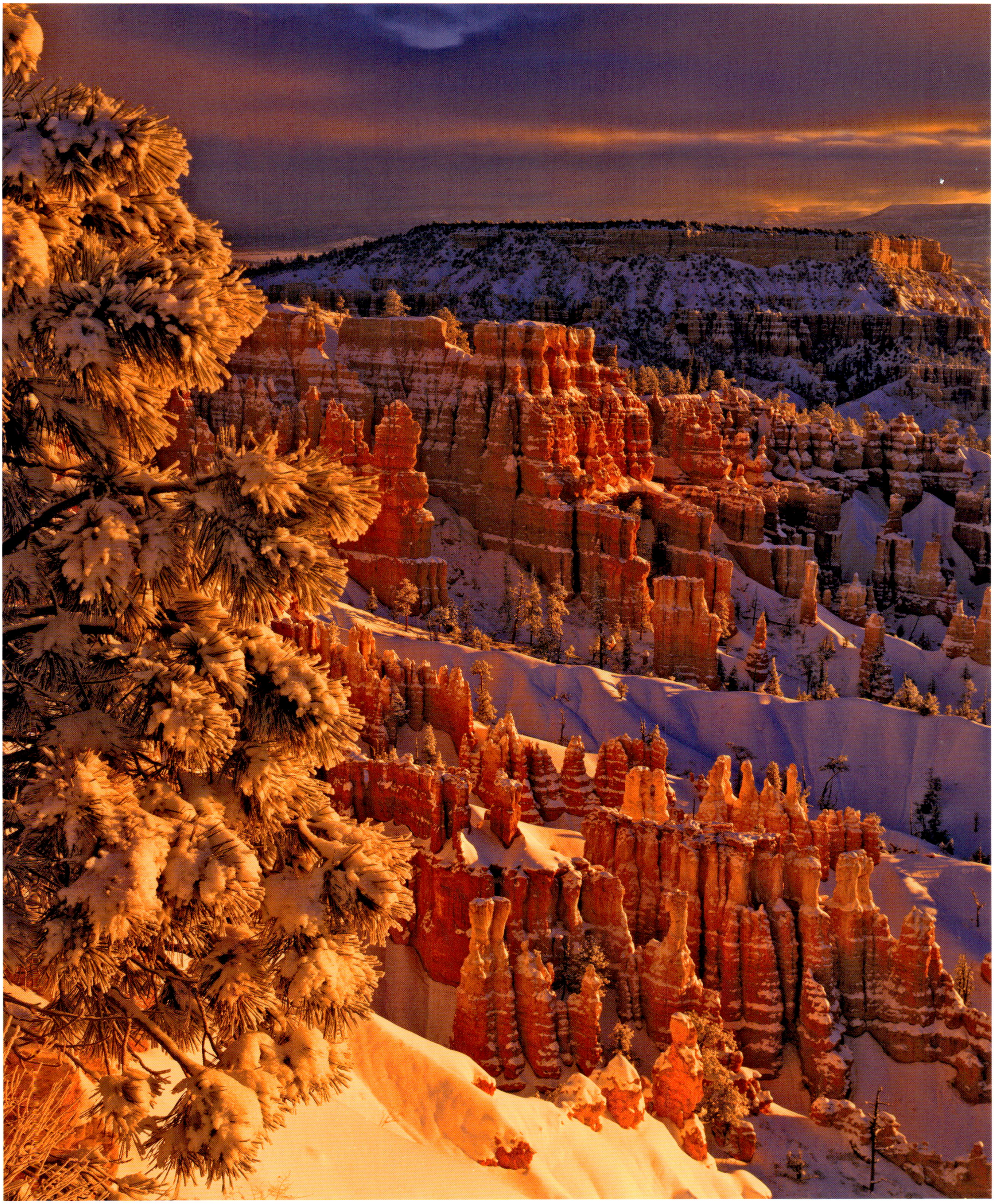

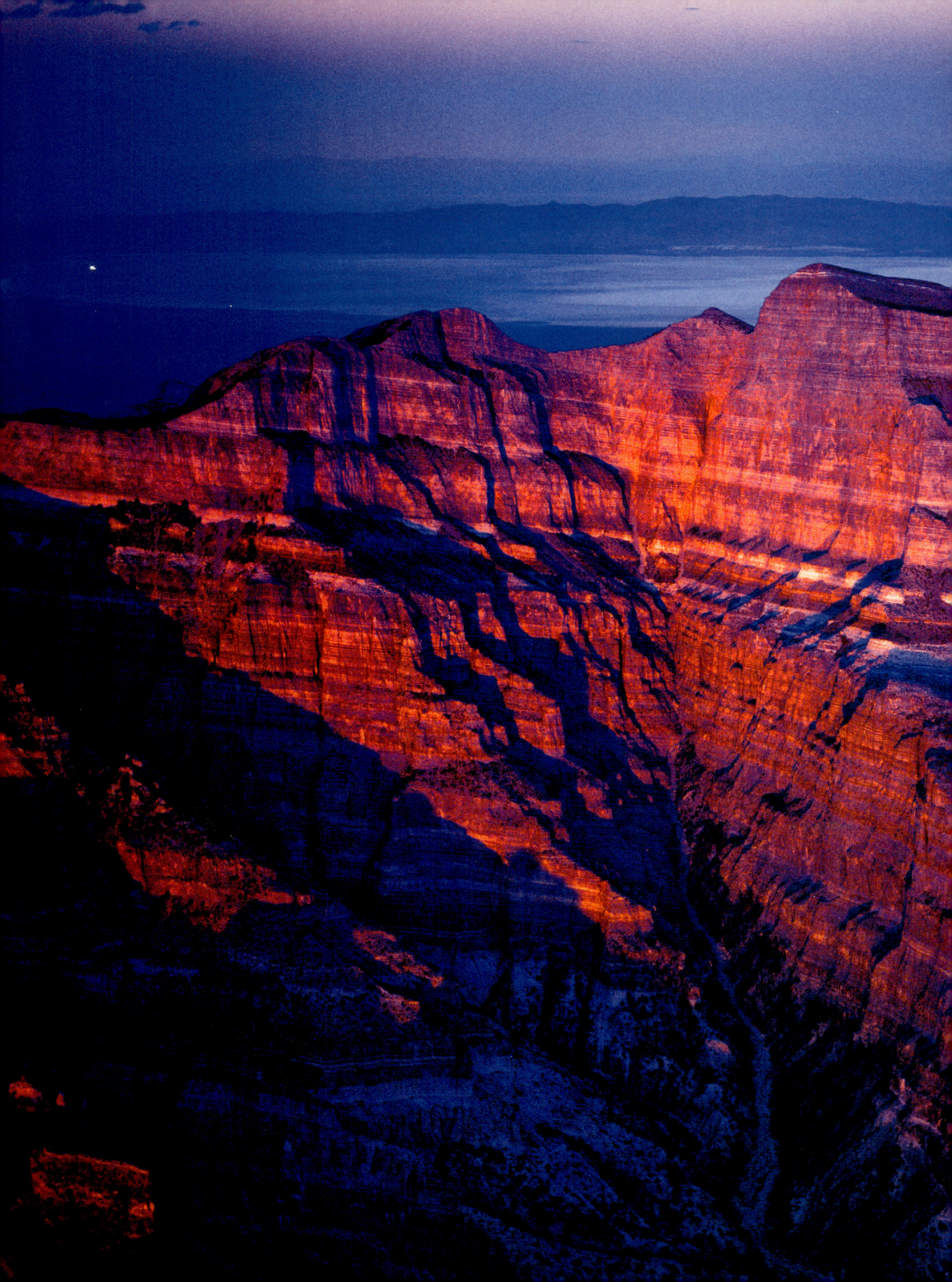

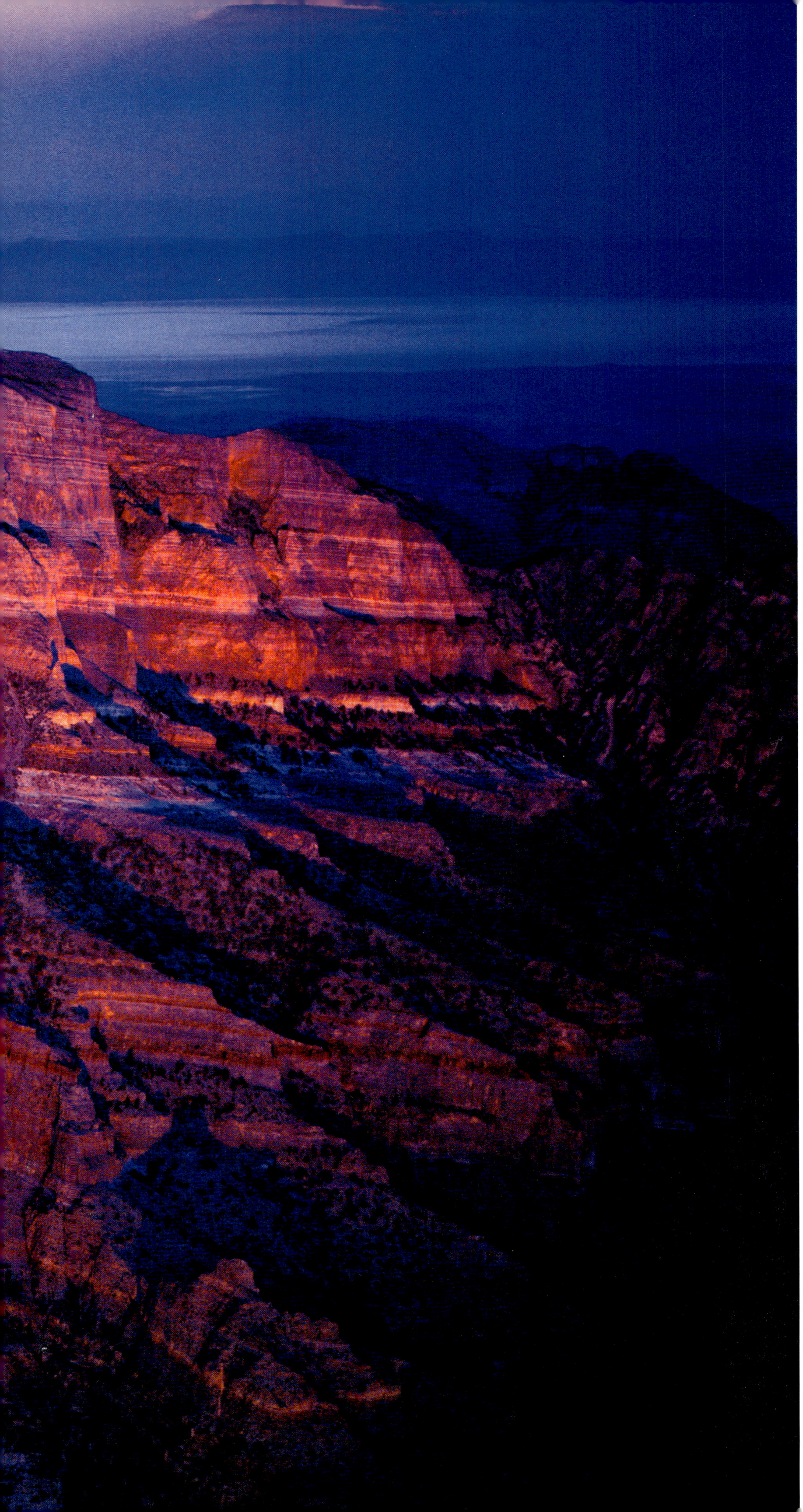

PREVIOUS PAGE:
A winter sunrise at Bryce Canyon National Park at five degrees below zero fahrenheit is warmed by the sun's momentary glow.

LEFT:
Light falls on the giant north-facing cliff of Notch Peak for only a few weeks during June and July. This huge limestone facade is one of the largest mountain cliffs in America.

Beyond Notch Peak, the dry lakebed that is sometimes the home of the Sevier River is lost in the blues of a Great Basin sunset.

NEXT PAGE:
A receding Lake Powell leaves behind enormous beautiful beaches like this on the Utah/ Arizona border.

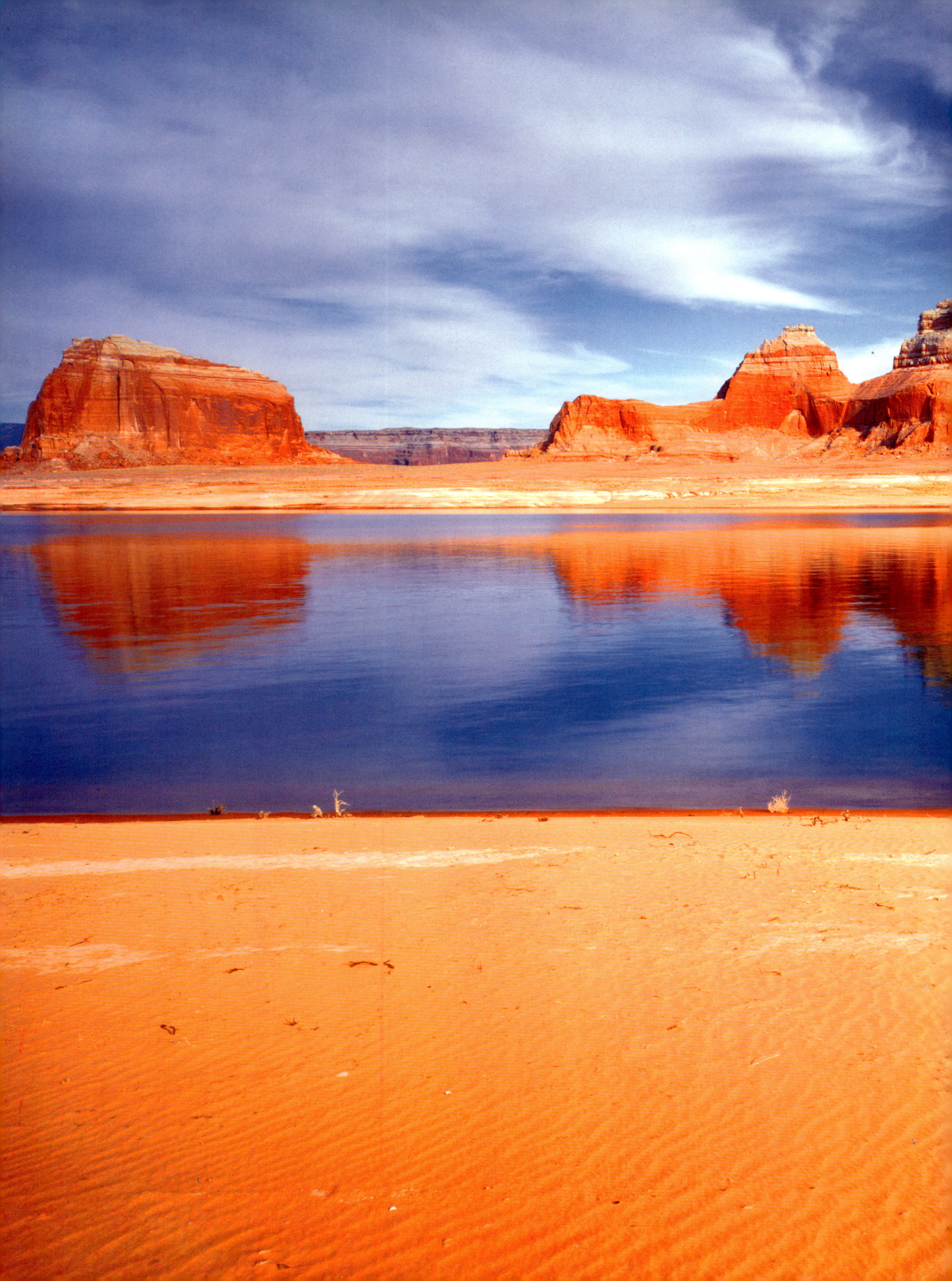

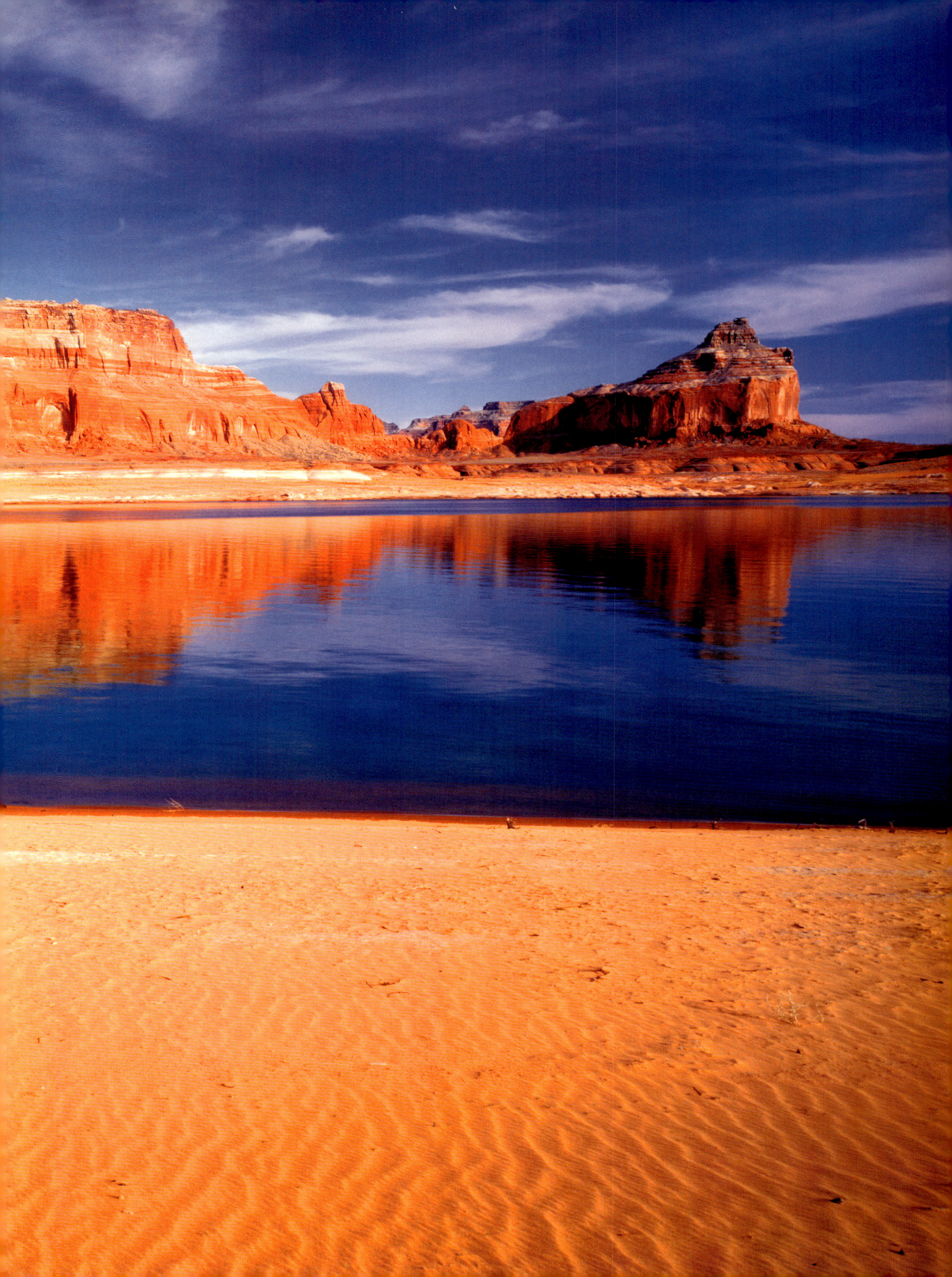

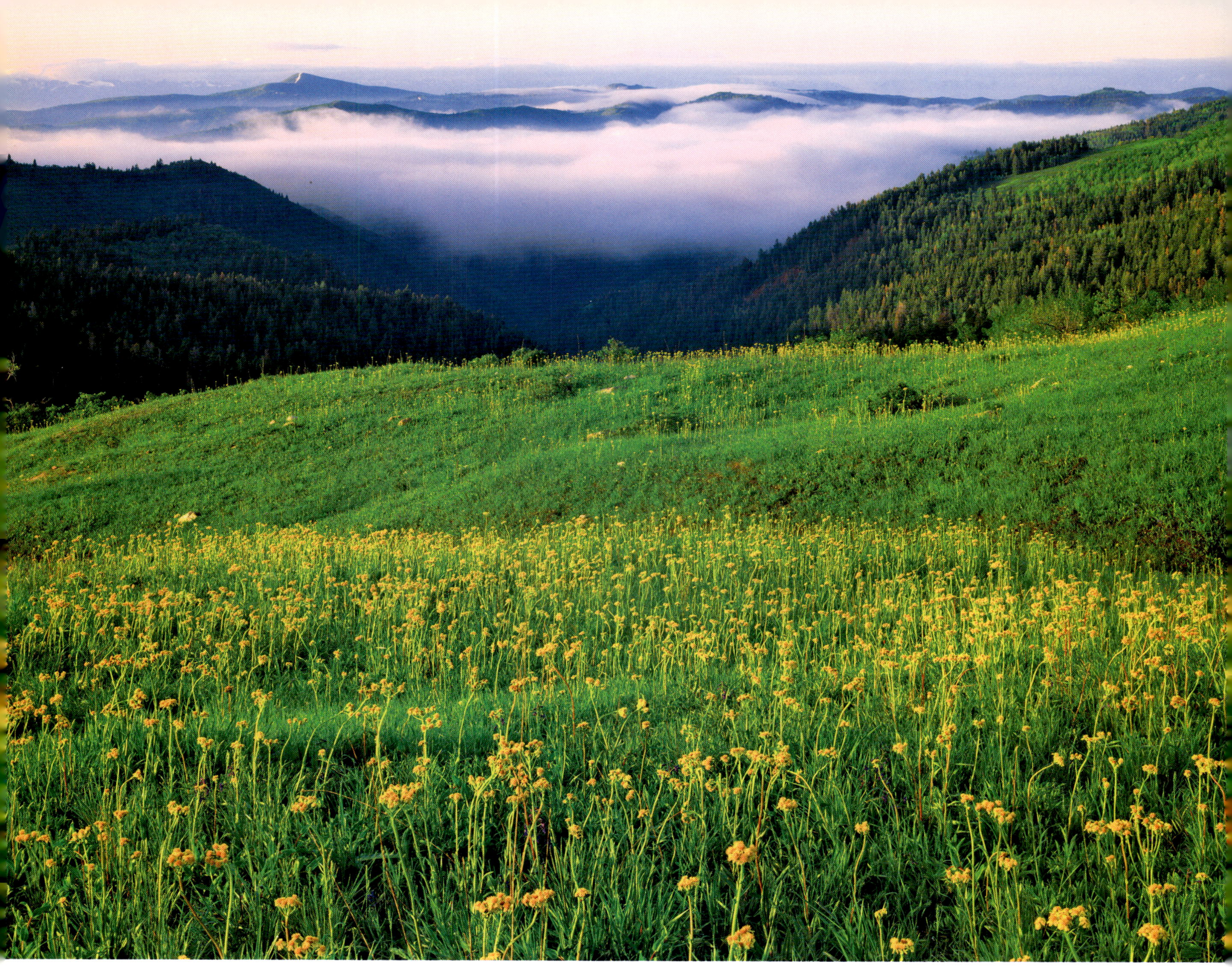

ABOVE:
On an early summer morning, rich greens and foggy skies refute the lie that Utah is a complete desert. This view was along the Nebo Loop near Nephi.

BELOW:
Cottonwoods blaze in autumn glory at Capitol Reef National Park.

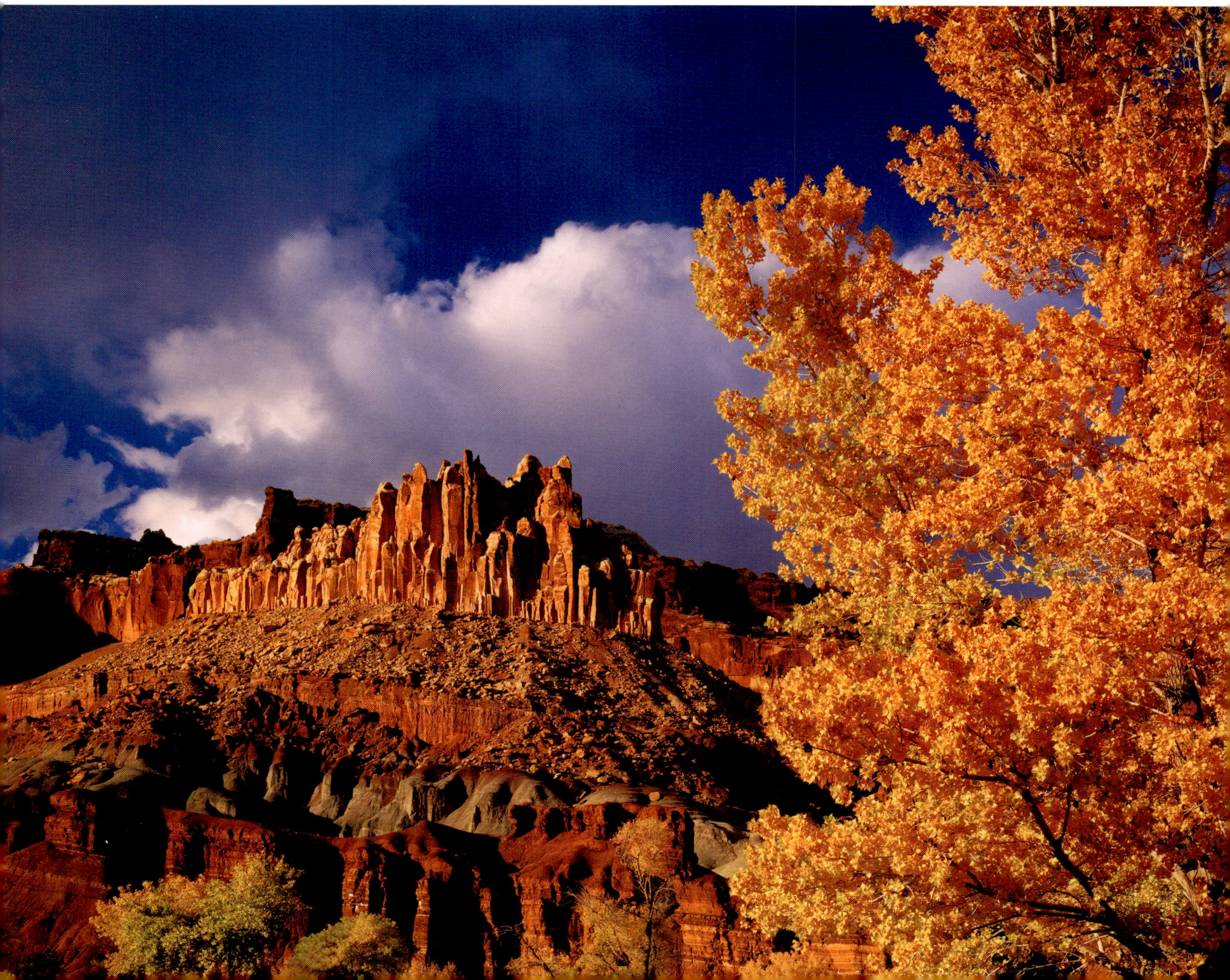

RIGHT:
This image of the formations at Red Canyon in Dixie National Forest was made a number of years ago when my children were little and was never used in any of my books. Since I didn't edit many of my works, the images were usually someone else's choice, not mine. I have fond memories of my kids playing in the snow while I worked, and I have always liked the image and hoped it would be seen someday.

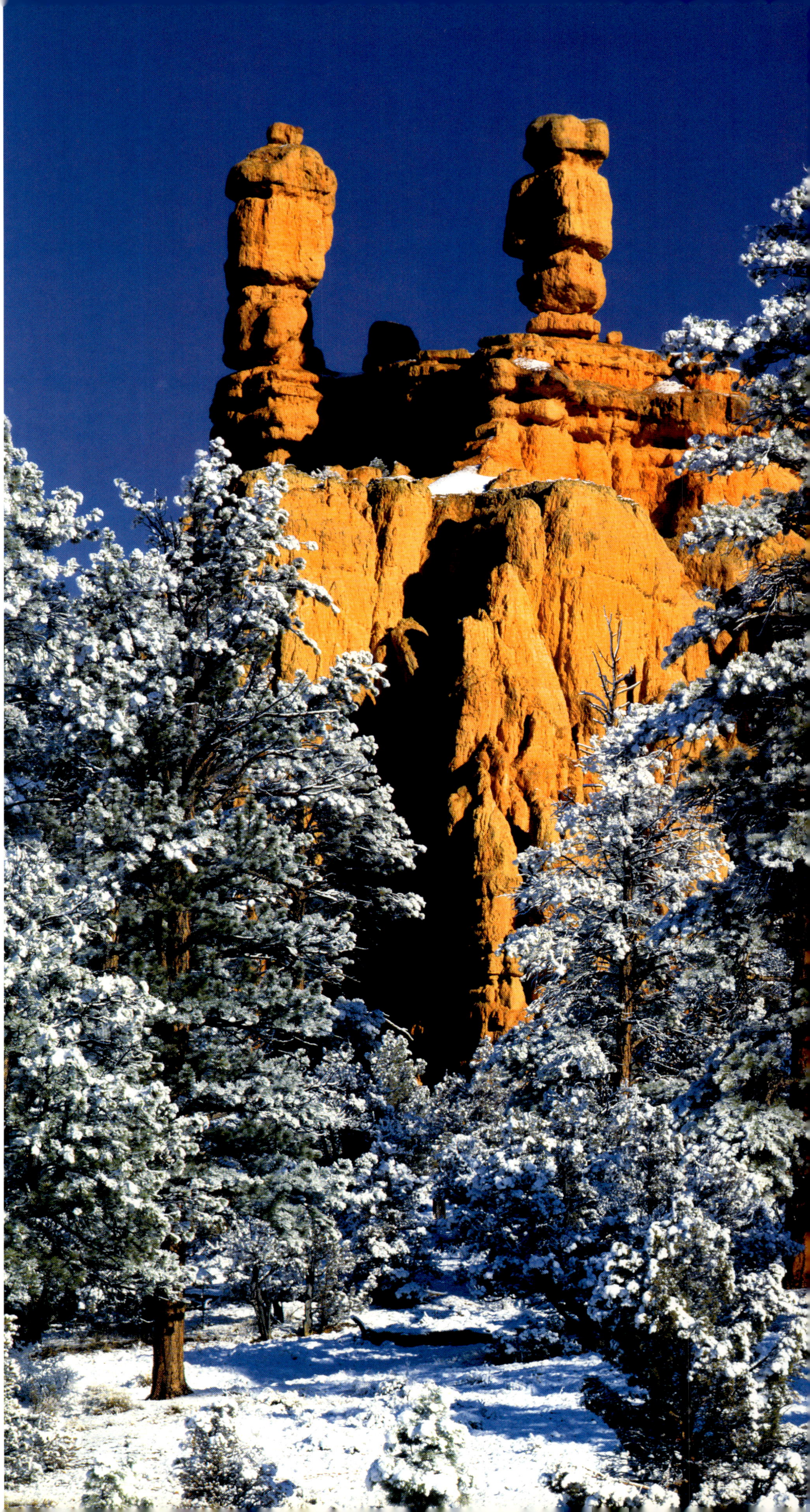

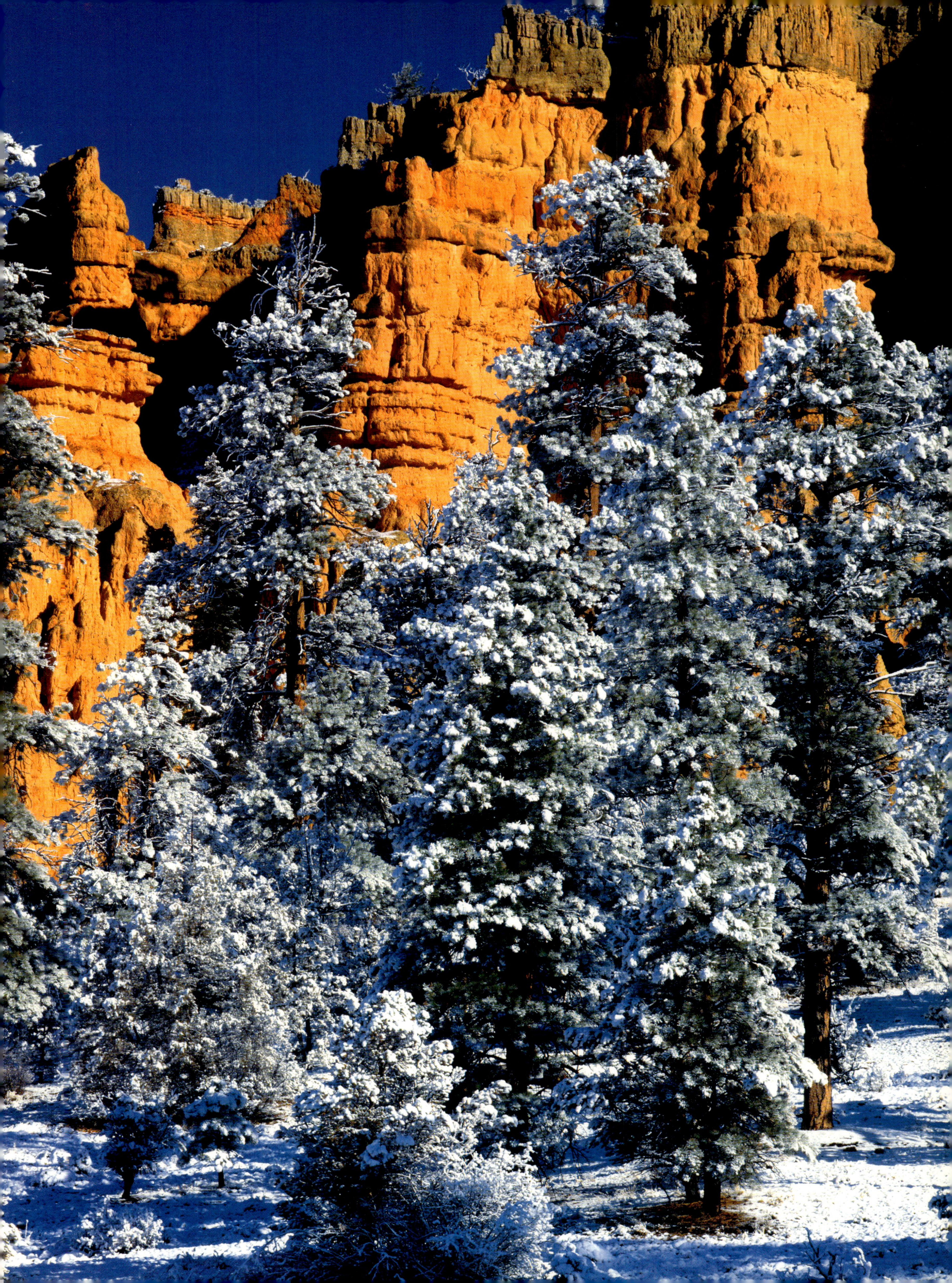

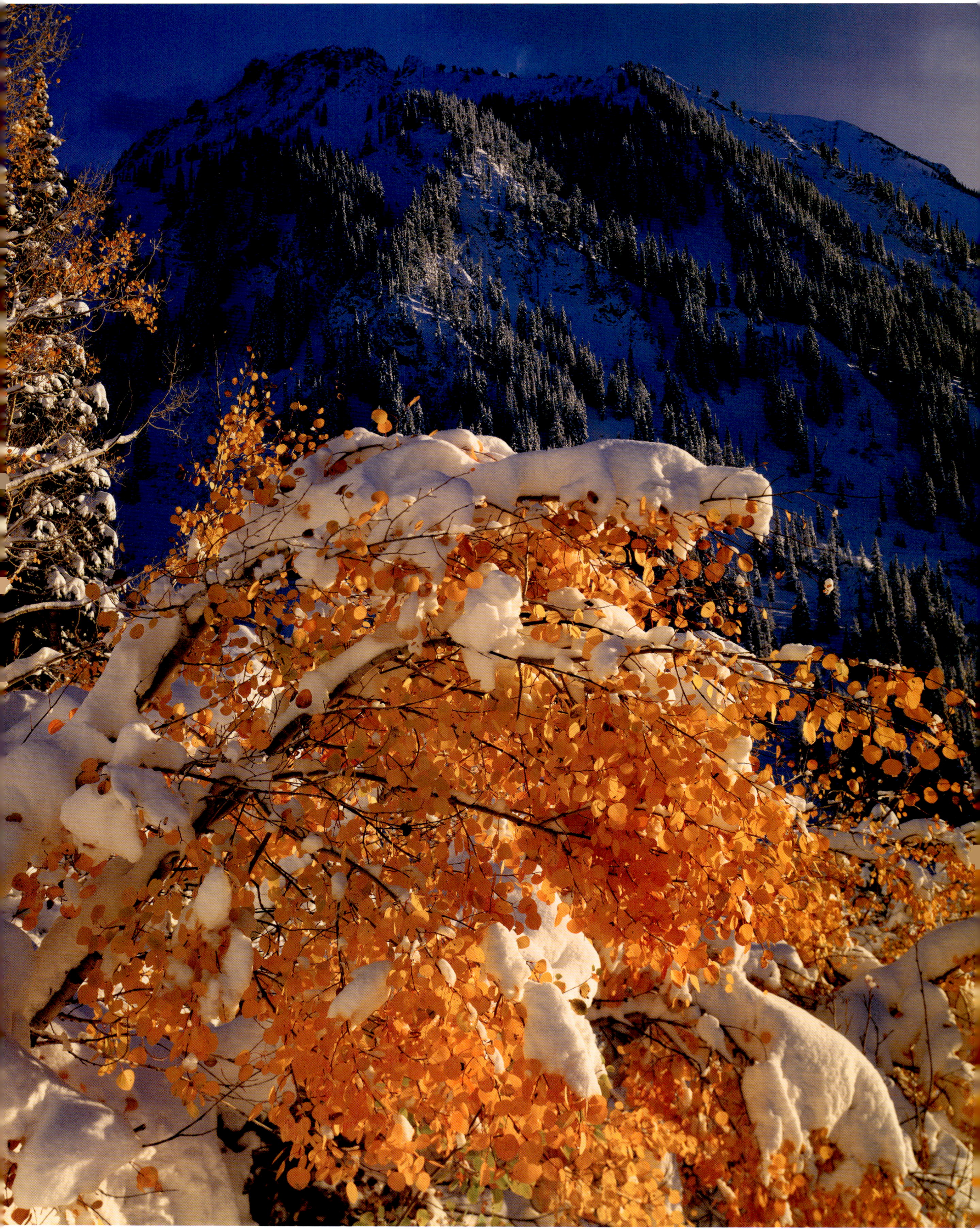

BELOW:
Clouds hang around above the Monument Valley Mittens, enhancing a sunset scene. Clouds are a big part of my work. They function as subjects, light controllers, and as welcome shade on hot days.

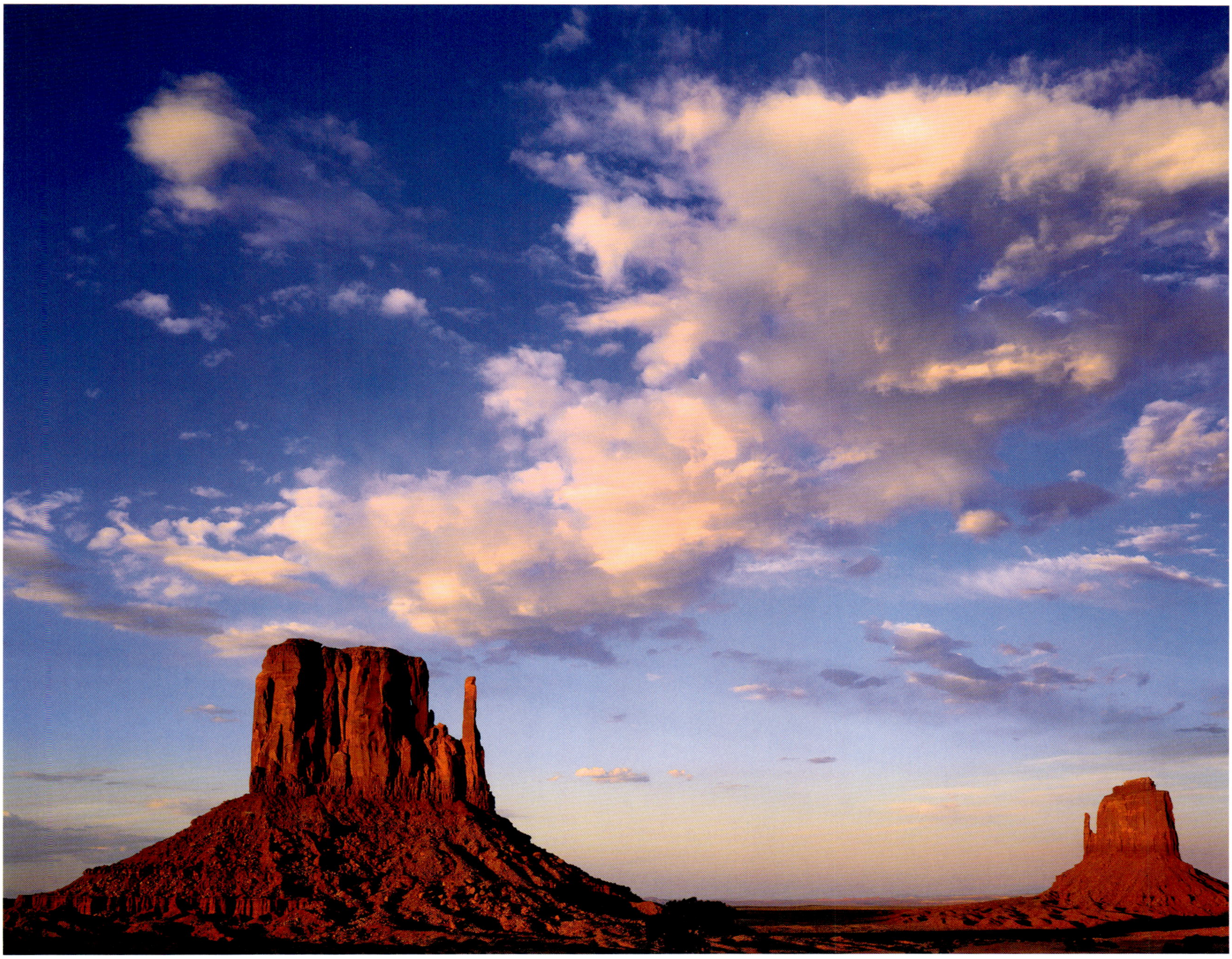

LEFT:
I like to find images that show the cusps of two seasons. I'm often asked about which images are my favorites, and although I have very few, this is one I've always liked. The intense blues of the shadowed distant mountain were not a surprise. Over the years I've tried to train my eyes to be sensitive to blues and to situations where film will perhaps register colors more blue than the eye sees. Which is correct, the eye or the film? I don't know, but I love the blue, and I like to explore it.

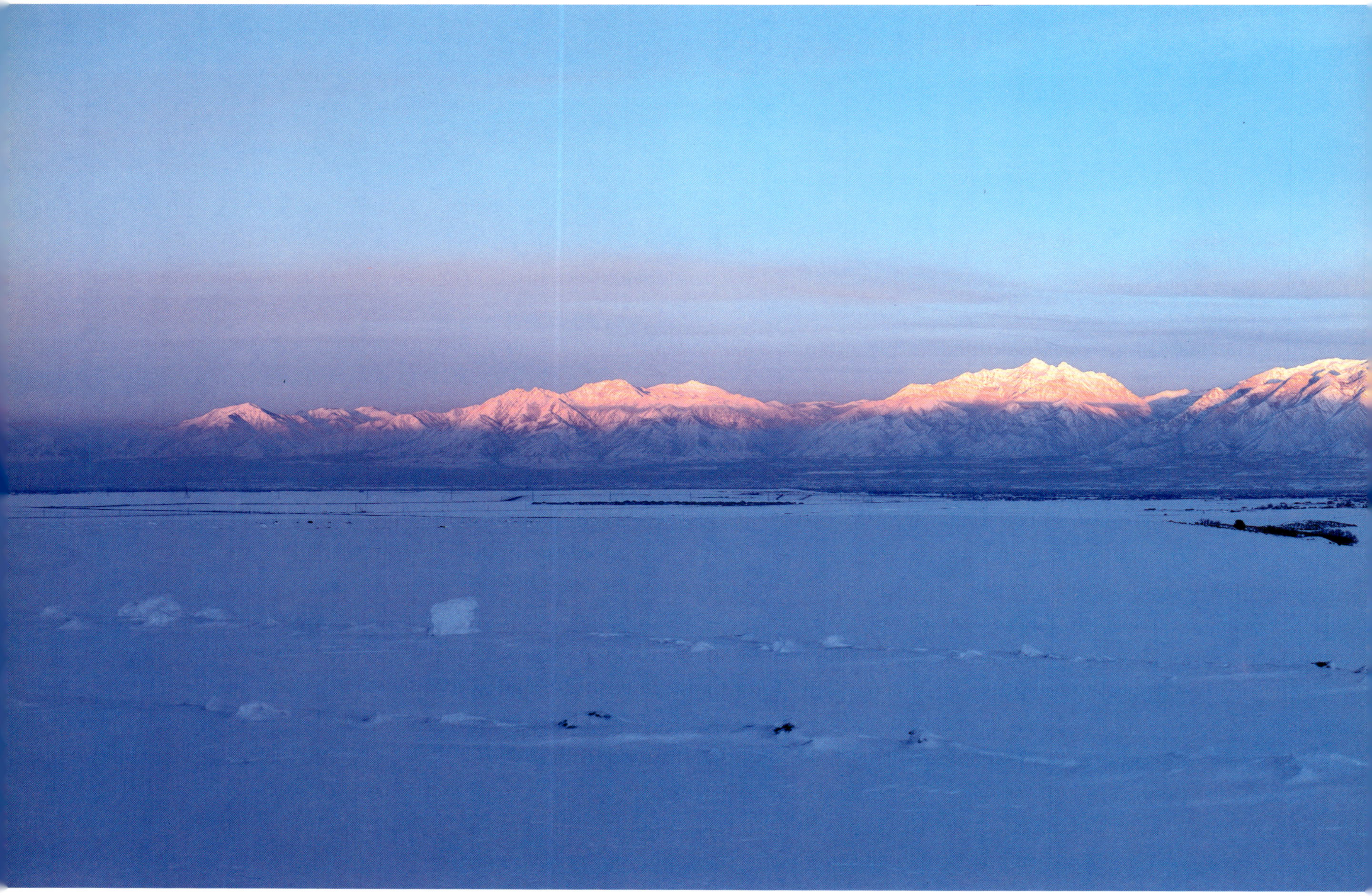

ABOVE:
From this vantage point, the Salt Lake Valley appears deserted. The panoramic image takes in a winter view from the Northern Wasatch to Mt. Timpanogos.

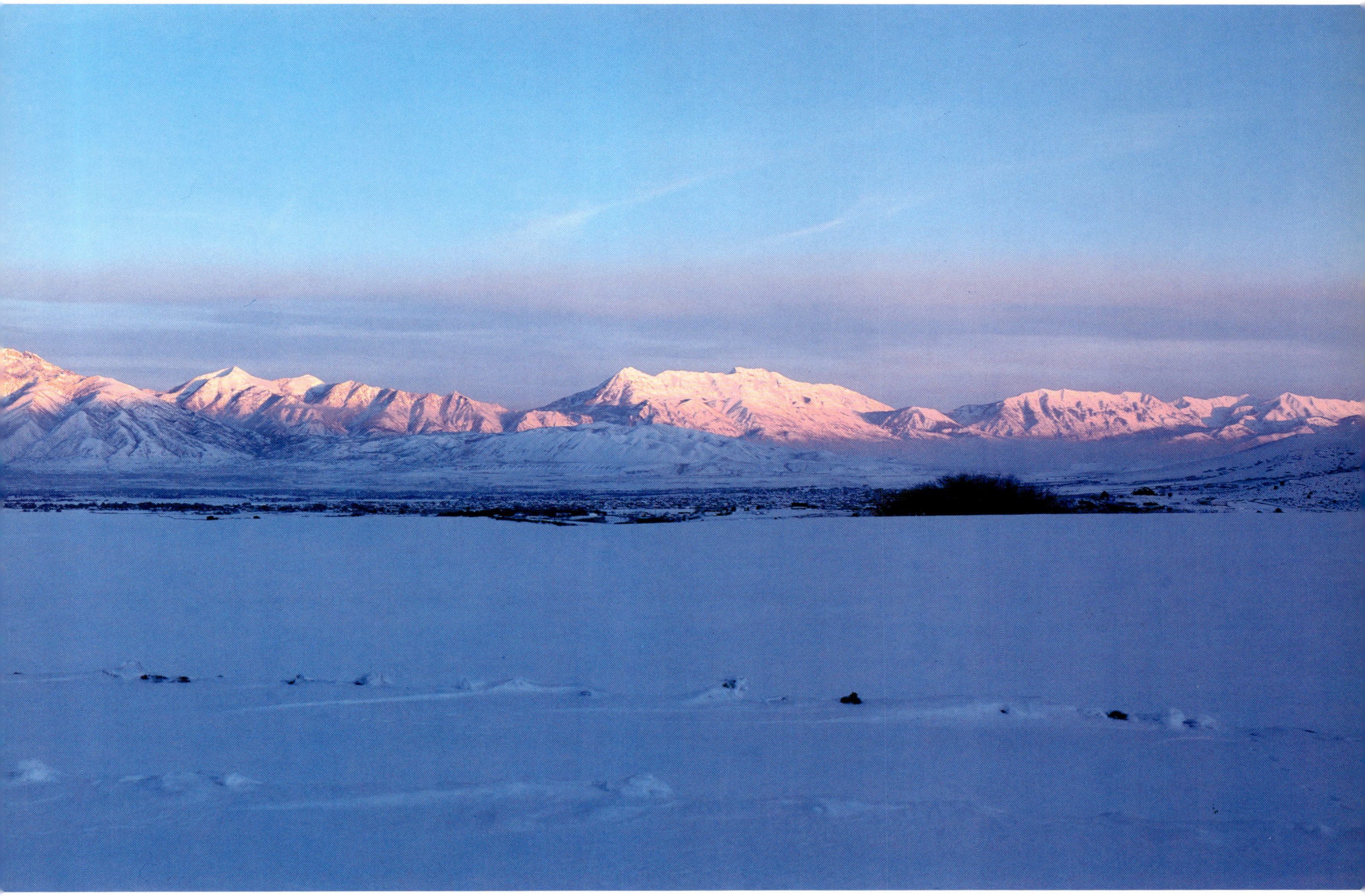

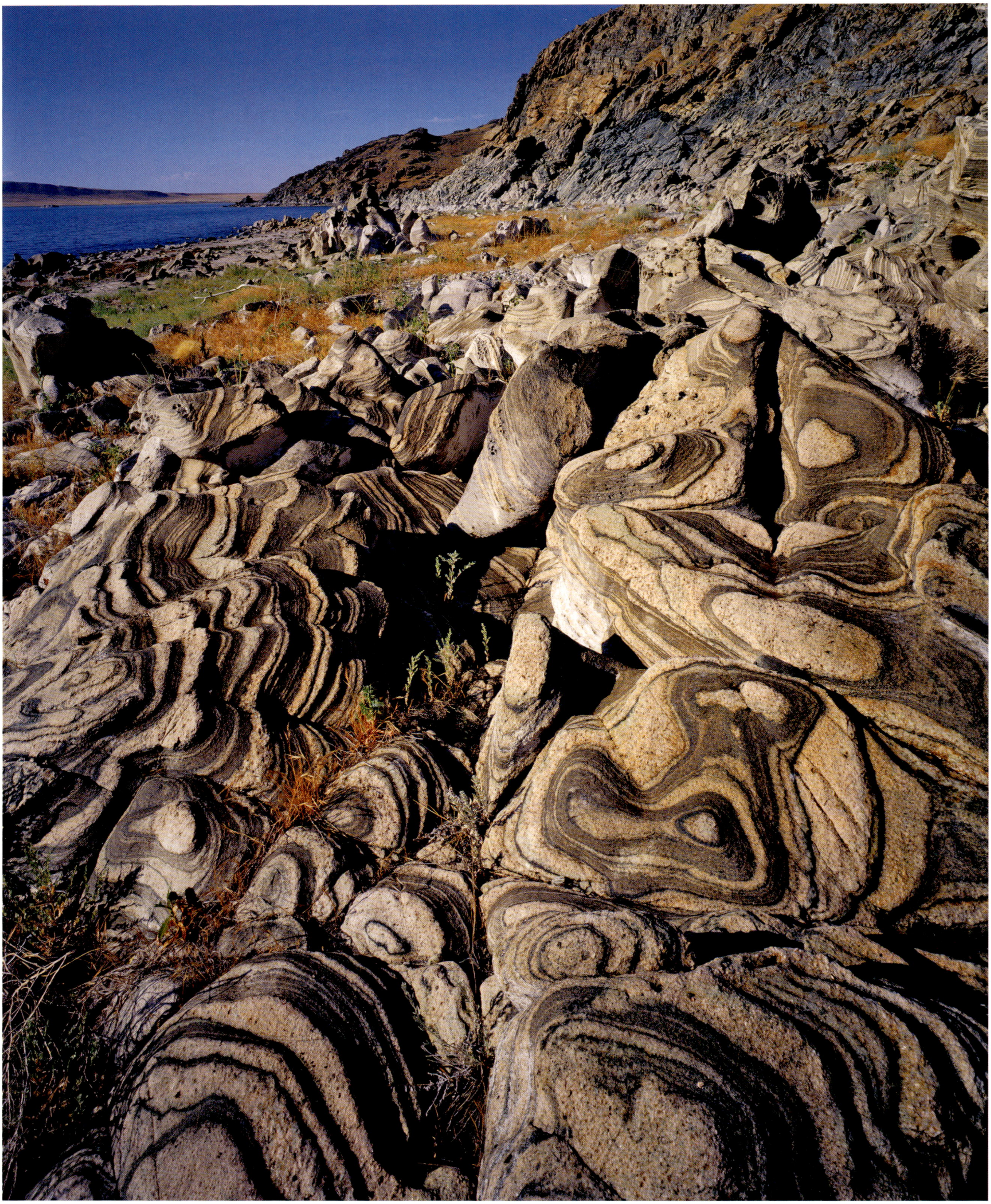

ABOVE:

In Antelope Island State Park, numerous areas are home to spectacularly polished shore rocks. The beauty of the patterns and their many manifestations are breathtaking and a photographer's dream. I kayaked across the lake to reach these formations.

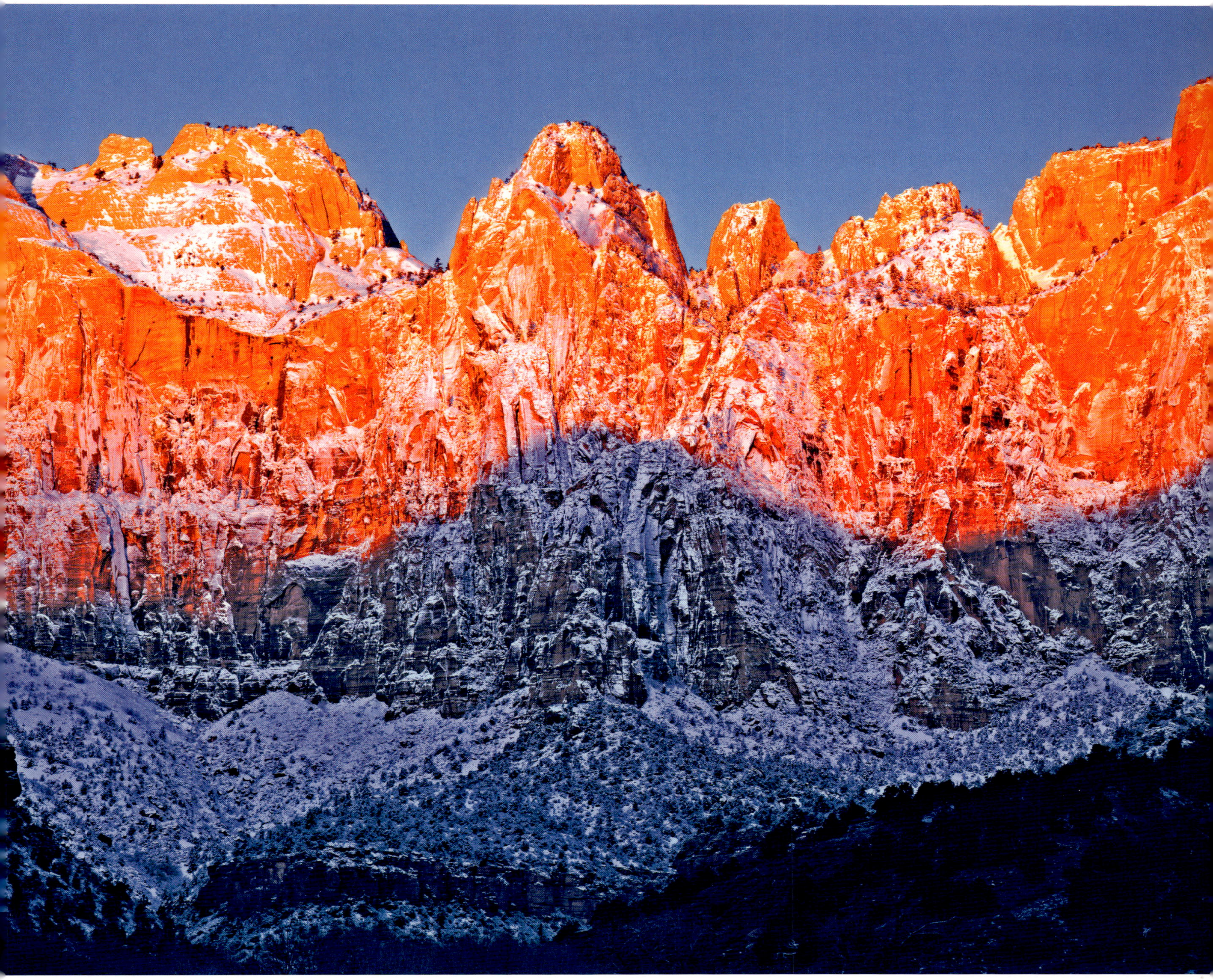

ABOVE:
After years of trying and countless mornings visiting the old Zion Visitor Center at dawn, I finally was able to luck into a morning with fresh snow on the Zion towers and a rosy winter dawn. There are many images I have tried to get for decades and have been unsuccessful. Landscape photography, it seems to me, is a very long-term project, with certain goals obtained only after years of striving. On the other hand, certain photos come so easily that they can be only thought of as gifts, dropping into my hands just because I took the time and effort to show up.

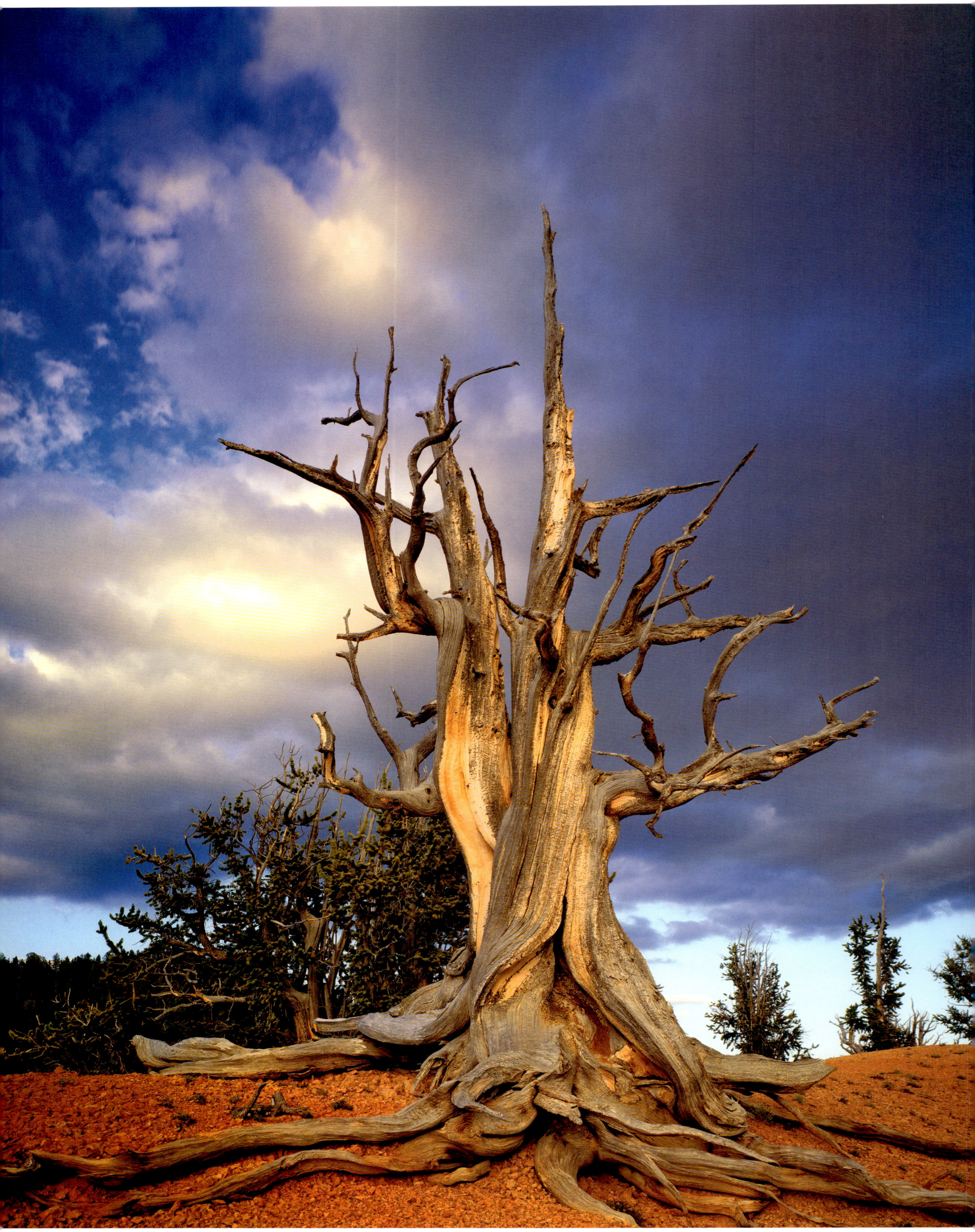

LEFT:
Ashdown Gorge Wilderness in the Dixie National Forest is home to some of Utah's most beautiful bristlecone pine forests. Among the earth's oldest living things, bristlecone snags like this can stand sentinel for centuries.

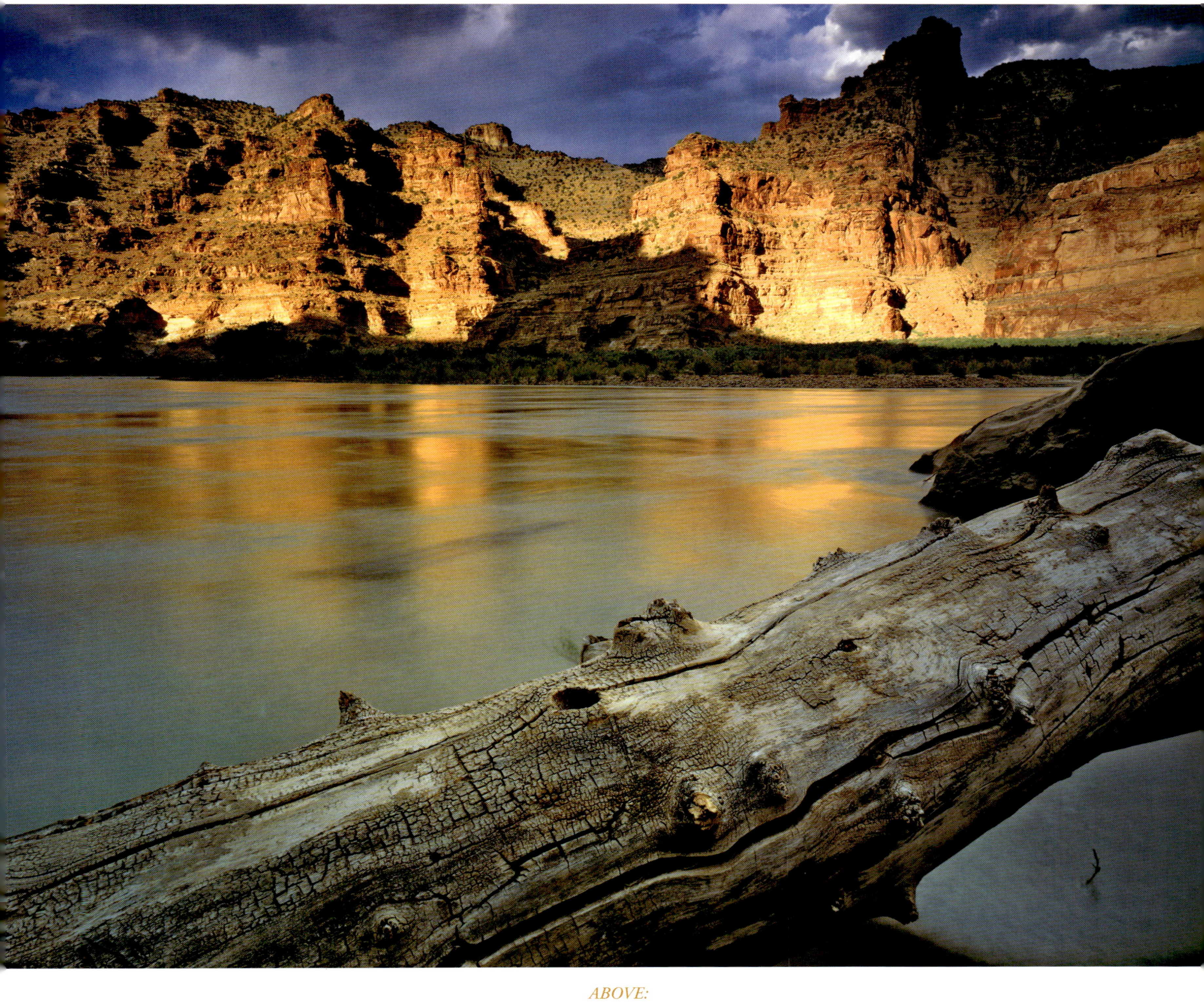

ABOVE:
Driftwood is stranded on a beach in Desolation Canyon Wilderness Study Area. One of the jewels of Utah's proposed BLM wilderness, the canyon is threatened by frantic oil and gas exploration encroaching on its rims.

BELOW:

Strange ice patterns appear on a lake in the High Uintas Wilderness in the Wasatch/Cache National Forest. The unusual abstract designs seem to be caused by the initial formation of ice on the lake in late fall.

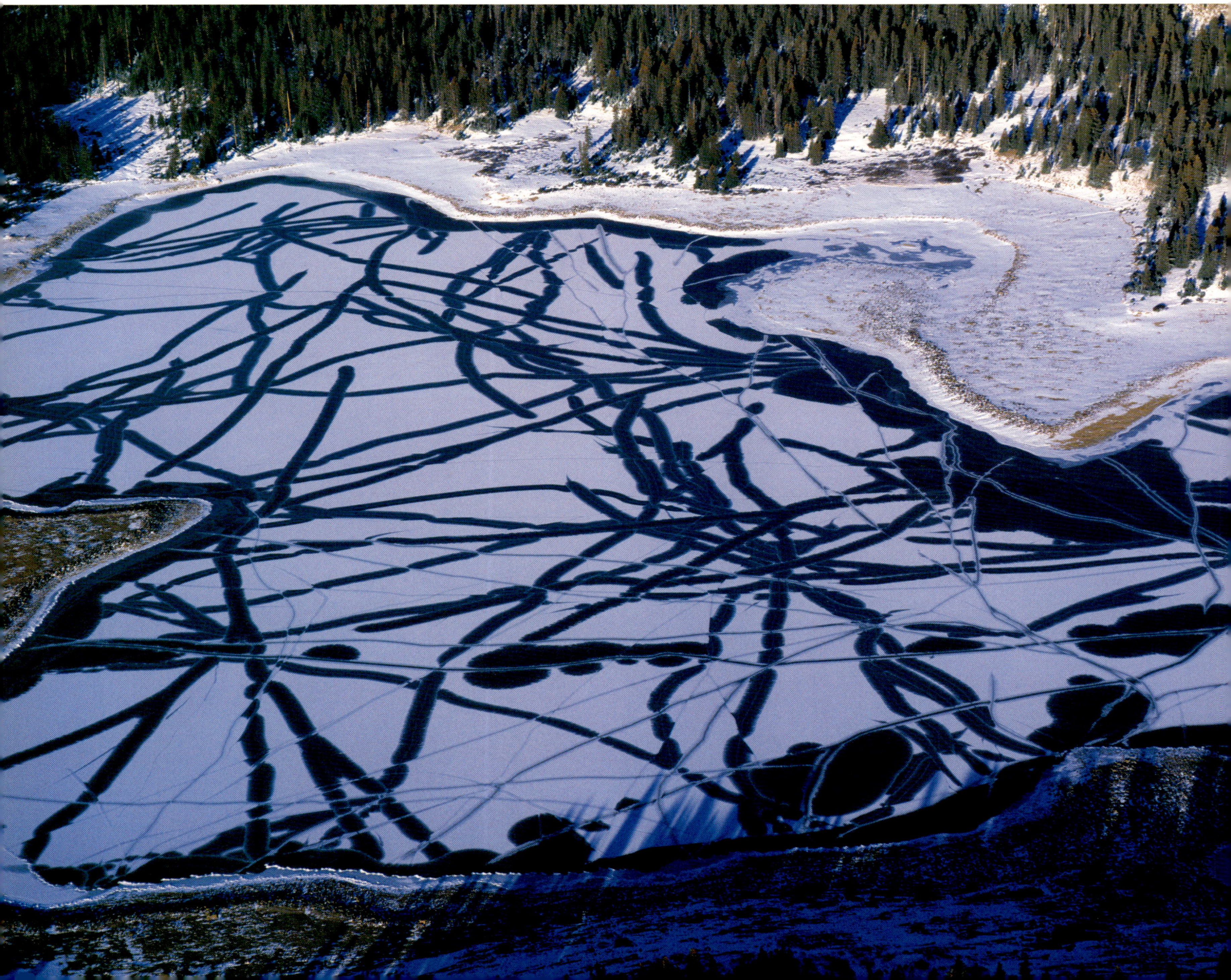

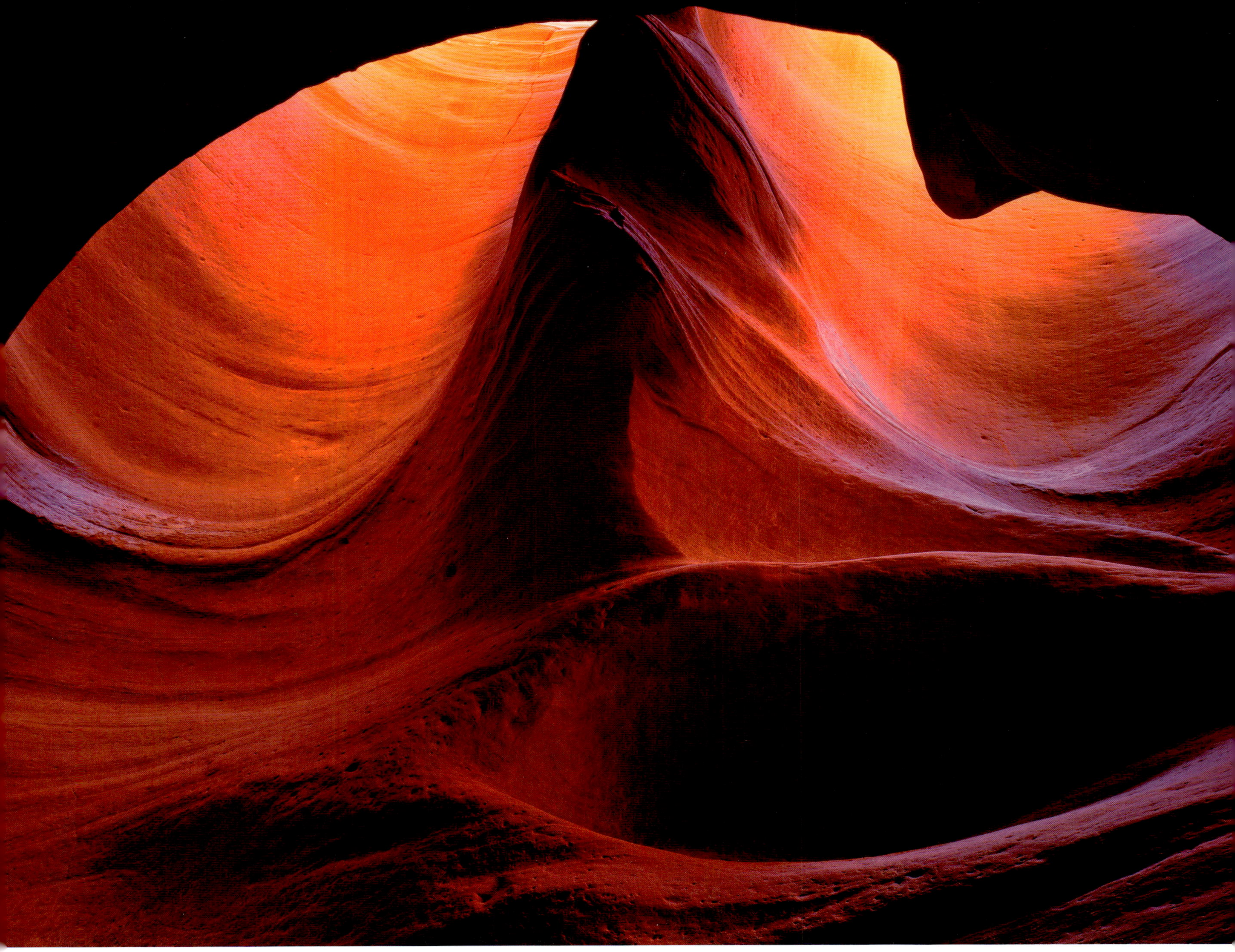

ABOVE:
Though this slot canyon resembles the beauty of the famous slots near Page, Arizona, it is actually firmly inside the borders of Utah, as well as inside a BLM Wilderness Study Area and Proposed Wilderness.

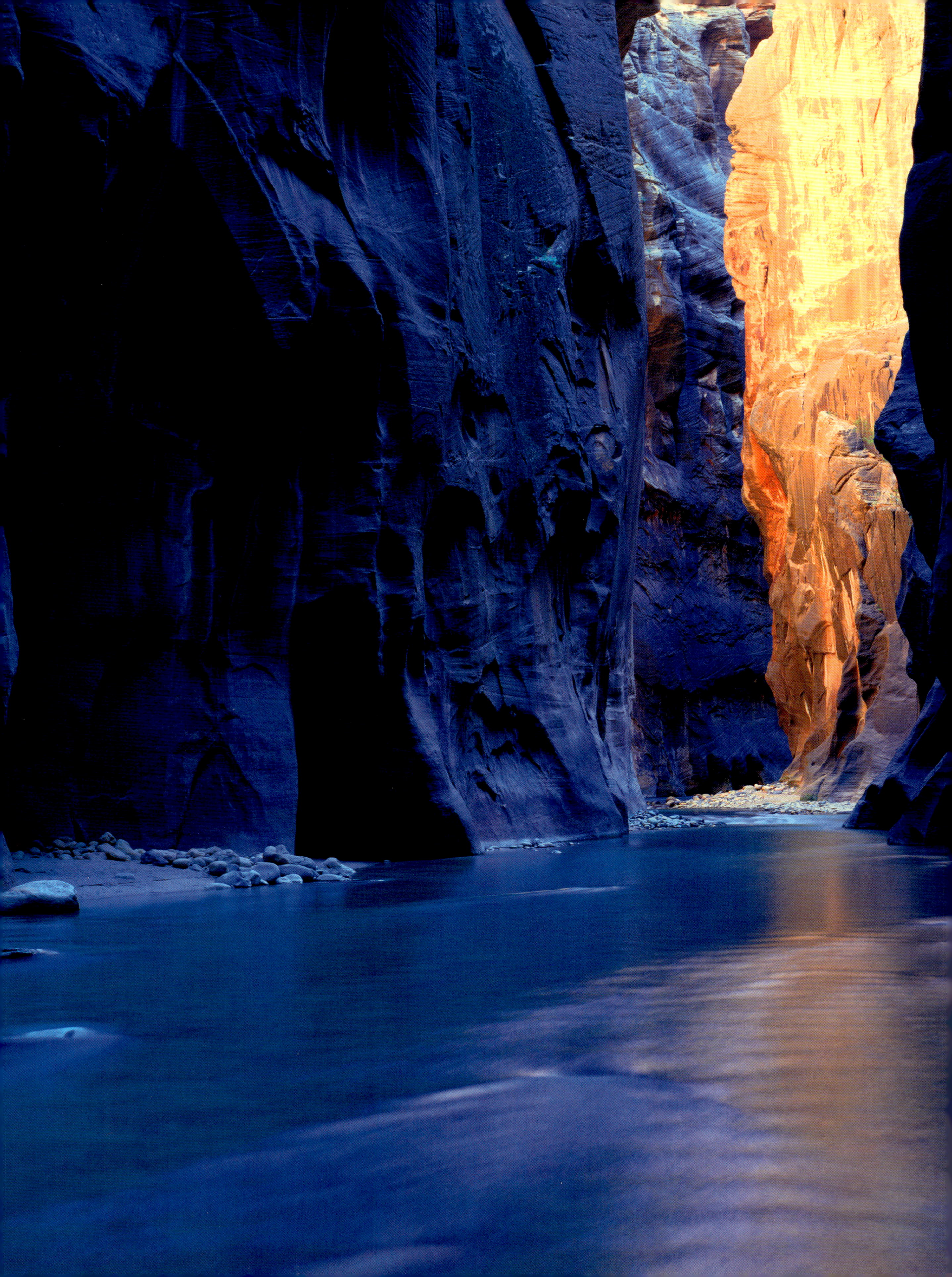

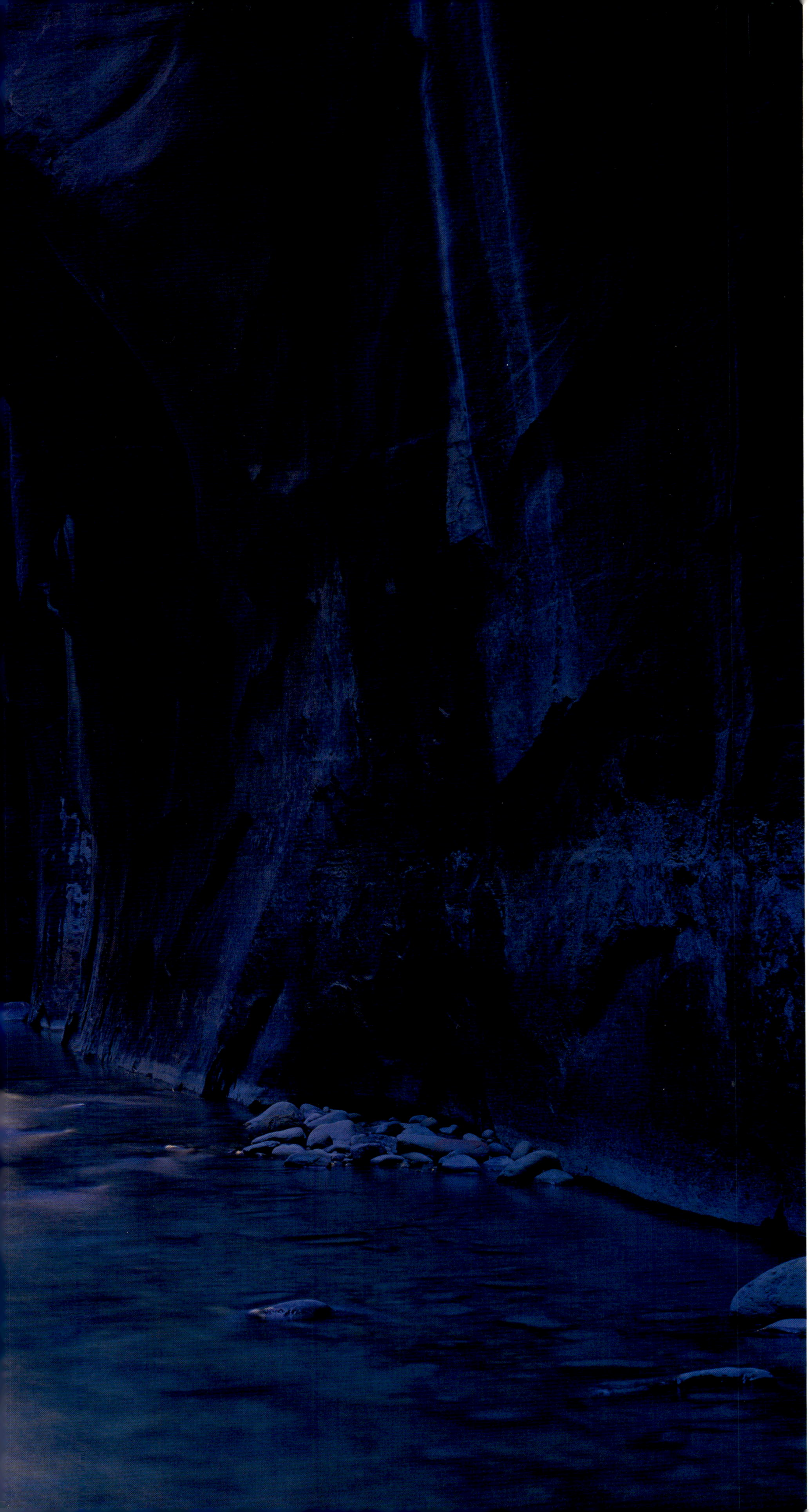

LEFT:
Inside the deep walls of Zion Narrows, light does amazing and unpredictable things. A recent National Geographic list of the world's highest cliffs listed the Zion Narrows as a runner-up, and as light bounces around down these endless walls, colors are bent, shaped, twisted and mutated, usually in dramatic and beautiful ways.

BELOW:
Usually shot from below, I hiked the rim of Calf Creek Canyon to photograph the Lower Falls from above, highlighting the rich greens of the microenvironment surrounding this desert oasis. Now part of Grand Staircase/ Escalante National Monument, Calf Creek Falls is one of America's most beautiful desert cascades.

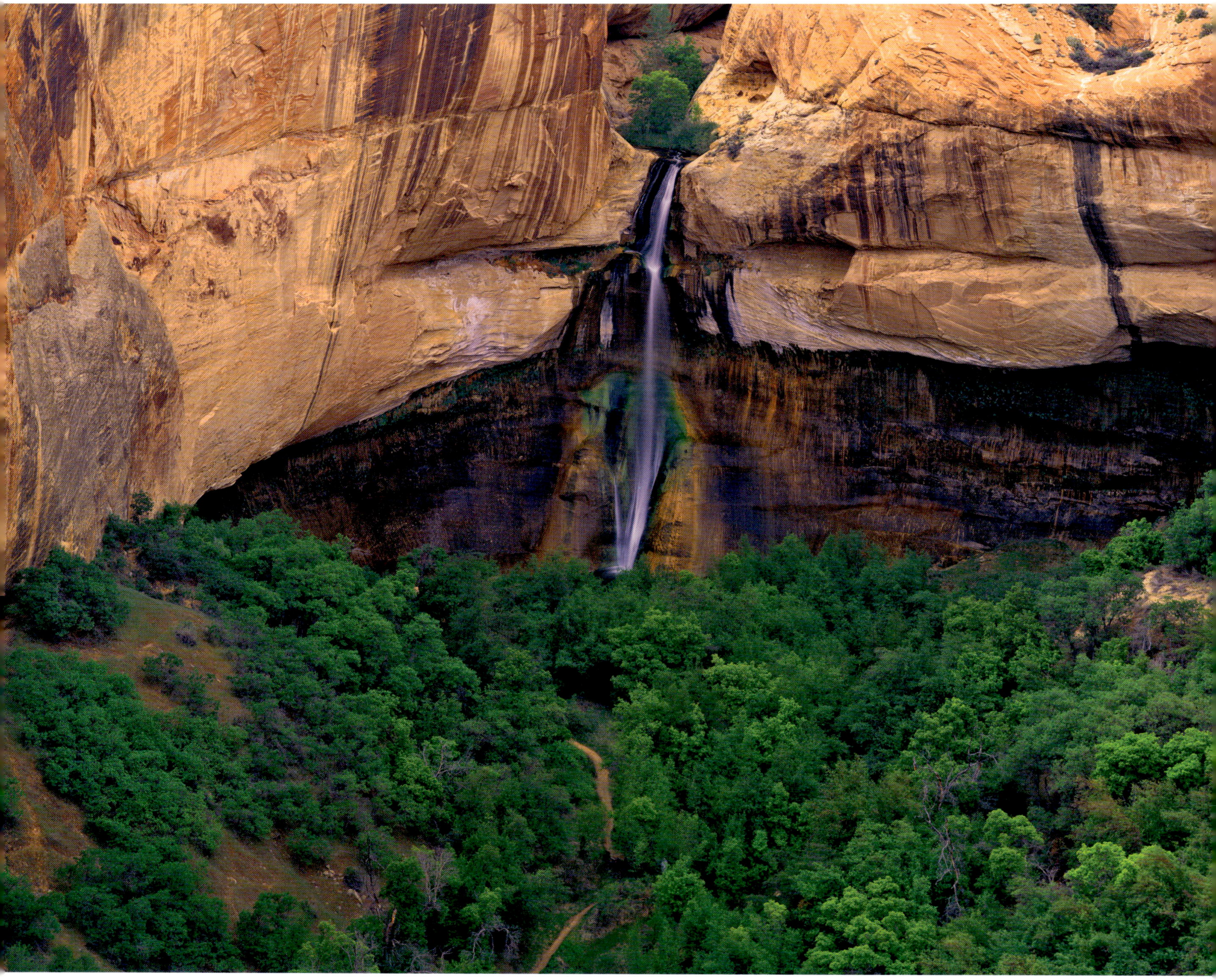

RIGHT:
Rock forms glow at sunset near Sundial Peak in Twin Peaks Wilderness, Wasatch/Cache National Forest.

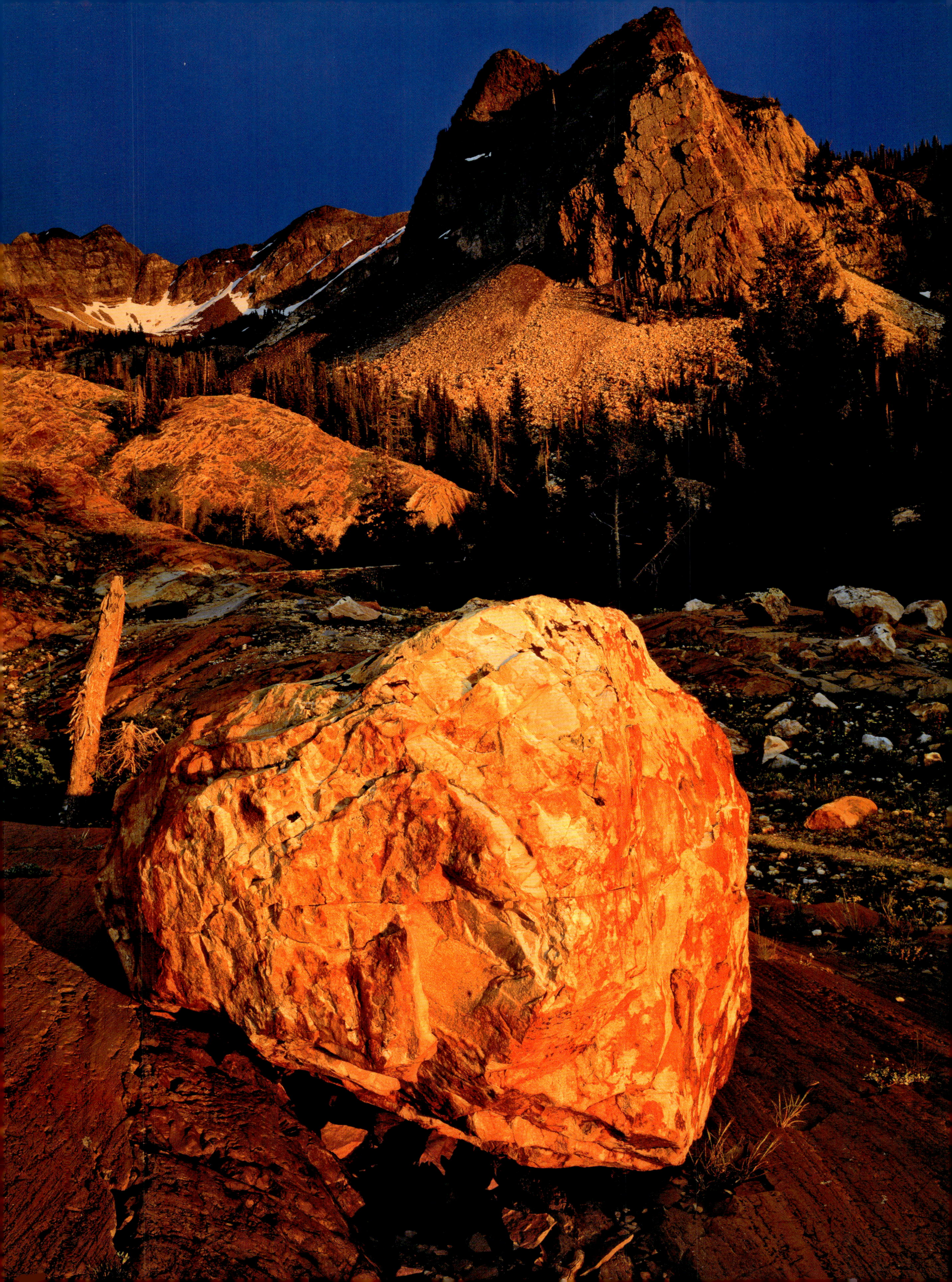

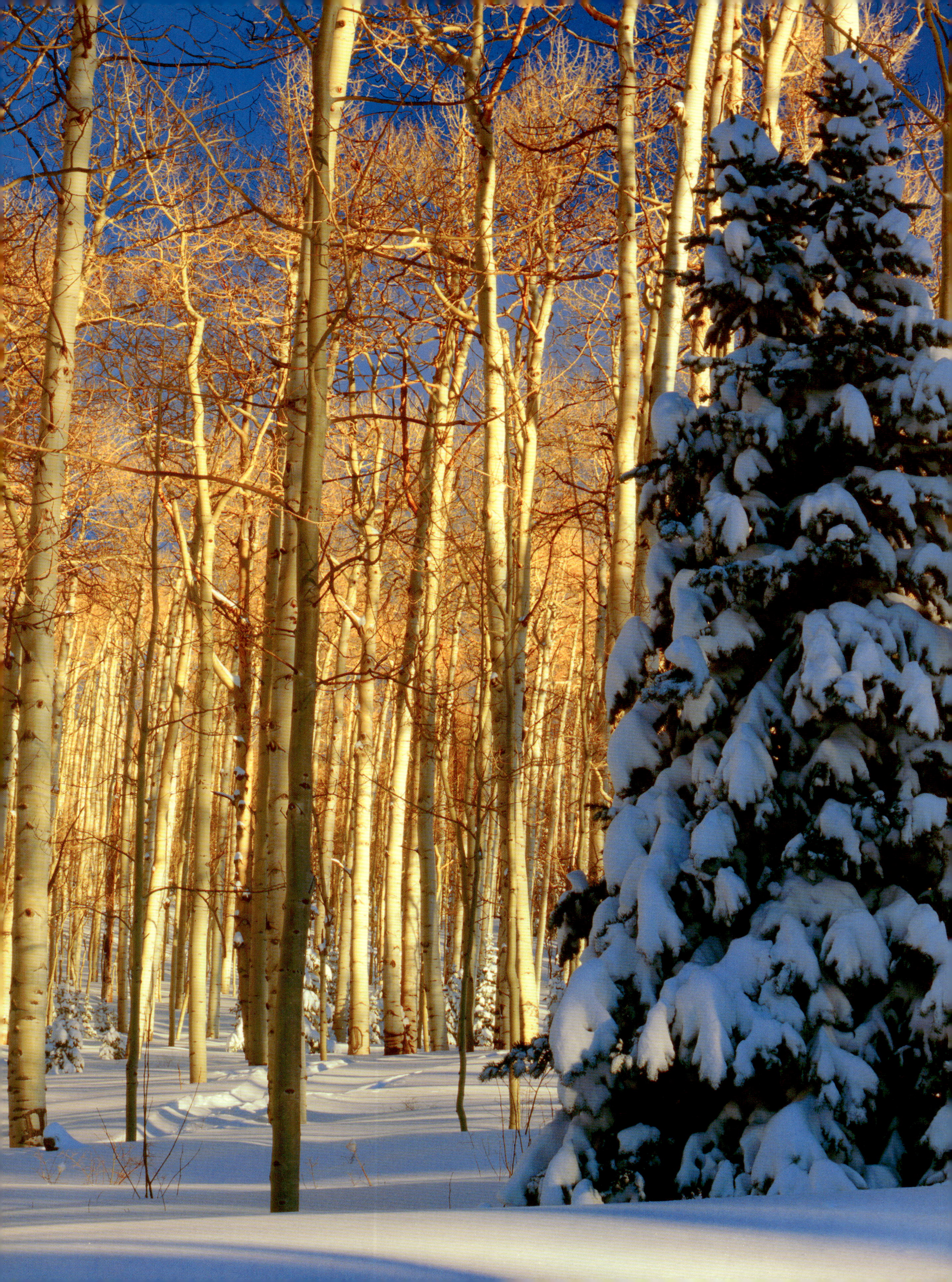

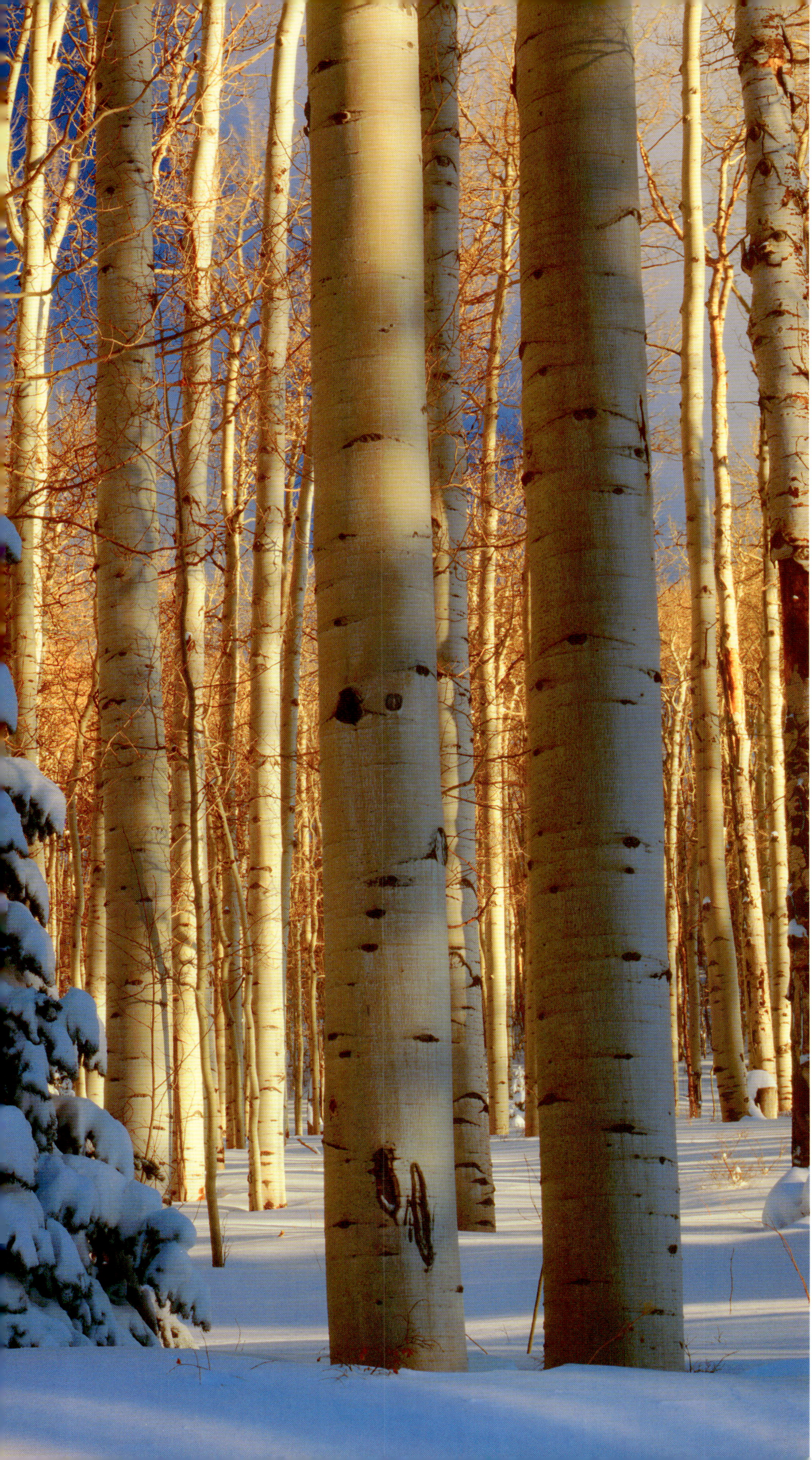

LEFT:
Snow and evening light evoke a peaceful moment in the La Sal Mountains in the Manti-La Sal National Forest.

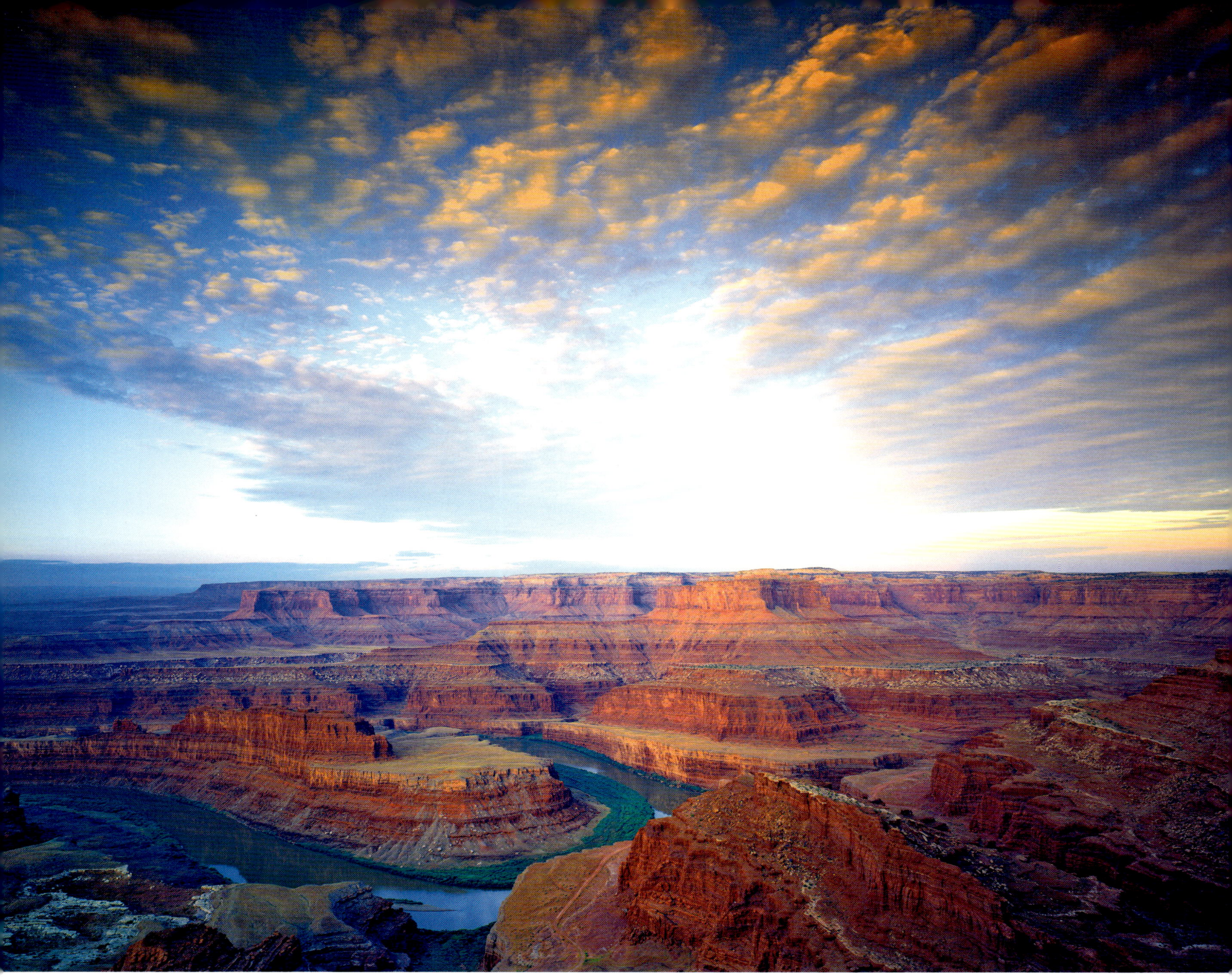

ABOVE:
Clouds glow with the dawn over Canyonlands as seen from Dead Horse Point.

BELOW:
On the north side of the Mt. Nebo Loop, brilliant maples are set off by fields of yellow rabbitbrush.

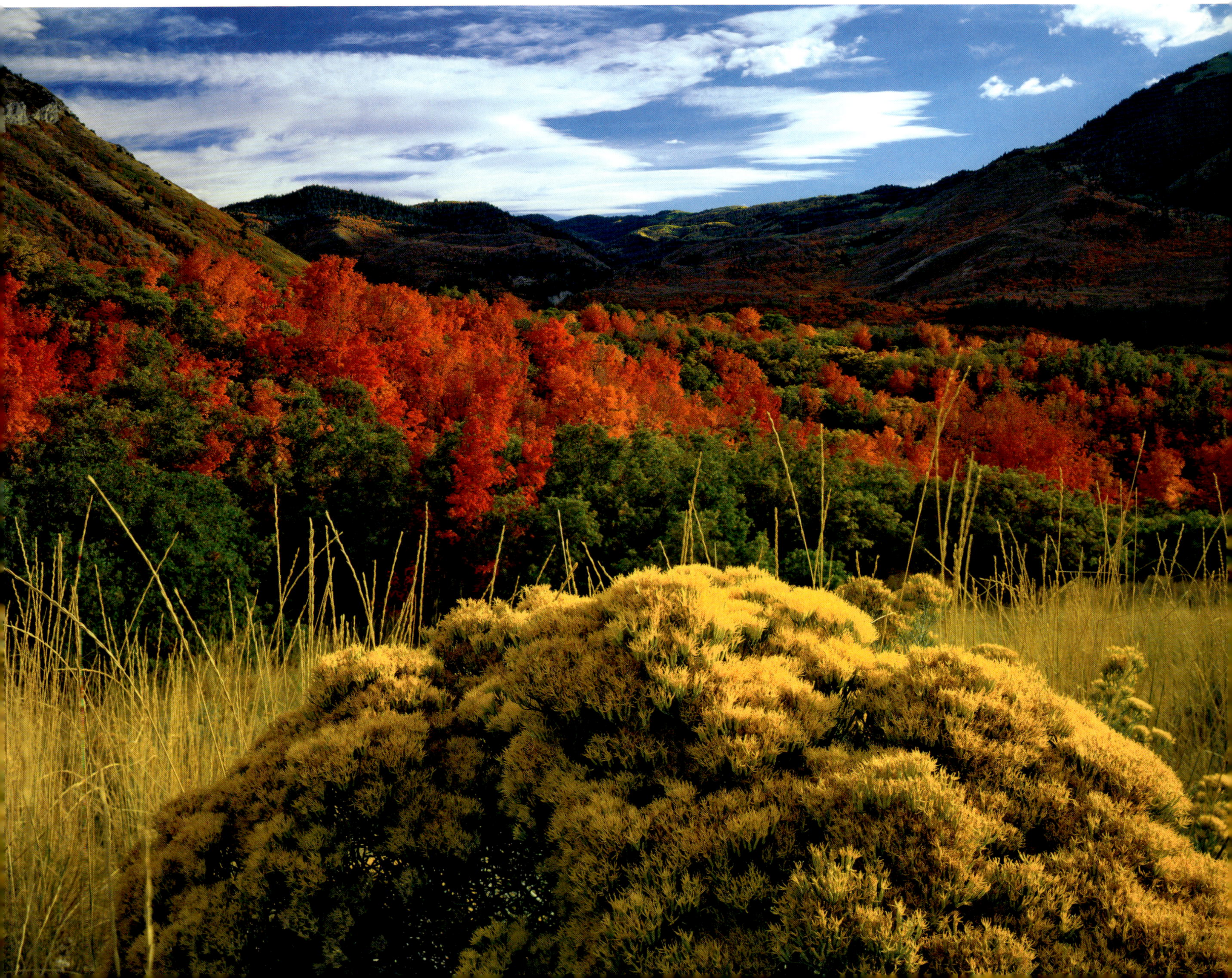

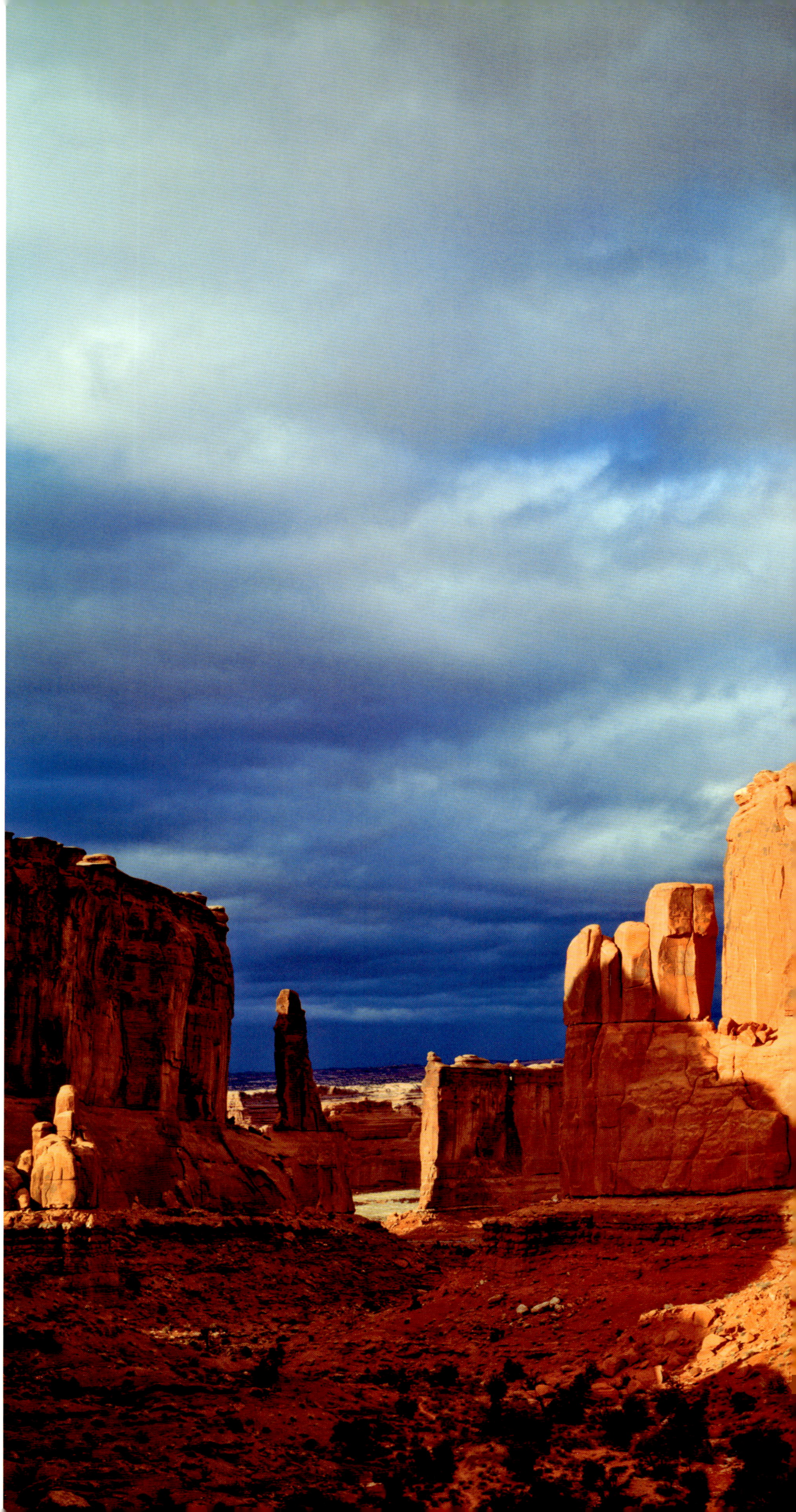

RIGHT:
Black chiaroscuro-forming clouds contrast with warm sandstone in Park Avenue in Arches National Park.

This light against dark contrast is my favorite form of lighting, even though I find the Italian word difficult to say or spell.

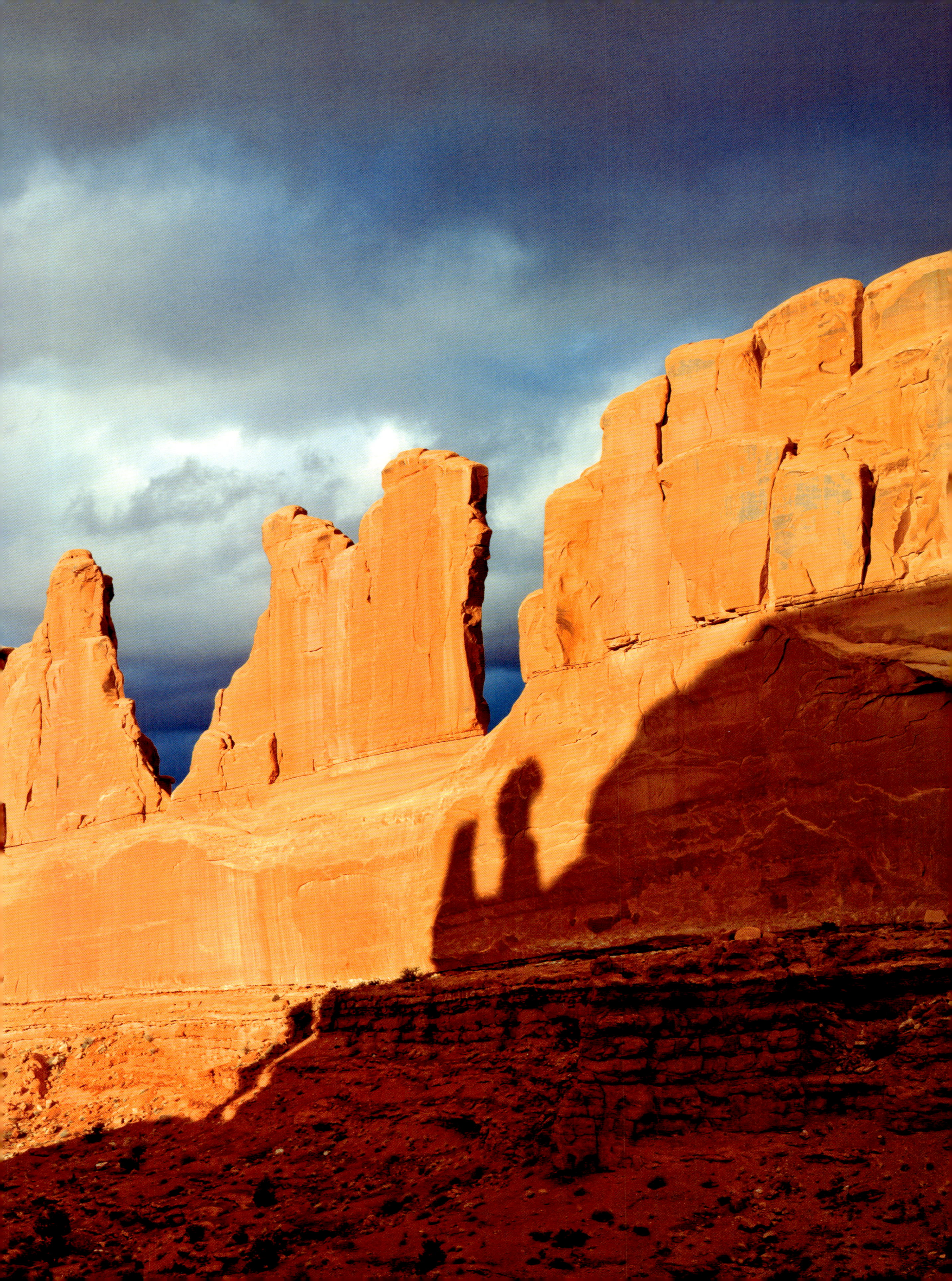

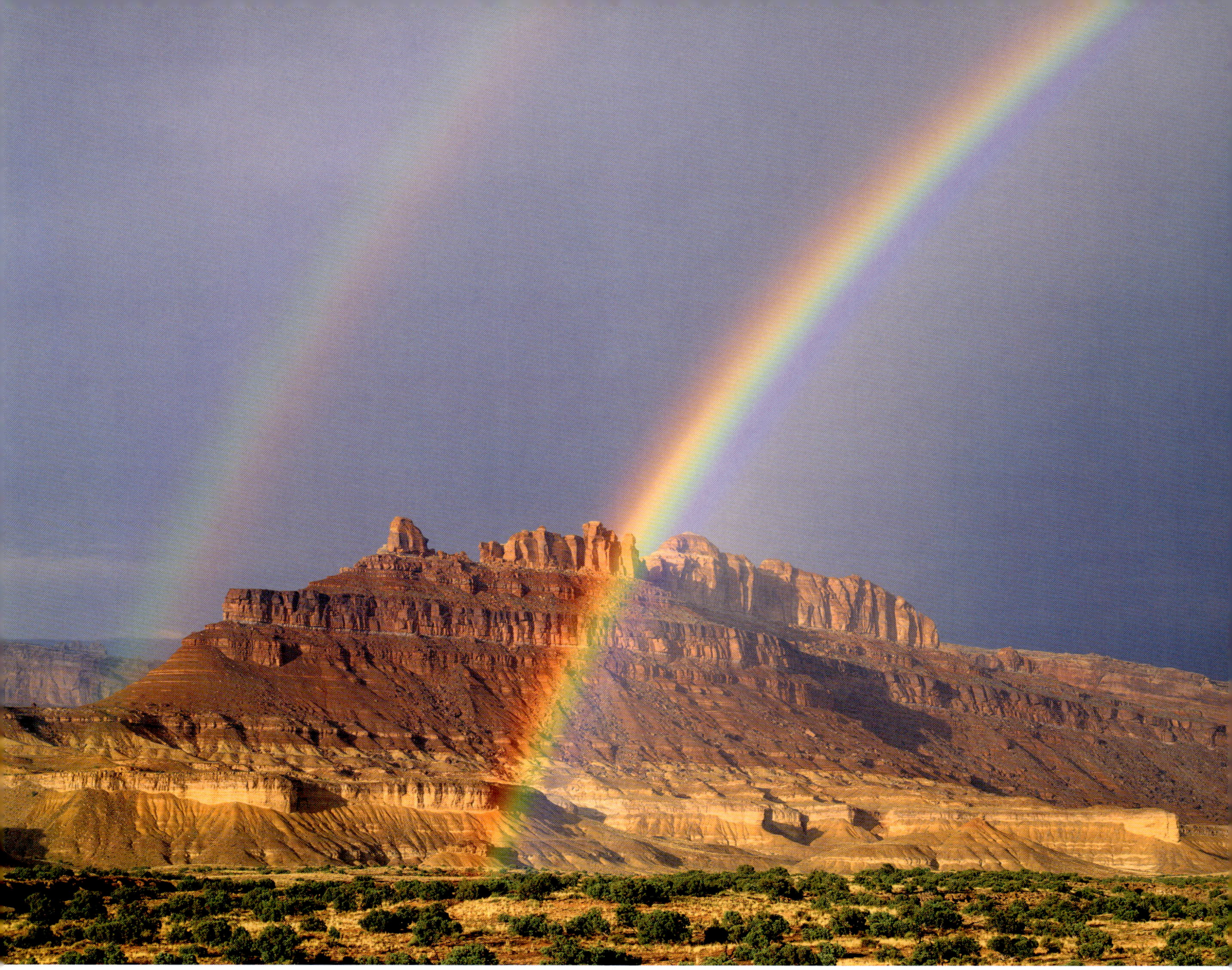

ABOVE:
A double rainbow forms over Mexican Mountain Wilderness Study Area and San Rafael Swell Proposed Wilderness. The San Rafael Swell needs to be Utah's sixth national park. The scenic and cultural resources of the Swell are so large and varied and on such a spectacular scale that National Park designation is the only policy that makes sense.

BELOW:

A week-long river trip down the Escalante River was one of the most rewarding but difficult wilderness journeys of my life. The river itself was high and fast, with constant obstacles. This beautiful wall, near Scorpion Gulch, was one of many sculpted alcoves we passed on our journey.

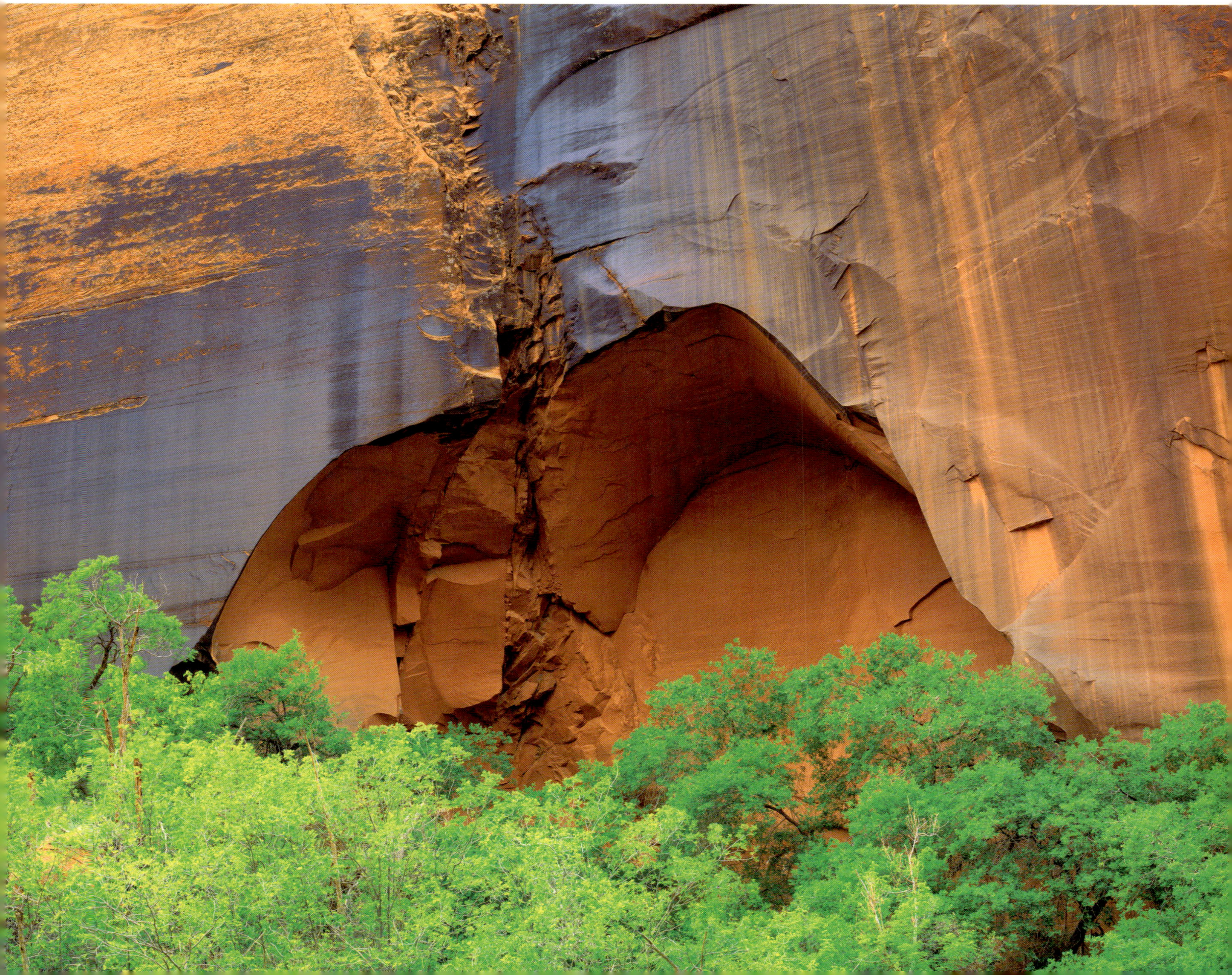

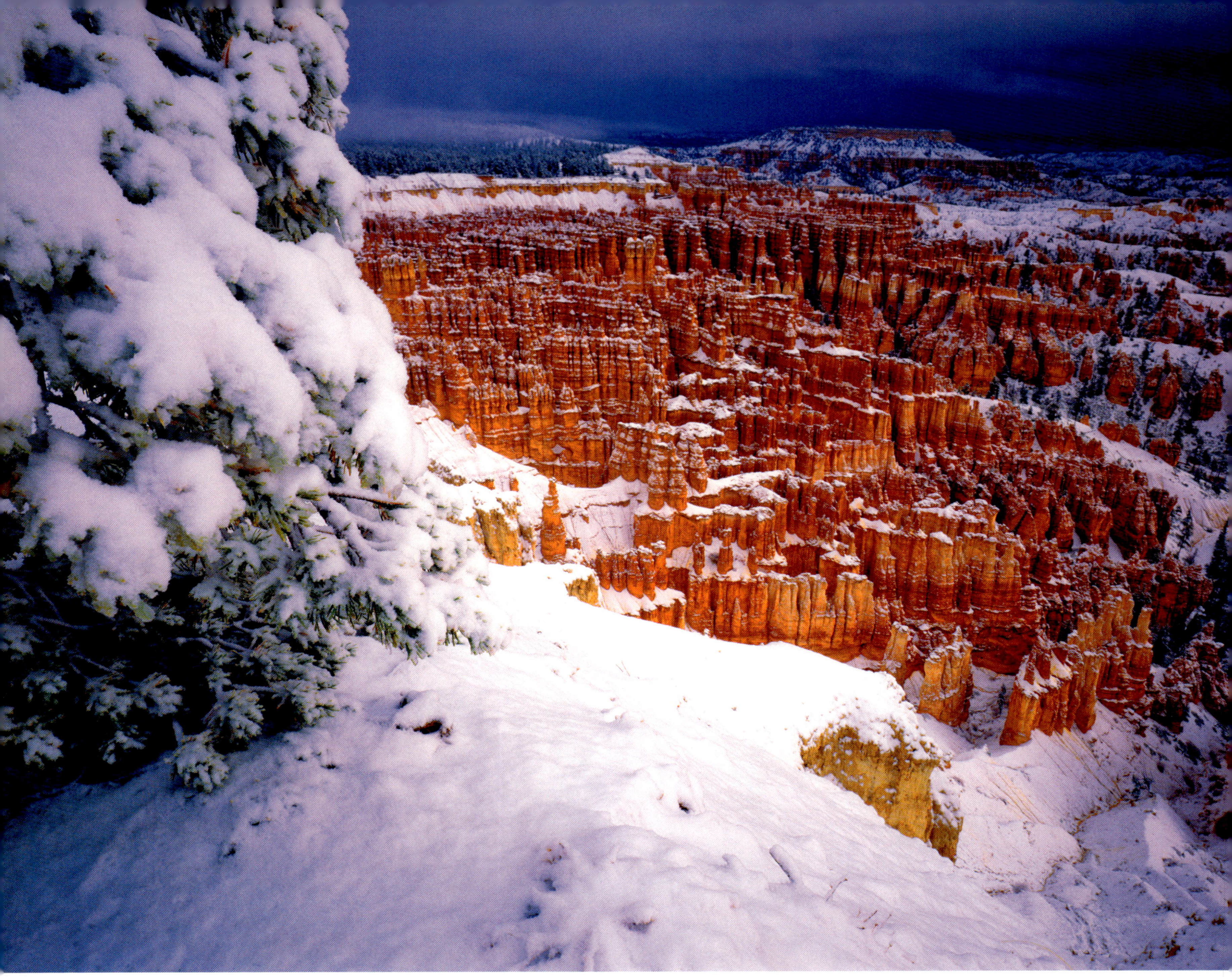

ABOVE:

"Bad weather means good pictures" has been a mantra of mine during my entire career. Storms move and excite me, and I love their story-telling potential. They have beginnings, middles, and endings and they are all unique. Mark Eubank, long-time Salt Lake City weatherman is a personal hero of mine, and I was sad to see him retire. This storm blanketed Bryce with a heavy load of snow — not an unusual occurrence, but always an exciting one.

RIGHT:

Grafton is Utah's most spectacular ghost town, as well as Utah's most spectacular town. The backdrop of Mt. Kinesava and the towering cliffs of Zion are unmatched. The Grand Canyon Trust and other groups deserve a great deal of credit for preserving and refurbishing the remains of Grafton, including this church/school building reflected in a rainwater pool.

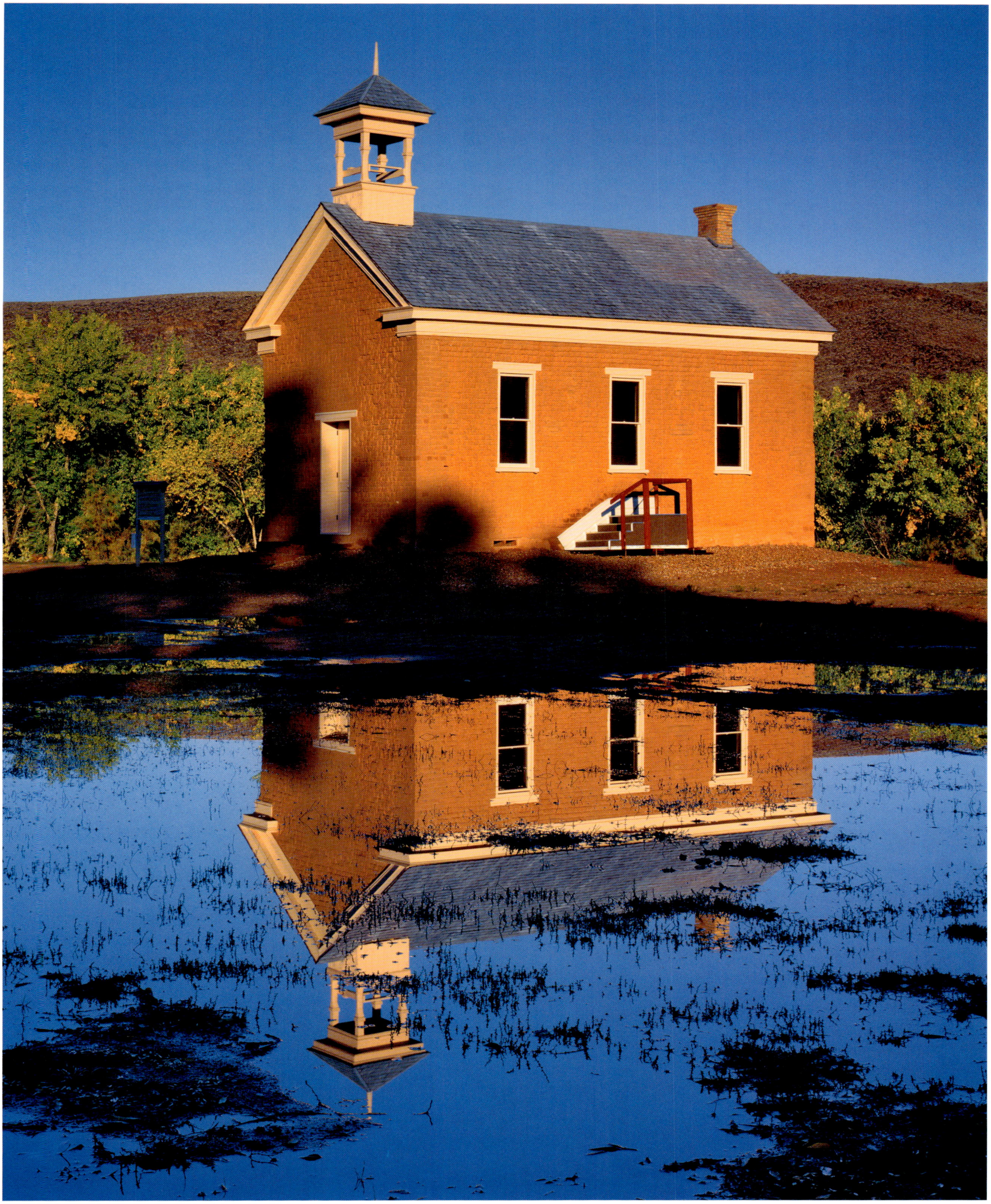

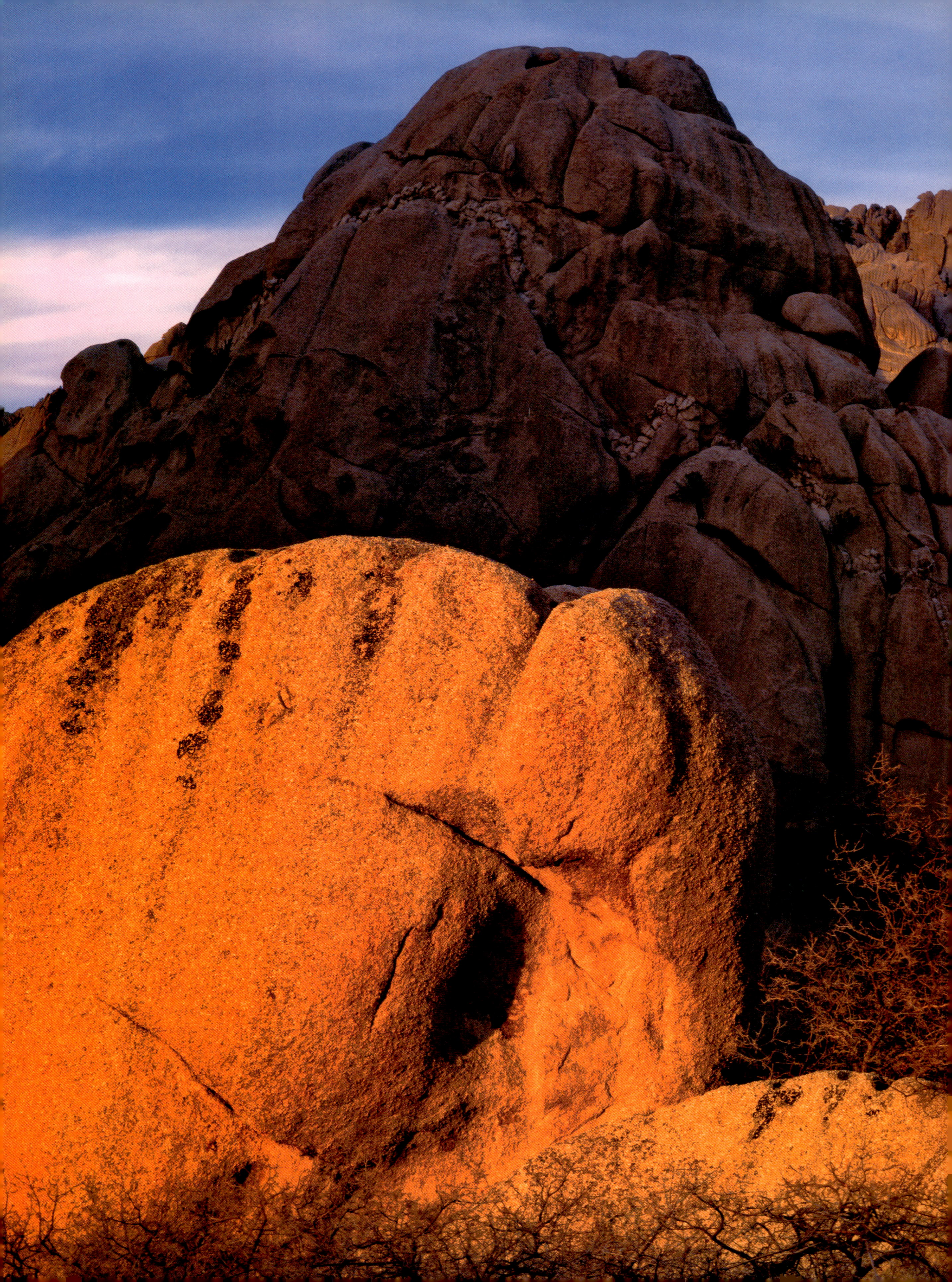

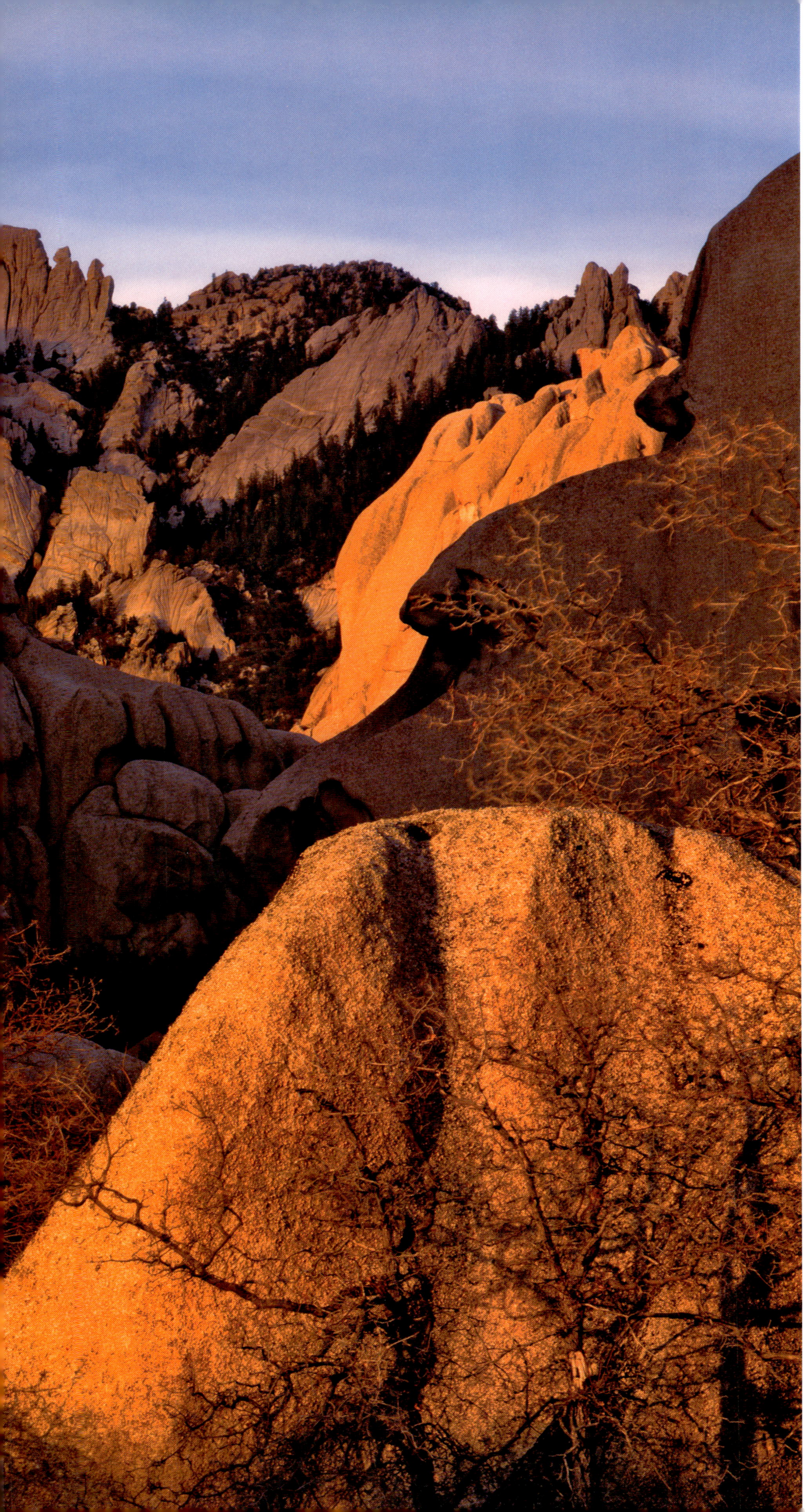

LEFT:
Light plays among the granite upthrusts of the proposed Granite Peak Wilderness in Utah's West Desert.

Rustic Reminders:
Park City Barns

The barns of Park City remind us of a simpler time, when cows outnumbered condos and pastures stood where luxury second homes now bloom. I love photographing barns. Perhaps it comes from my farm boy heritage. I spent a lot of my youth playing in our family's barn and in the barns of my uncles.

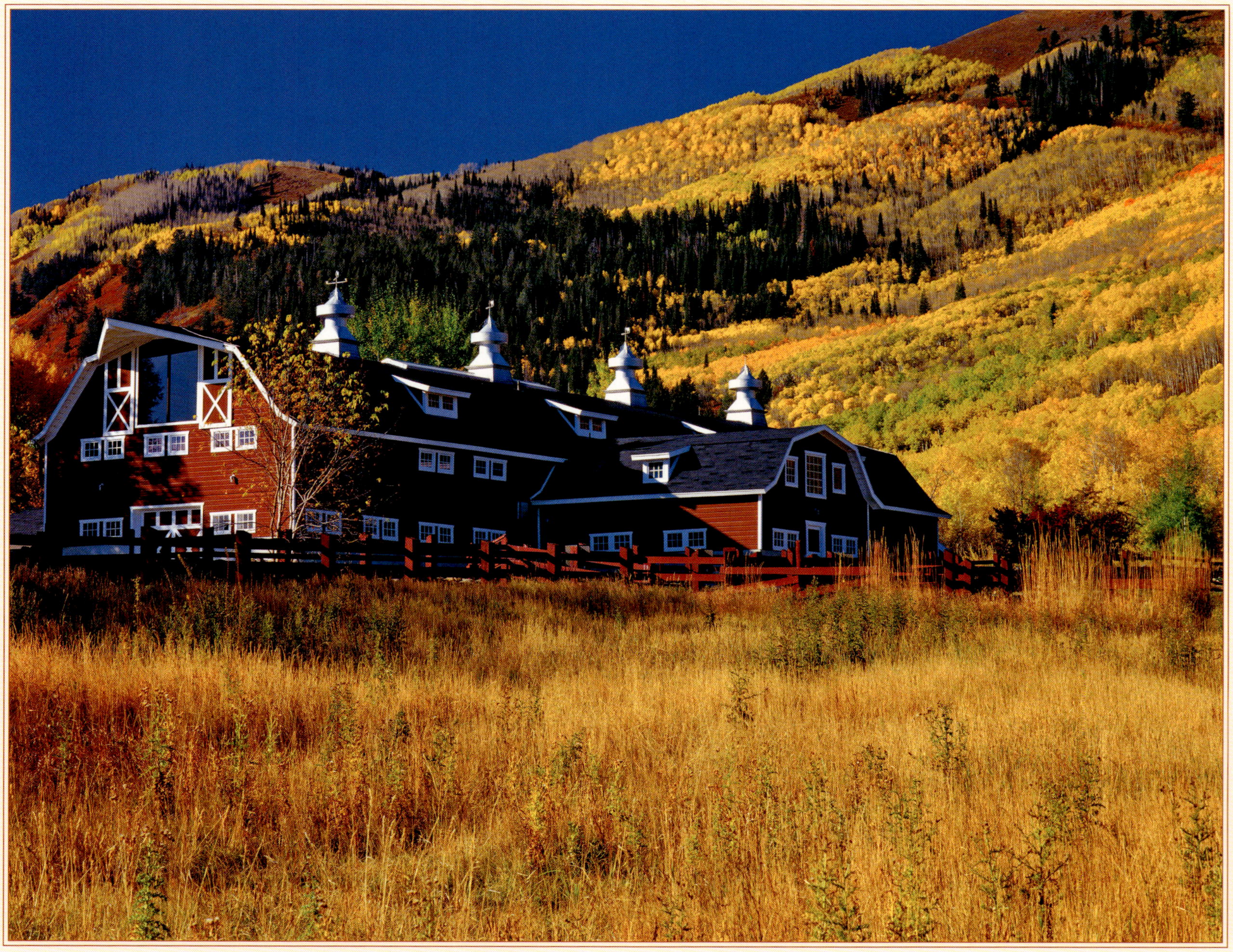

Mel and Kerry Armstrong are owners of this barn, originally built in 1922. It stands just outside the Park City ski slopes.

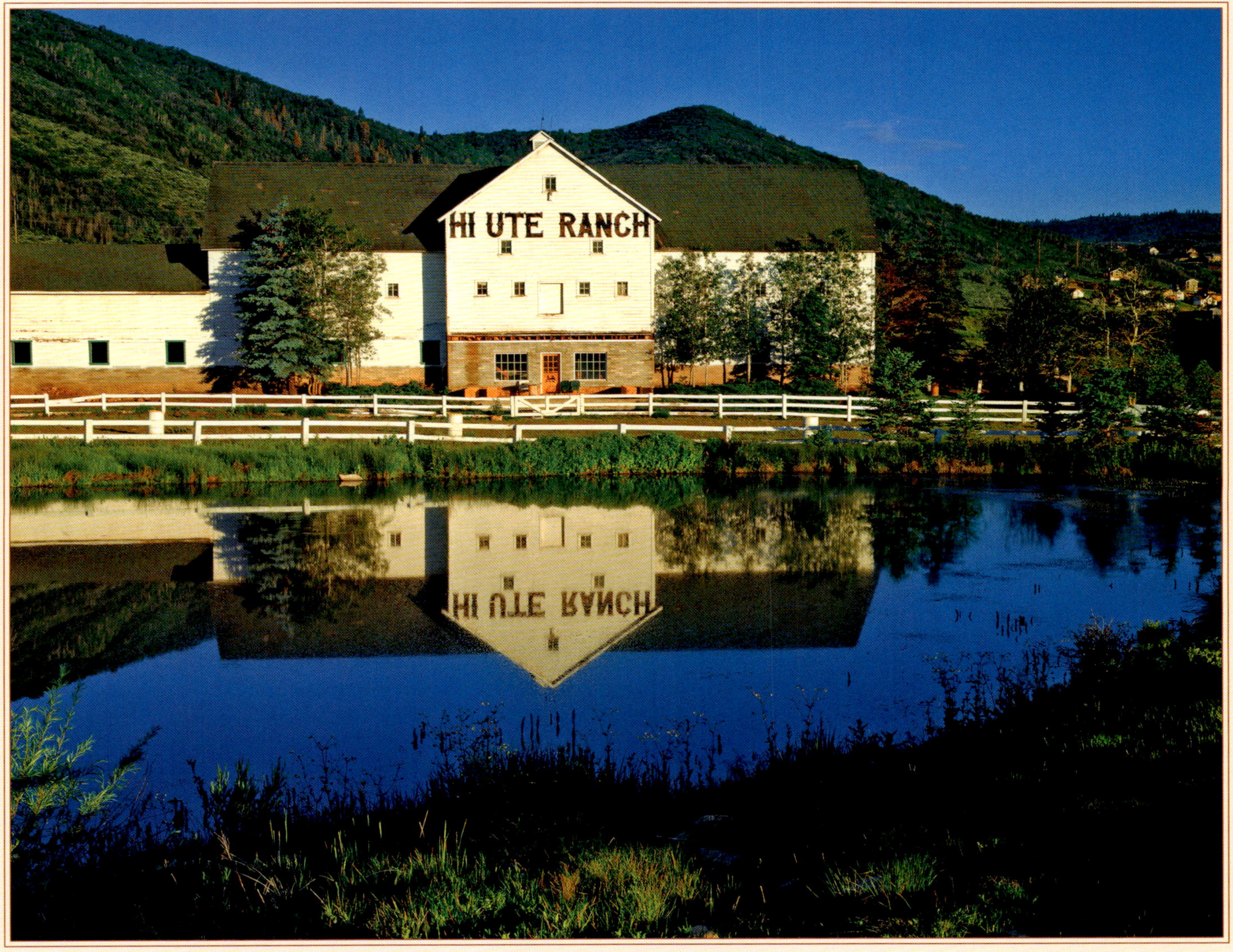

Hi Ute Ranch is a property under the management of Utah Open Lands. Along with the barn, the group holds ranch lands that will remain undeveloped.

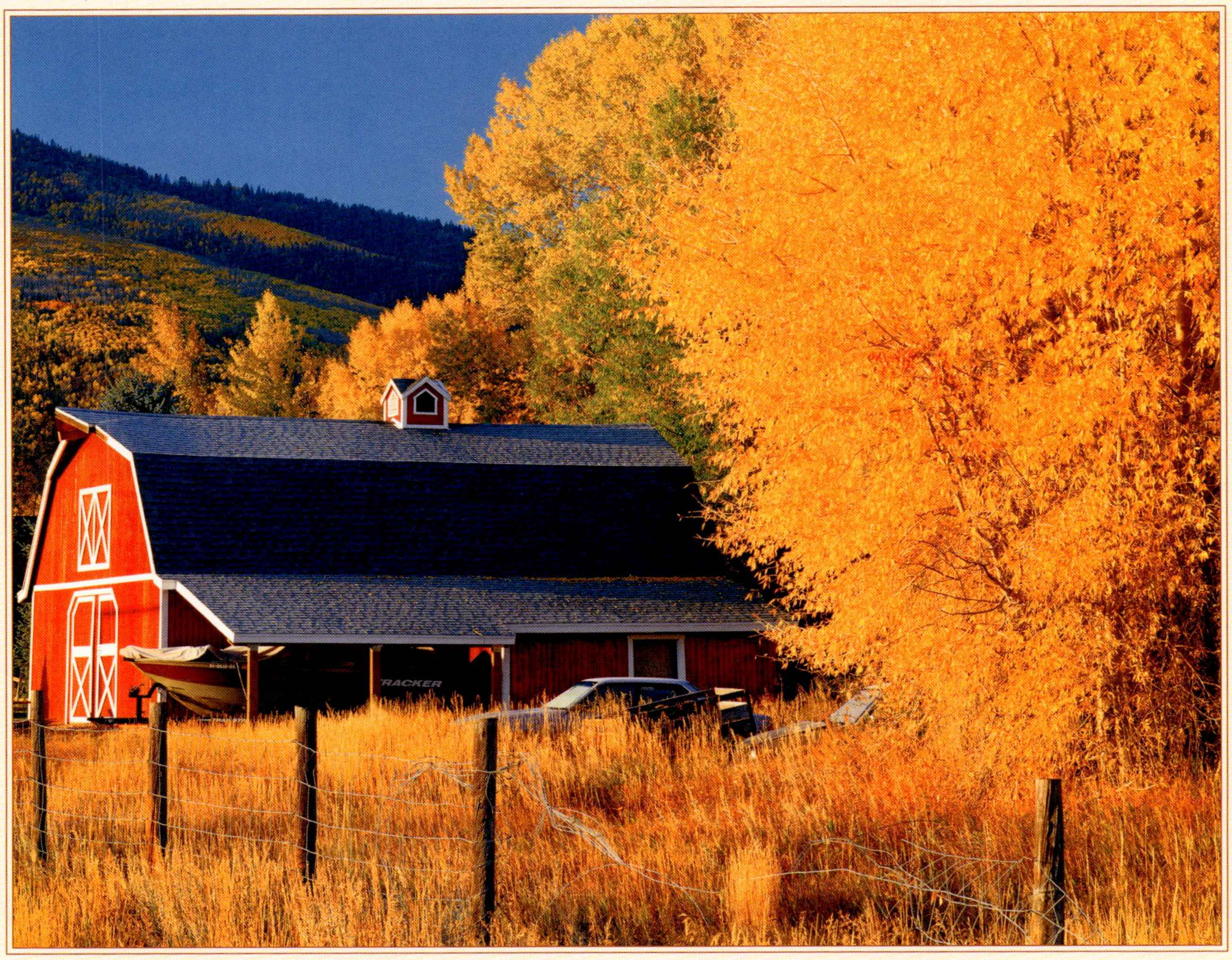

There are very few red barns in Utah, and this one was irresistible, as it stood next to a beautiful fall tree.

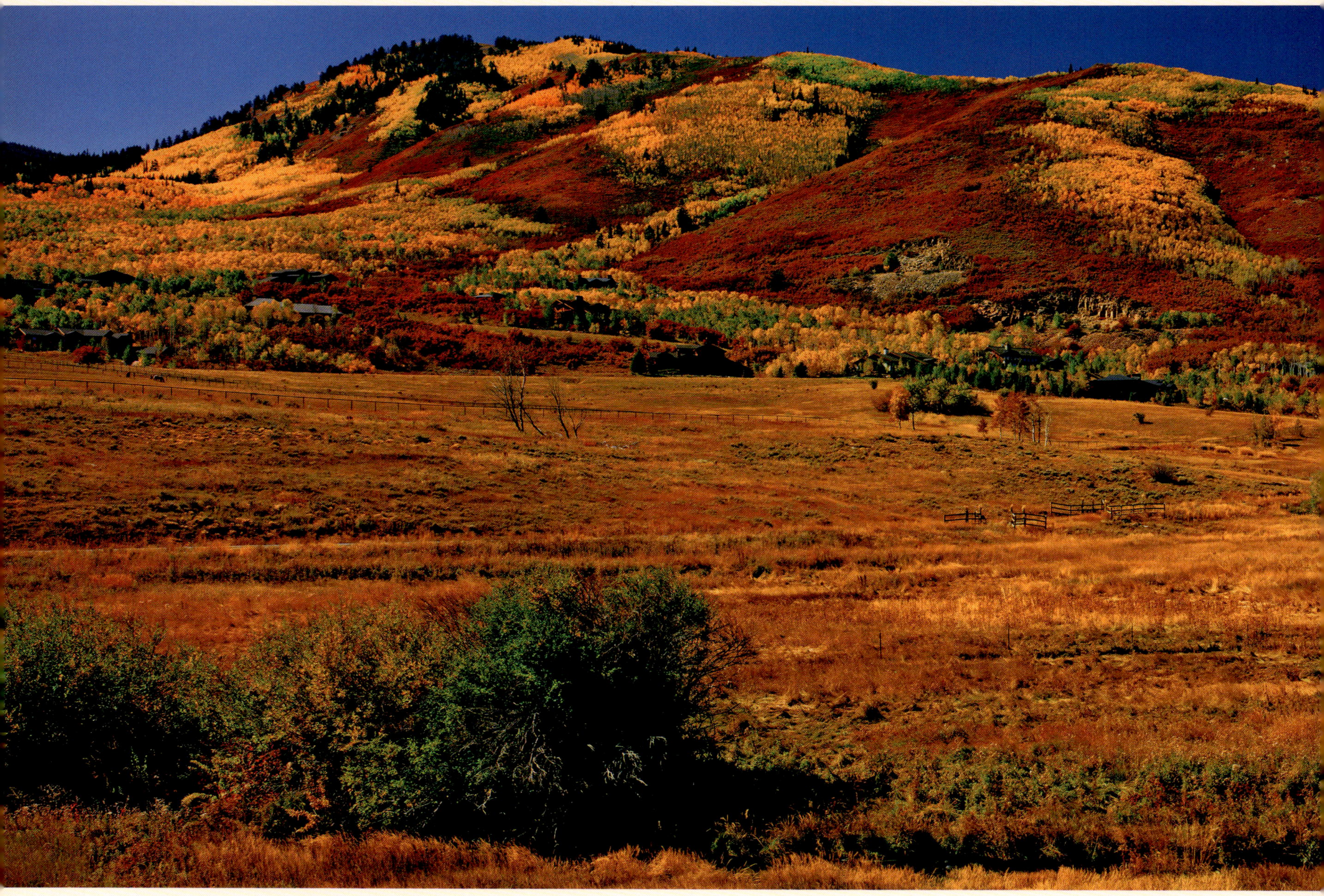

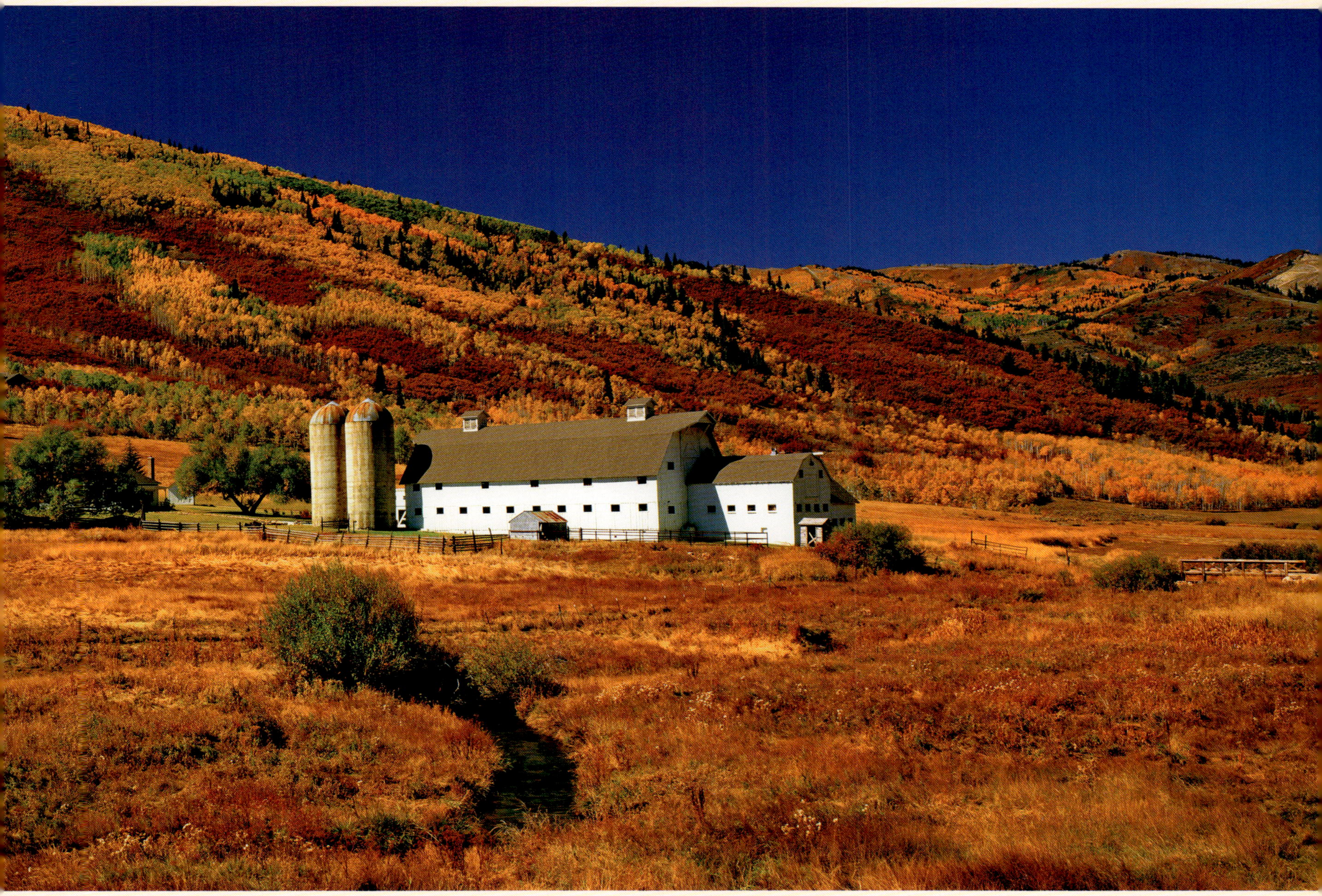

Park City's best-known barn stands below a ridge of oaks and aspens, resplendent in fall draperies.

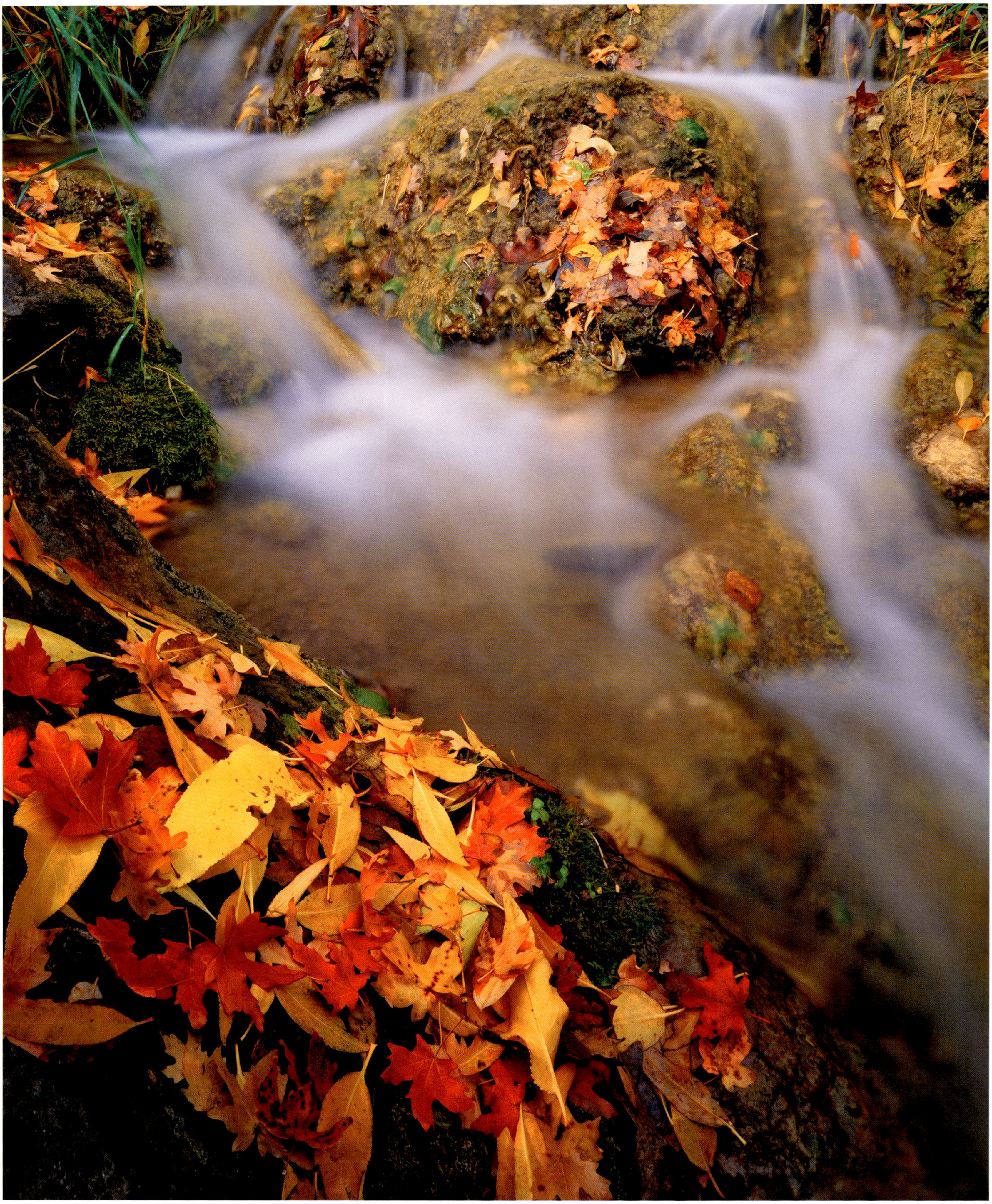

ABOVE:
A leaf pileup decorates a waterfall in Mill Creek Canyon in the Wasatch/Cache National Forest.

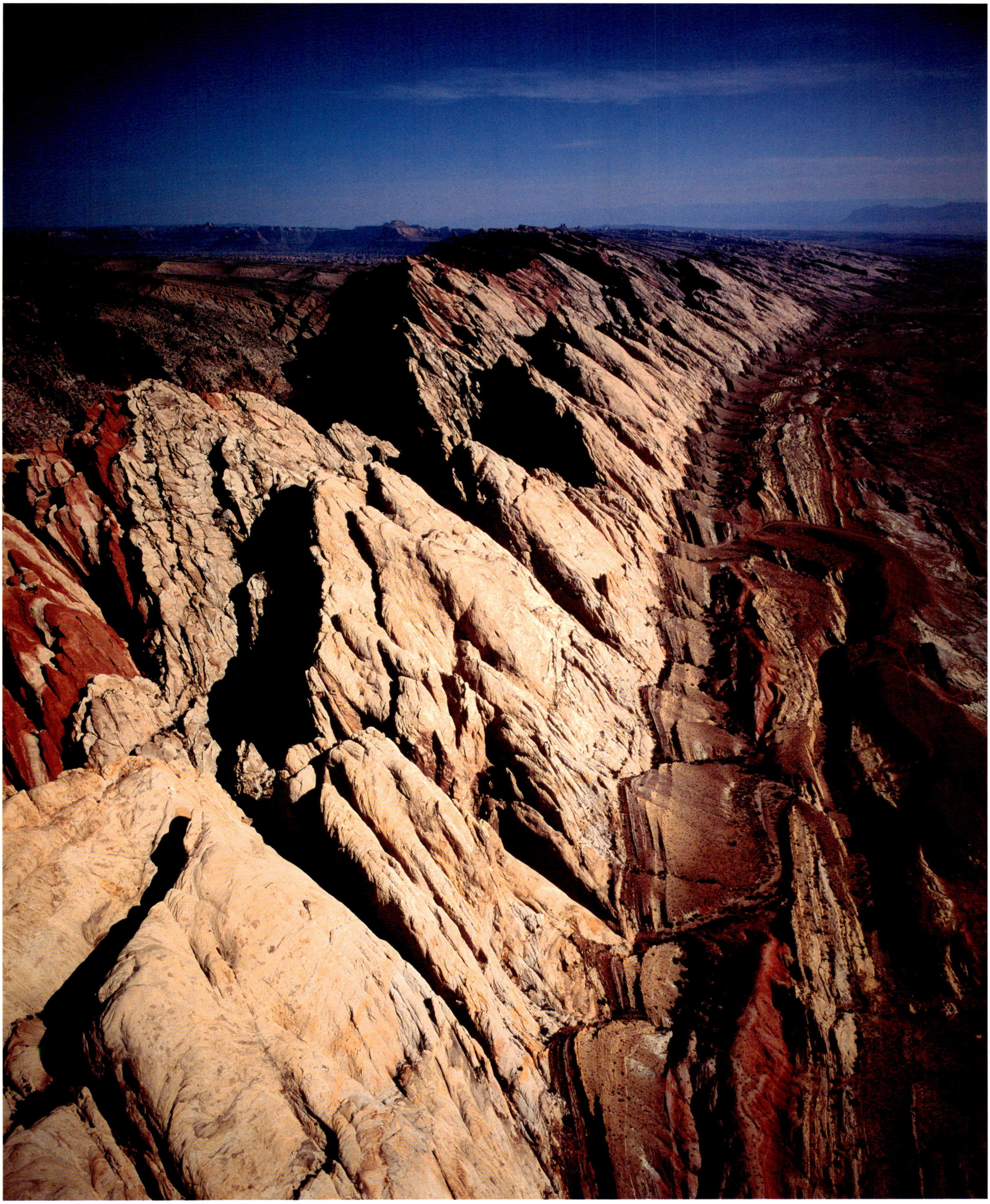

ABOVE:
The front massif of the San Rafael Swell rises like a giant tsunami above the Green River Desert Forest.

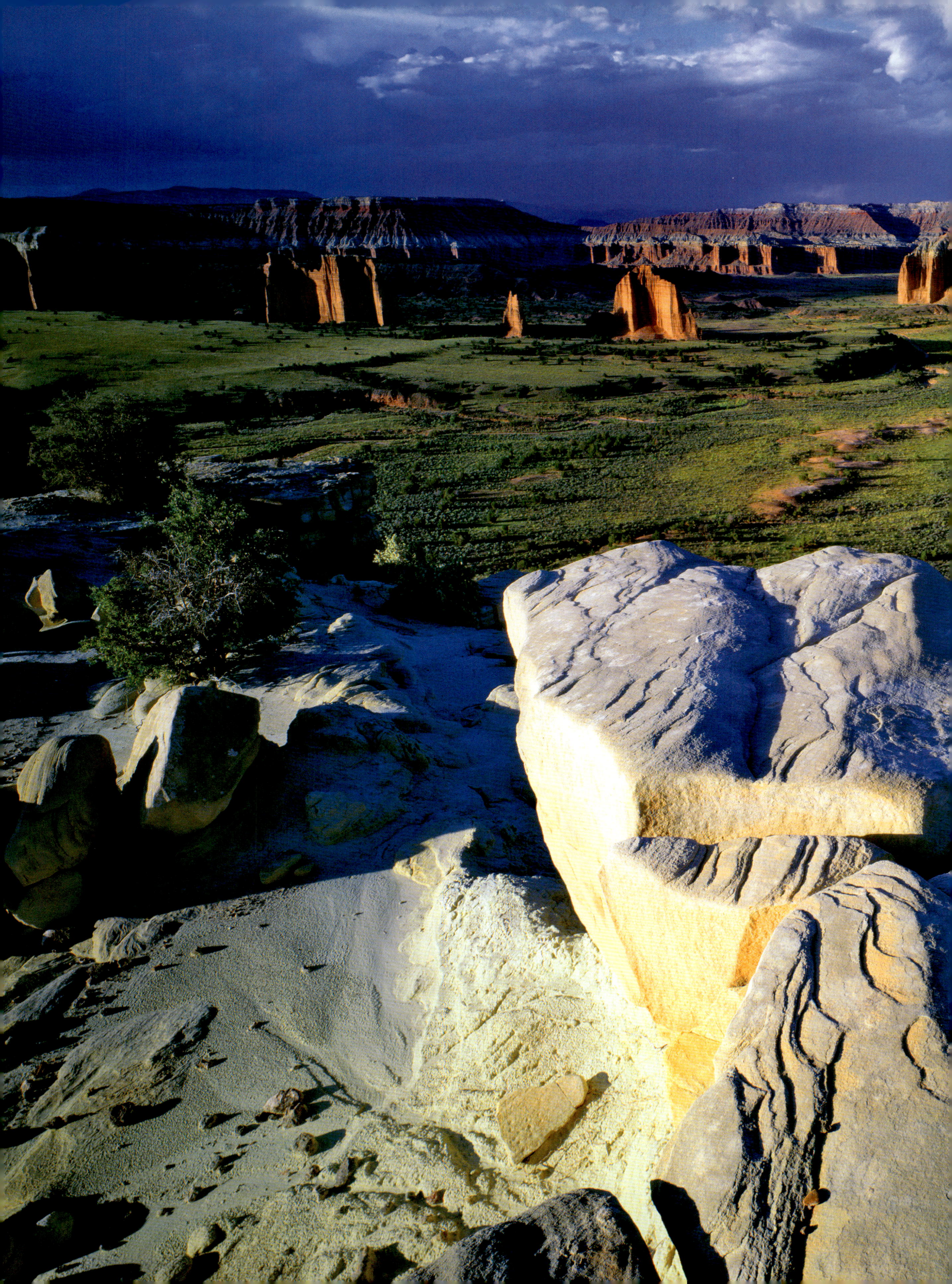

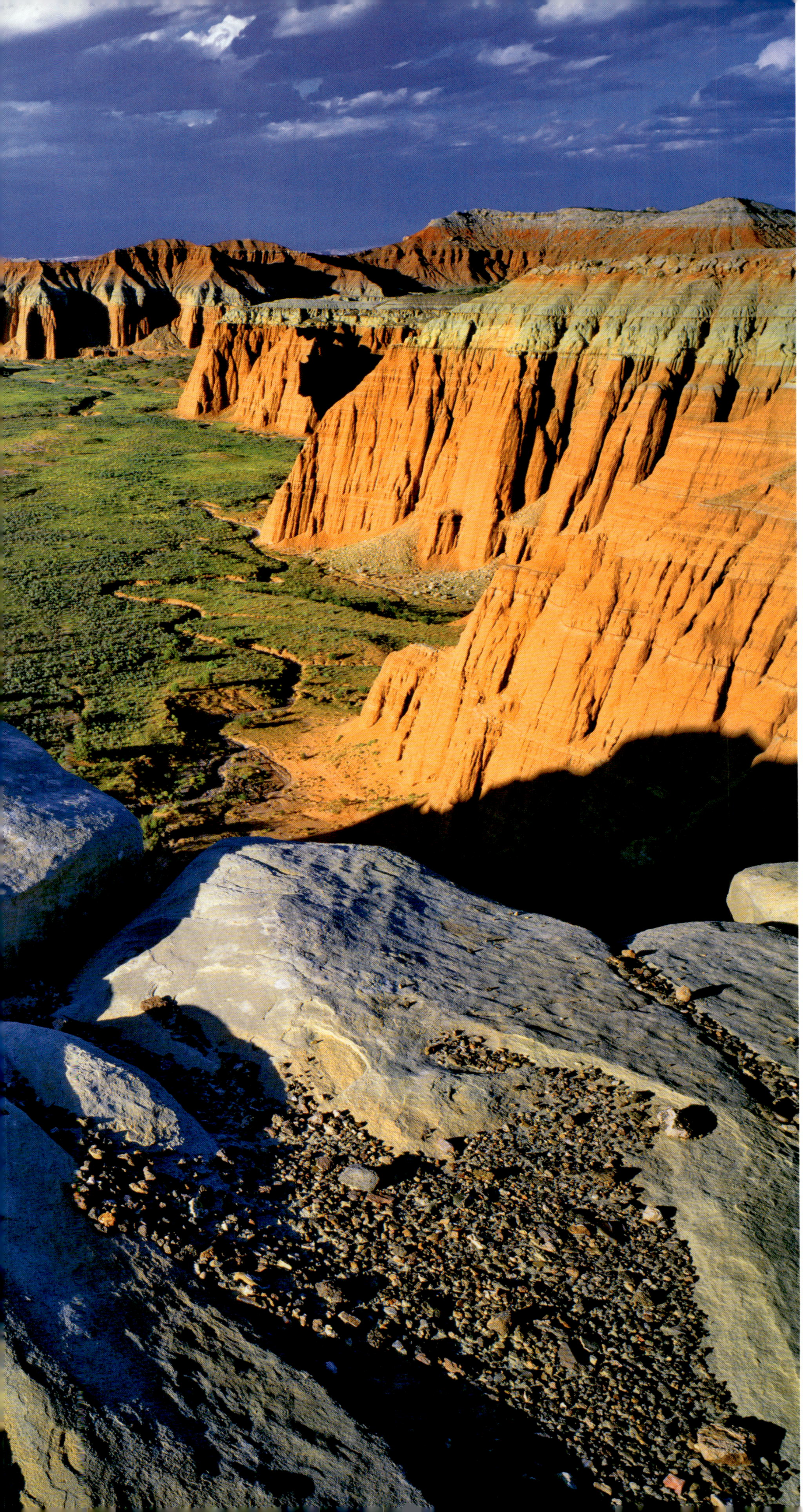

LEFT:
After a day spent shooting multiple rainbows and flashfloods, I photographed this sunset with a very wide-angle lens above Upper Cathedral Valley in Capitol Reef National Park.

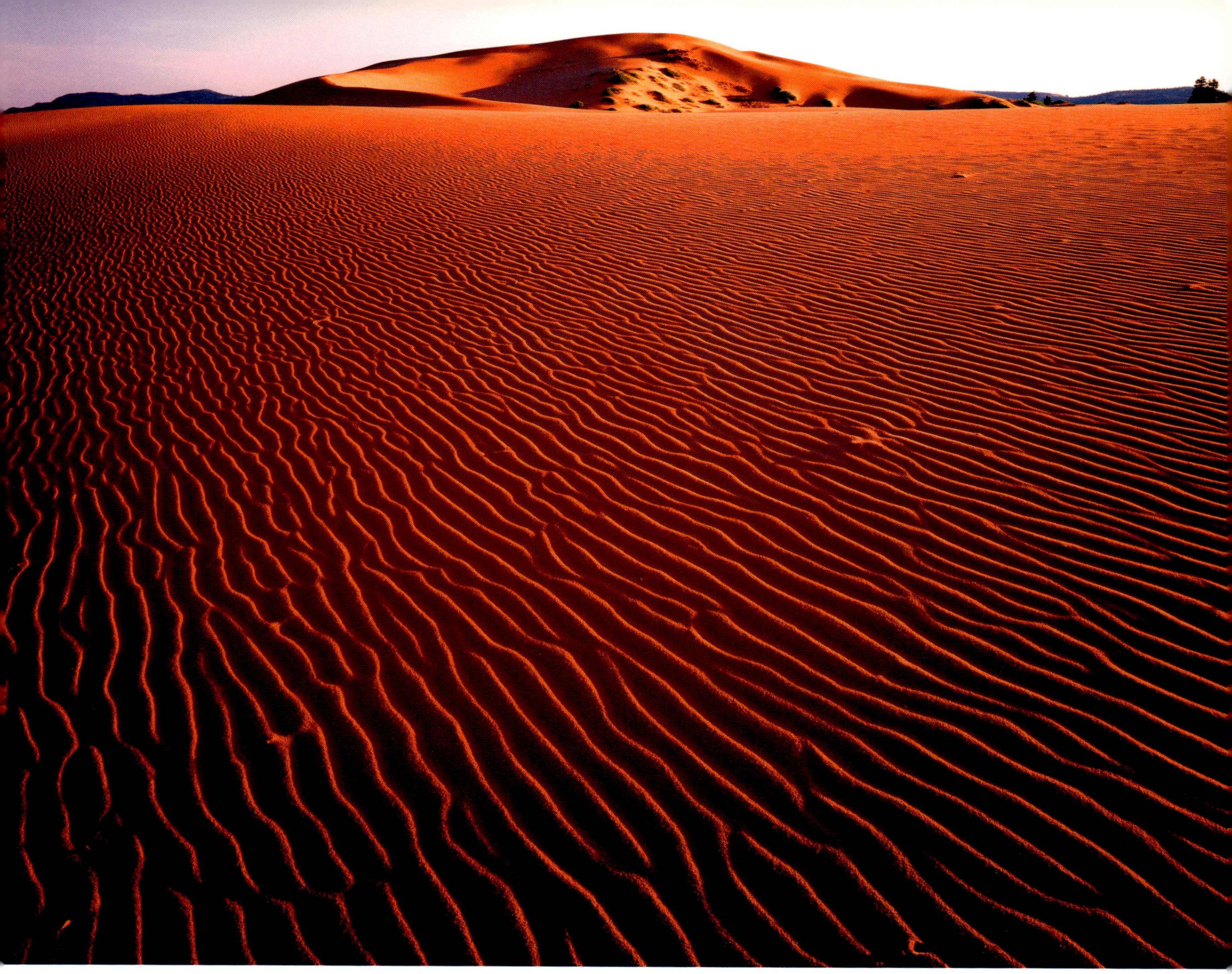

ABOVE:
Sand patterns at Coral Pink Sand Dunes State Park are true to their name, glowing with an inner fire at sunset.

BELOW:
The snow-white Bonneville Salt Flats reflect sunrise-blue storm clouds.

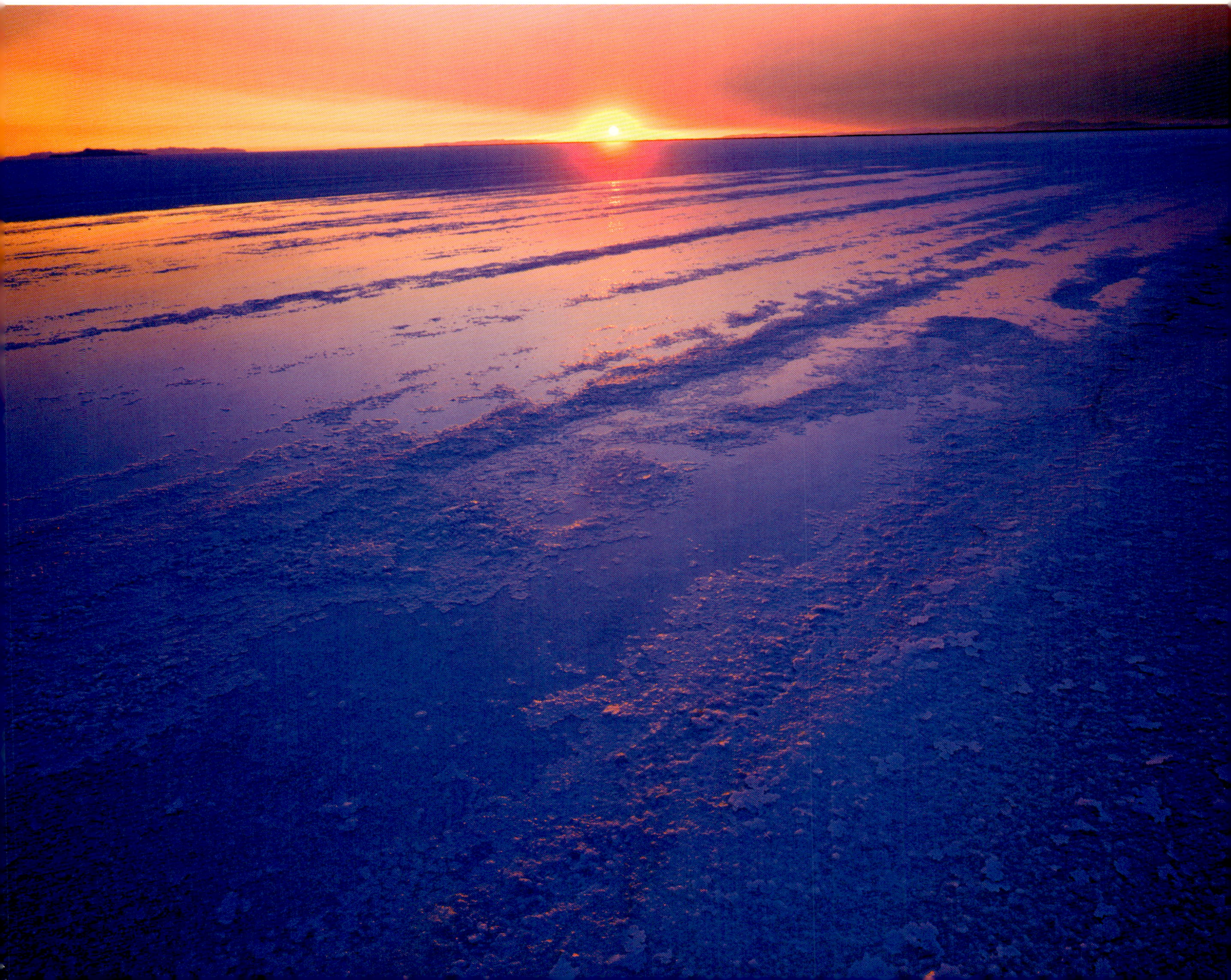

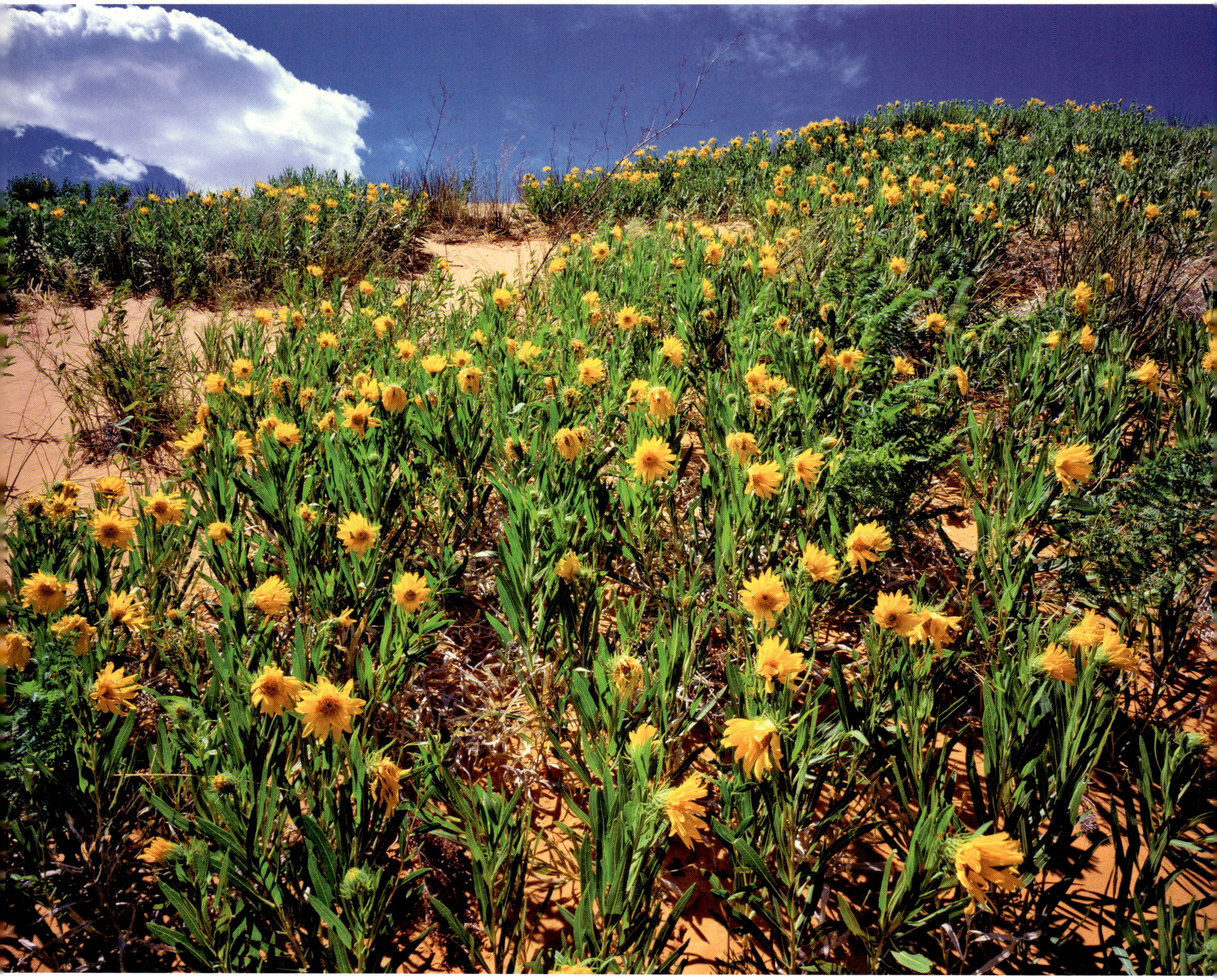

ABOVE:
Bursting forth from the shifting sands of Moquith Mountain Wilderness Study Area, fields of mule ear flowers cover the slopes of the dunes.

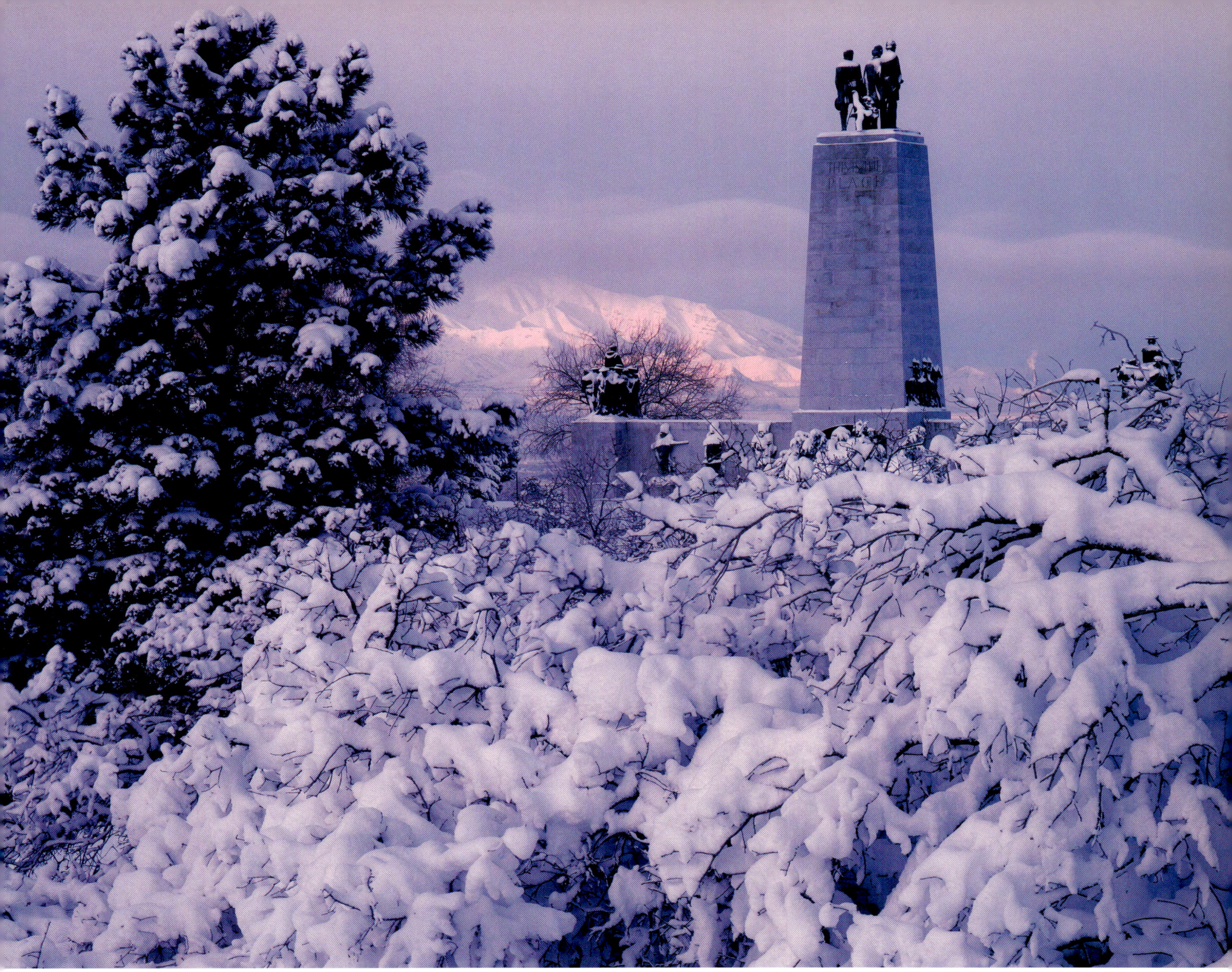

ABOVE:
A faint sunrise glow shines on the Oquirrih Mountains behind This is the Place Monument in Emigration Canyon.

RIGHT:
Clouds and late light highlight the walls of Zion Canyon. This image, along with many others in this portfolio, was made using a simple device called a graduated neutral density filter.

The filter does not add color, but instead evens out the dark and light parts of any scene so that they are more easily recorded by the film, which has a latitude much smaller than the human eye.

To get closer to what I really see, the gnd, as it's called, has a dark area that blocks the brightest part of the scene, and a clear area where the darker area goes.

Almost every outdoor scene you see in a movie was made using similar filters, and cinematographers have made the use of gnds an art form. I can only carry a few with me, but I use them a great deal.

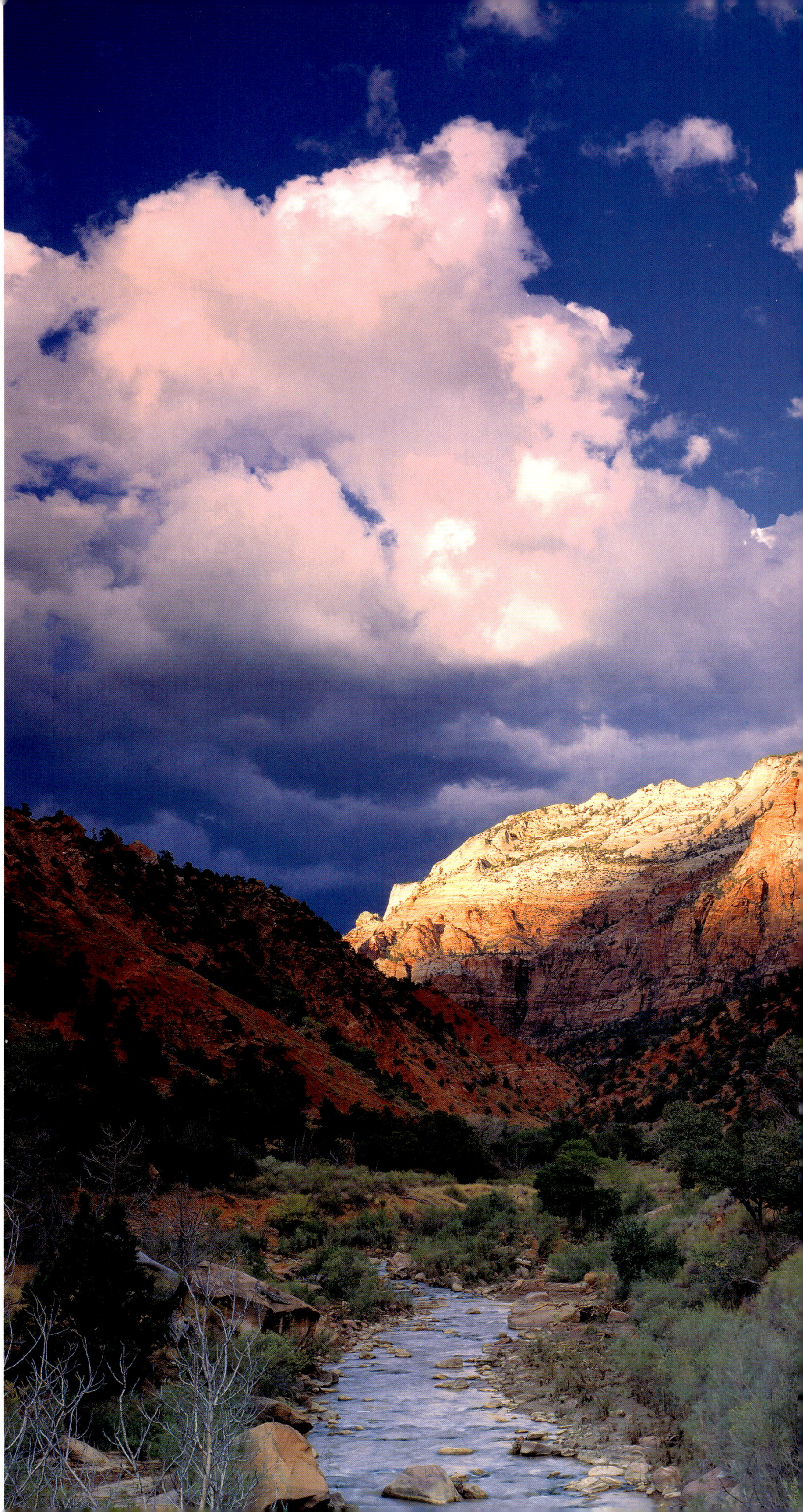

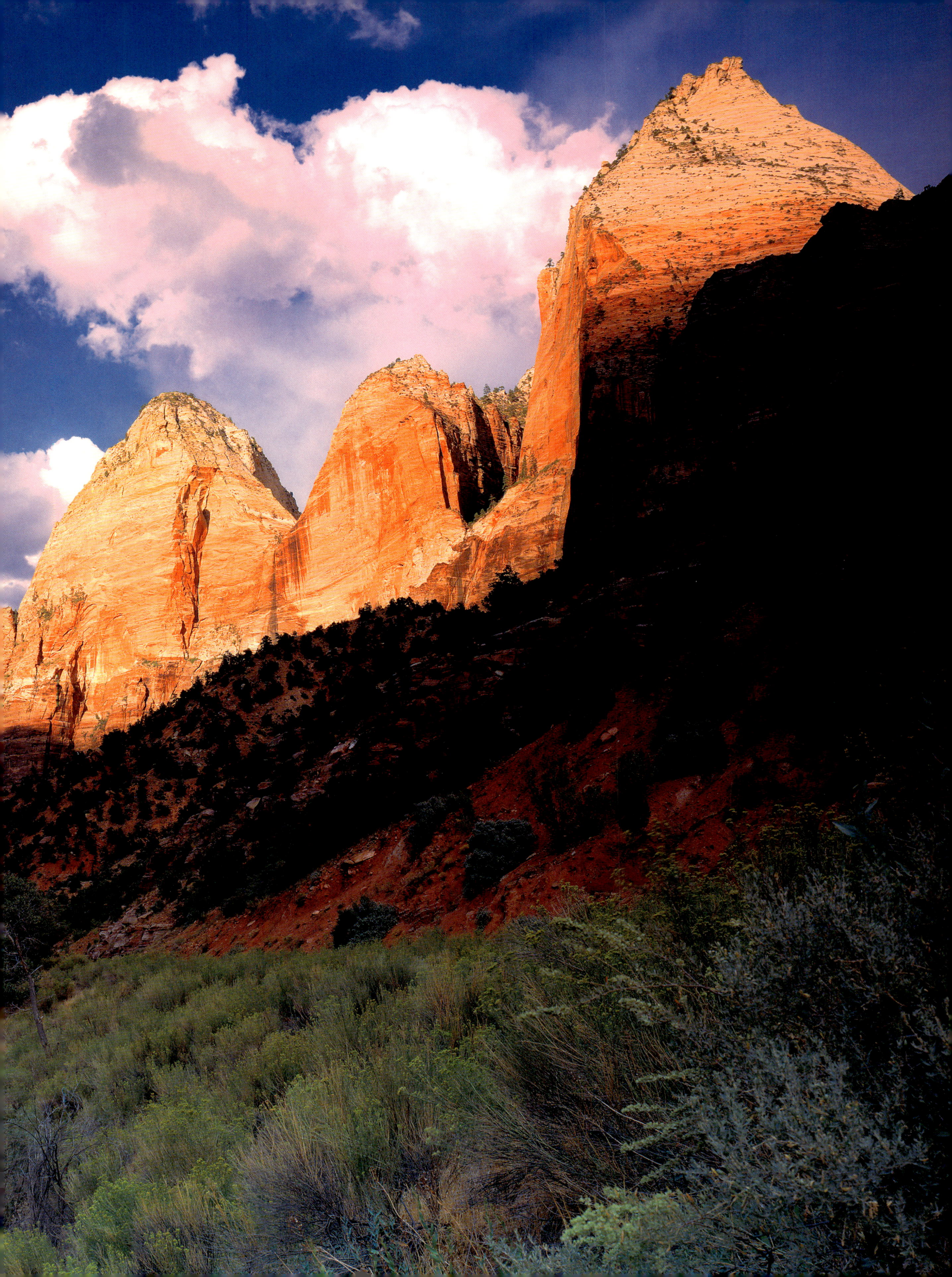

BELOW:
Mt. Timpanogos rises above morning fog on Deer Creek Reservoir.

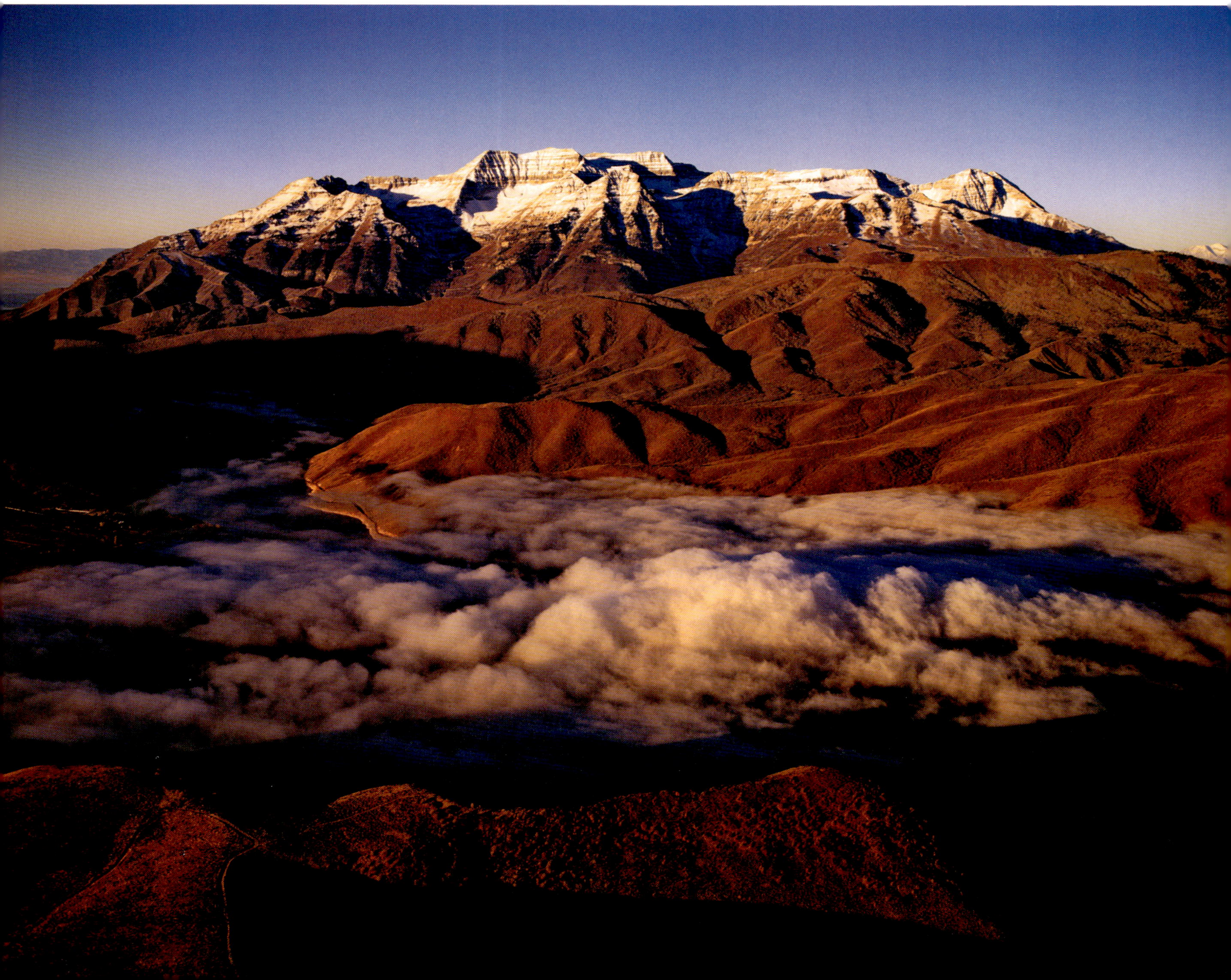

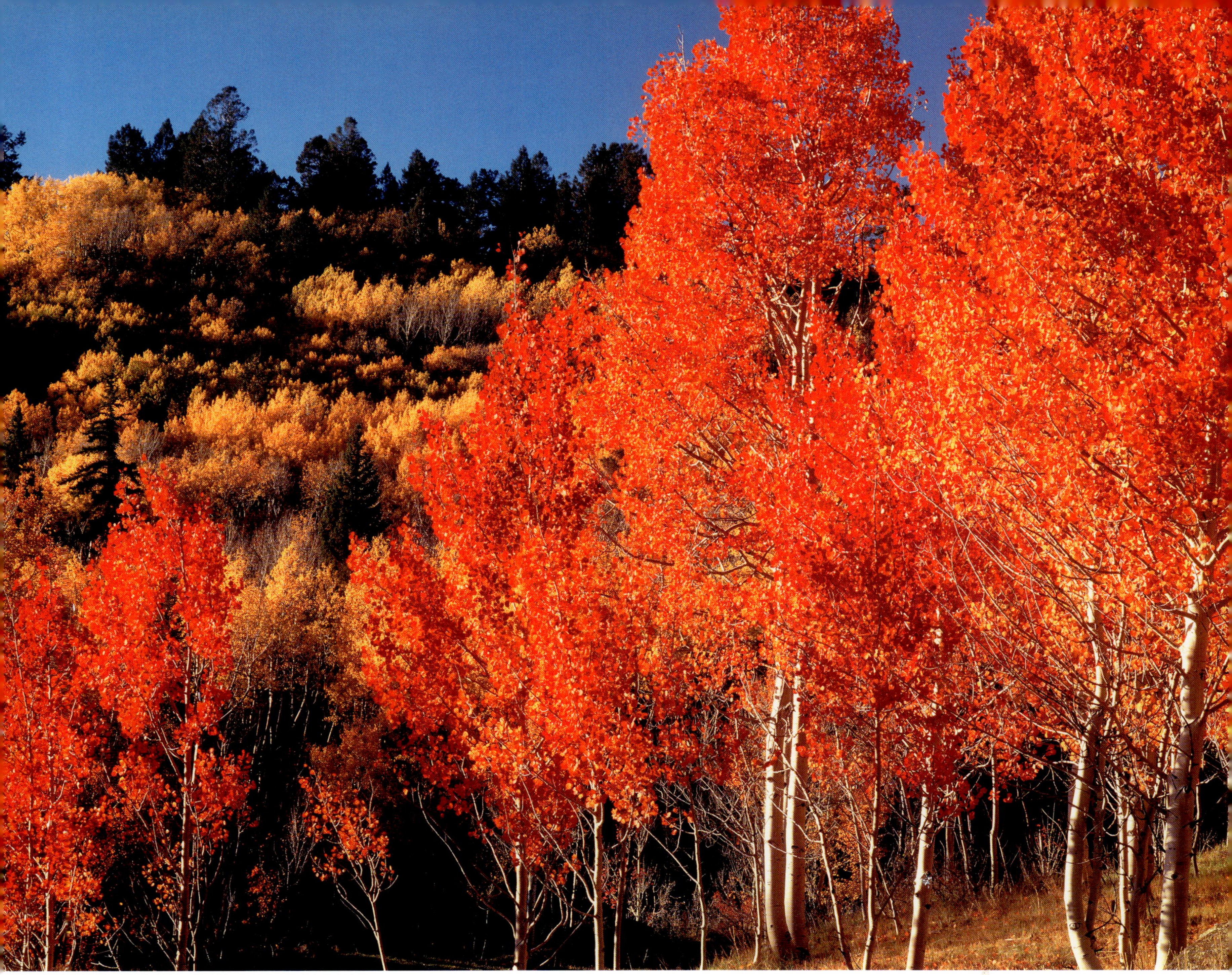

ABOVE:
This small stand of aspen on Boulder Mountain in Dixie National Forest always turns brilliant red instead of the standard yellow. I even saw an image of these trees by an amateur on the Mark Eubank weather report a year after I made this shot. In recent years, aspen groves have been found to be single organisms consisting of many trees above ground connected below through their roots. Some researchers have speculated that the tree systems may be very old, and their combined biomass may make them among the earth's largest living things.

BELOW:
It's rare when a lake as big as the Great Salt Lake is calm enough to reflect the sky, especially in the afternoon when the sun-warmed air is usually unstable. It helps that the lake is shallow, as in this view from Antelope Island State Park.

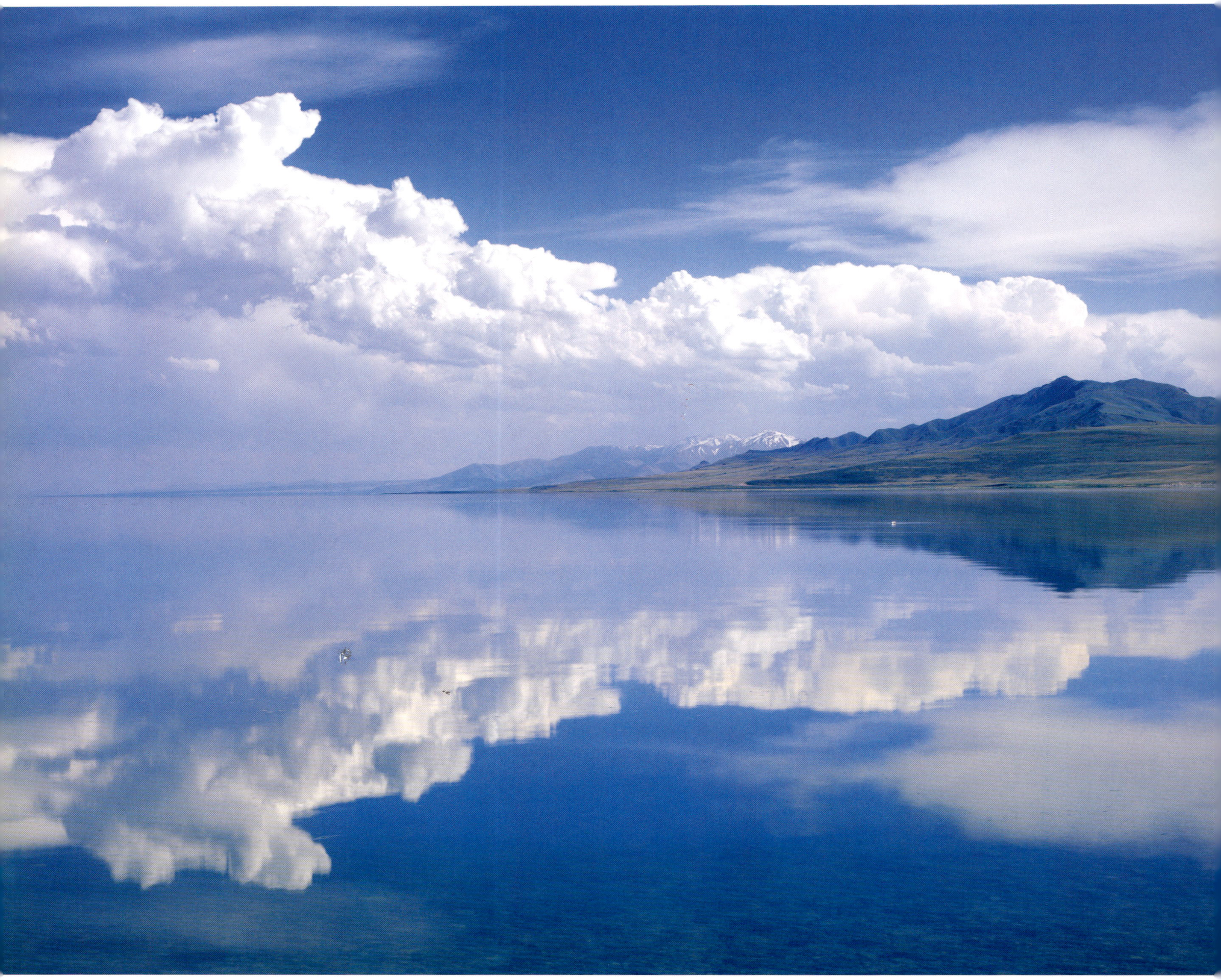

RIGHT:
The color of ice can vary from black to deep blue, as you will see in other examples in this book. Ice patterns are as different as snowflakes, each a work of nature's random art.

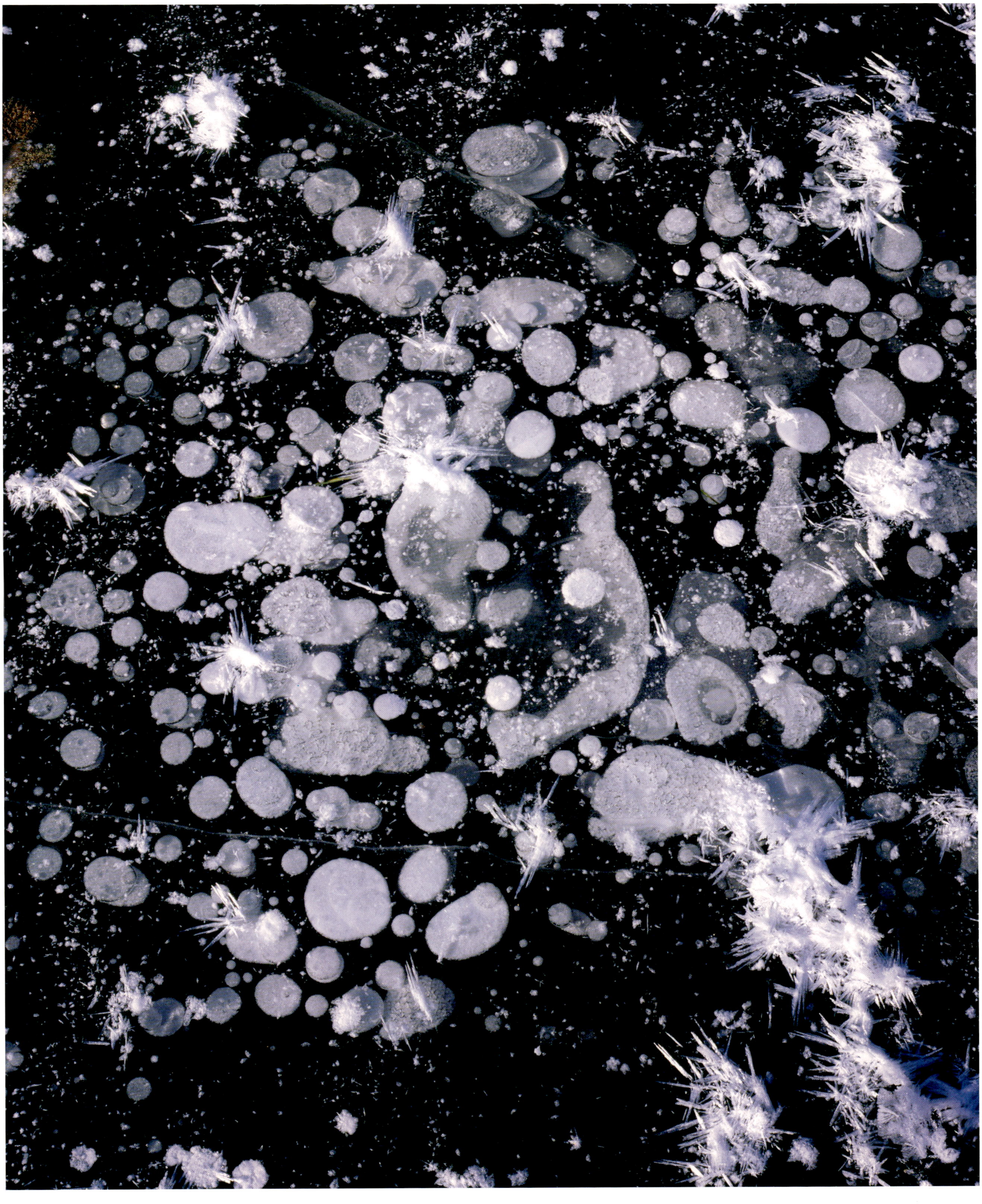

RIGHT:
A predawn hike to Ruple Point in Dinosaur National Monument brought me to this view of Split Mountain Canyon of the Green River, one of my favorite Utah canyons.

I have hiked all over the rims on both sides of the Canyon, searching for interesting and unusual views.

After the sun rose and I finished my work with this shot, I began the long hike back to my truck. As the sun rose higher, I witnessed a strange phenomenon — the ground began to move. Even more frightening, the trail I was on was moving, too. Wherever the sun's ray hit the ground, movement began.

I was witnessing the awakening of tens of thousands of Mormon crickets, an ugly insect resembling a mutated grasshopper. The hatch occasionally bursts forth in plague-of-locust numbers in the Dinosaur area.

For the next hour, my goal was to make it back to my vehicle without having some of the thousands of creatures climb up my legs.

Though I tried hard not to crush any, it was impossible to walk without killing or maiming hundreds of the bugs, if not thousands. I still have nightmares about it.

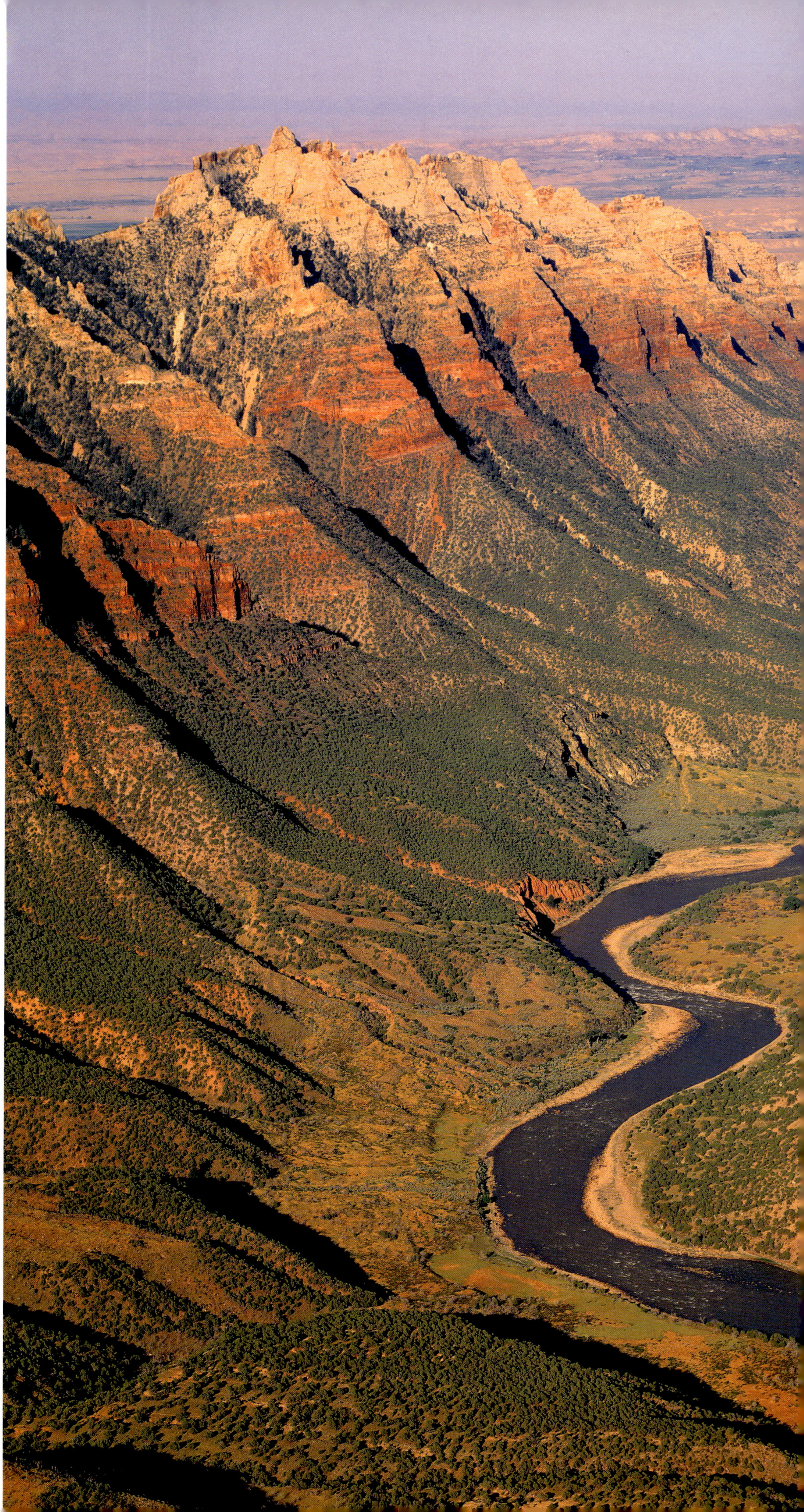

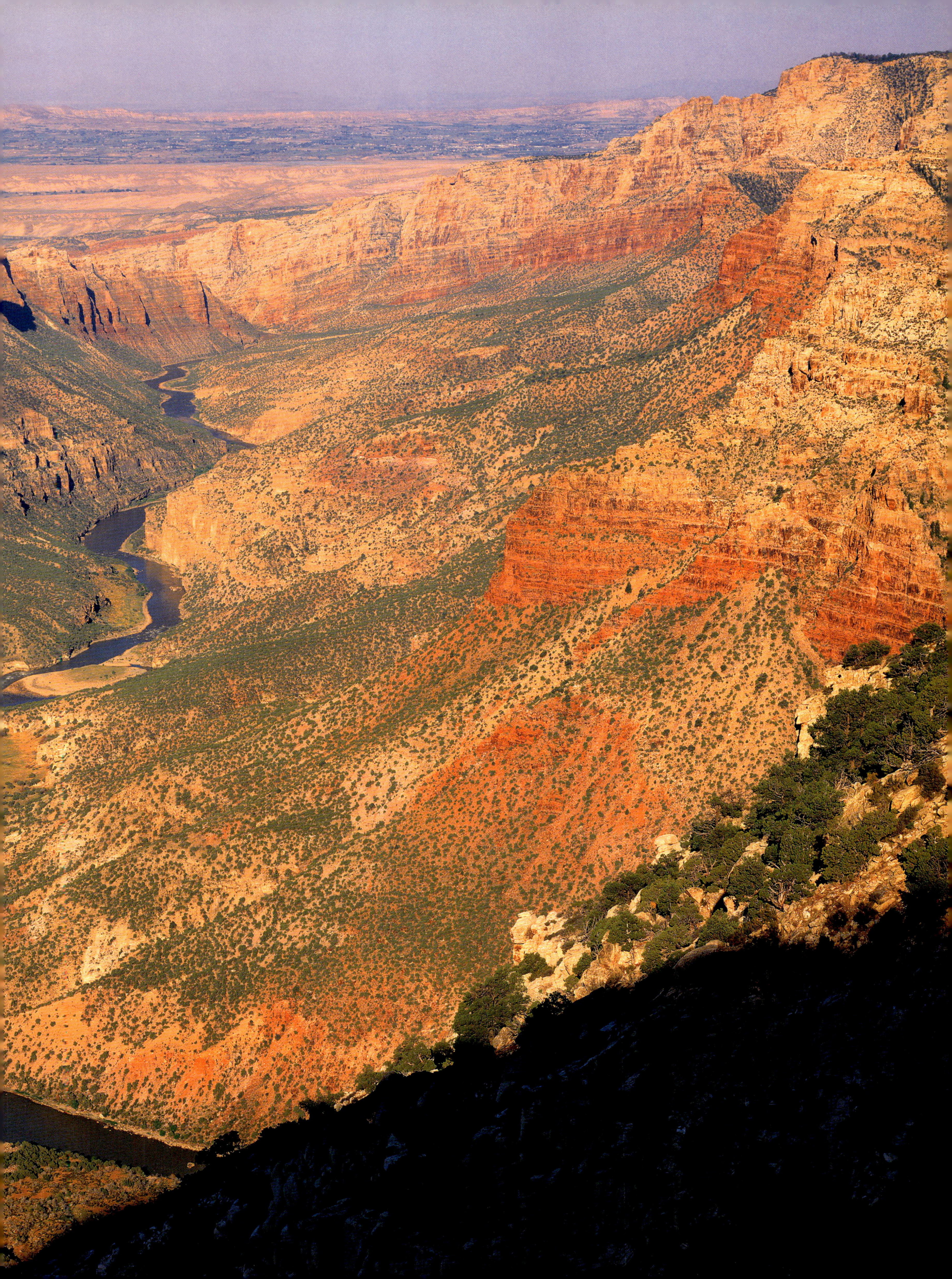

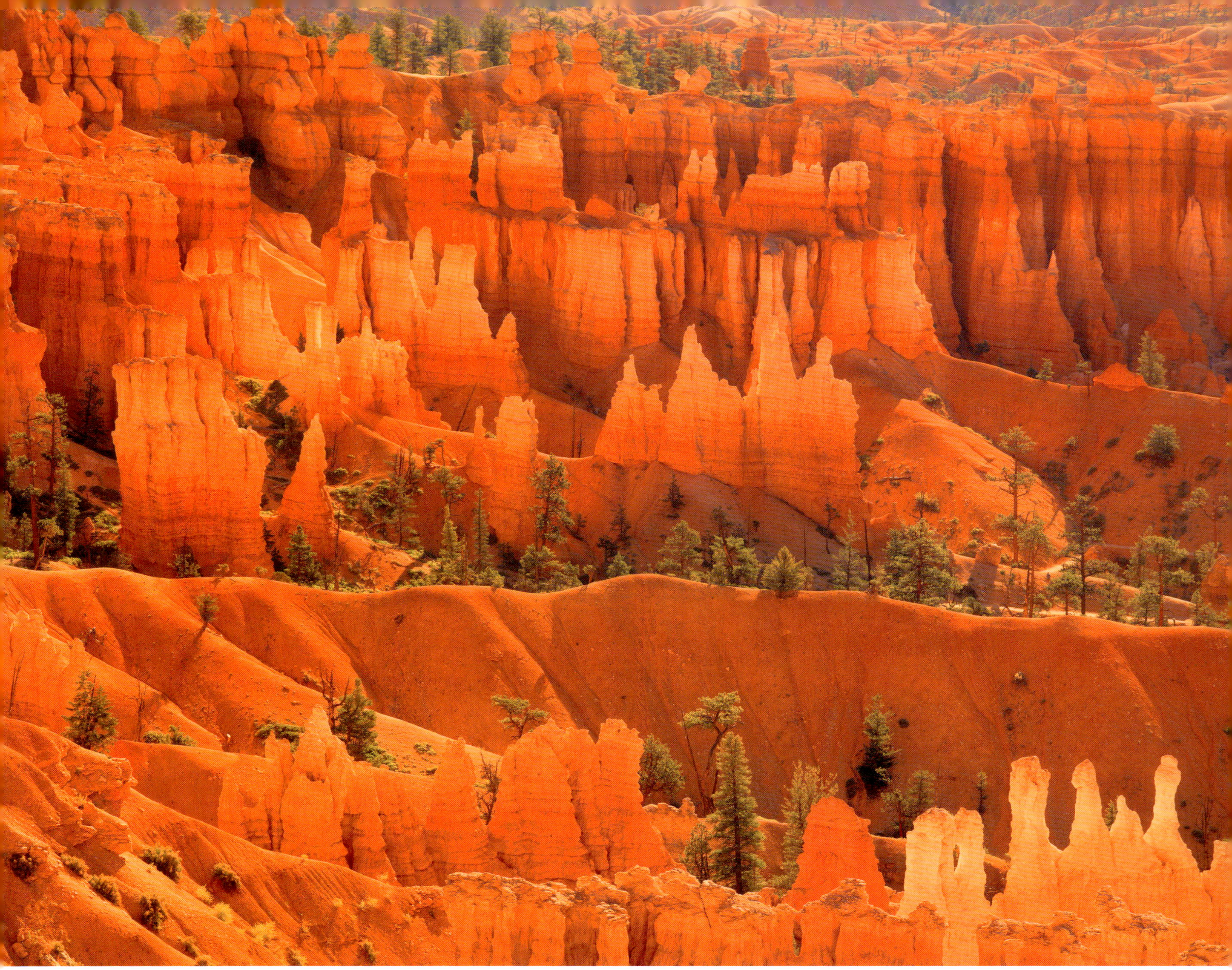

ABOVE:
The colorful pinnacles of Wasatch limestone that make up the hoodoos of Bryce Canyon National Park reflect light unto their neighbors, filling their shadows with rich color. I call it "ghosting," and it's a lighting effect I've seen nowhere else in the world.

BELOW:
A rainbow appears above the city of Provo.

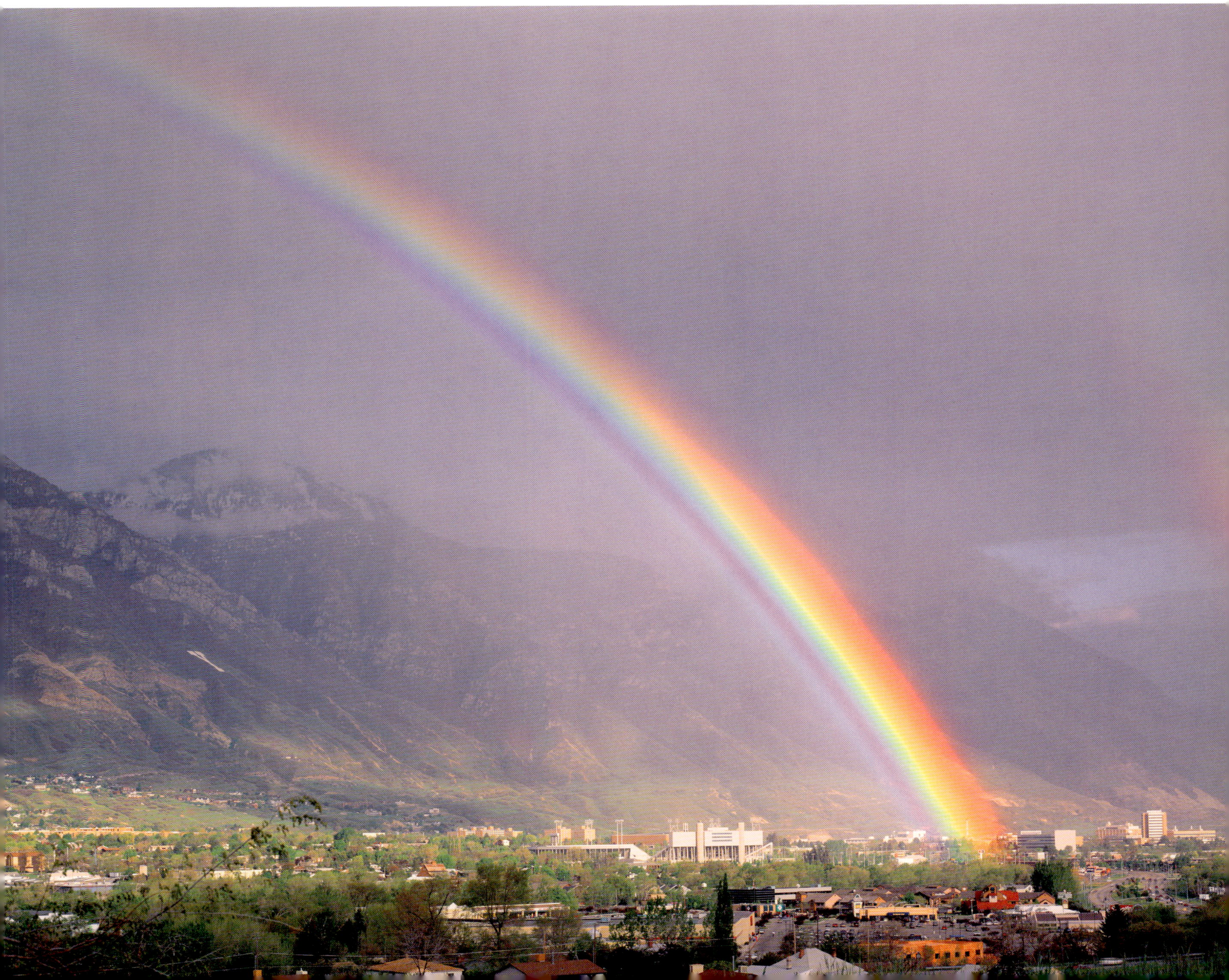

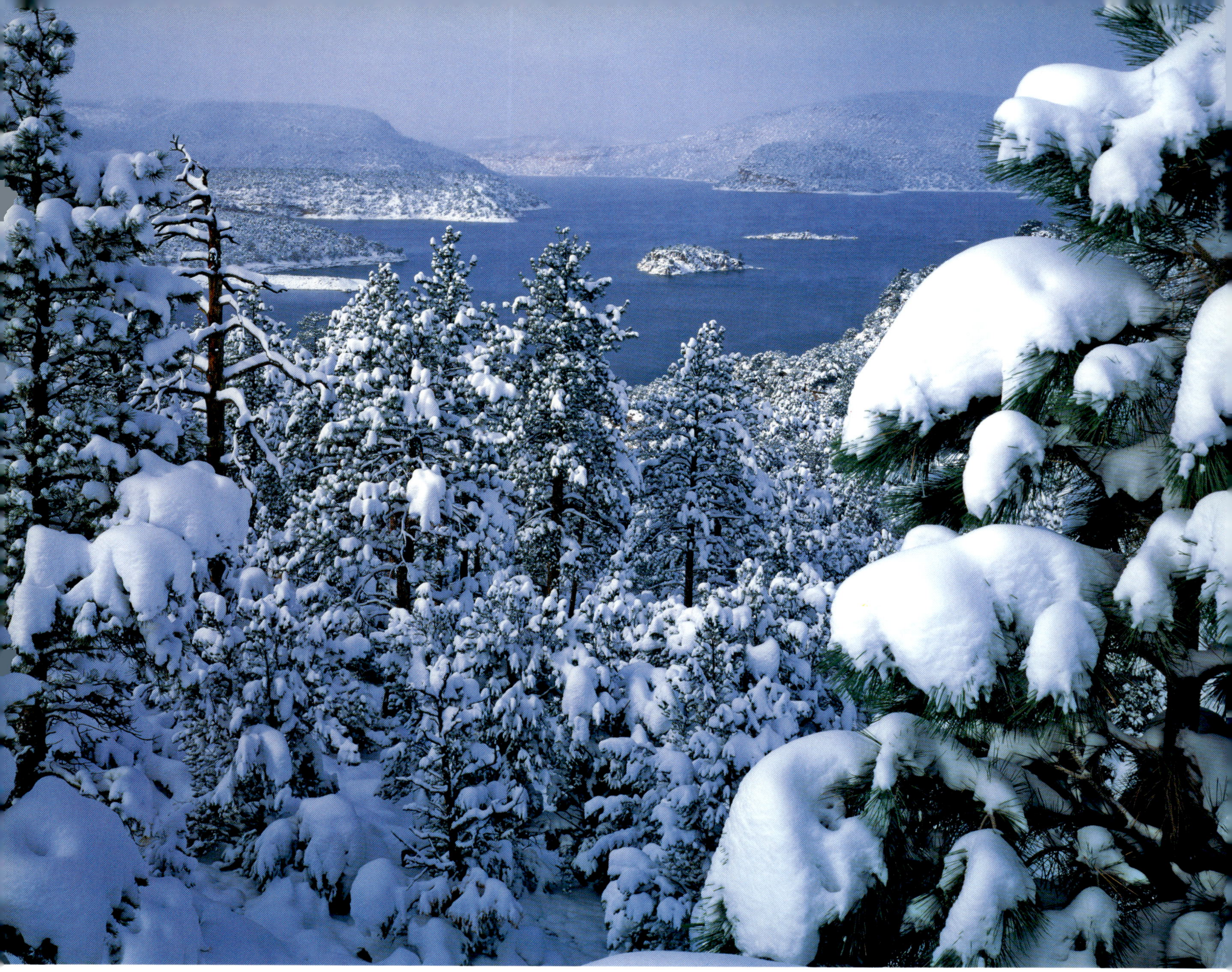

ABOVE:
My family and I have good friends, the Solawetz family, who lived in Dutch John for fifteen years. We loved the Flaming Gorge area, especially in summer when it was a cool vacation getaway from Moab. Over the many years, and after hundreds of hikes, river trips, and motorboat jaunts, we explored the area in depth. When we tired of the high country, we headed for the desert to visit Dinosaur or Fantasy Canyon. We experienced many wonderful snowstorms at Dutch John, something that happens less often at home. This storm is the kind I love, the first wet snow of the season that flocks the trees beautifully.

RIGHT:
Near the top of Notch Peak in the West Desert, a snag defies the assault of scorching summers and frigid winters. Nearby, large aggressive rattlesnakes seemed to appear at every turn of the summit trail.

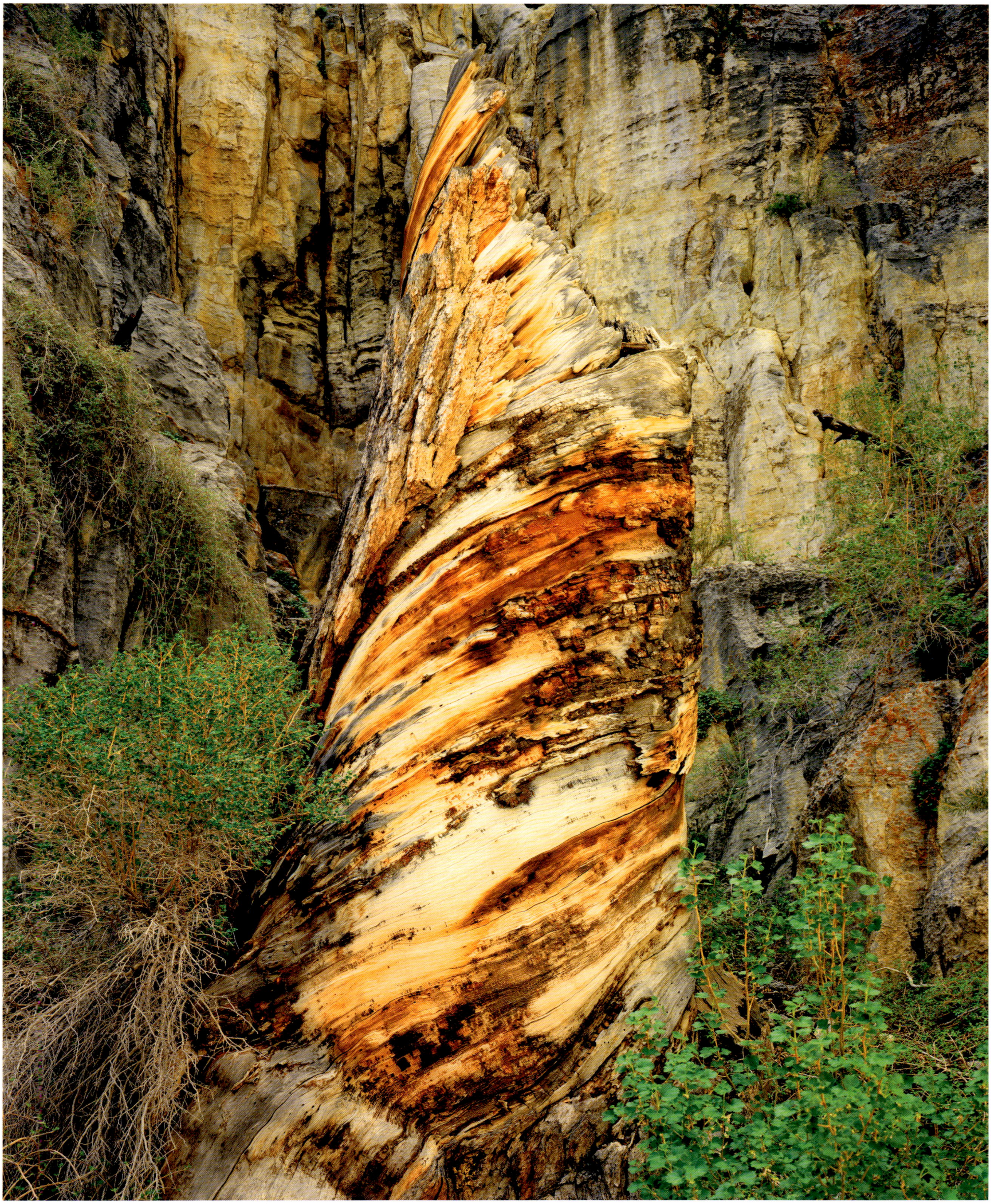

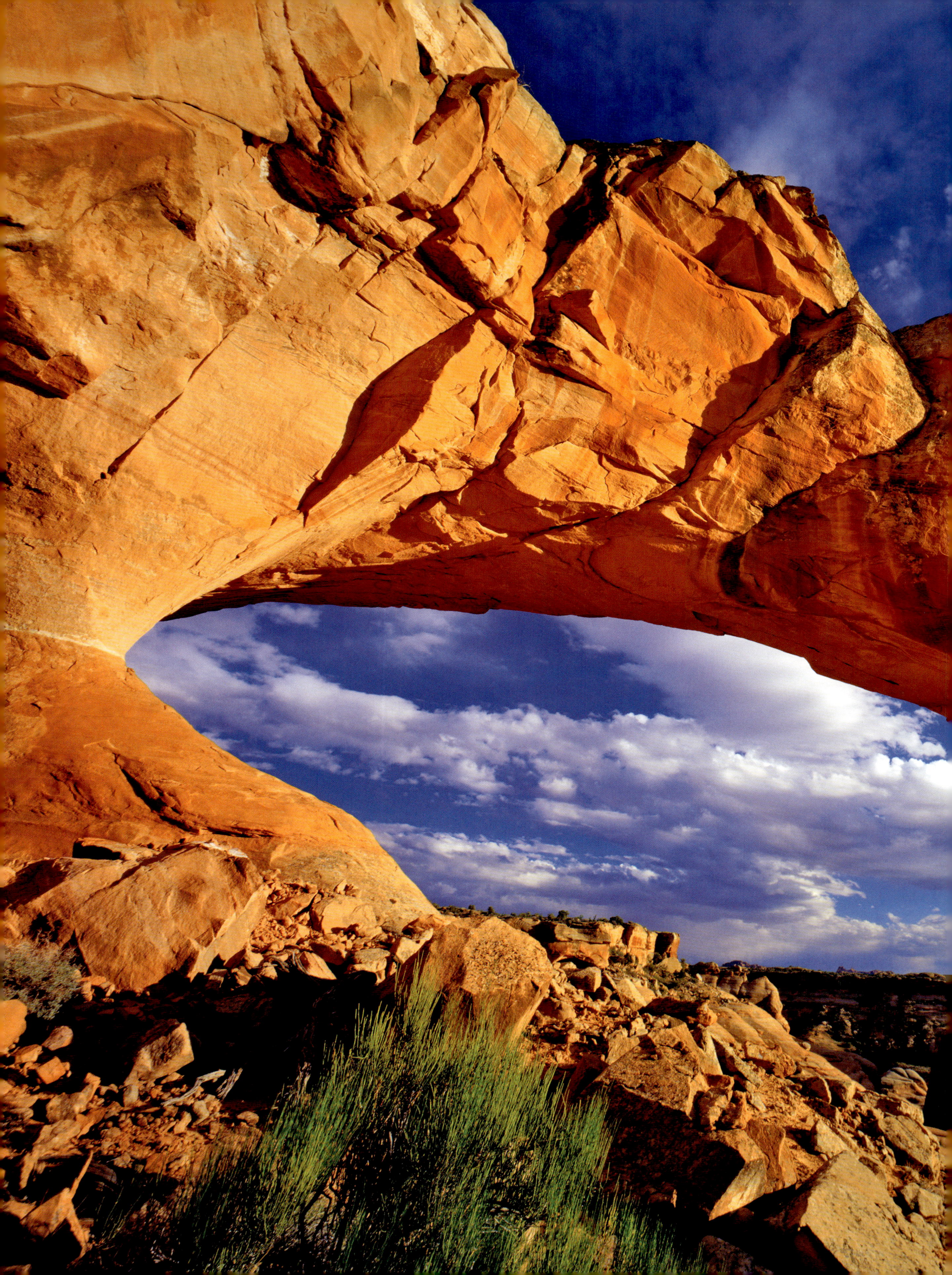

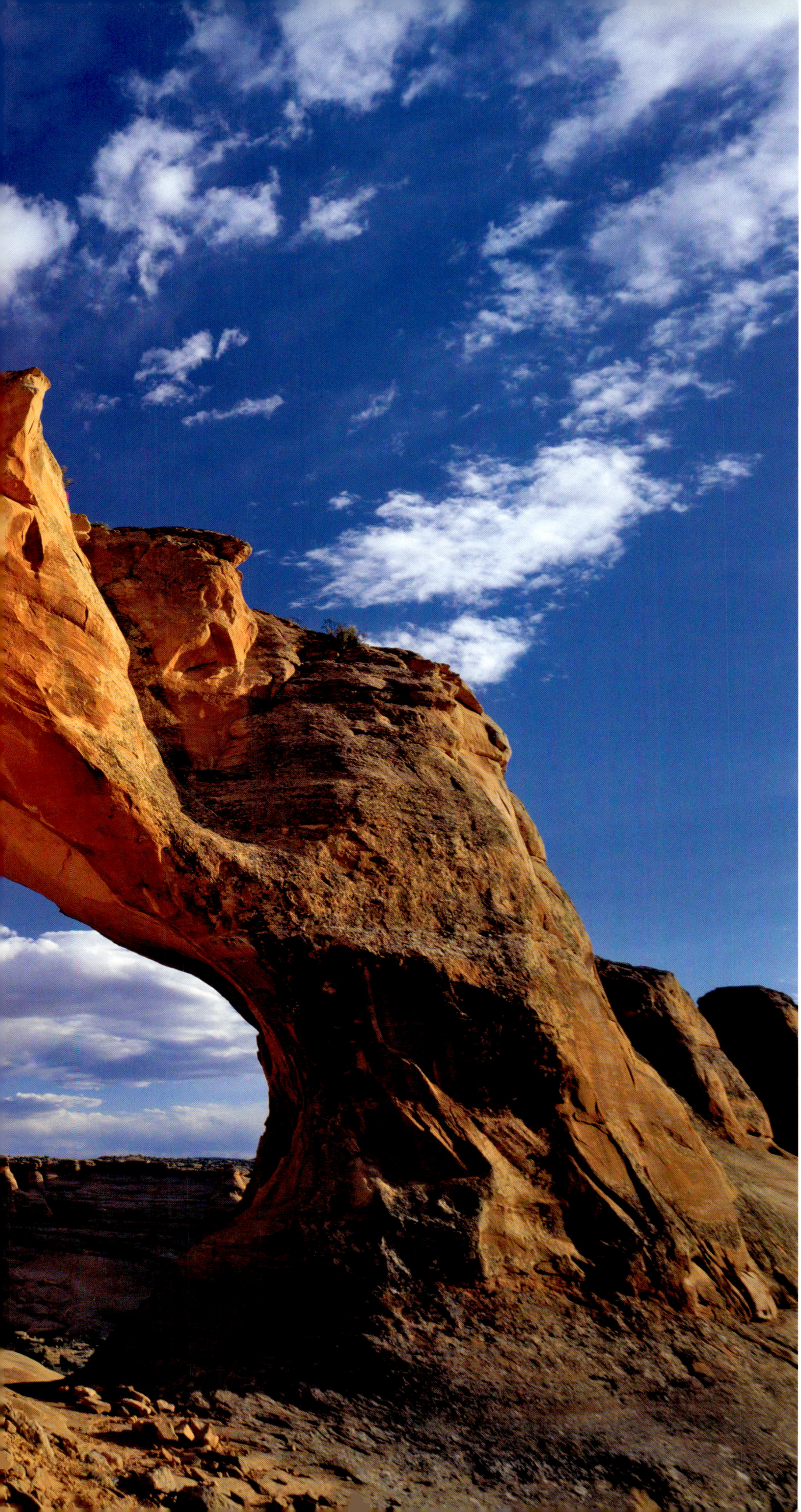

LEFT:
Obtaining this shot of Covert Arch required numerous trips.

The steep canyon walls on each side of the arch allow the photographer to get no closer than a few feet, and the arch itself is very large. Also, it's lined up almost perfectly on an east/ west axis.

Since I was so close, I knew the opening would be a big part of the scene, and I needed good clouds to fill that space.

I finally got what I wanted with a very wide-angle lens, near the summer solstice, and, as luck would have it, a good cloudscape.

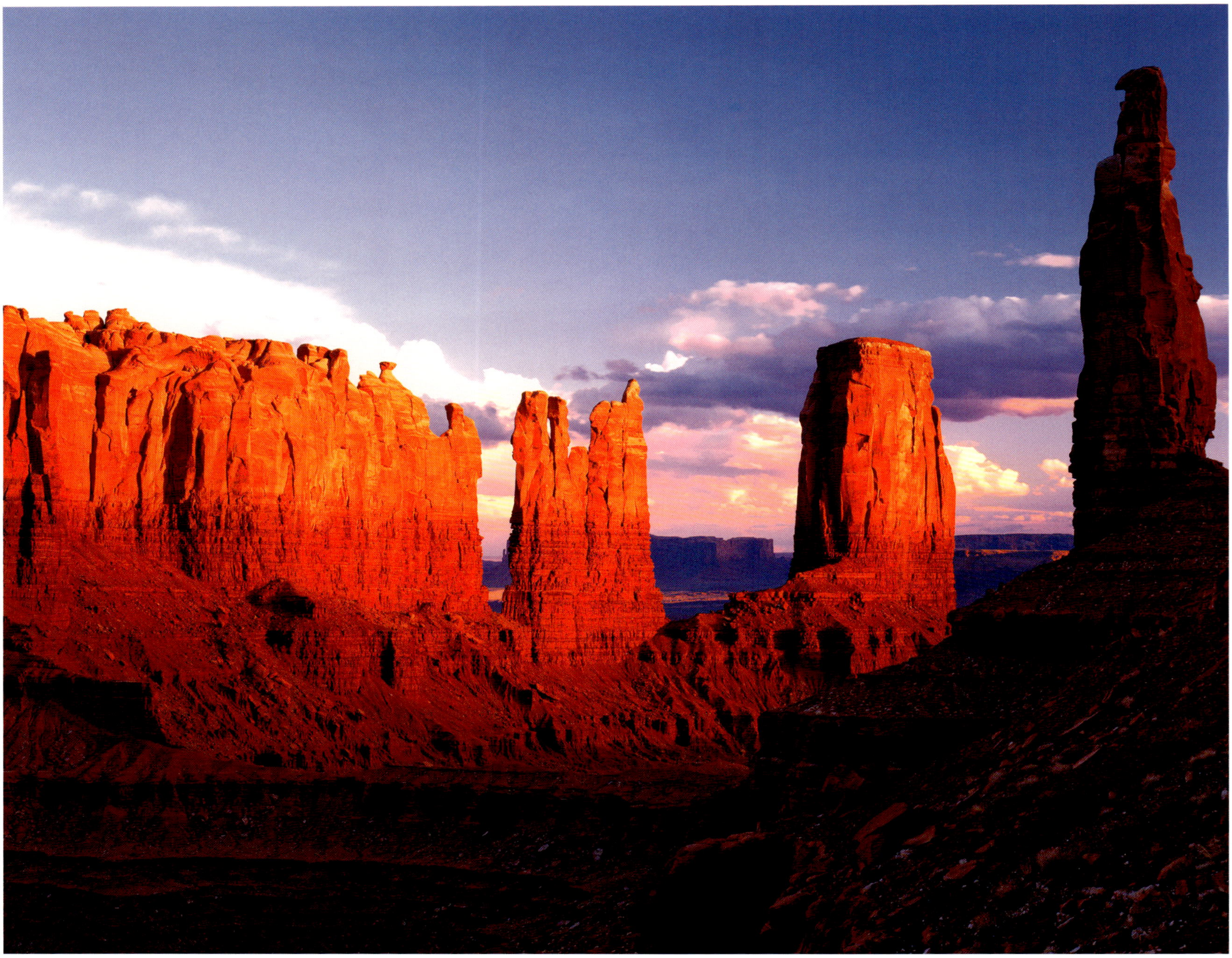

ABOVE:
These towers of Monument Valley are all firmly on the Utah side of the state line. Since the border of Utah and Arizona passes right though Monument Valley, mistakes are sometimes made. The State of Arizona had an image of these Utah towers on its state maps for several years, while an advertising campaign for Utah tourism showed a family camped on Hunts Mesa, easily ten miles into Arizona.

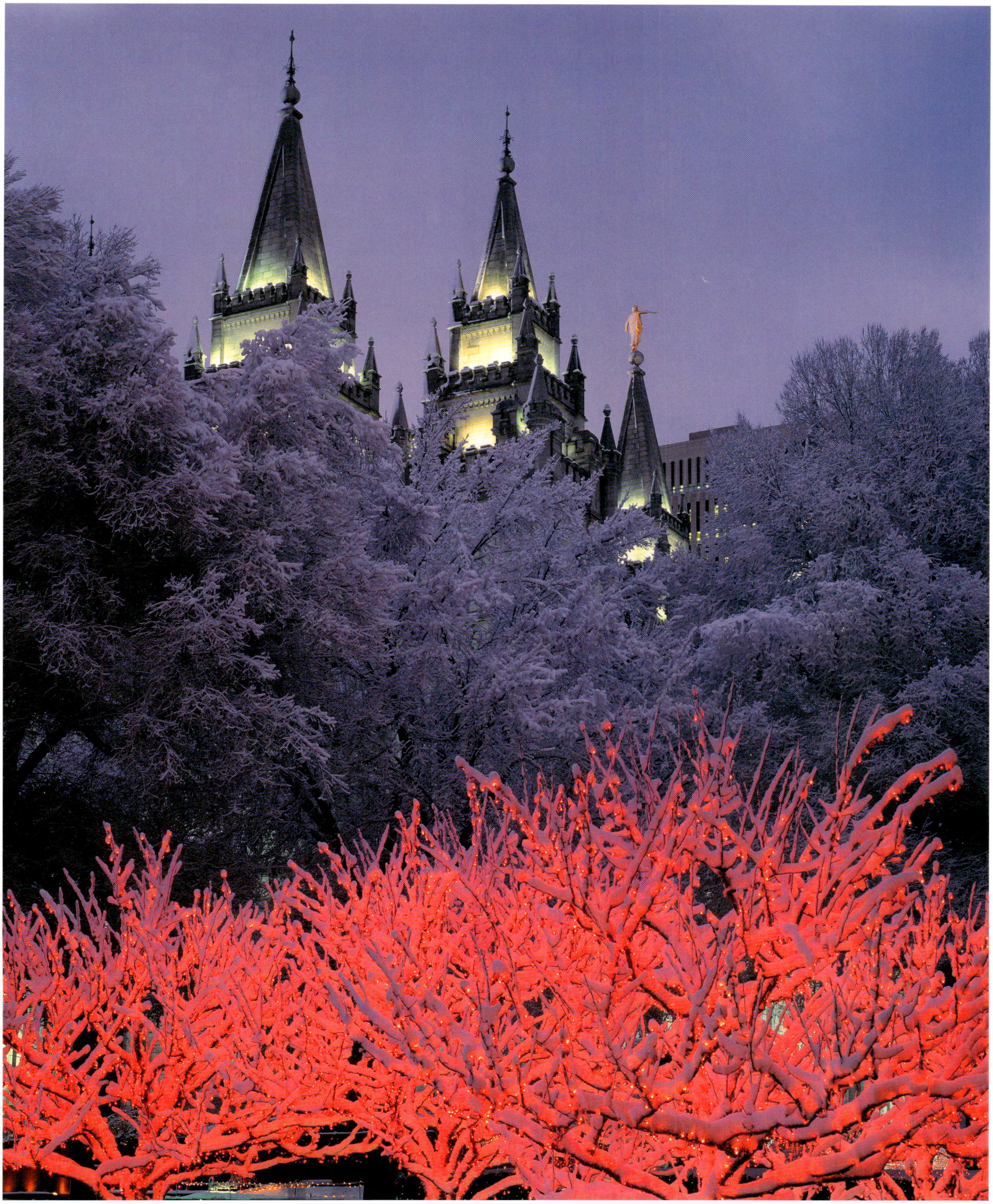

ABOVE:
Fresh snow provides a colorful focal point in this Christmas view of the Salt Lake City Church of Jesus Christ of Latter Day Saints Temple on Temple Square. The Temple decorations are always an inspiring sight, and combined with snow they are particularly stunning.

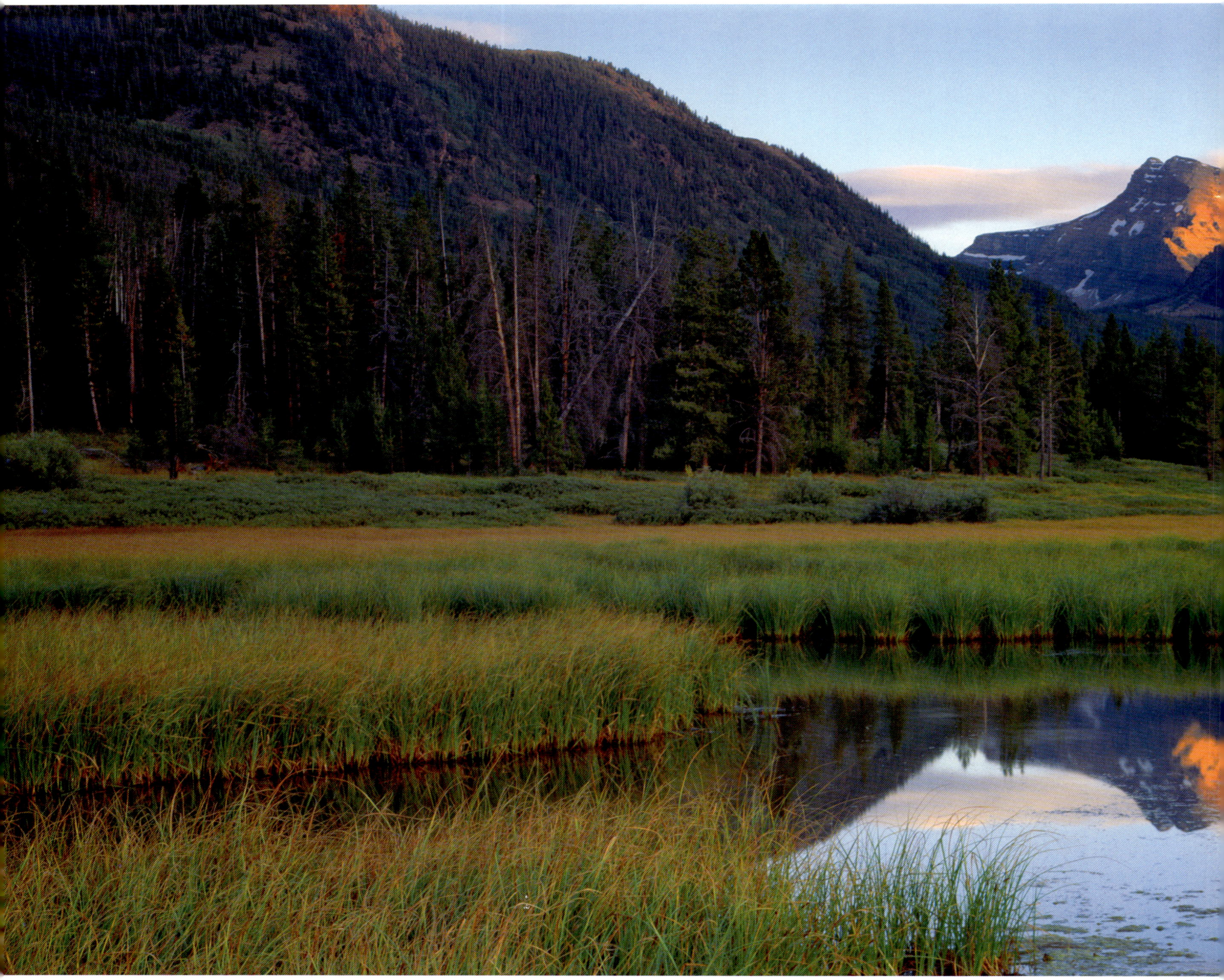

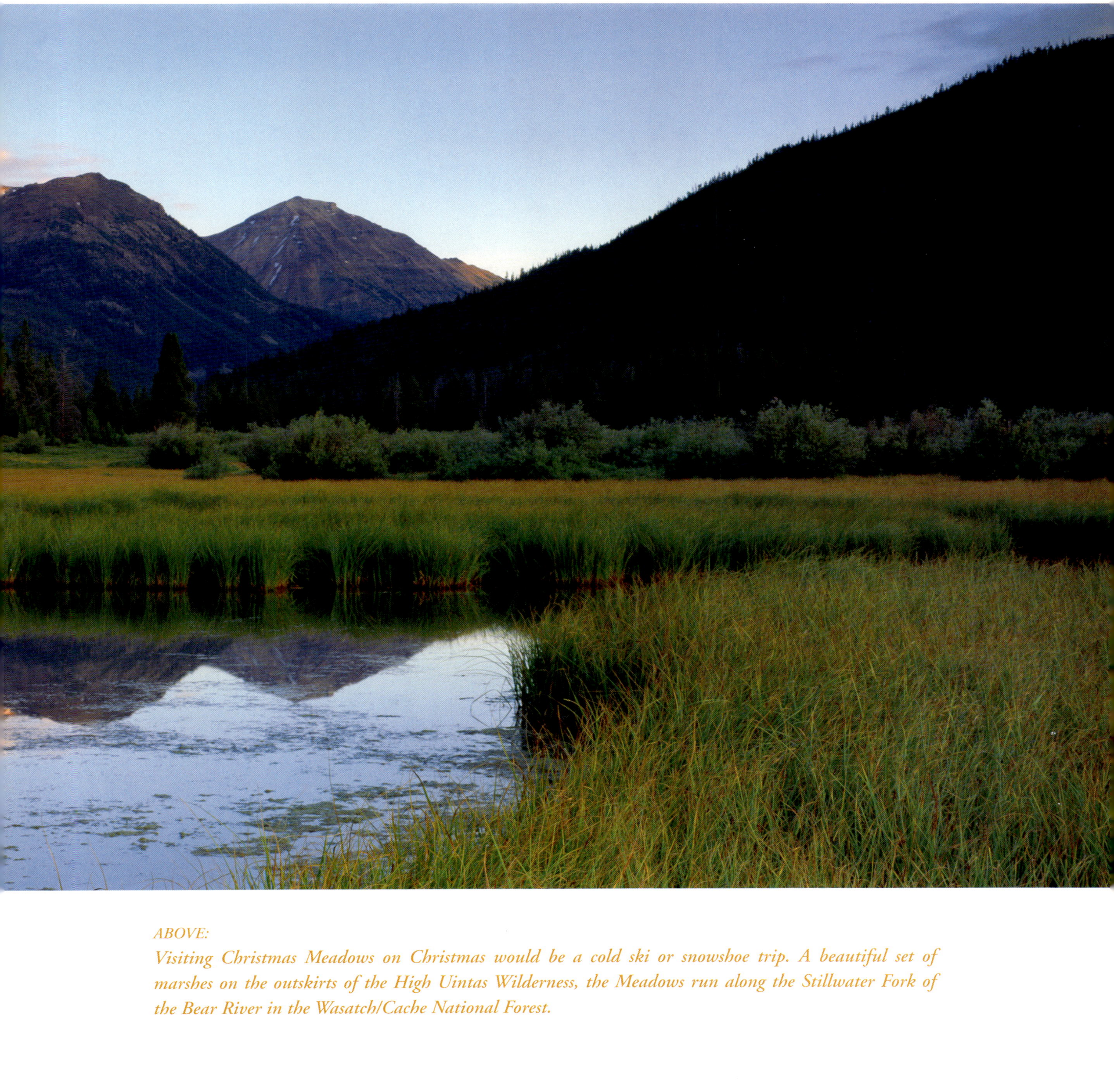

ABOVE:
Visiting Christmas Meadows on Christmas would be a cold ski or snowshoe trip. A beautiful set of marshes on the outskirts of the High Uintas Wilderness, the Meadows run along the Stillwater Fork of the Bear River in the Wasatch/Cache National Forest.

RIGHT:
High in the isolated House Range of Utah, in Utah's West Desert, a huge limestone cave opening reflects the late day sun.

The cave is reminiscent of Leviathan Cave in Nevada, and both require a long slog to the top of the range. The fact that these huge caves occur at the very top of their respective mountain ranges has always struck me as amazing and weird.

This cave is said to have the largest opening of any in Utah, although a sandstone cave near Moab also has a very large entrance.

After photographing the cave, my GPS malfunctioned and I was as lost as I have ever been. After struggling up and down ridge after ridge for hours and watching my water supply dwindle, I finally found my truck. As they say in Australia, "When you least expect it, this country will reach up and bite you on the ass."

The cave and surrounding area are part of the House Range Proposed Wilderness.

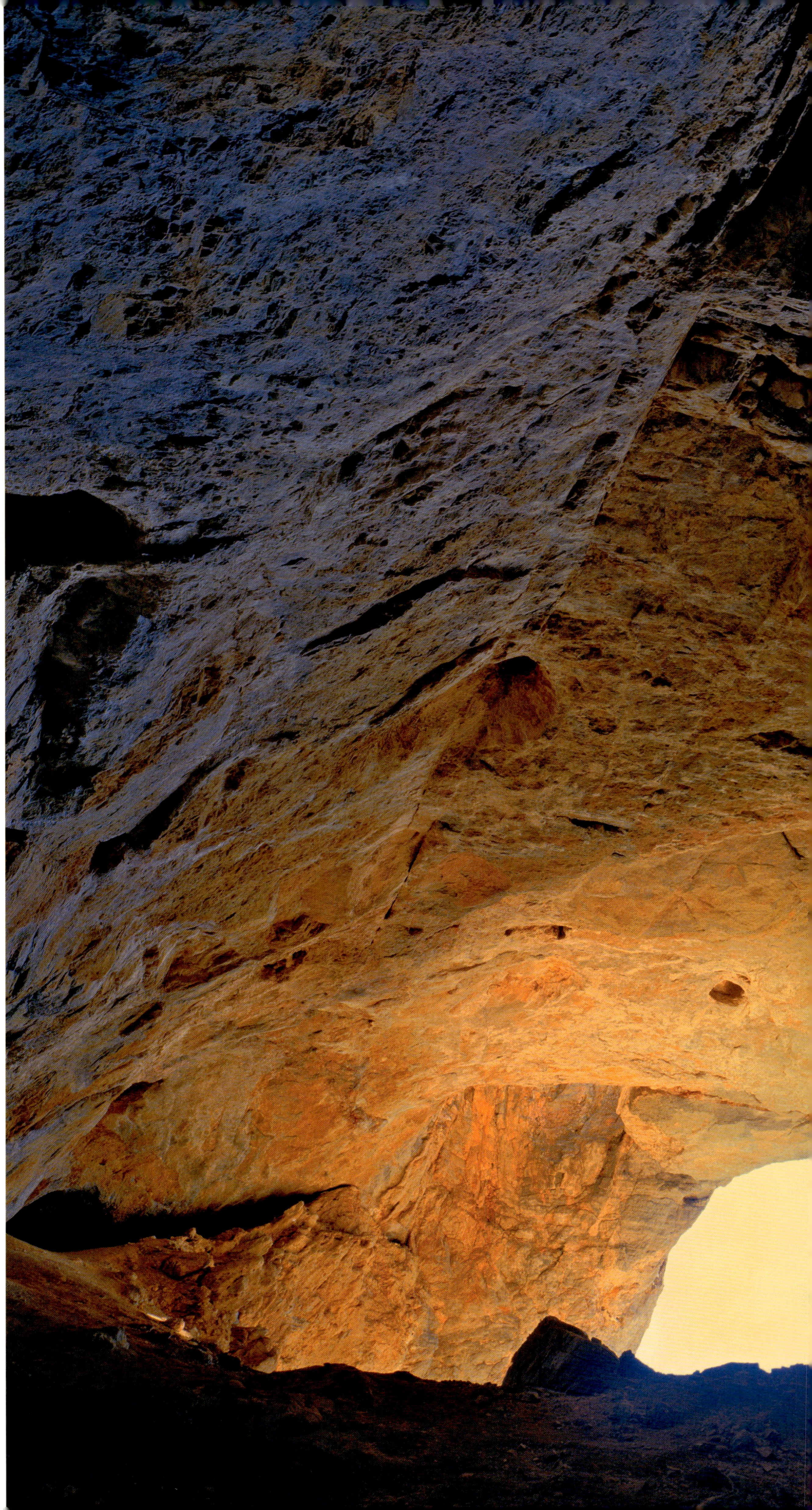

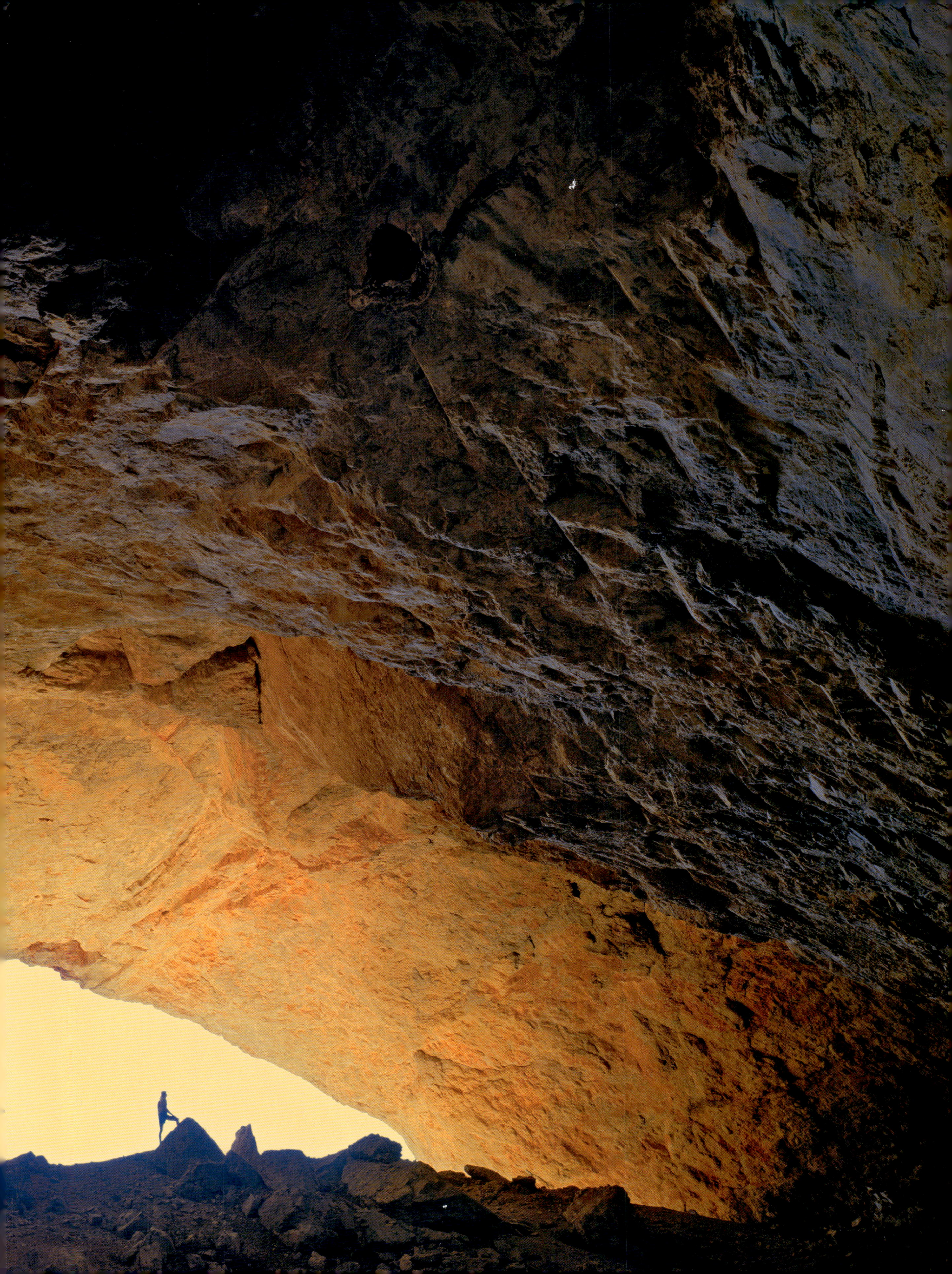

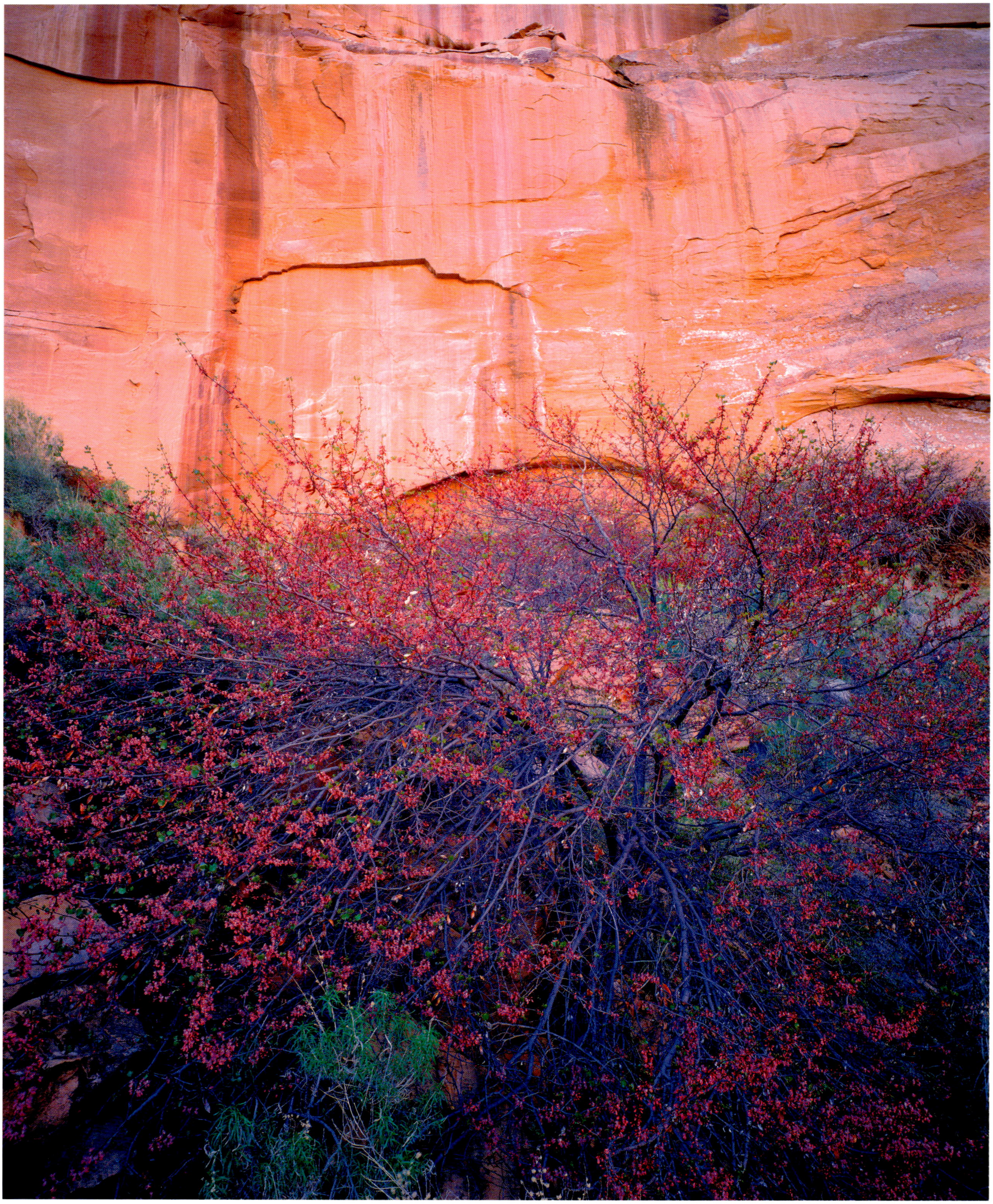

ABOVE:
Western redbud trees are rare in Utah. They inhabit only a few side canyons of Lake Powell and, so I've heard, some small niches in Grand Gulch. This tree is part of a redbud "forest", the only large concentration of the trees known.

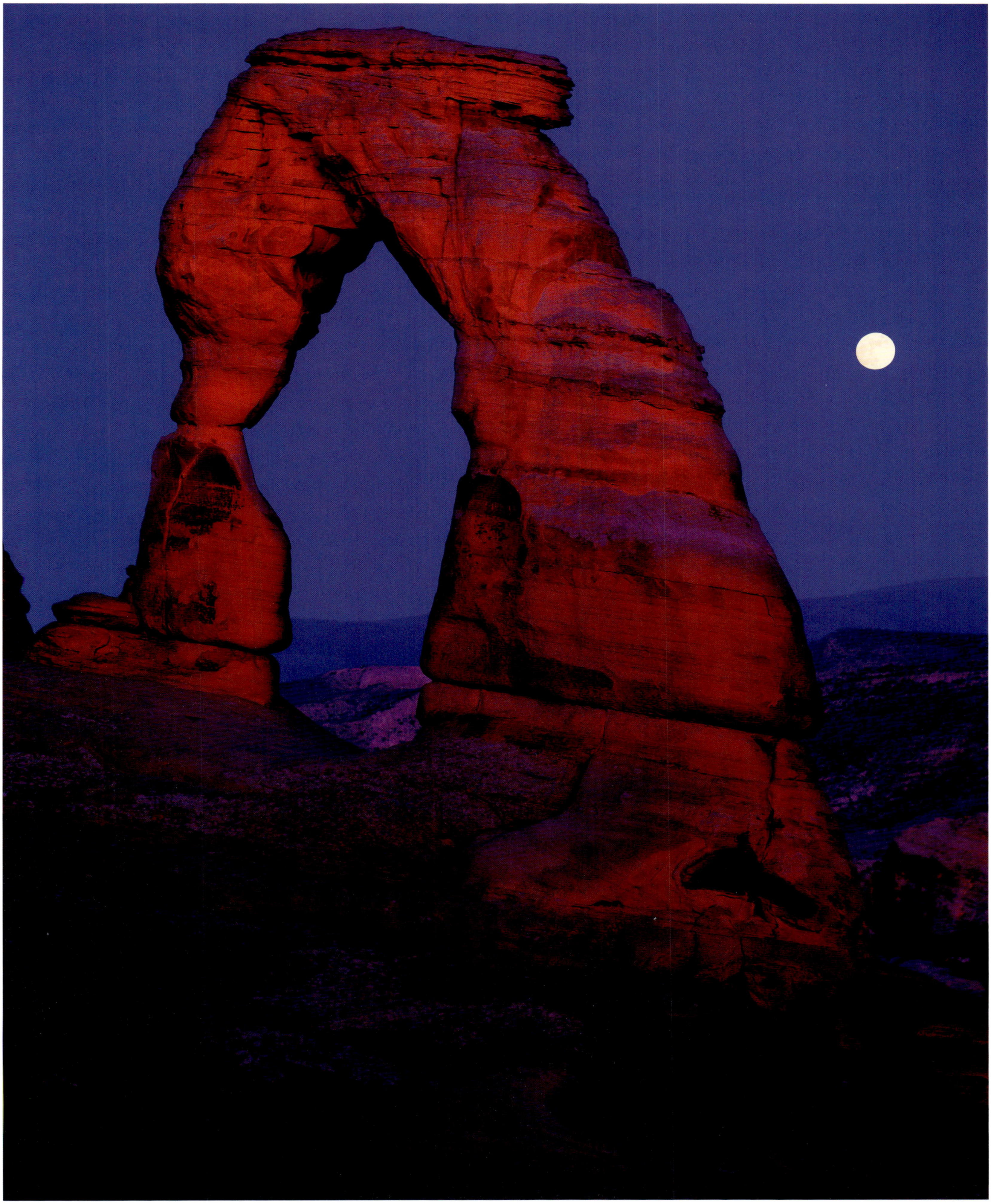

ABOVE:
A full moon rises behind Delicate Arch, which glows from a glorious sunset in the western sky. Sunsets themselves can add an unusual-looking warmth to a subject by reflecting their colors back to the east. Most of the photographs of Delicate Arch you may have seen with the moon directly inside the arch are double exposures.

BELOW:

Snow at Goblin Valley State Park would usually be a short-lived event. Most snow in Southern Utah melts quickly when the sun appears. Once in awhile, though, it gets really cold. After this snowfall, the temperature stayed below freezing for several days, dropping well below zero at night.

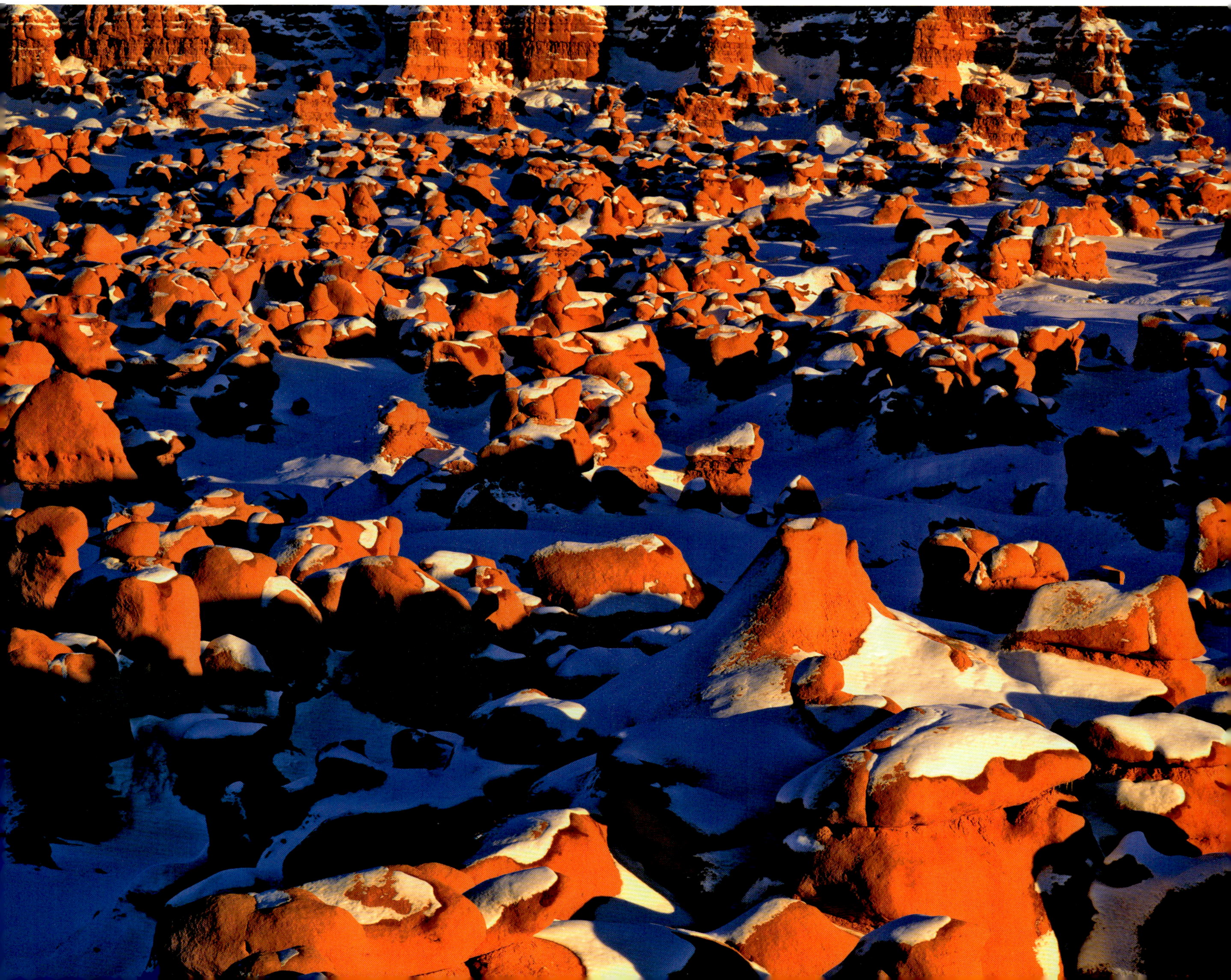

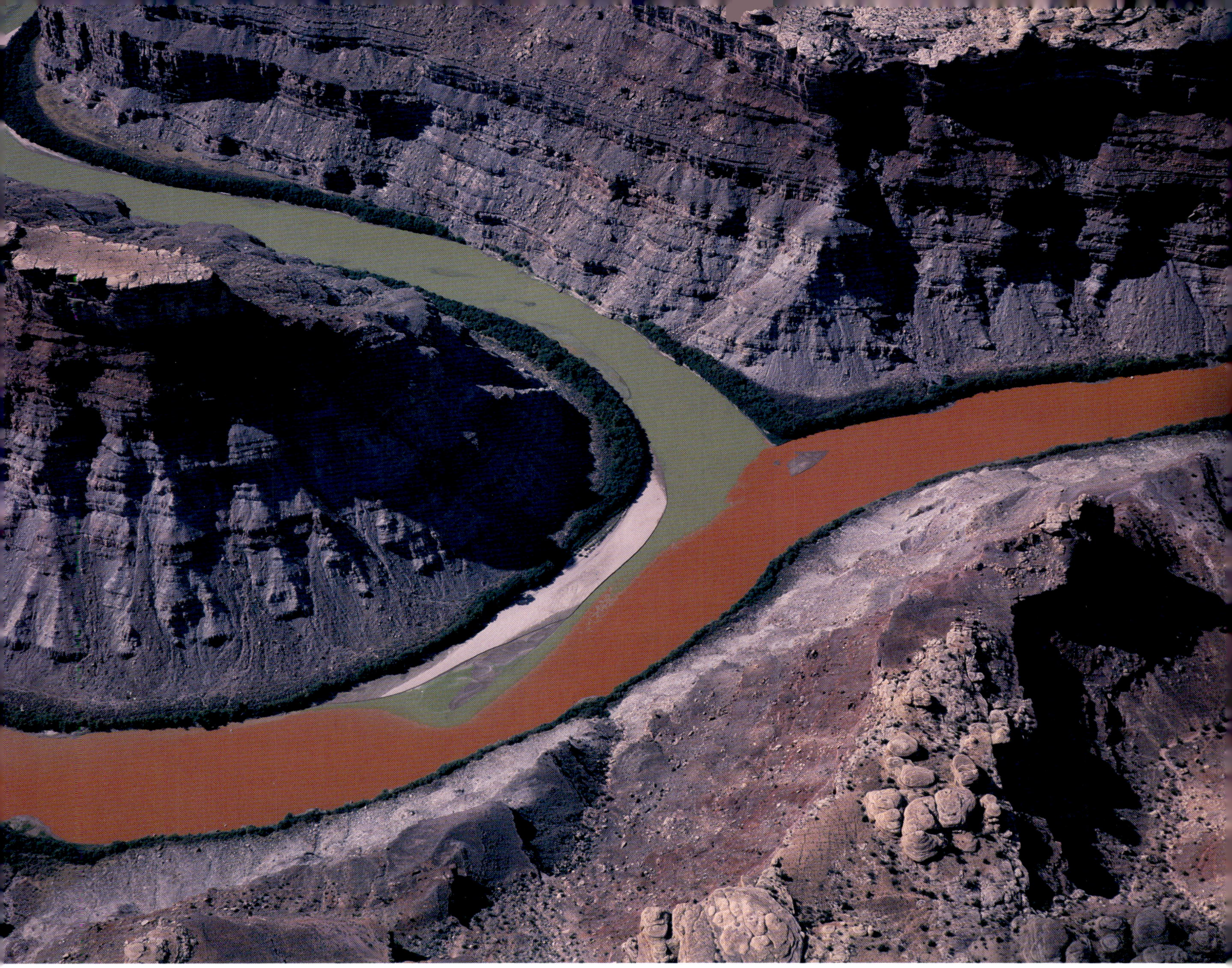

ABOVE:
The Green and Colorado (red) rivers combine at the Confluence in Canyonlands National Park. Due to heavy rains and the flooding of certain washes (one is called Bloody Mary) on the Colorado side of the drainage, the river can run blood red. In the Green River drainage, if no downpours or cloudbursts have happened, the river maintains its prescribed green color, providing a brilliant contrast when they meet. I asked the pilots at Canyonlands Field near Moab to call me if they ever saw such an event happening, and Tim Martin, famous for flying his airplane through many arches in the Moab area, alerted me that a red surge was headed down the river to the Confluence. I rushed to the airport and flew with Tim down to the park, where we were treated to the proverbial meeting of colored waters.

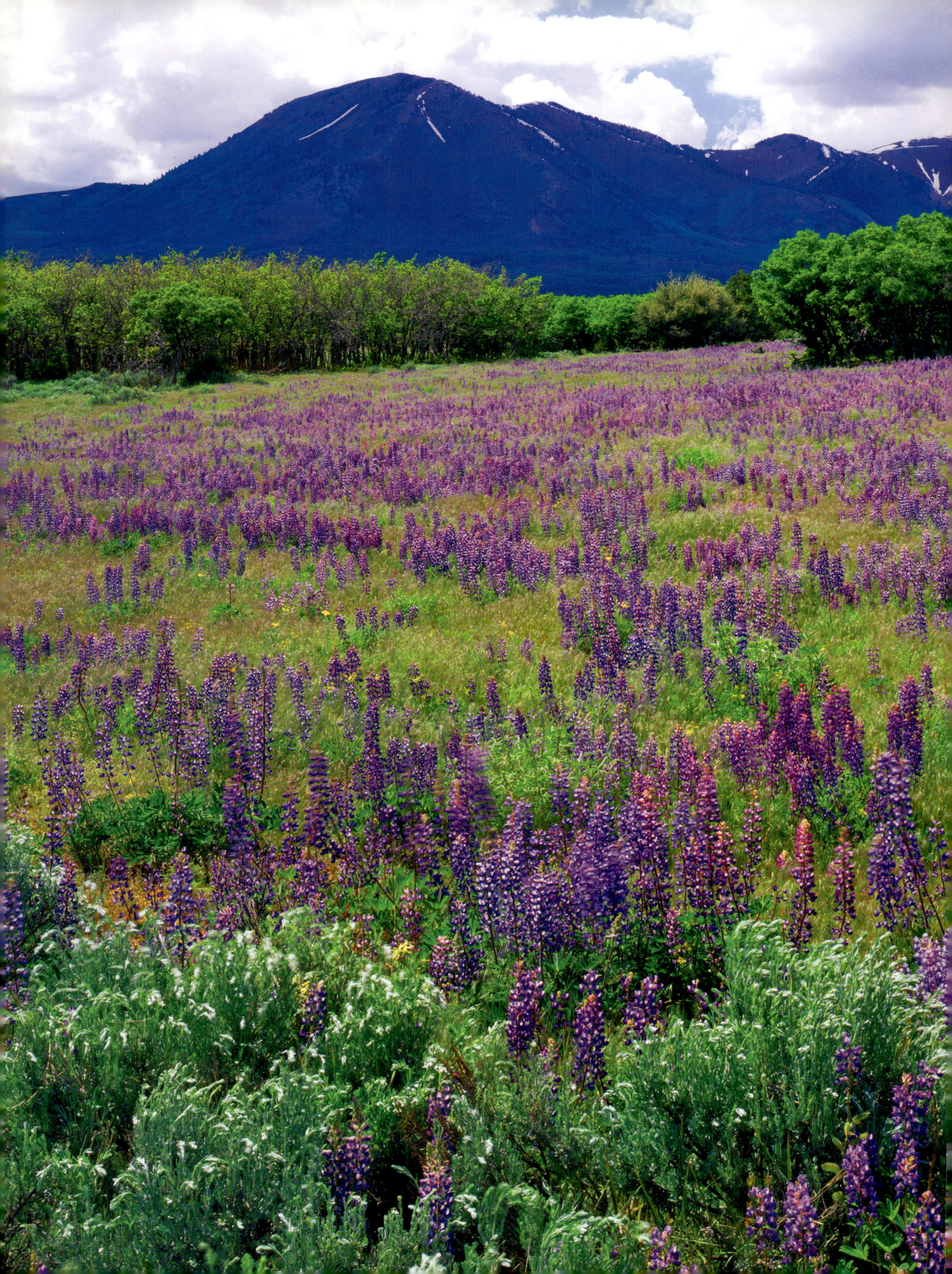

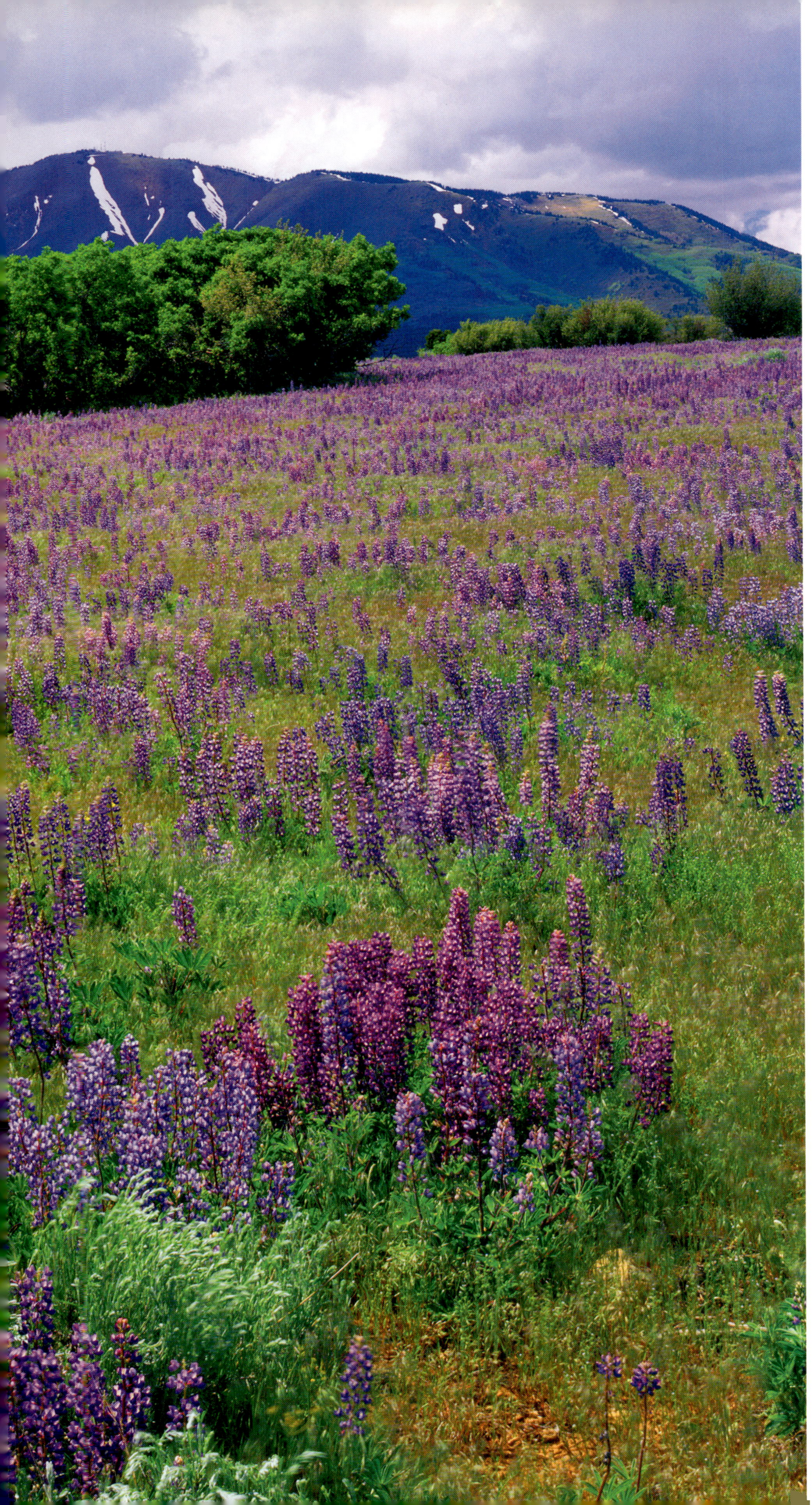

LEFT:
A field of lupine adds a splash of color below the Abajo (Blue) Mountains in the Manti-La Sal National Forest.

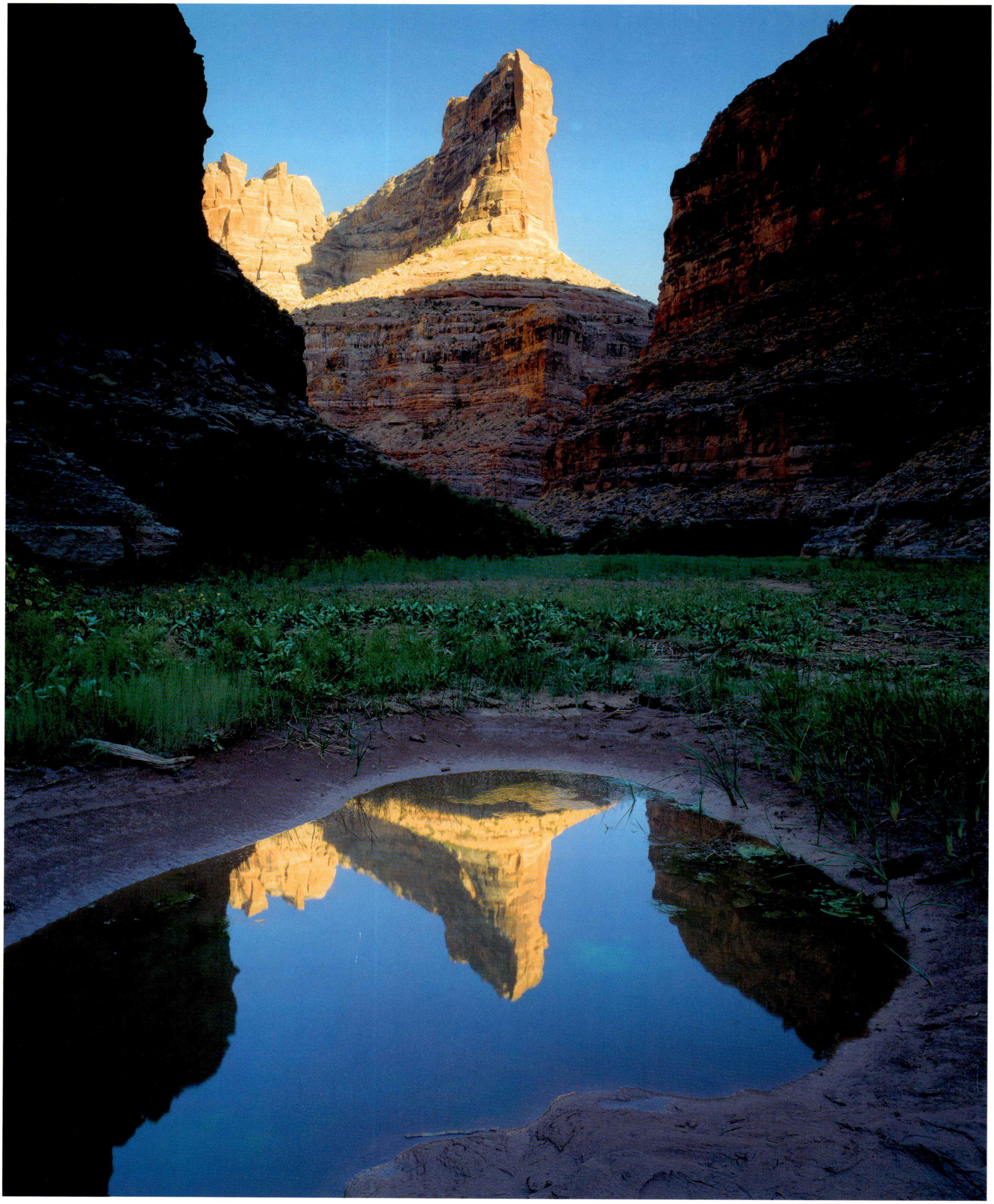

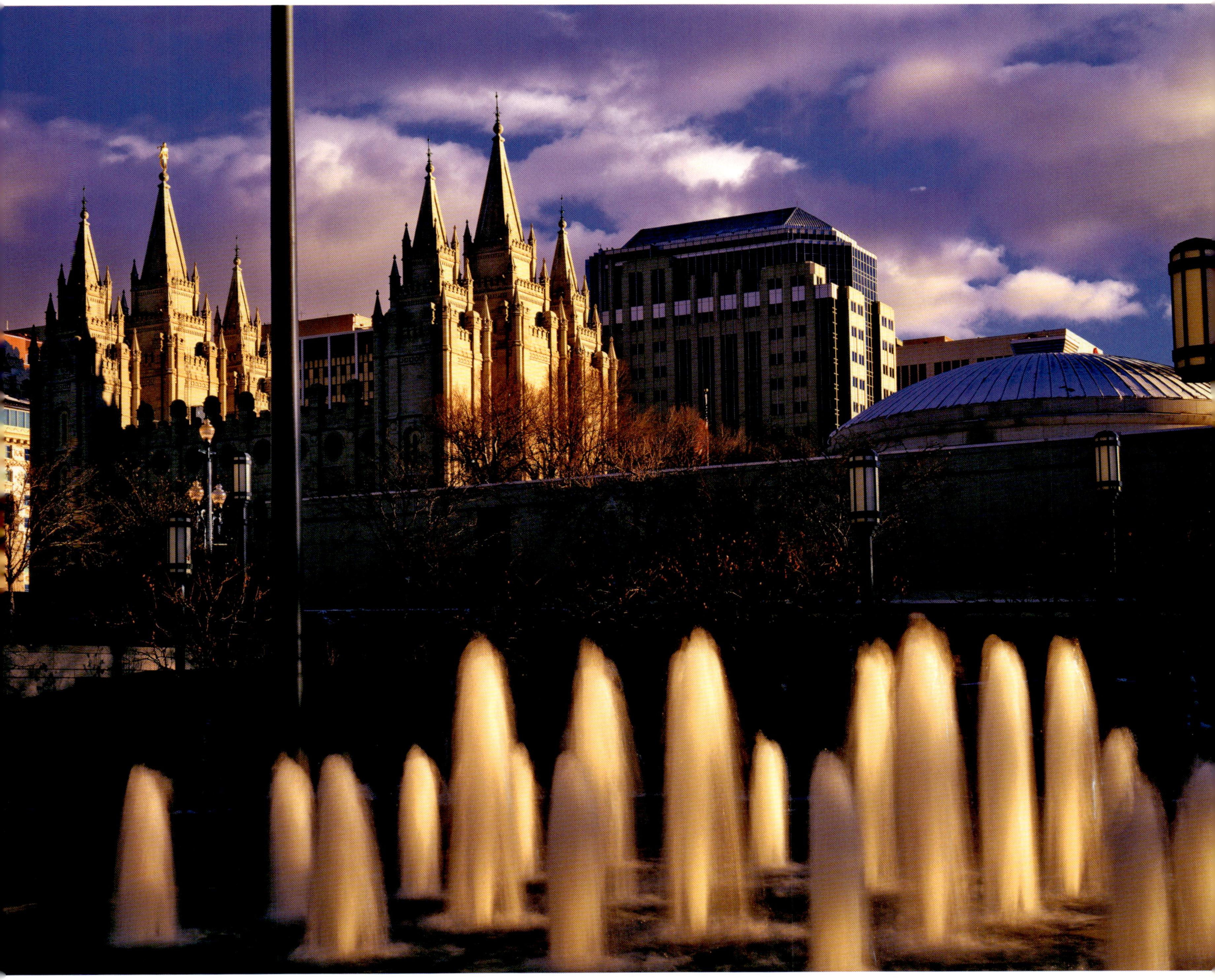

ABOVE:
Fountains near the new LDS Conference Center provide a background for the Salt Lake Temple.

LEFT:
A wonderful pinnacle in Dark Canyon is reflected in a small pool. Dark Canyon is a big, long canyon which empties into lower Cataract Canyon, now a part of Lake Powell. The first time I flew over Dark Canyon, I was amazed at its size and complexity. Part of the canyon is a designated wilderness, while the BLM portion is still only a wilderness study area.

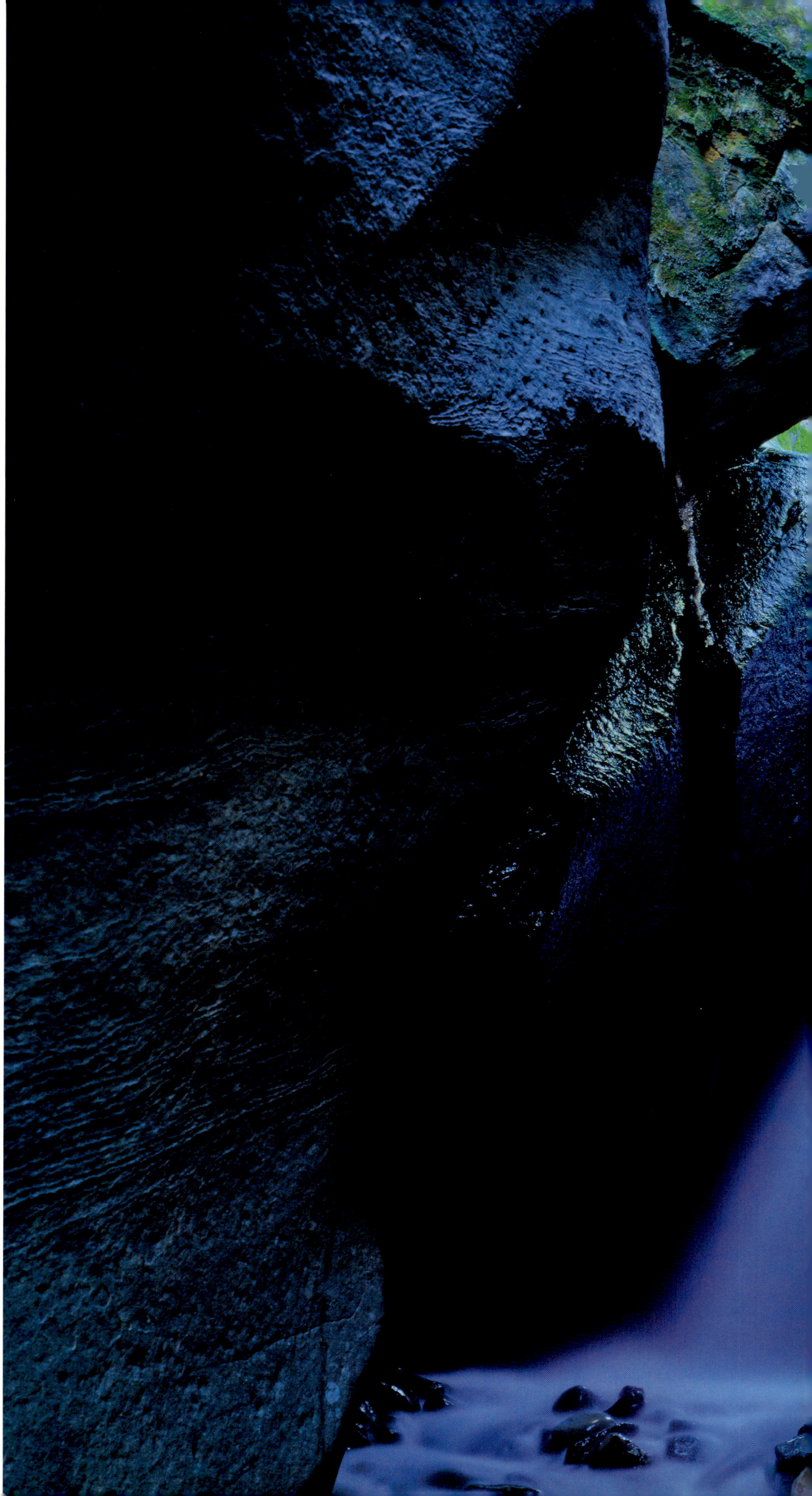

RIGHT:
Inside an alpine slot canyon, a waterfall crashes through a narrow cave in the La Sal Mountains. Approaching this location required some rope work and wading through limb-numbing frigid waters.

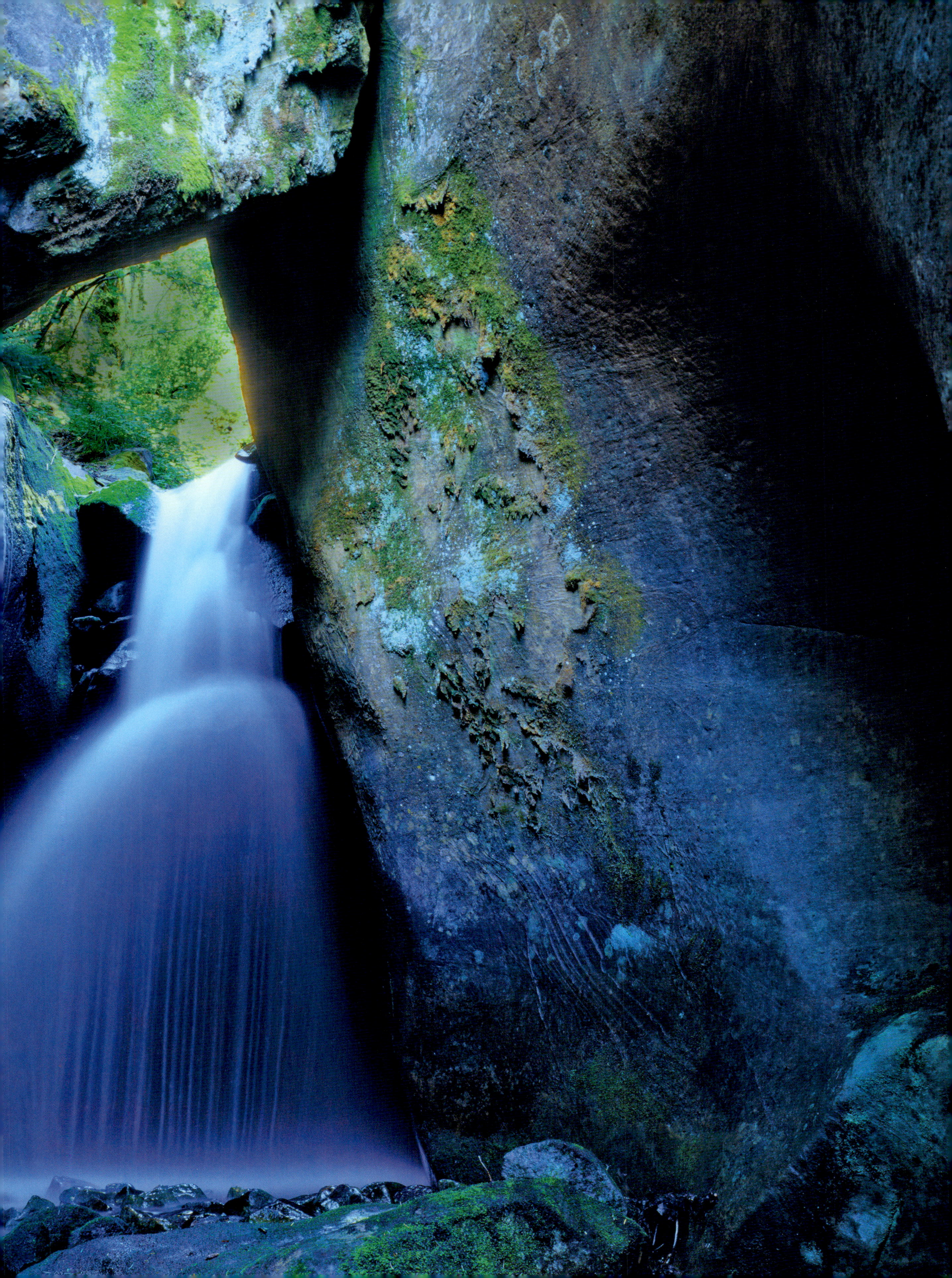

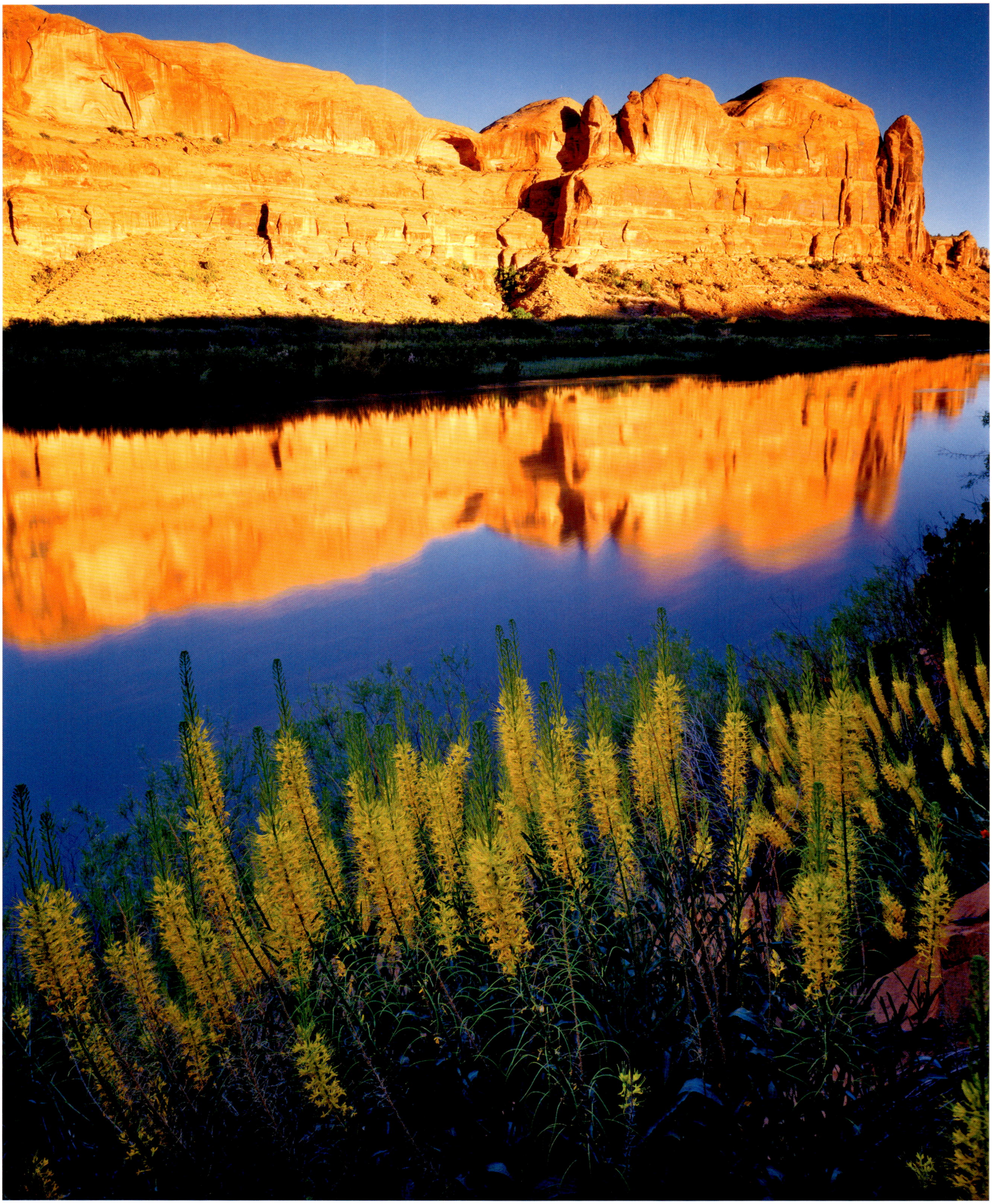

ABOVE:
Prince's plume blooms glow yellow at dawn on the Colorado River near Moab.

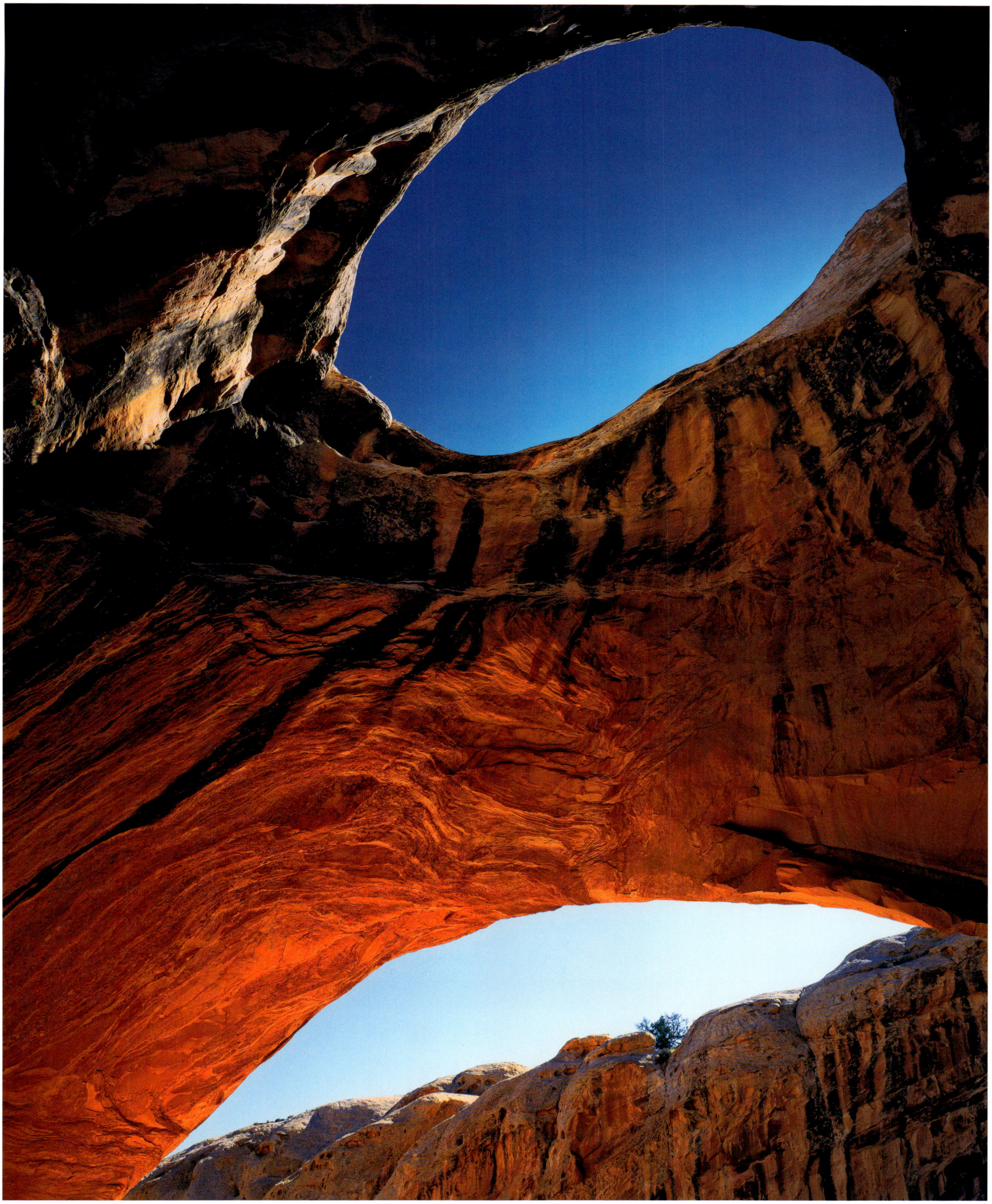

ABOVE:
A double arch glows from reflected light inside the San Rafael Swell. These rock openings are one of many spectacular features in this area, including Mystery Arch, another double span that stands high on the slopes of the Swell.

BELOW:
Though I rarely photograph wildlife, I was able to capture this detail of a peregrine-falcon wing. The image was made of a living bird that was recuperating in a Moab raptor hospital. It was reintroduced into the wild a short time later.

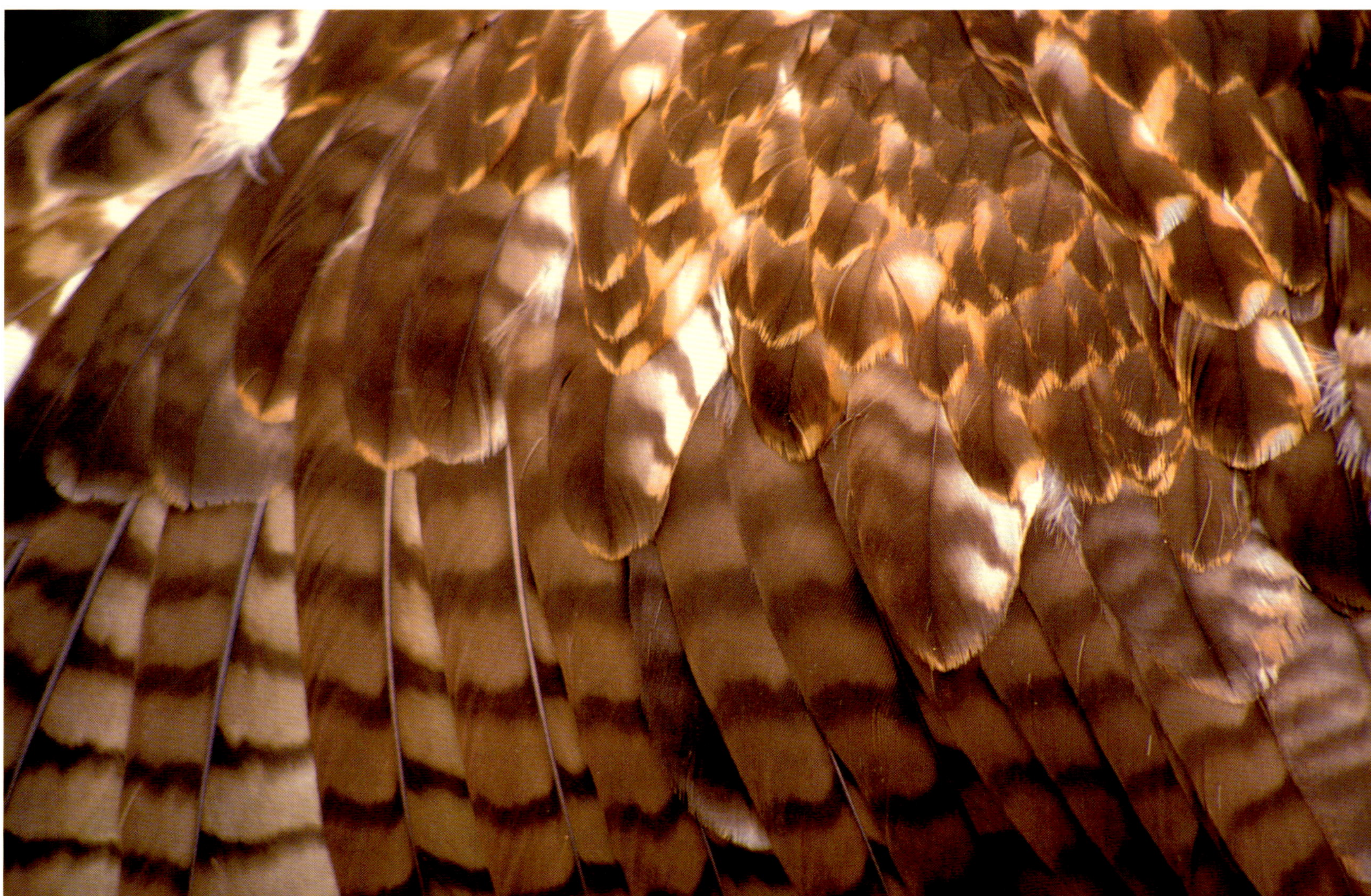

RIGHT:
During some spring seasons, the stars are right for prolific blooms of prickly-pear cactus. This beautiful group of flowers was found in Arches National Park.

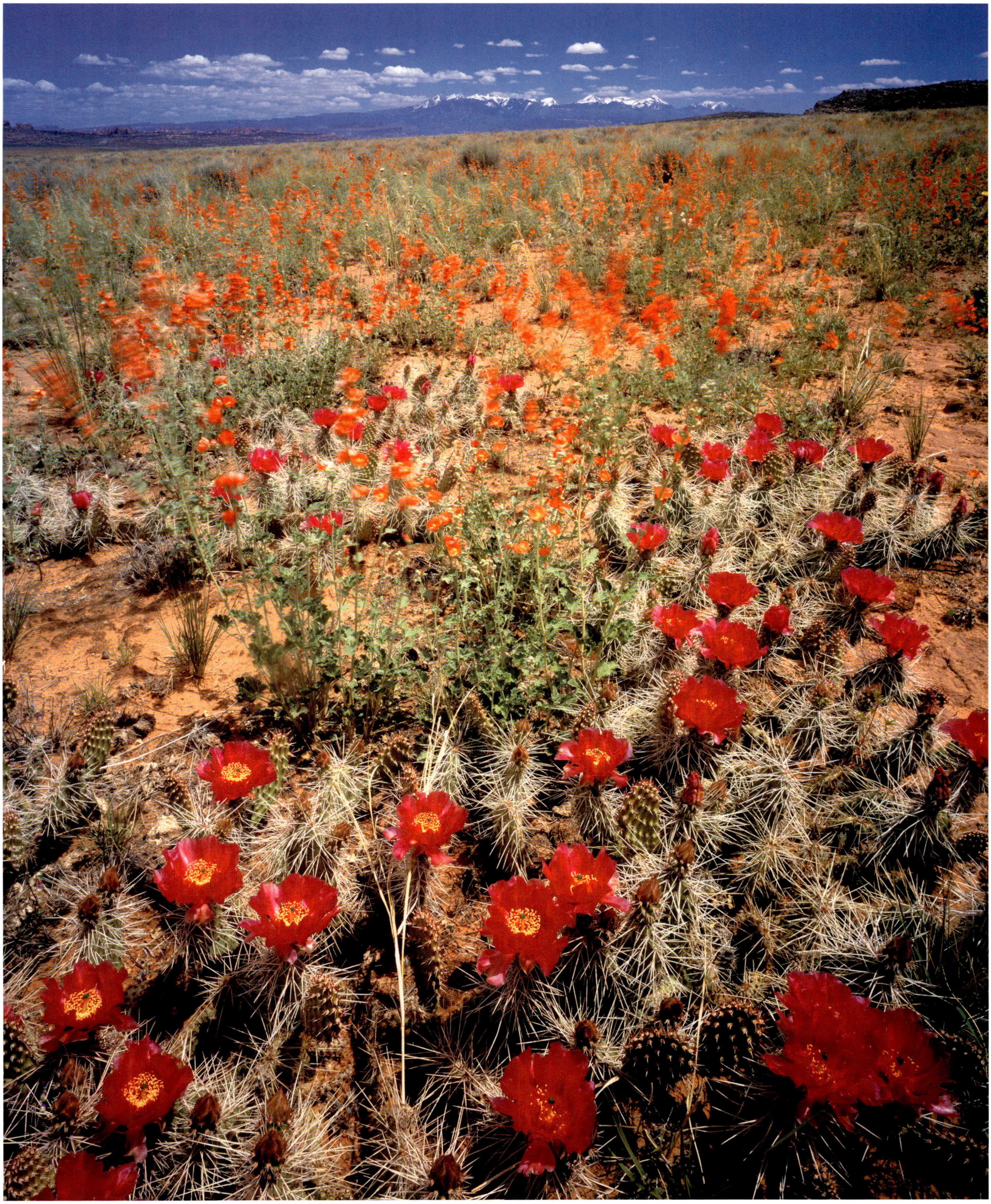

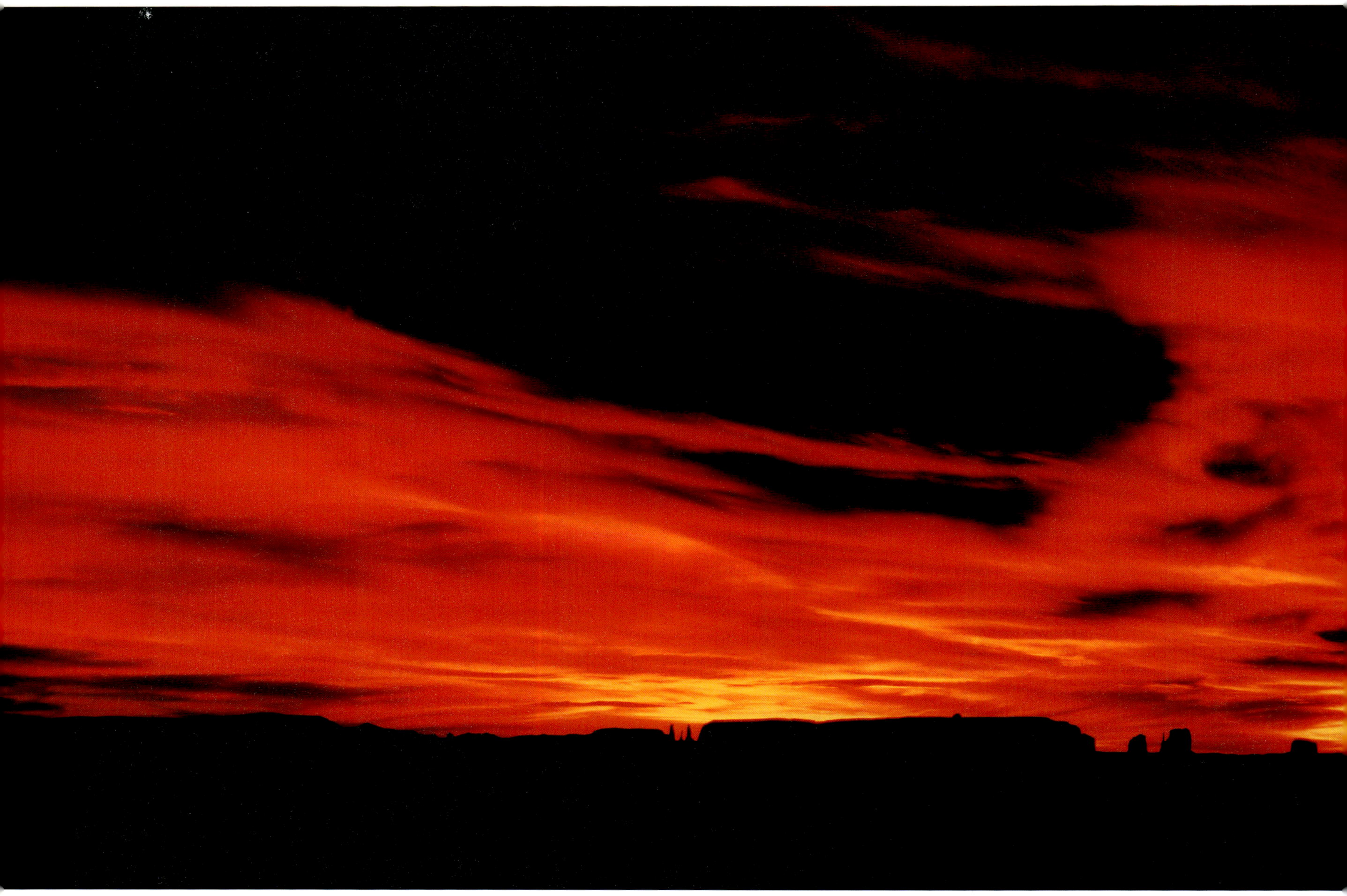

ABOVE:
The many spires of Monument Valley stand below a magnificent sunset.
In looking at the image upside down, another interesting landscape appears.

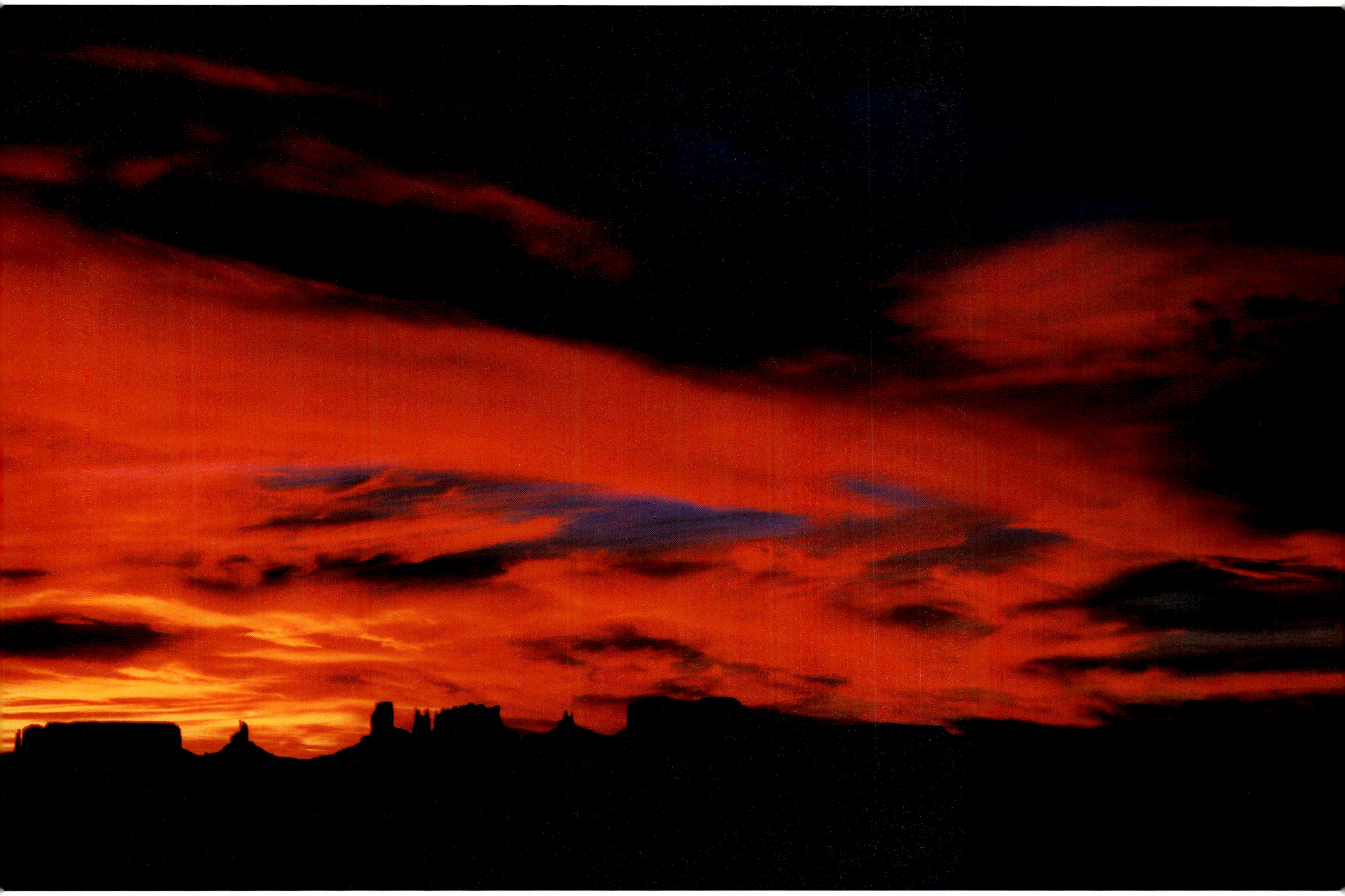

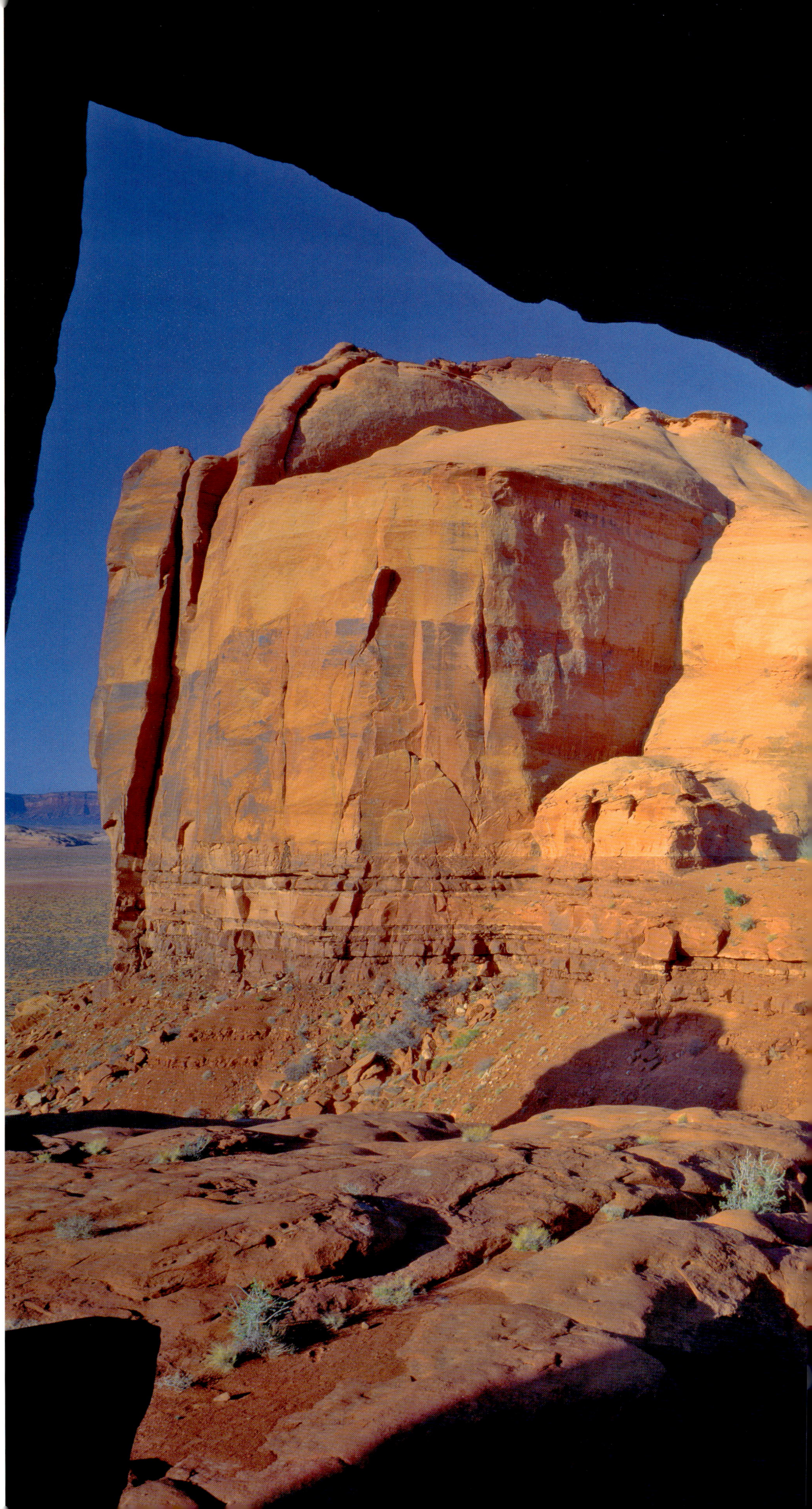

RIGHT:
Tucked away and hidden from the frenetic pace of modern life, an Ancestral Puebloan ruin stands as it has throughout the centuries, so far unscathed.

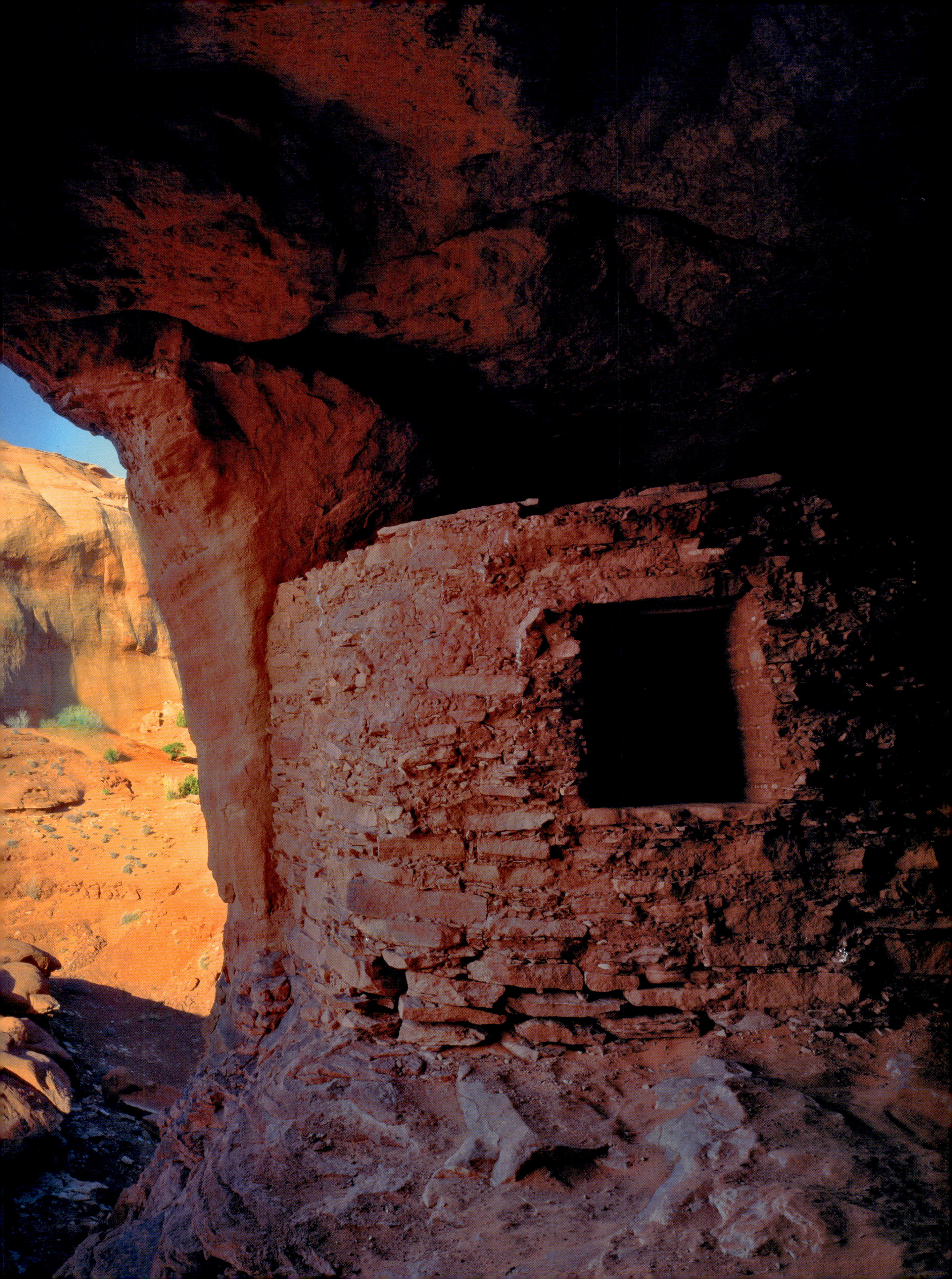

BELOW:

I hate to whine, but lugging fifty pounds of 4x5 camera gear to the top of Deseret Peak was an epic hike. After using all my film on this beautiful snag at the top of the mountain, I committed the cardinal sin for a professional photographer. I ran out of film while an over-the-top sunset played out over the Great Salt Lake before me. This has happened to me four times in my career and each event is still an unhealed wound.

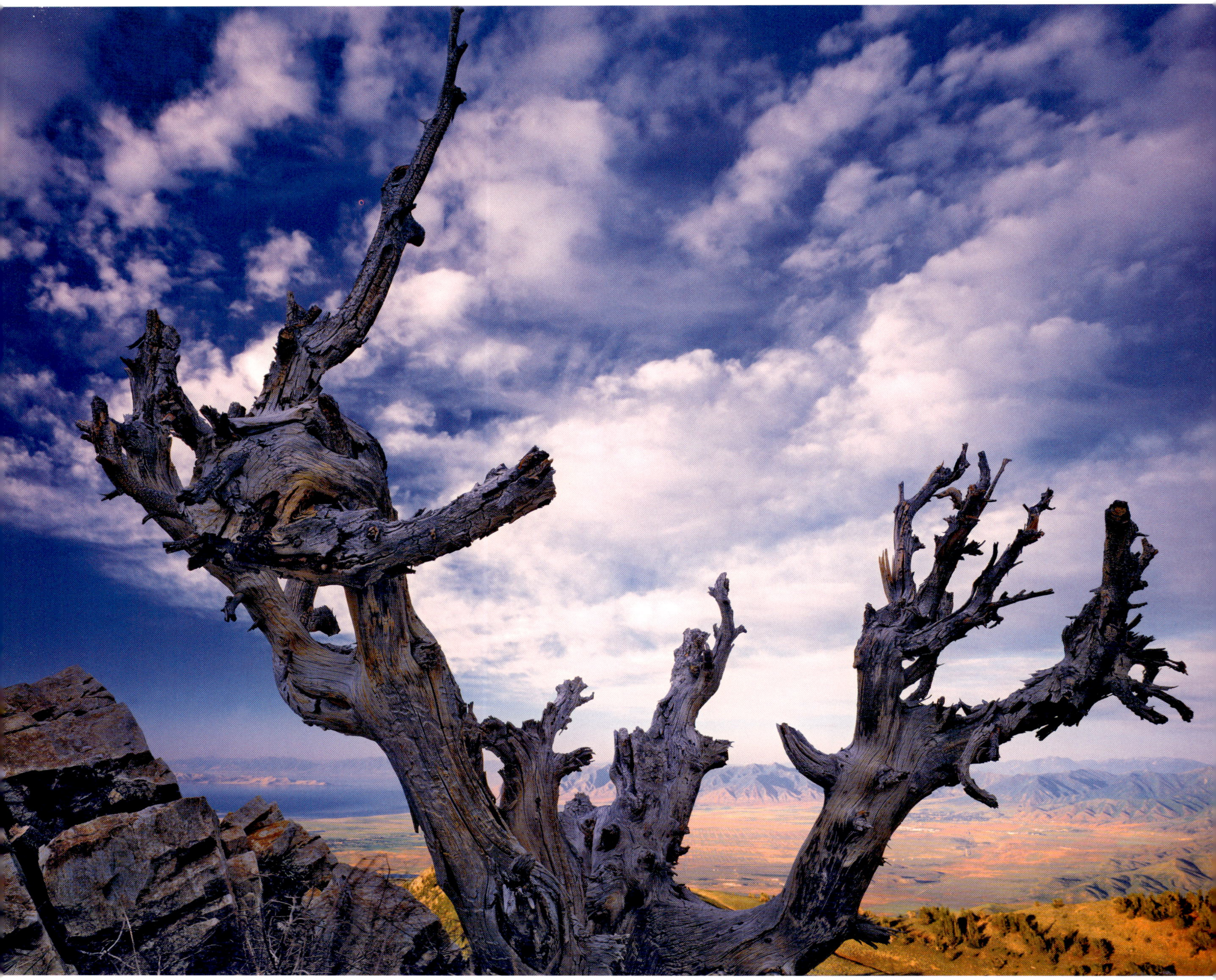

RIGHT:

These fragile towers stand deep in the wilderness of Grand Staircase/Escalante National Monument. After ten years of fighting the designation of this spectacularly beautiful piece of Utah landscape, opponents were finally all but stopped in 2006 when the courts sided with the government and agreed that President Clinton was within his rights in creating this park, using the same law that created Grand Canyon, Zion, and dozens of other parks that we take for granted today.

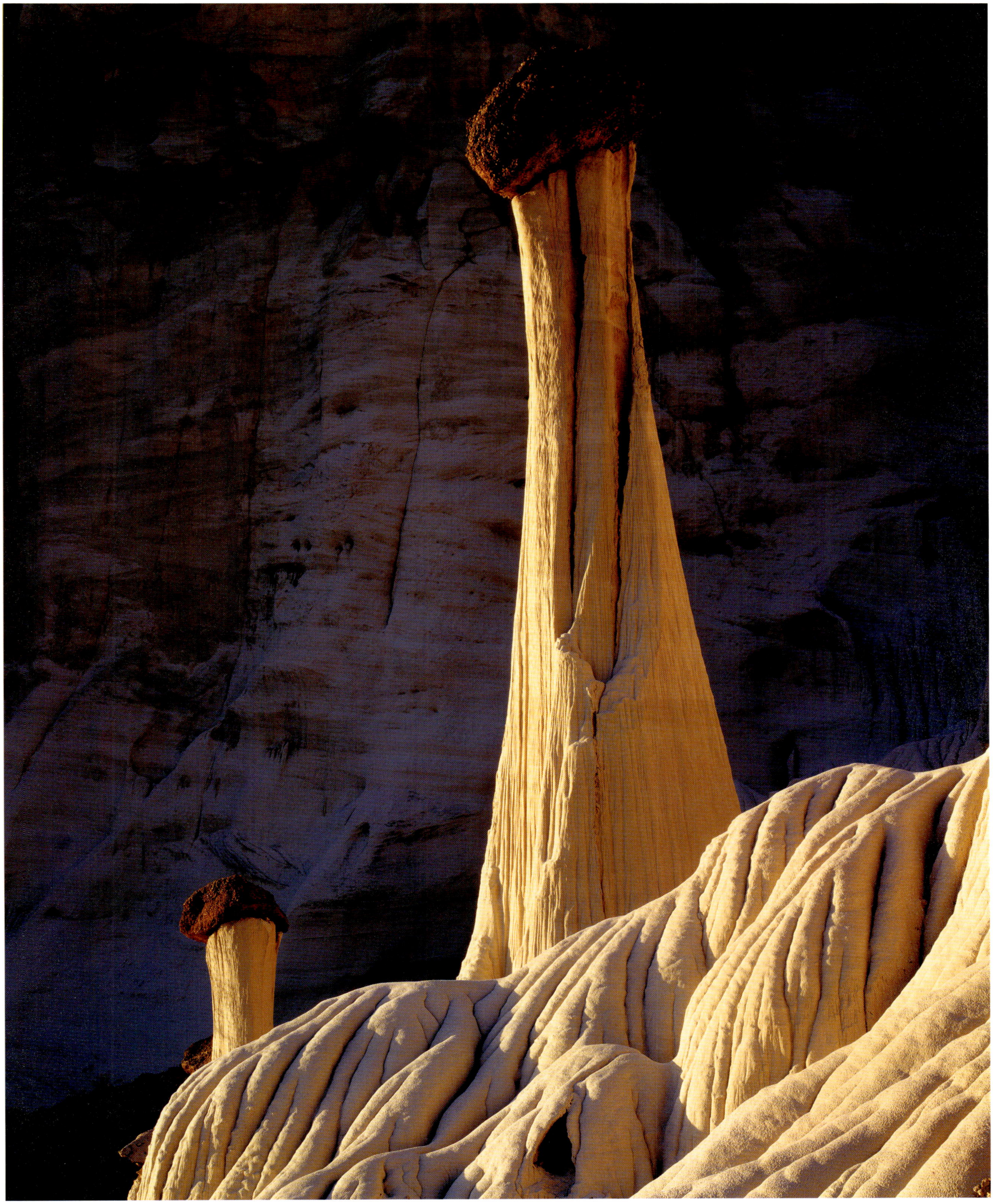

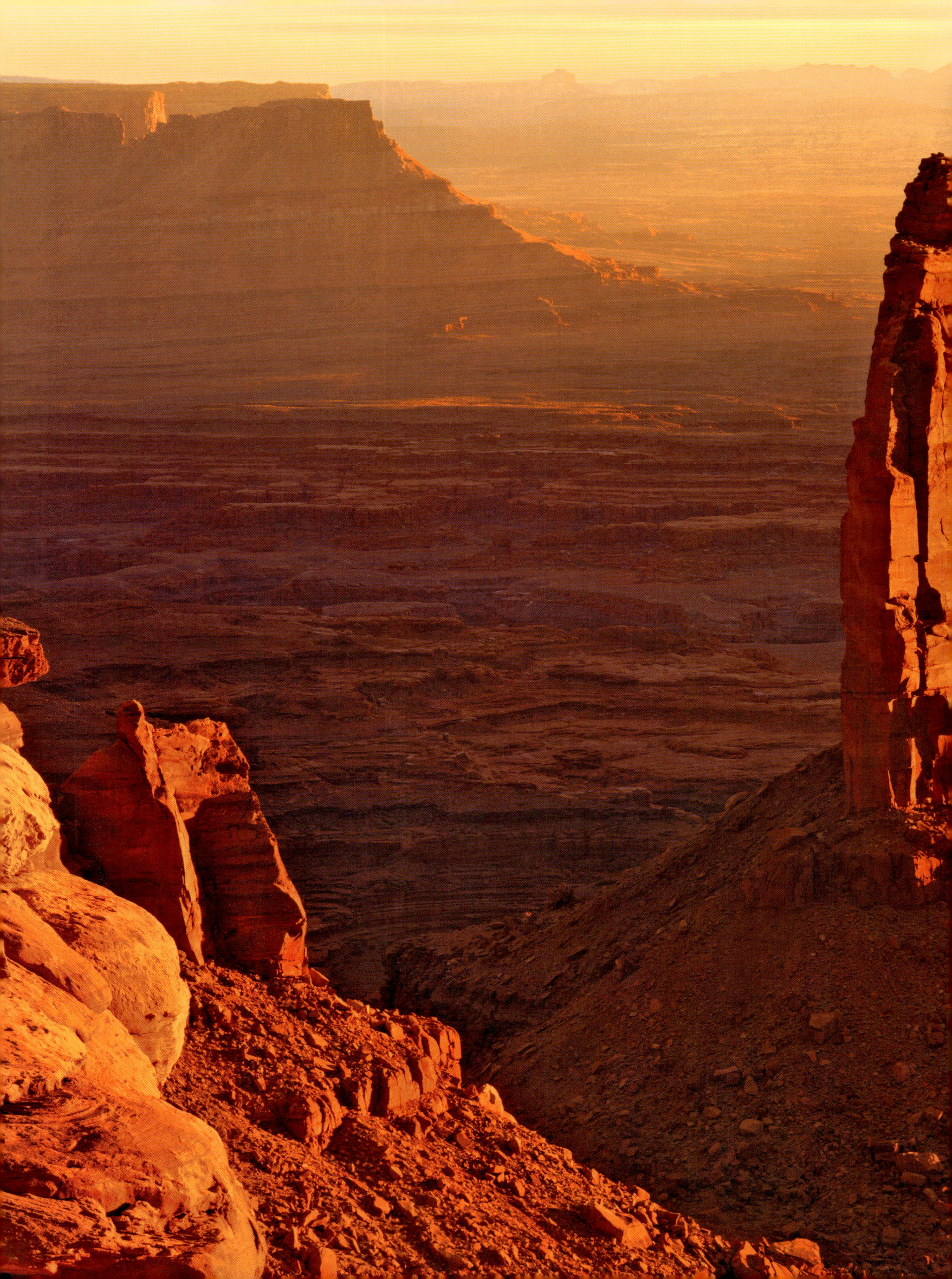

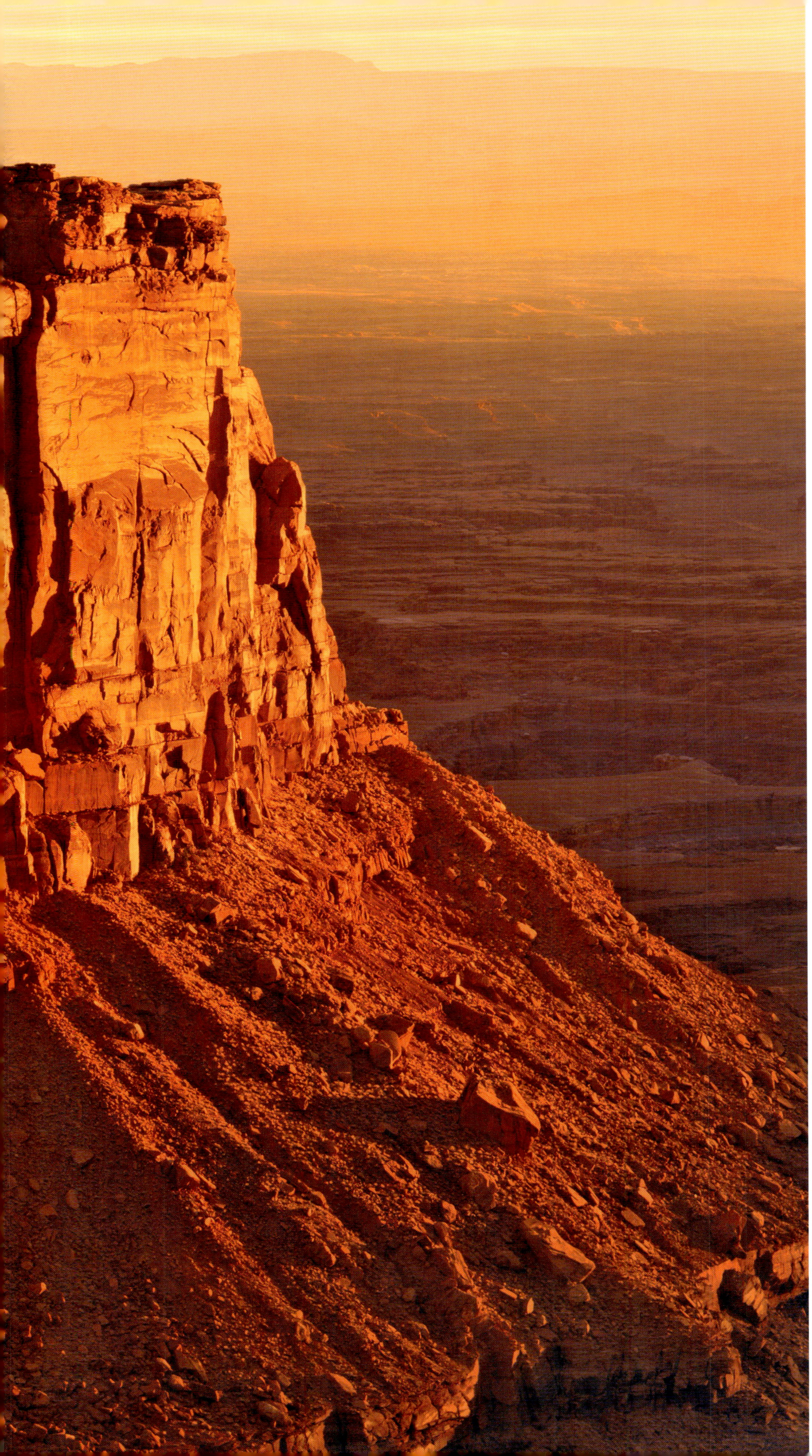

LEFT:
A huge butte seen from the eastern rim of the Canyonlands Basin is highlighted by forest-fire haze.

Environmentalists have always had a dream of a rim-to-rim park with Canyonlands, which would protect the landscape in this scene and thousands of acres of beautiful wild lands.

Several areas in this vicinity are important to the energy exploration industry, so in the present climate this dream may never become a reality.

Planet Utah:
the Great Salt Lake

When I showed some of these aerial photographs of the northeastern arm of the Great Salt Lake to friends, they said the psychedelic imagery reminded them of photos on the surface of Mars or the African Rift Valley. Salt is the main agent at work here, producing startling landscapes even for Utah.

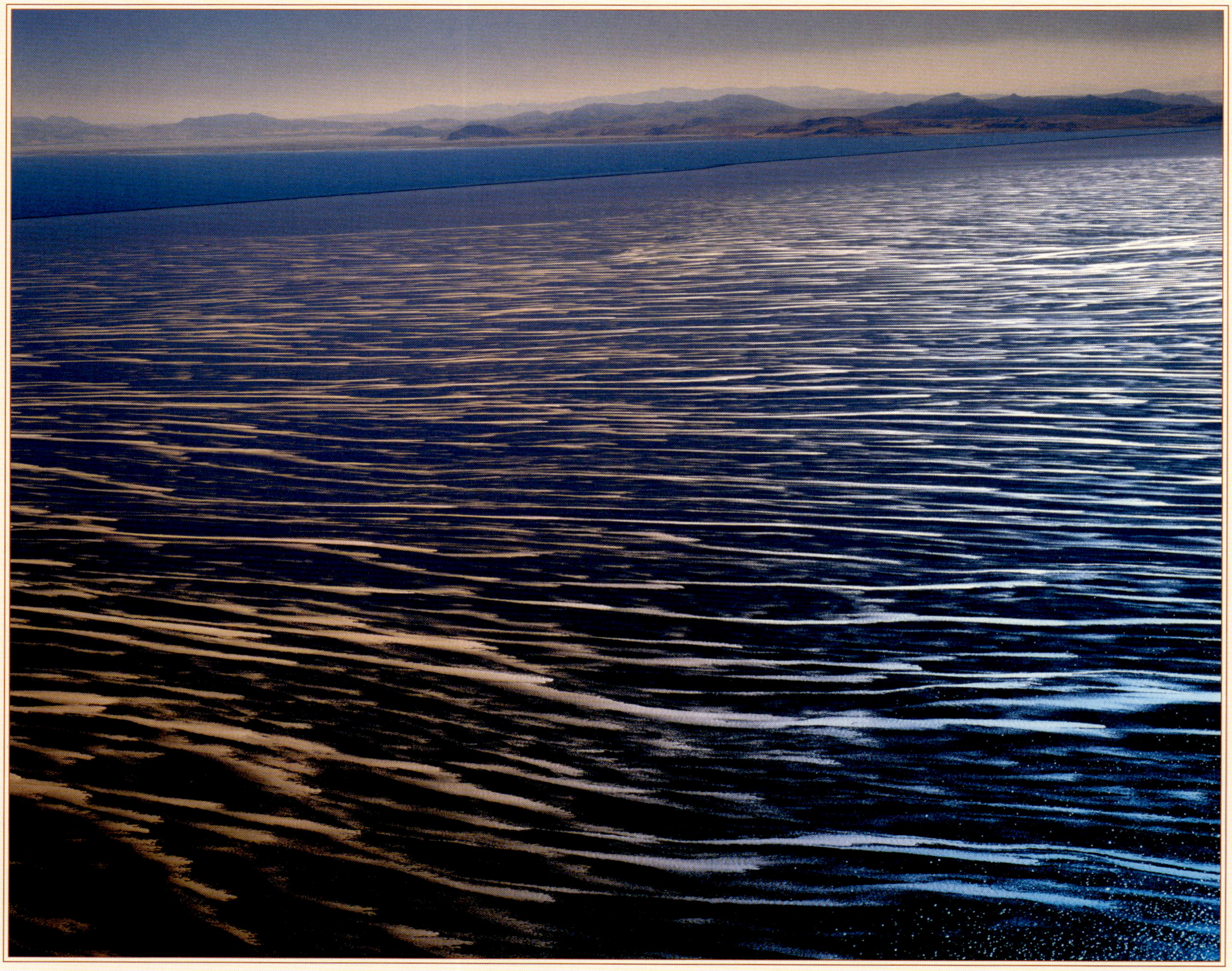

Salt forms create amazing patterns as they are shepherded by the wind.

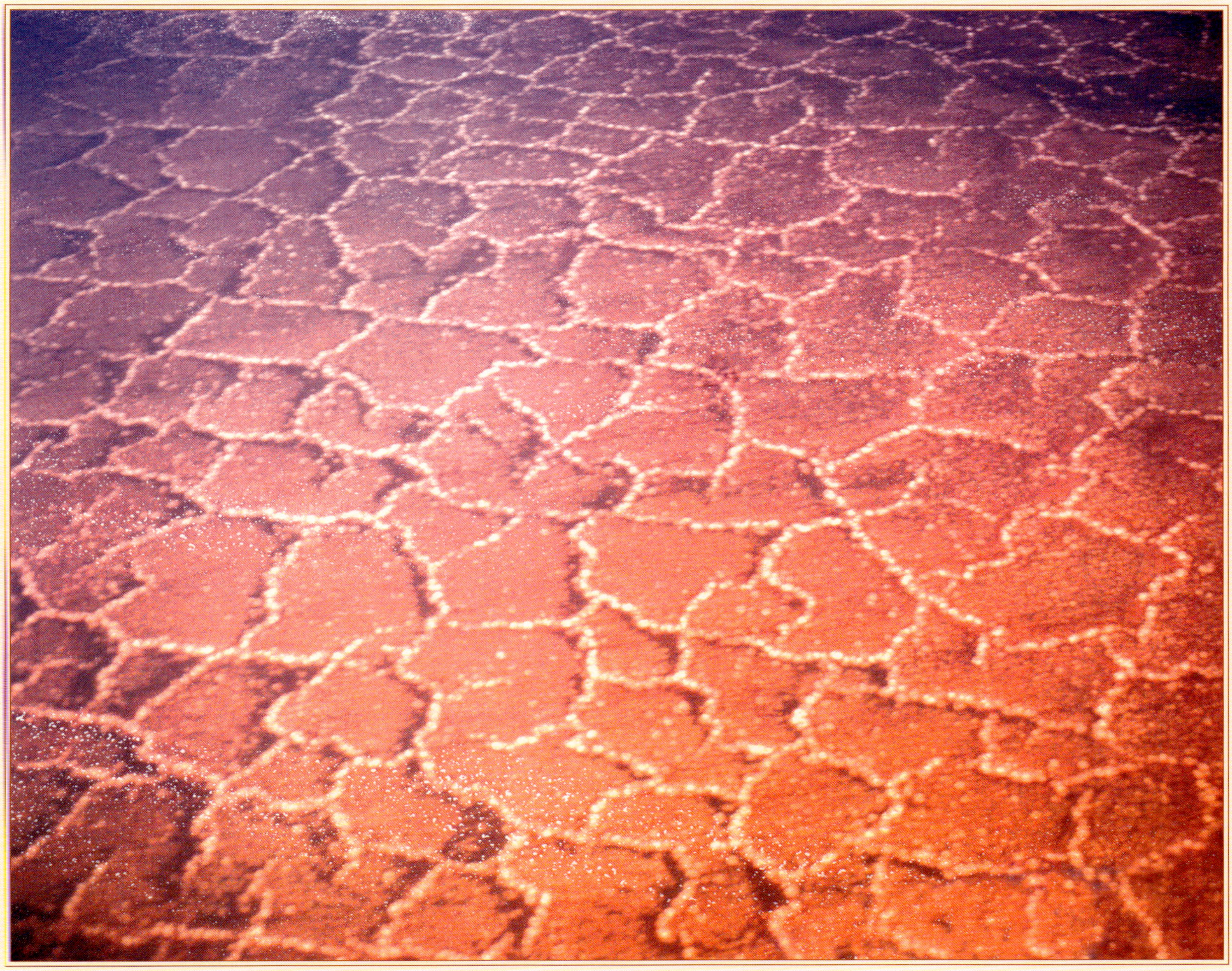

Under shallow lake water colored red by an algae bloom, these large salt formations are forming on the lakebed just under the surface. The image appears unsharp due to the bending of light rays from the underwater patterns by the lake's waters.

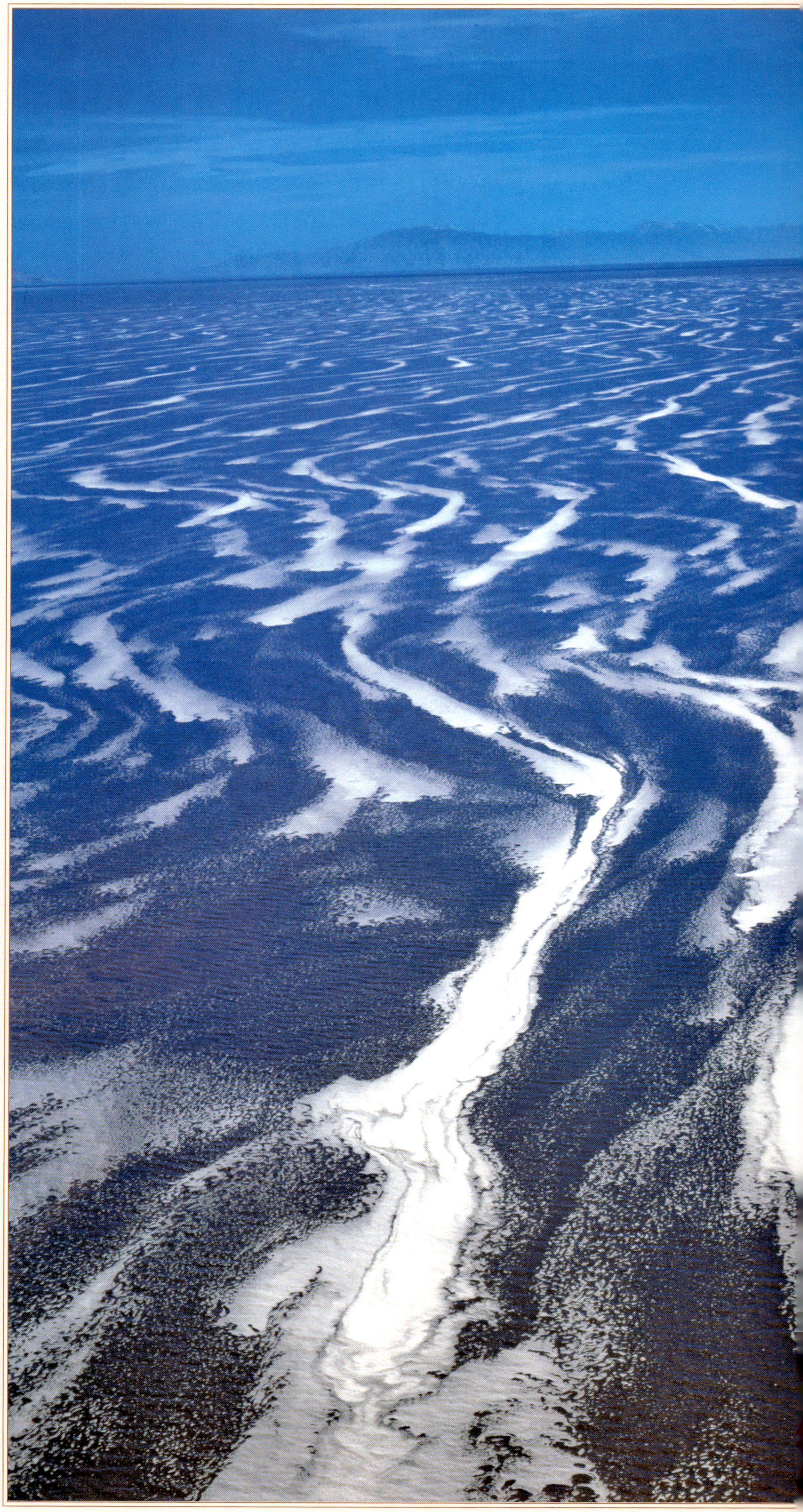

Salt and other minerals float on the Great Salt Lake's surface. The view is south toward the main part of the Lake.

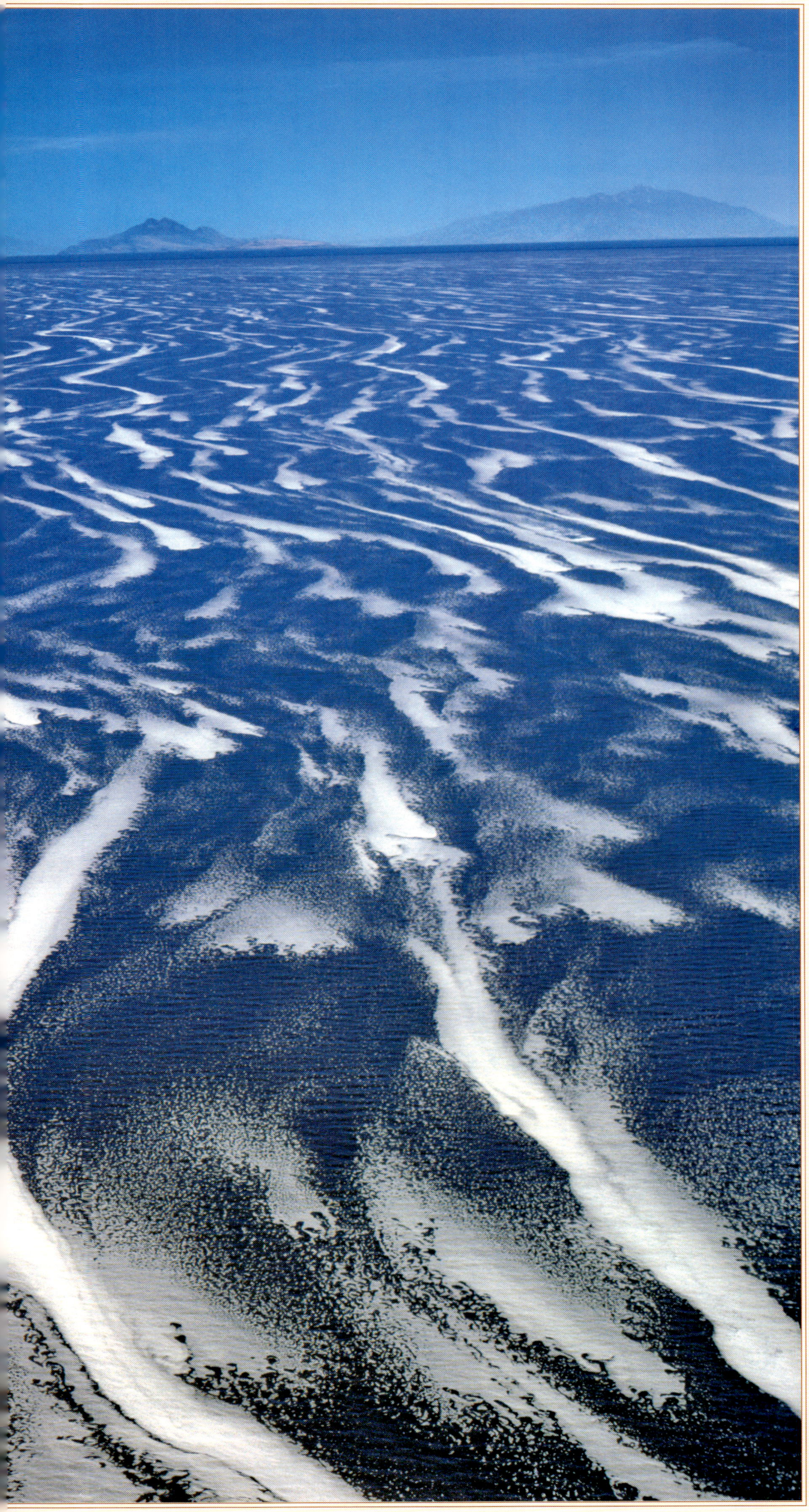

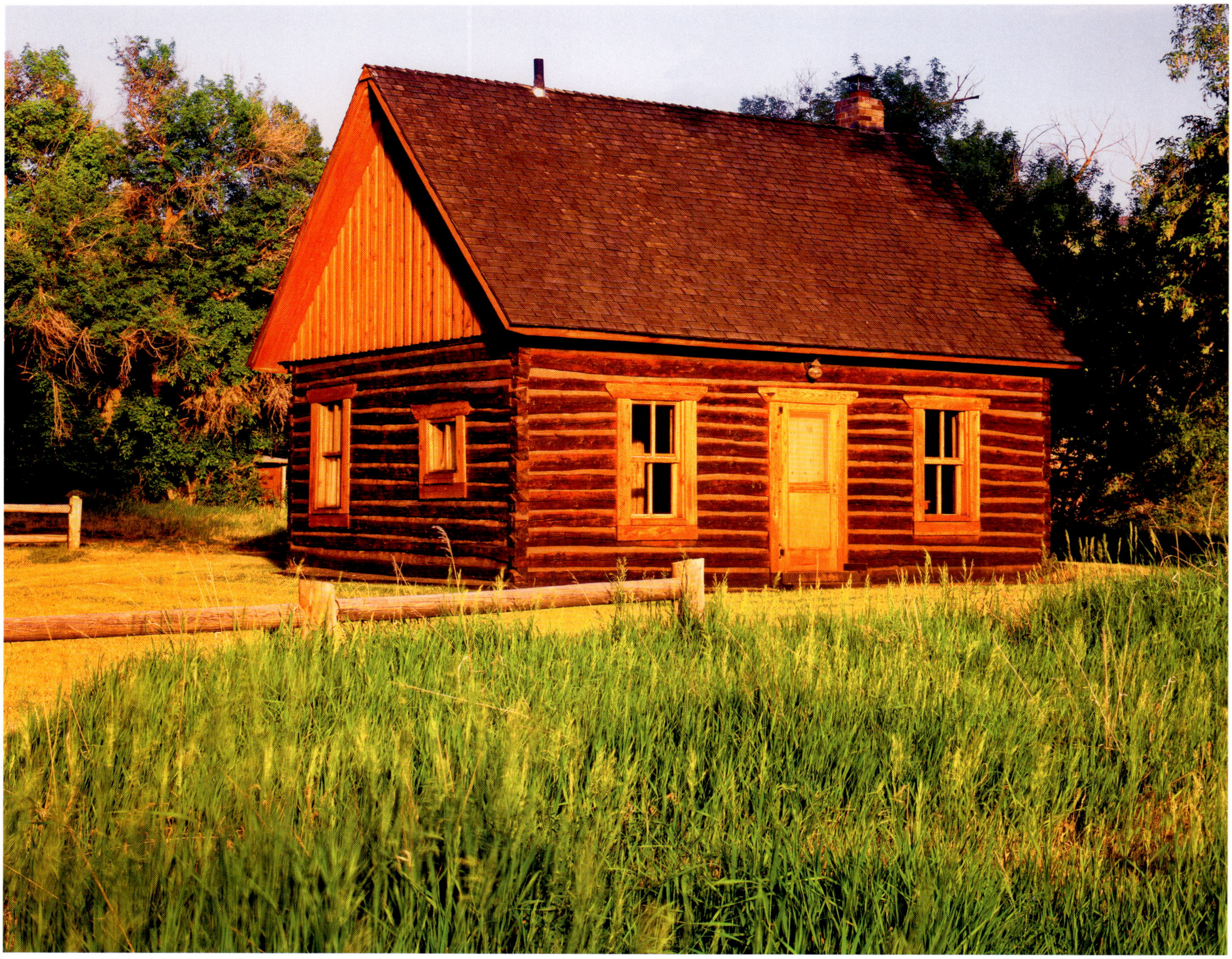

ABOVE:
Peaceful Valley Ranch in Morgan County is home to this beautifully restored Pony Express Cabin.

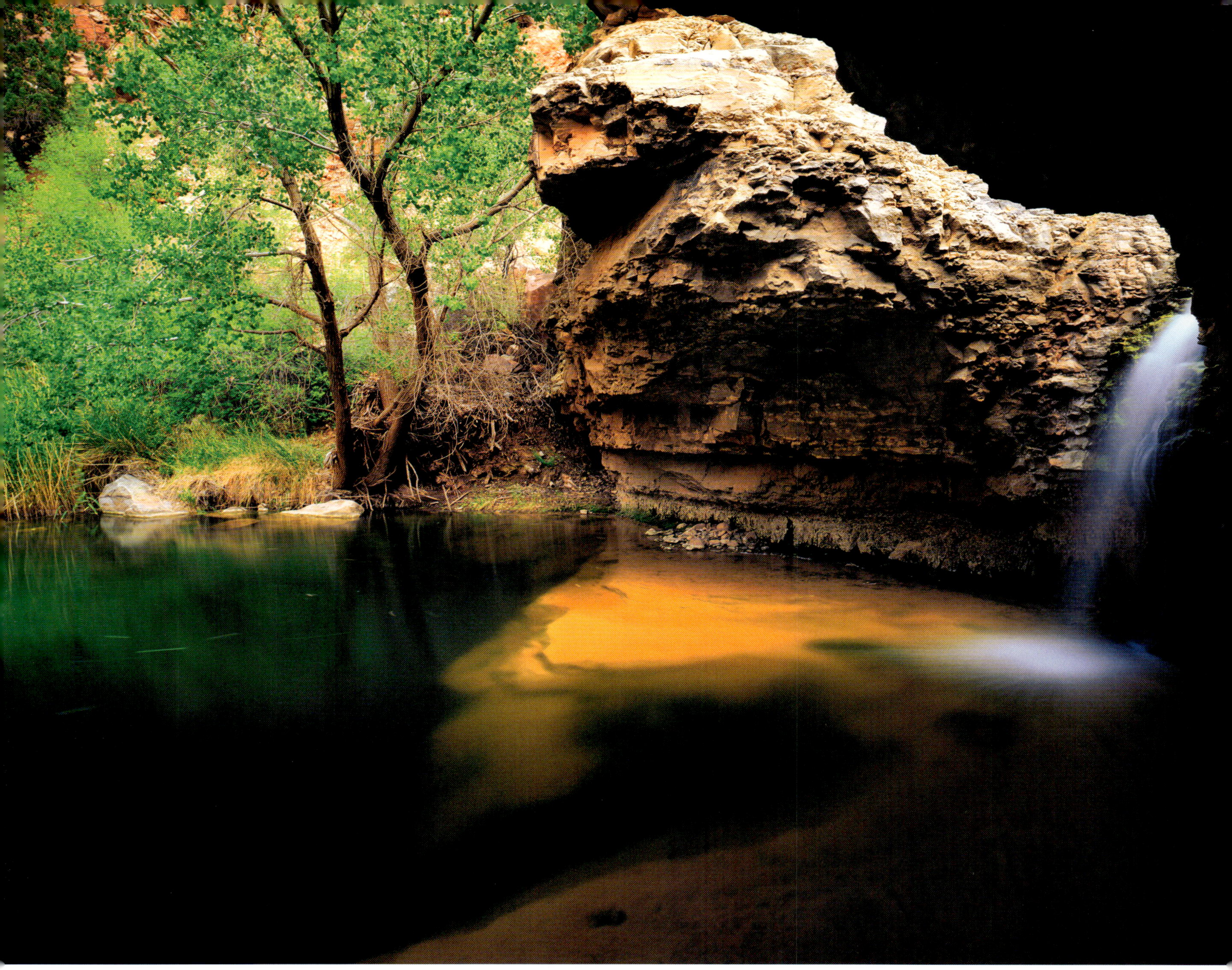

ABOVE:
Lush water-cooled canyons, like Gypsum Canyon, are made for exploration. Waterfalls, deep pools, and verdant greenery appear around every corner.

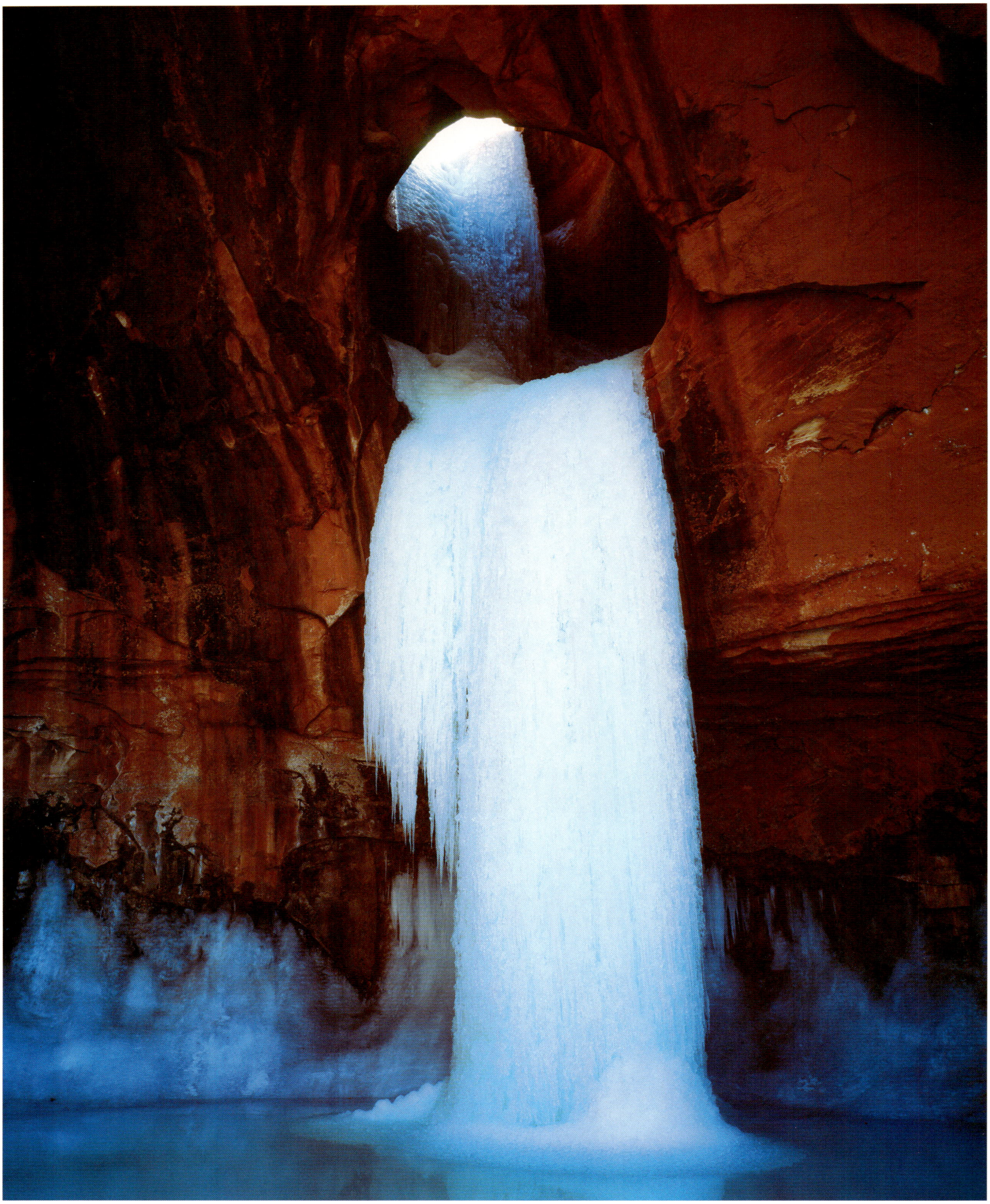

ABOVE:
Under normal conditions, this arch with a waterfall flowing through it is amazing enough, but when frozen it is particularly wonderful, although dangerous. On one visit we found evidence that the frozen waterfall had recently collapsed. Had this happened when we were nearby, we would surely have been killed or injured.

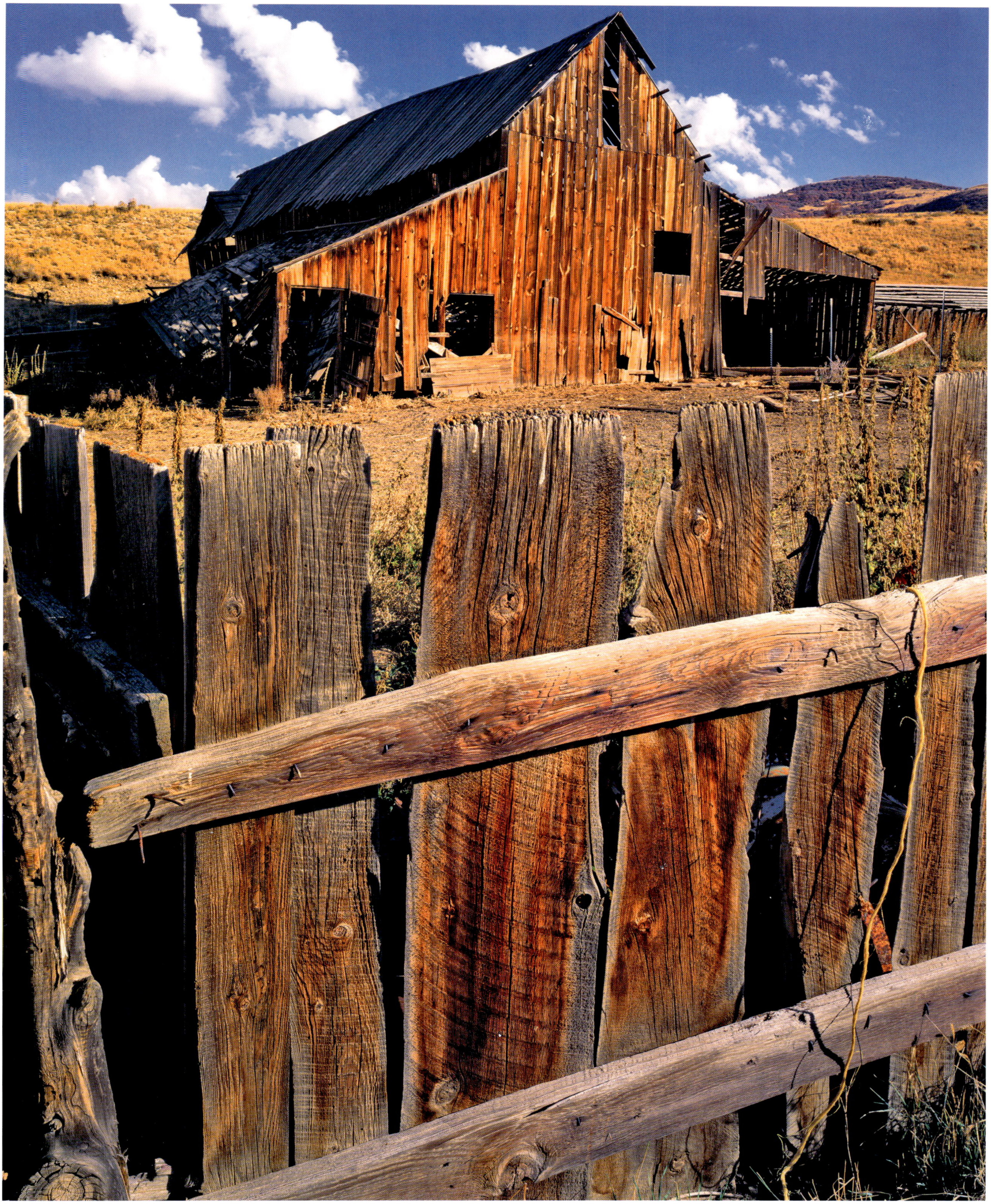

ABOVE:
A weathered barn fights the elements atop Soldiers Summit on the Wasatch Plateau. Many of Utah's beautiful old barns have fallen to the elements, and the life expectancy of this one appears to be short.

BELOW:
Pink sunset light highlights the ridges of Cedar Breaks in Cedar Breaks National Monument.

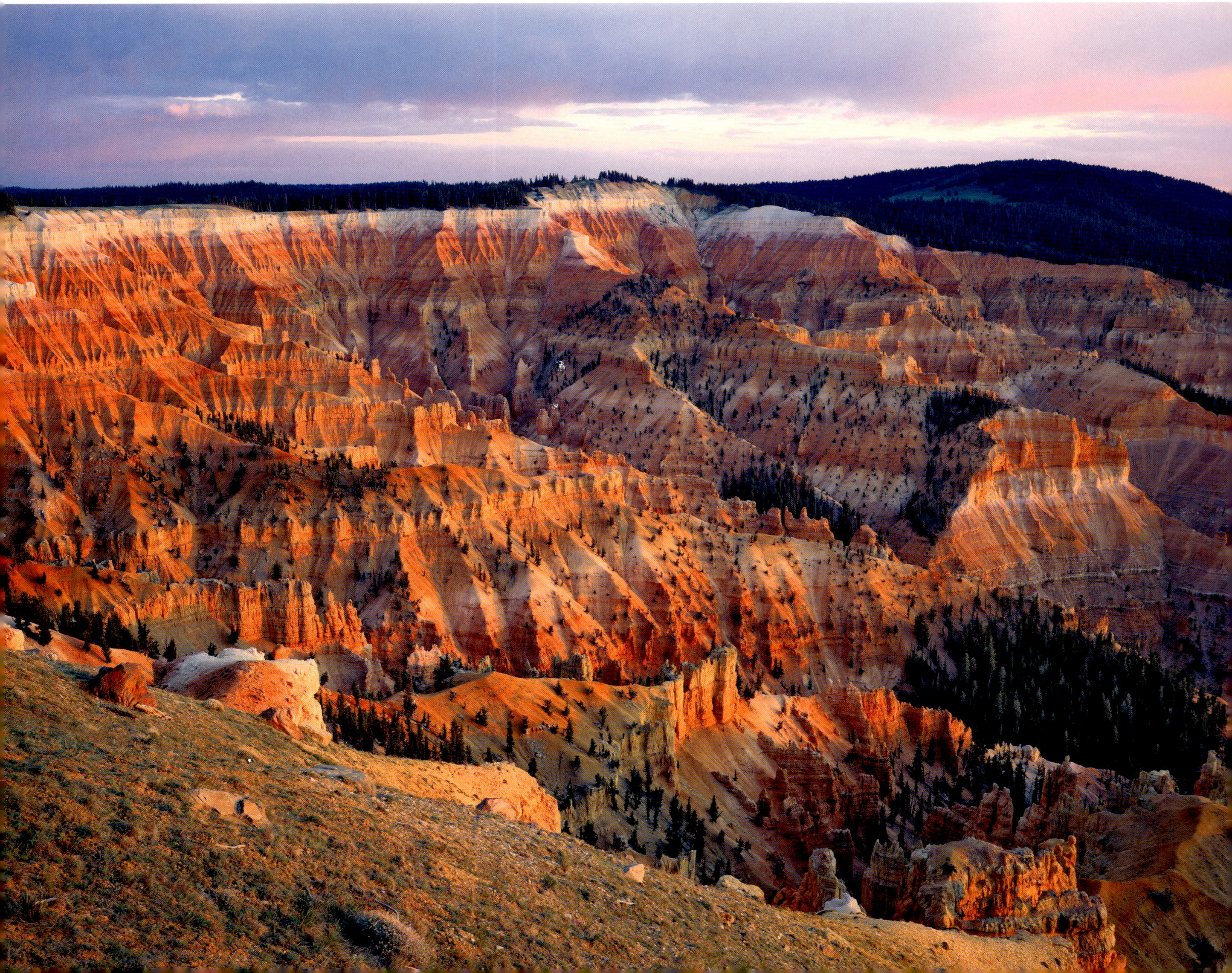

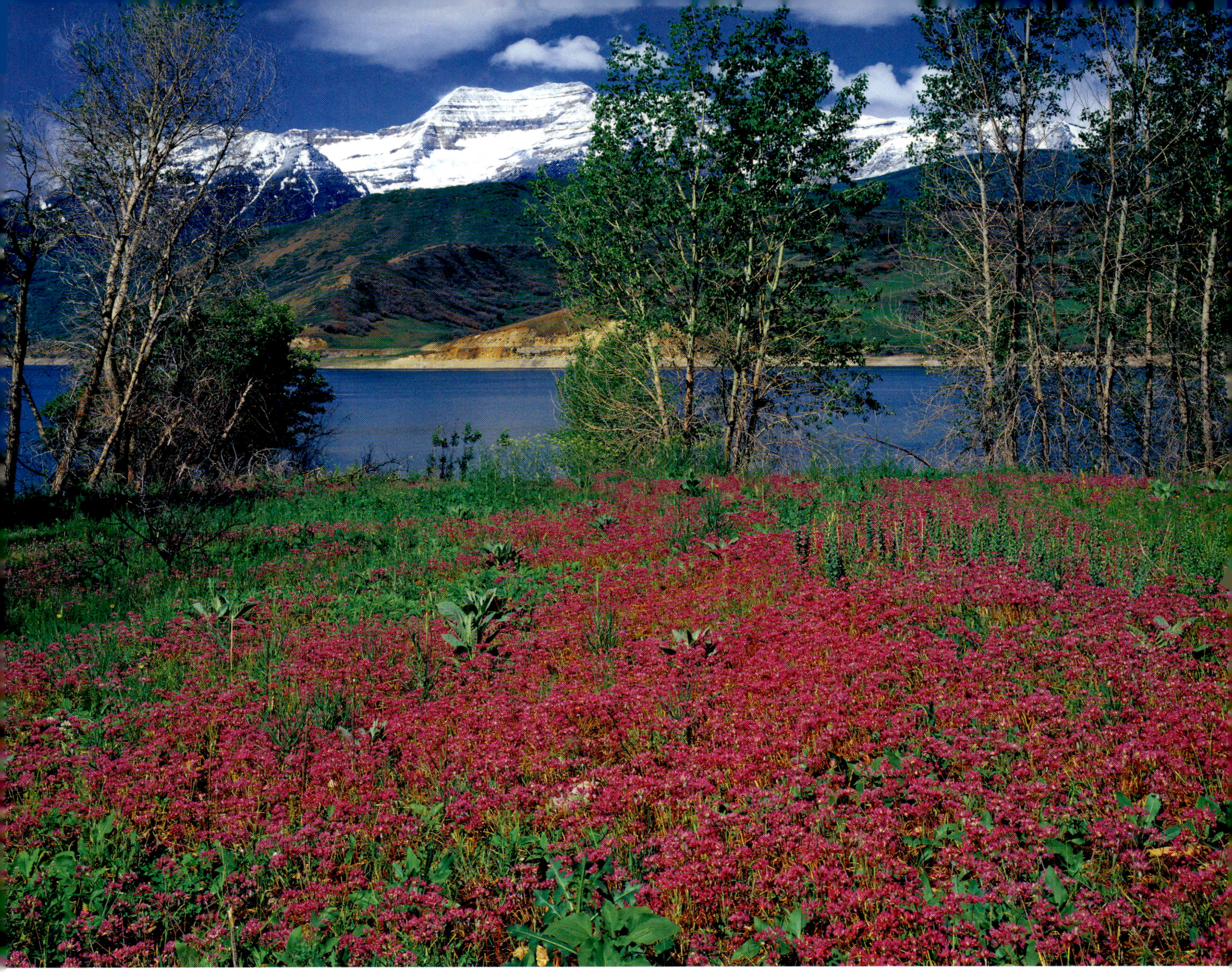

ABOVE:
A field of wild onion graces the shores of Deer Creek Reservoir. Beyond, Mt. Timpanogos, mantled with spring snow, commands the distant Wasatch skyline.

BELOW:
Since I'm based in Moab, I've constantly tried to produce different and new photographs of the astounding local scenery. A lot of my attention has been spent on Arches National Park. After hiking around and in the Fiery Furnace for years, I finally found this angle, which I think is best for showing the wilderness of fins of the Furnace with the distant La Sal Mountains. The added accent of a very rare heavy snowfall and a right angle sun further delineates this wonder of erosion.

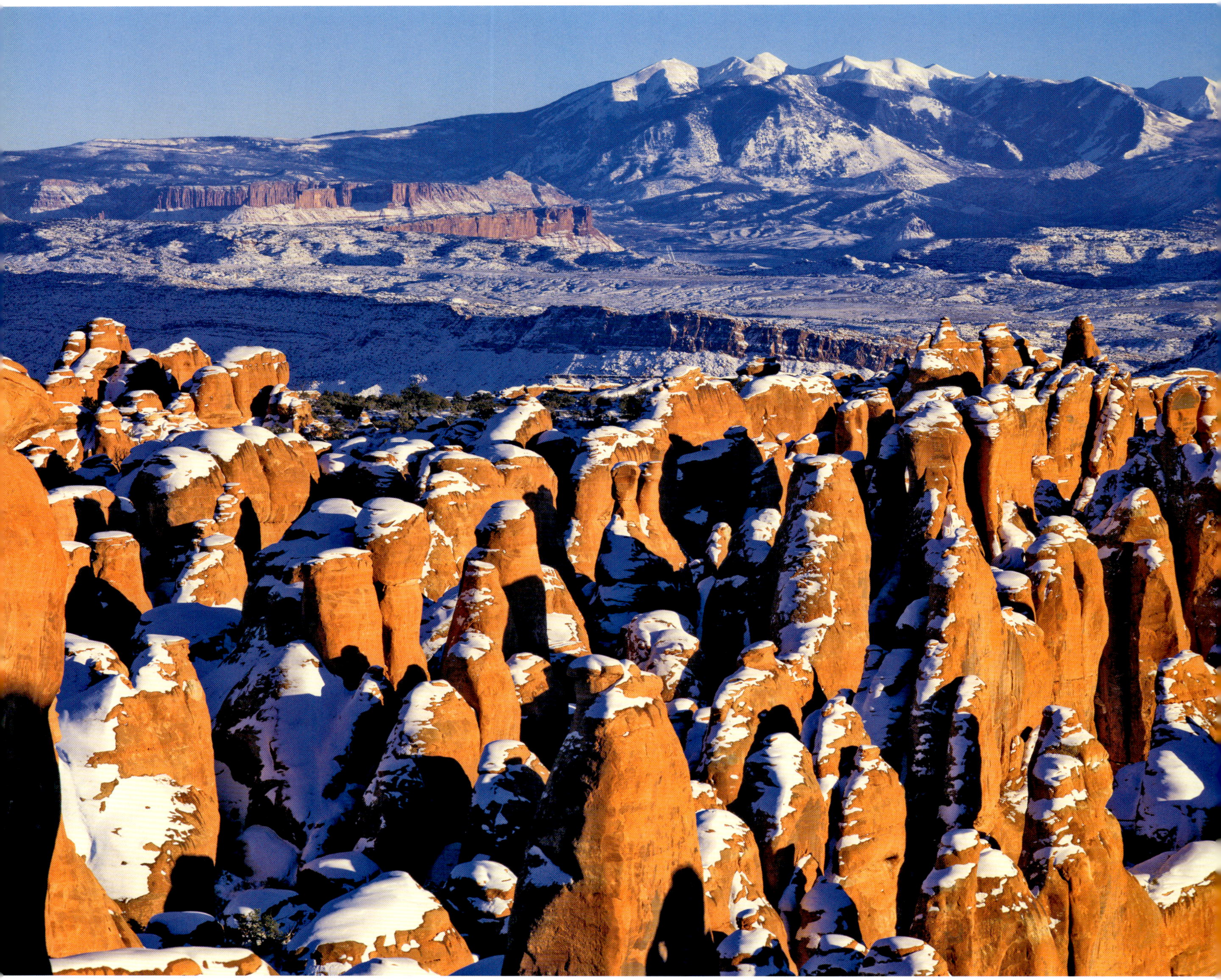

RIGHT:
Inside a slot canyon in the San Rafael Swell, rich blues from the intensely clear day reflect on the narrow walls. Though not a national park, the Swell harbors a wide range of treasures that make it a prime national park candidate. These include numerous world-class natural arches, dozens of peerless slot canyons, some of the best Ancestral Puebloan rock art in the West, pioneer cabins, many of the world's largest free-standing buttes, and rivers that can be hiked or run in small kayaks or inner tubes.

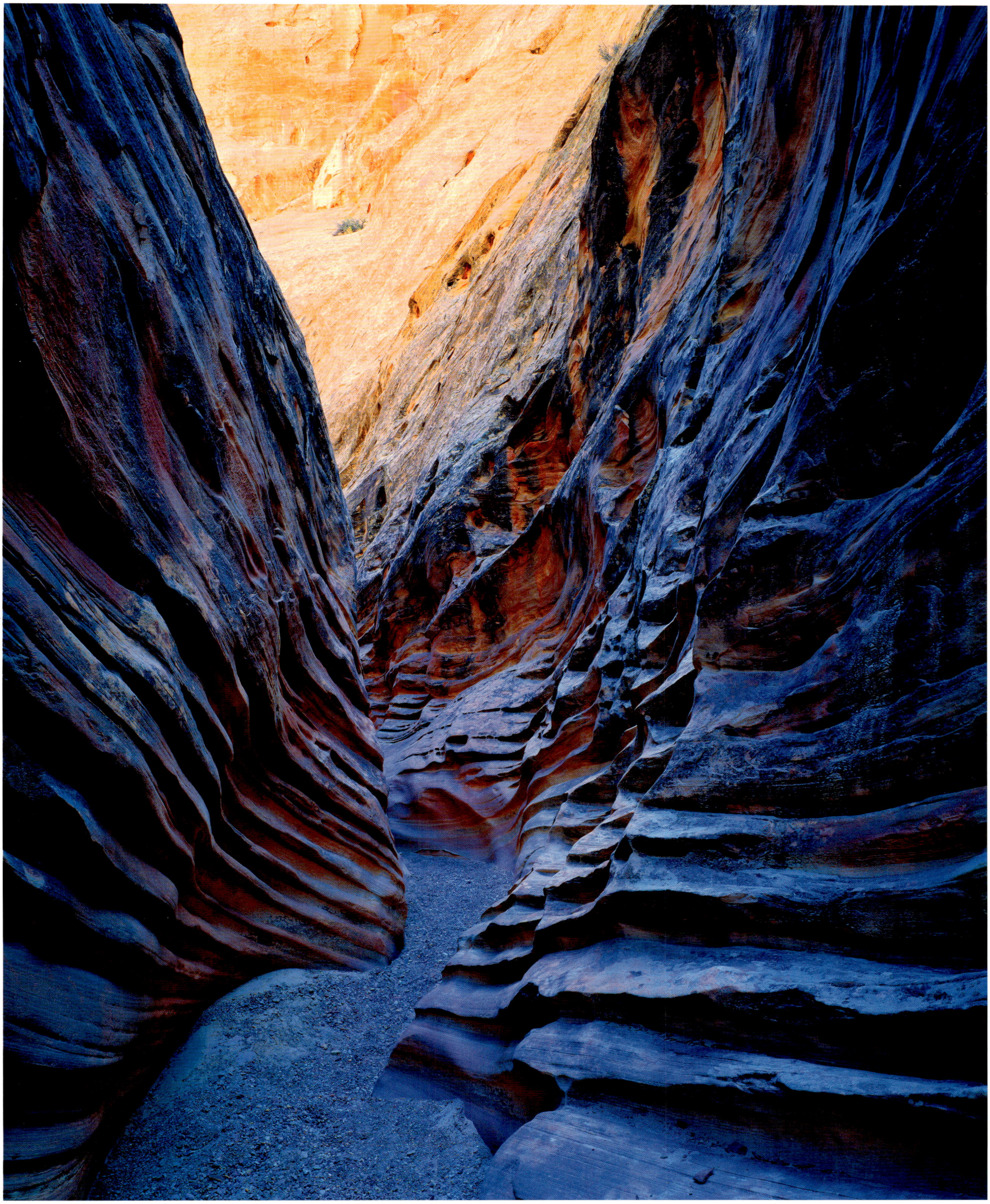

BELOW:
Ancestral Puebloan rock art adorns a red wall in Southern Utah.

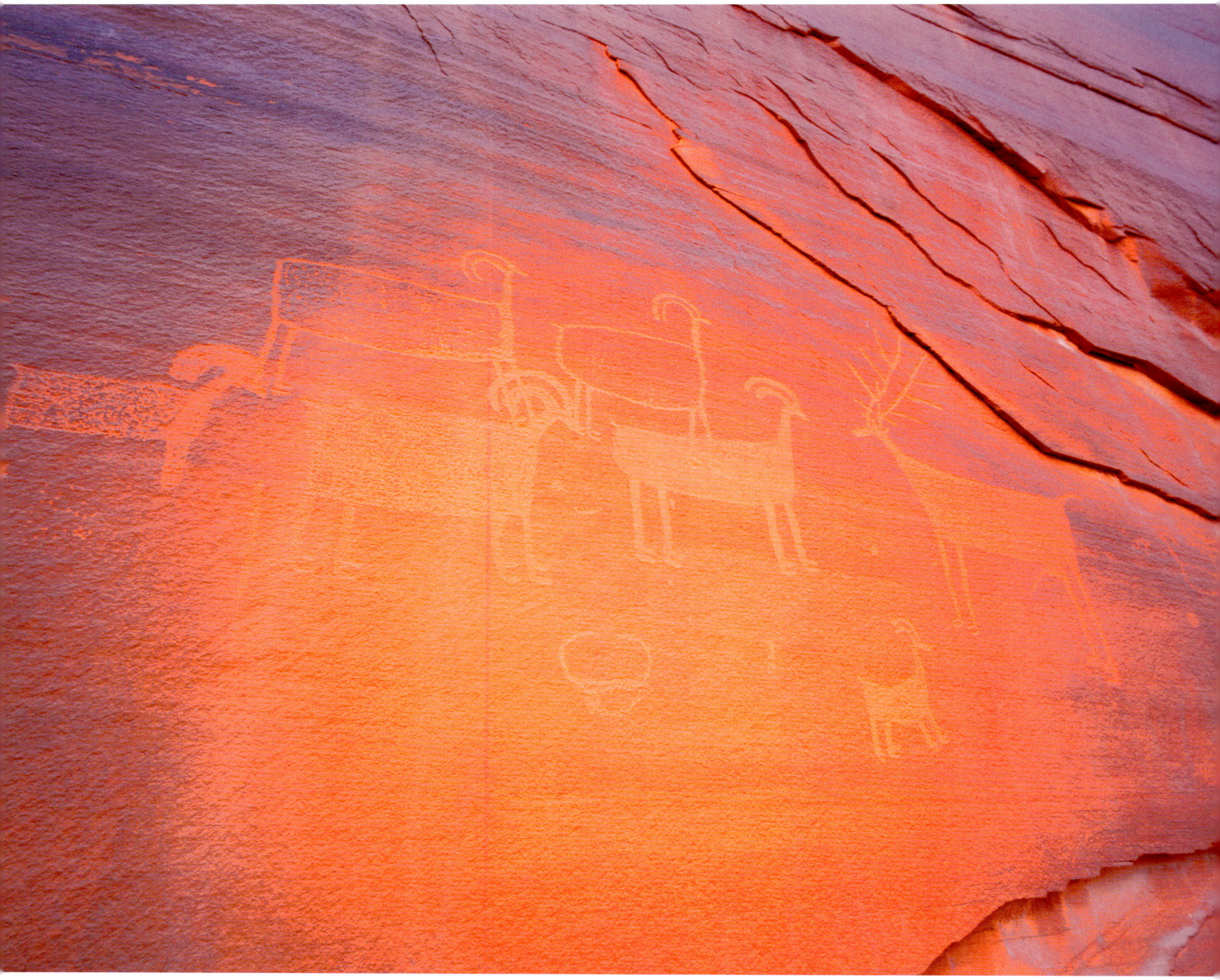

RIGHT:
Morning Glory Arch is one of the world's largest. The size of large trees at its base gives some scale of the arch's massive span. Difficult to photograph because it is a wall arch, I used a 38mm lens on my 4x5 camera (equivalent to about 10mm on a 35mm camera) to try and capture as much of the arch as possible in the image.

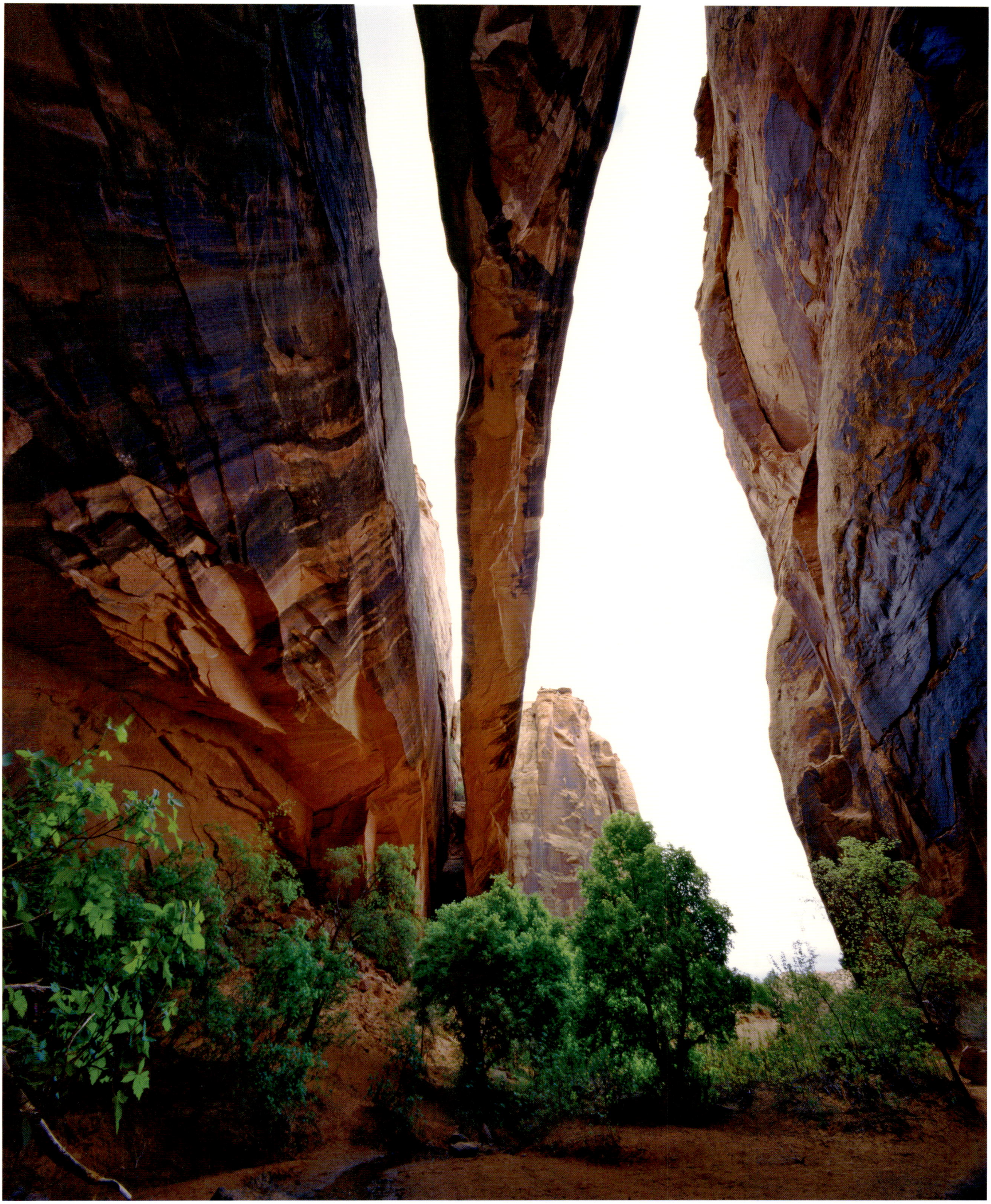

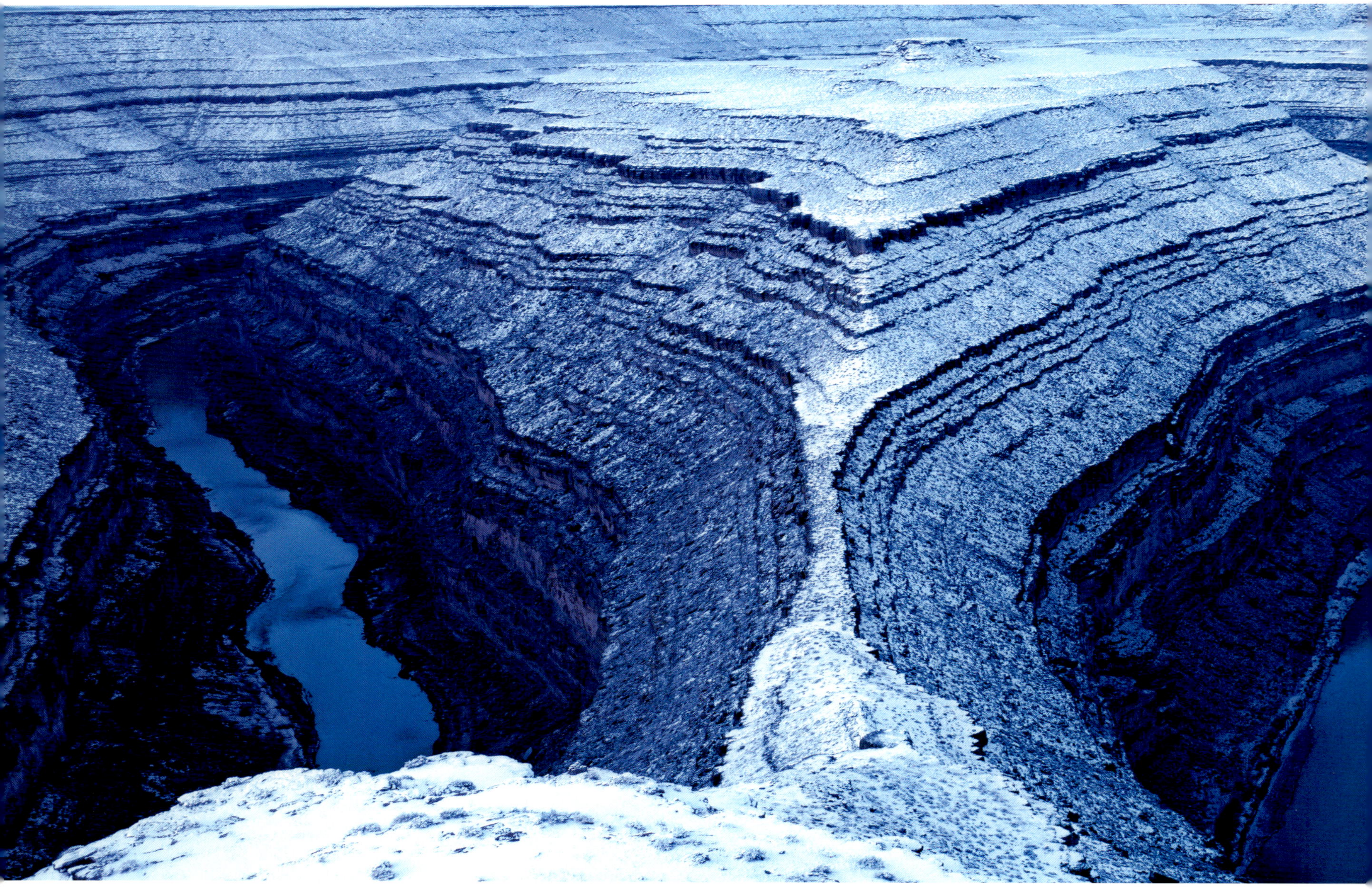

ABOVE:

Winter snow outlines the rock strata of the Goosenecks of the San Juan State Park. Only rare winter storms reach down to the bottom of the deep canyon. Shot before sunrise, the film recorded the intense blues of the snow in the predawn light.

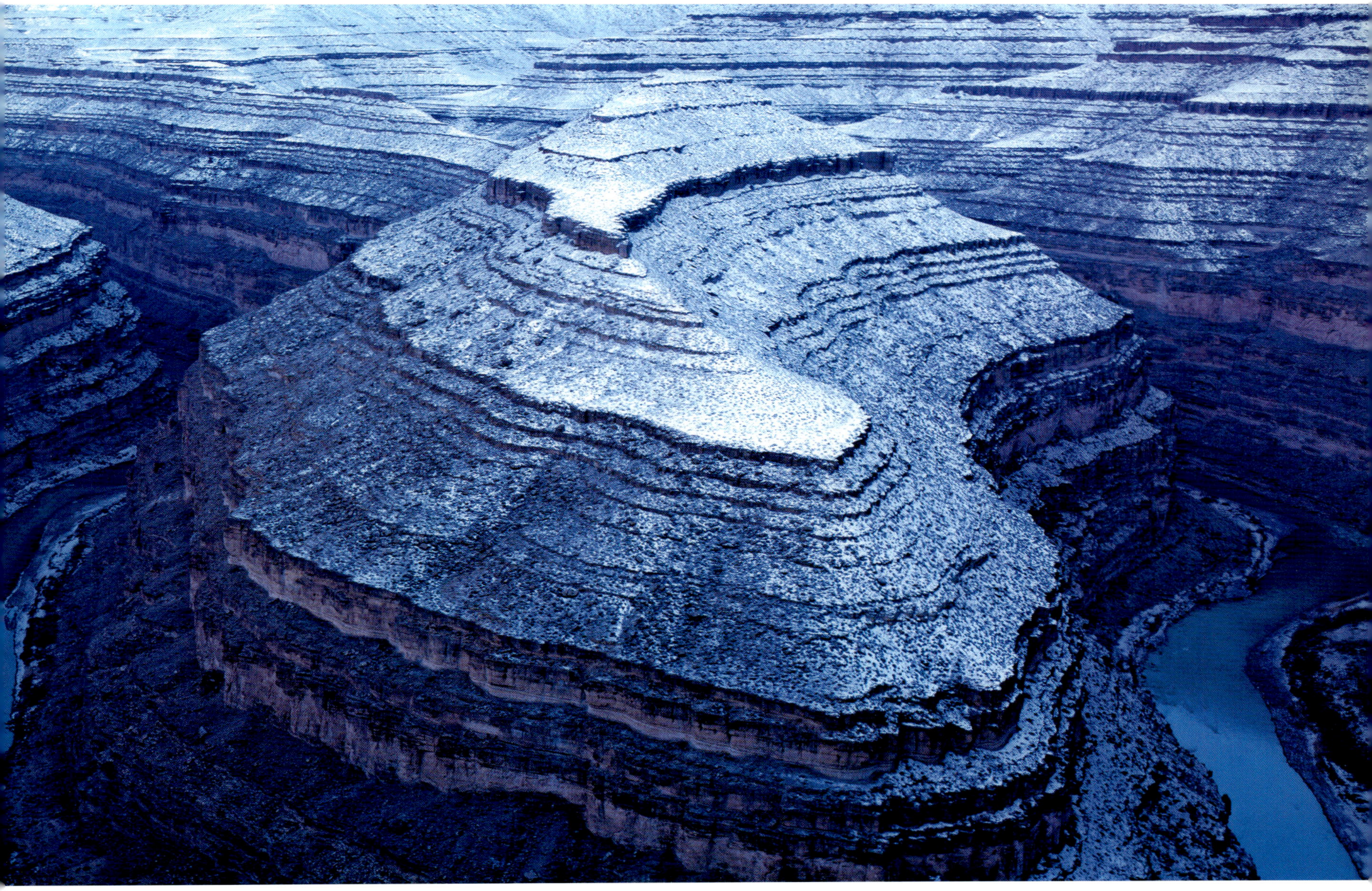

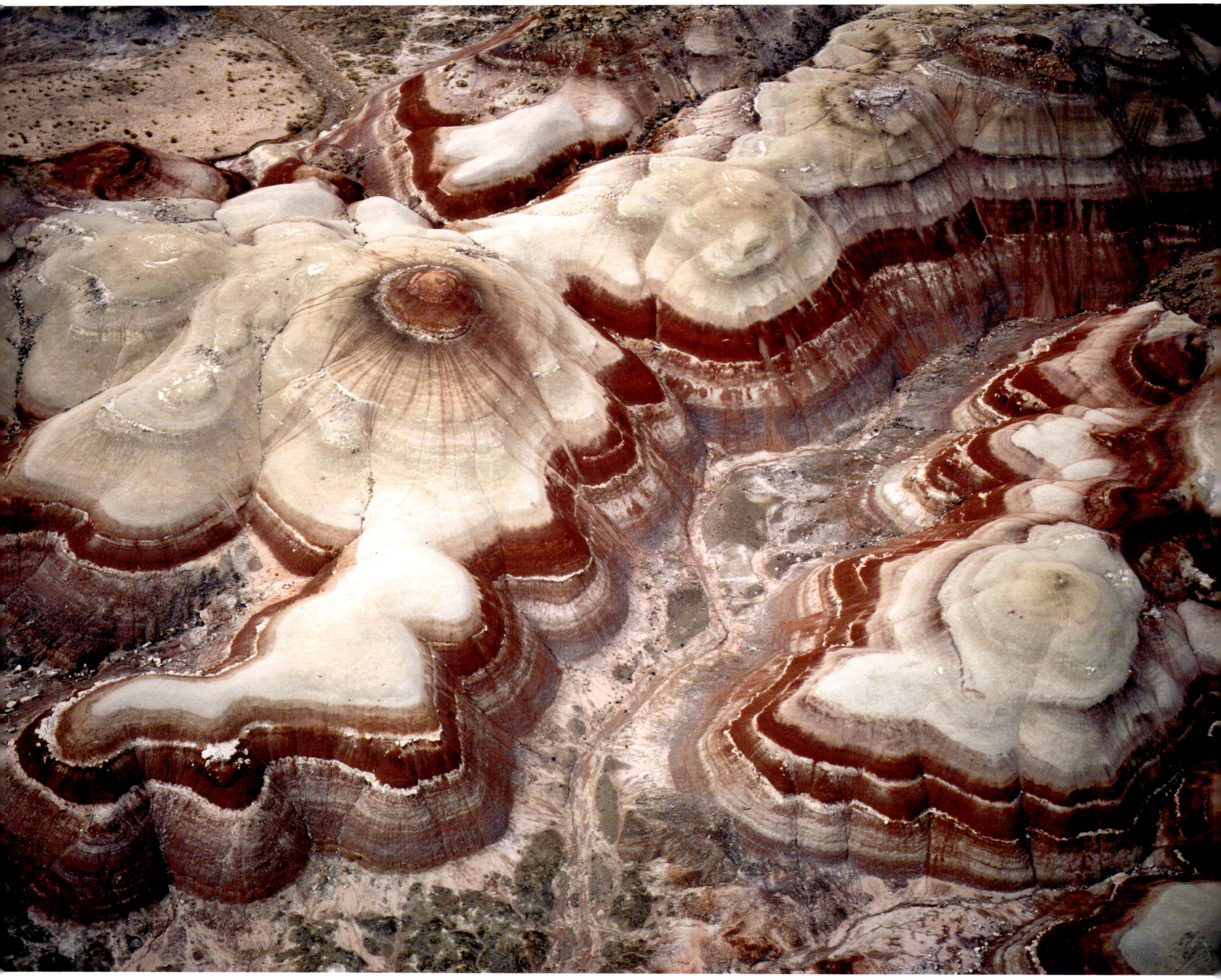

ABOVE:
Several days of extremely heavy rains in Southern Utah left these badlands in Capitol Reef's Hartnet Desert saturated — emboldening their colors and heightening the contrast of their abstract forms and orange stripes.

BELOW:

Whether you are a member of the Mormon Church or not, the architecture and beauty of many LDS temples is striking. The Manti Temple is my favorite. Made from stone that seems to glow from within and standing on a high hill where it catches the best afternoon and evening light, the Temple is an inspiring creation.

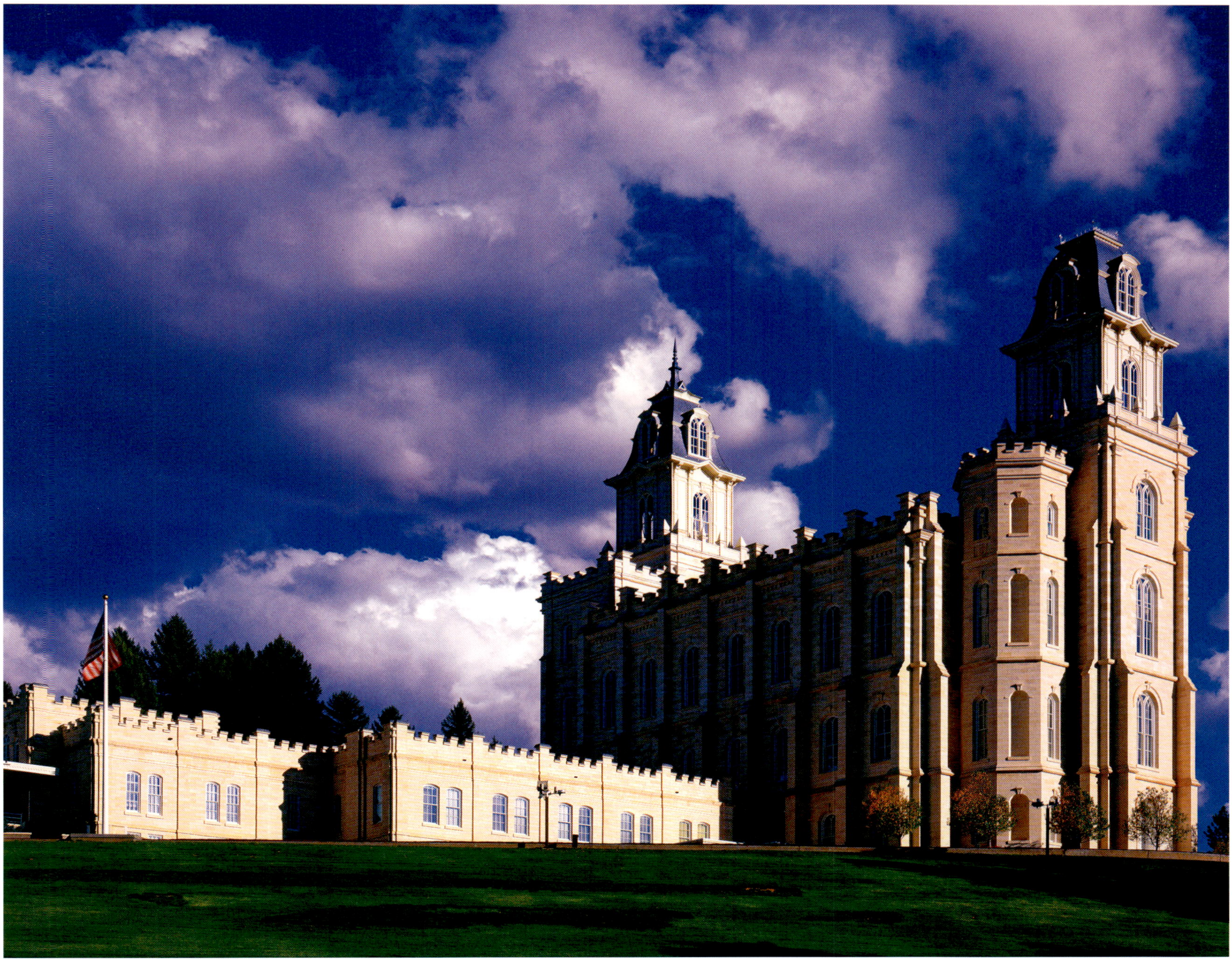

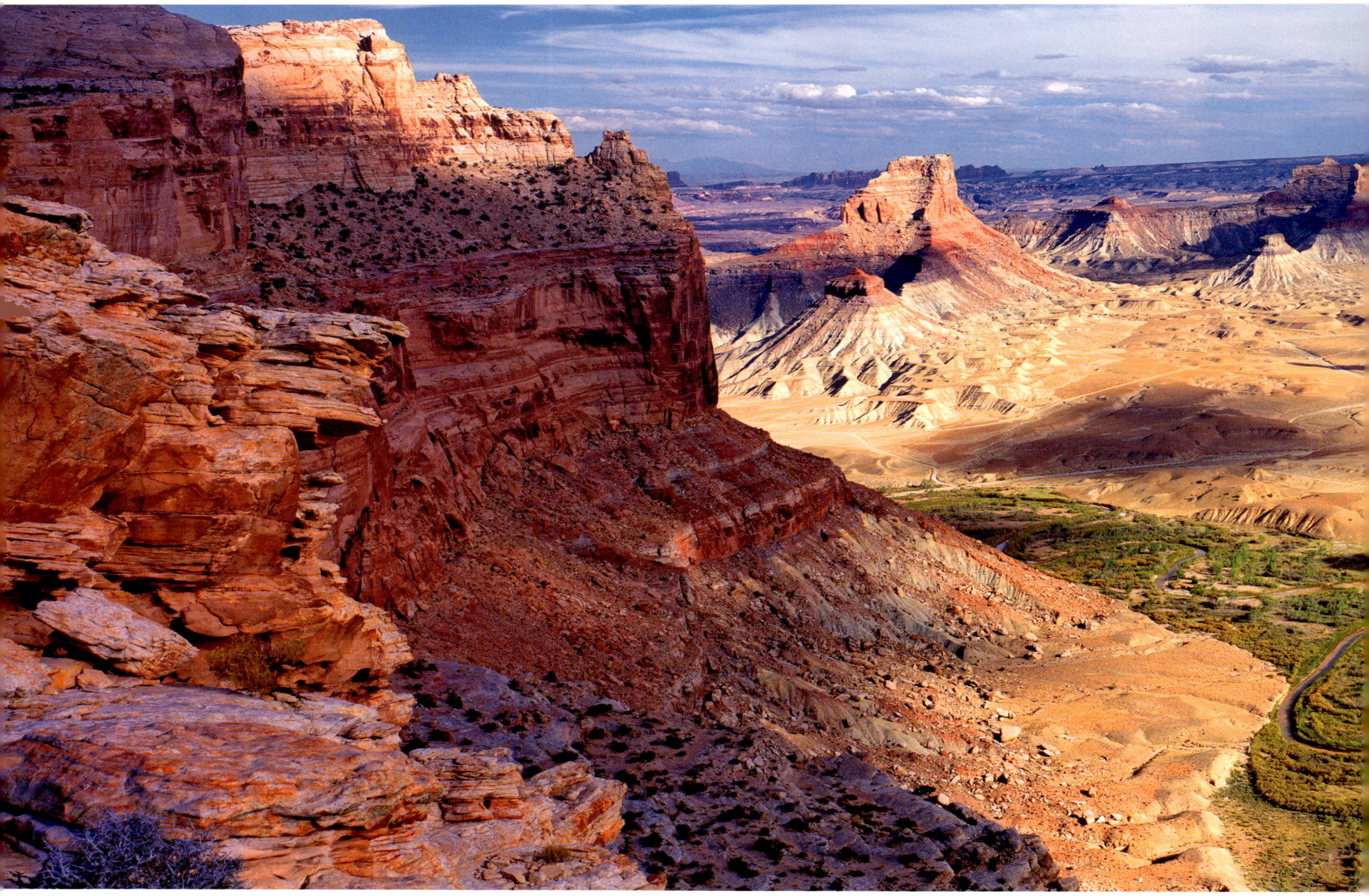

ABOVE:
As the Grand Canyon of the San Rafael River ends, the river canyon opens into an area of monumental buttes, including Bottleneck, Window Blind, and Assembly Hall. The image is not an aerial, but taken from high on the rim above the amazing view. This is an example of a "planned" image. I had the idea for the shot, even going so far as to draw a sketch of what I though it might look like. By hiking a long distance from the road, I was able to realize my previsualization of a panoramic overhead view of this amazing landscape.

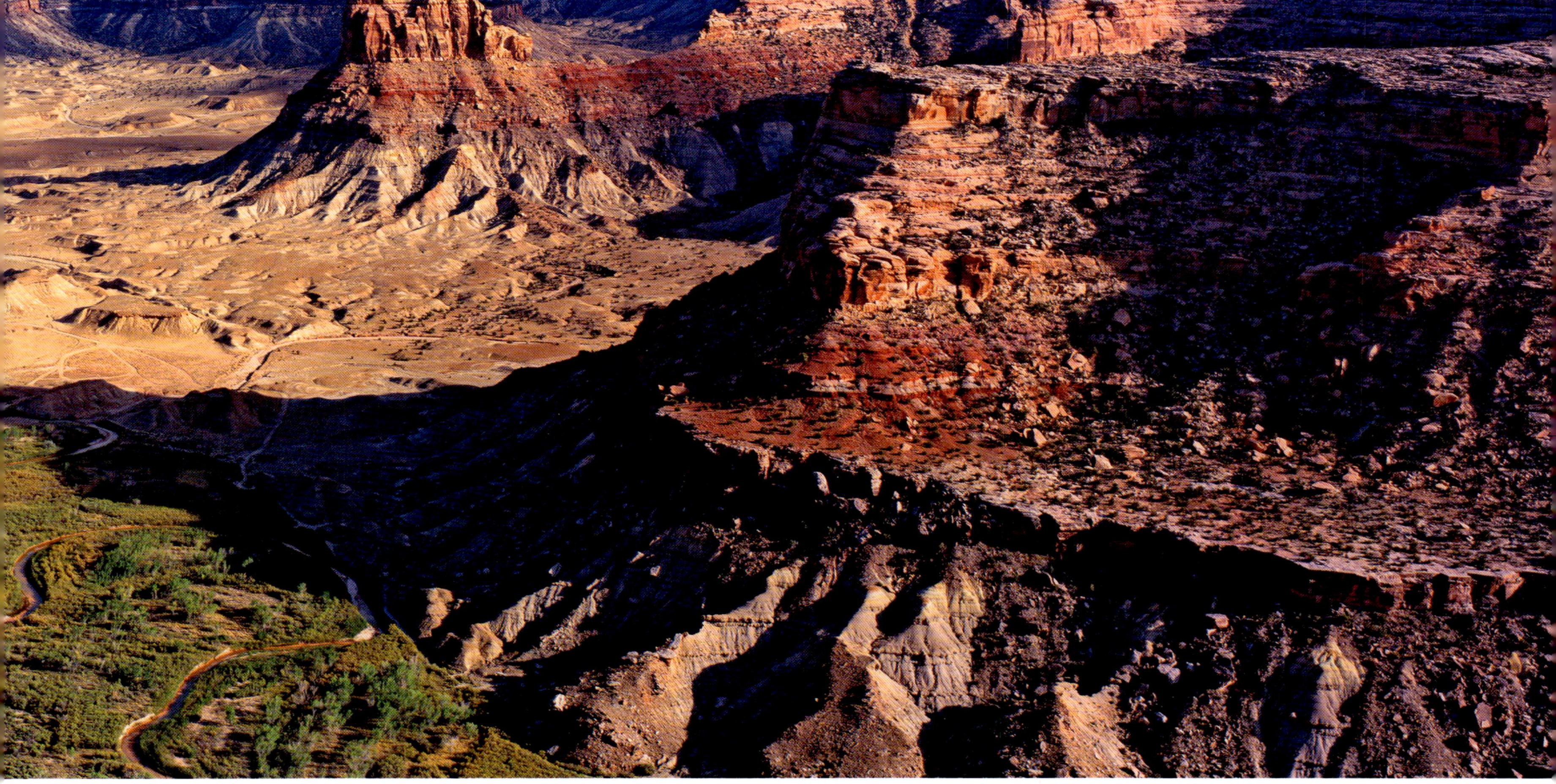

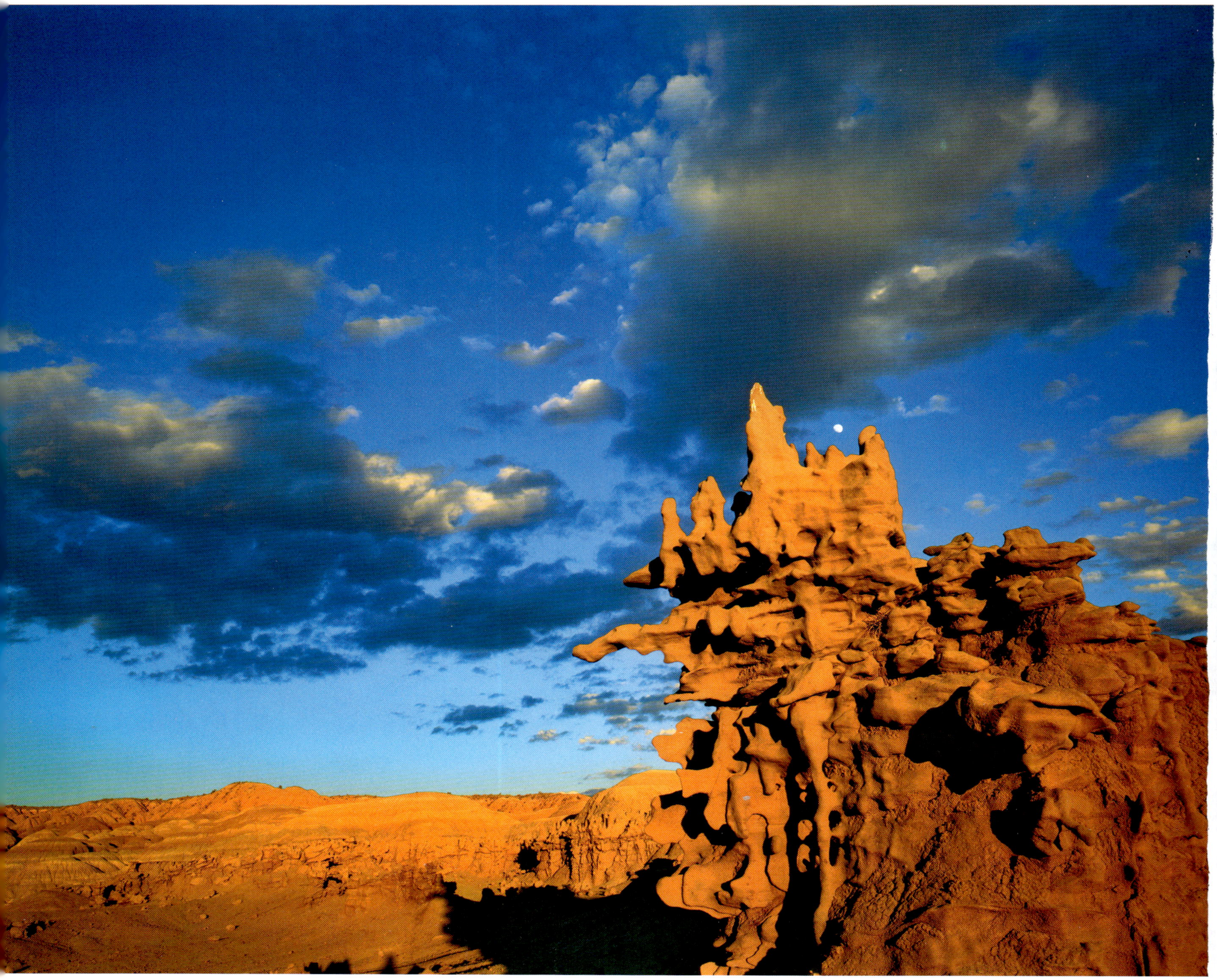

ABOVE:
Outlandish rock forms are the norm at Fantasy Canyon. Unfortunately, in 2006, one of the most famous and photogenic formations was destroyed either by vandalization or natural erosion.